ASIAN DEVELOPMENT OUTLOOK 2022
UPDATE

ENTREPRENEURSHIP IN THE DIGITAL AGE

SEPTEMBER 2022

ADB

ASIAN DEVELOPMENT BANK

© 2022 Asian Development Bank
6 ADB Avenue, Mandaluyong City, 1550 Metro Manila, Philippines
Tel +63 2 8632 4444; Fax +63 2 8636 2444
www.adb.org

Some rights reserved. Published in 2022.

ISBN 978-92-9269-754-9 (print); 978-92-9269-755-6 (electronic); 978-92-9269-756-3 (ebook)
ISSN 1655-4809 (print)
Publication Stock No. FLS220405-3
DOI: http://dx.doi.org/10.22617/FLS220405-3

The views expressed in this publication are those of the authors and do not necessarily reflect the views and policies of the Asian Development Bank (ADB) or its Board of Governors or the governments they represent.

ADB does not guarantee the accuracy of the data included in this publication and accepts no responsibility for any consequence of their use. The mention of specific companies or products of manufacturers does not imply that they are endorsed or recommended by ADB in preference to others of a similar nature that are not mentioned.

By making any designation of or reference to a particular territory or geographic area, or by using the term "country" in this document, ADB does not intend to make any judgments as to the legal or other status of any territory or area.

Corrigenda to ADB publications may be found at http://www.adb.org/publications/corrigenda.

Notes:
In this publication, "$" refers to US dollars.
ADB recognizes "China" as the People's Republic of China, "Hong Kong" as Hong Kong, China; "Korea" as the Republic of Korea; "Siam" as Thailand; "Vietnam" as Viet Nam; and "Russia" as the Russian Federation.

Cover design by Anthony Victoria.

Cover artwork by Demosthenes Campos/2017.

CONTENTS

FOREWORD

Developing Asia continues to recover as many economies ease restrictions from the coronavirus disease (COVID-19) pandemic. However, global uncertainties are undermining prospects for a return to strong and lasting growth. Among the top concerns is the Russian invasion of Ukraine, which has contributed to rising food and fuel prices, and monetary tightening in advanced economies.

In this update to the *Asian Development Outlook 2022* released in April, we have revised down our growth forecasts for developing Asia from 5.2% to 4.3% for 2022 and from 5.3% to 4.9% for 2023. Economic prospects have dimmed in particular for the People's Republic of China, which faces recurring hard lockdowns under its zero-COVID strategy. Inflation in the region is trending higher, driven by rising food and energy prices. While remittances remain healthy and tourism is recovering, signs of a slowdown are emerging, evidenced by weaker export orders and worsening financial conditions.

As the region continues to emerge from the pandemic, new growth drivers are needed to build and sustain momentum. The theme chapter of this report examines the very promising area of entrepreneurship in the digital age. As the pandemic demonstrated, digitalization helps foster entrepreneurial resilience. Entrepreneurs with online presences navigated the lockdowns and related challenges especially well. Embracing digital entrepreneurship in the post-pandemic era can open a world of opportunities for innovation and equip the region's mostly middle-income economies to sustain rapid growth.

Digital entrepreneurship is largely a private endeavor, but it is nevertheless essential for economies to create an environment that allows entrepreneurship and digitalization to prosper. Because the economies of developing Asia are at different stages in their development, tailored policies are needed to advance digital entrepreneurship while ensuring inclusive access to the tremendous opportunities entrepreneurs can unlock. Sound institutions that reinforce strong property rights, honest and effective governments, reliable legal systems, and open and competitive markets, will also be critical to nurturing entrepreneurship. Improving public perceptions of entrepreneurship through education will support all these efforts.

I hope the *Asian Development Outlook 2022 Update* continues to be a useful resource as we tackle issues that are vital for the region's development. Preparing this report is part of our commitment to provide comprehensive policy analysis and sound policy advice so that the region can confront the current challenges effectively.

The Asian Development Bank remains optimistic about the region's prospects and will remain steadfast in its support to achieve a more prosperous, inclusive, resilient, and sustainable Asia and the Pacific.

MASATSUGU ASAKAWA
President
Asian Development Bank

ACKNOWLEDGMENTS

Asian Development Outlook 2022 Update was prepared by staff of the regional departments and resident missions of the Asian Development Bank (ADB) under the guidance of the Economic Research and Regional Cooperation Department (ERCD). Representatives of these departments met regularly as the Regional Economic Outlook Task Force to coordinate and develop consistent forecasts for the region.

ERCD economists, led by Abdul Abiad, director of the Macroeconomics Research Division, coordinated the production of this report, assisted by Edith Laviña and Priscille Villanueva. Shiela Camingue-Romance, Cindy Castillejos-Petalcorin, David Keith De Padua, Nedelyn Magtibay-Ramos, Pilipinas Quising, Dennis Sorino, Mai Lin Villaruel, and Priscille Villanueva provided technical and research support. Emmanuel Alano, Gilliane Gorostiza, Jesson Pagaduan, Rene Cris Rivera, and Michael Timbang did additional research. Economic editorial advisors Robert Boumphrey, Eric Clifton, Joshua Greene, Srinivasa Madhur, Richard Niebuhr, and Reza Vaez-Zadeh made substantial contributions to the economic trends and prospects in developing Asia section.

The support and guidance of ADB Chief Economist Albert Park and Deputy Chief Economist Joseph E. Zveglich Jr. is gratefully acknowledged.

Authors who contributed the sections are bylined in each chapter. The subregional coordinators were Kenji Takamiya, Lilia Aleksanyan, and Fatima Catacutan for the Caucasus and Central Asia; Akiko Terada-Hagiwara, Marzia Mongiorgi, and Dorothea Ramizo for East Asia; Rana Hasan and Lani Garnace for South Asia; James Villafuerte and Dulce Zara for Southeast Asia; and Rommel Rabanal, Cara Tinio, and Remrick Patagan for the Pacific.

In addition to the contributors named in the bylines and the authors of the background papers and notes, the theme chapter benefitted from inputs from the ADB Digital Technology Thematic Group of the Sustainable Development and Climate Change department. The research studies that served as background materials for the theme chapter were supported by ADB under Knowledge and Support Technical Assistance Project 6711-REG Digital Entrepreneurship in Asia for Economic Resilience and Post-Pandemic Recovery, funded by the Government of the Republic of Korea, through the e-Asia and Knowledge Partnership Fund. Rick Chan edited the background papers and notes.

Peter Fredenburg and Alastair McIndoe edited *Asian Development Outlook 2022 Update*. Alvin Tubio and Jonathan Yamongan did the typesetting and graphics, assisted by Heili Ann Bravo, Fermirelyn Cruz, Elenita Pura, and Rhia Bautista-Piamonte. Art direction for the cover was by Anthony Victoria, with artwork from Demosthenes Campos. Kevin Nellies designed the landing page for *Asian Development Outlook 2022 Update*. Fermirelyn Cruz provided administrative and secretarial support. A team from the Department of Communications, led by David Kruger and Terje Langeland, planned and coordinated the dissemination of this *Update*.

DEFINITIONS AND ASSUMPTIONS

The economies discussed in *Asian Development Outlook 2022 Update* are classified by major analytic or geographic group. For the purposes of this report, the following apply:

- **Association of Southeast Asian Nations** (ASEAN) comprises Brunei Darussalam, Cambodia, Indonesia, the Lao People's Democratic Republic, Malaysia, Myanmar, the Philippines, Singapore, Thailand, and Viet Nam. ASEAN-5 are Indonesia, Malaysia, the Philippines, Thailand, and Viet Nam.

- **Developing Asia** comprises the 46 members of the Asian Development Bank listed below by geographic group.

- **Caucasus and Central Asia** comprises Armenia, Azerbaijan, Georgia, Kazakhstan, the Kyrgyz Republic, Tajikistan, Turkmenistan, and Uzbekistan.

- **East Asia** comprises Hong Kong, China; Mongolia; the People's Republic of China; the Republic of Korea; and Taipei,China.

- **South Asia** comprises Afghanistan, Bangladesh, Bhutan, India, Maldives, Nepal, Pakistan, and Sri Lanka.

- **Southeast Asia** comprises Brunei Darussalam, Cambodia, Indonesia, the Lao People's Democratic Republic, Malaysia, Myanmar, the Philippines, Singapore, Thailand, Timor-Leste, and Viet Nam.

- **The Pacific** comprises the Cook Islands, the Federated States of Micronesia, Fiji, Kiribati, the Marshall Islands, Nauru, Niue, Palau, Papua New Guinea, Samoa, Solomon Islands, Tonga, Tuvalu, and Vanuatu.

Unless otherwise specified, the symbol "$" and the word "dollar" refer to US dollars.

A number of assumptions have been made for the projections in *Asian Development Outlook 2022 Update*: The policies of national authorities are maintained. Real effective exchange rates remain constant at their average from 21 July to 31 August 2022. The average price of oil is $106/barrel in 2022 and $95/barrel in 2023. The 6-month London interbank offered rate for US dollar deposits averages 1.5% in 2022 and 3.6% in 2022, the European Central Bank refinancing rate averages 0.6% in 2022 and 1.8% in 2023, and the Bank of Japan's overnight call rate averages 0% in both years.

The forecasts and analysis in this *Update* are based on information available to 31 August 2022.

ABBREVIATIONS

ADB	Asian Development Bank
ADO	*Asian Development Outlook*
ASEAN	Association of Southeast Asian Nations
COVID-19	coronavirus disease
CPI	consumer price index
DFC	digital framework condition for entrepreneurship
DMC	developing member country
EFC	entrepreneurial framework condition
EFF	Extended Fund Facility
EIDES	European Index of Digital Entrepreneurship Systems
EU	European Union
FDI	foreign direct investment
FSM	Federated States of Micronesia
FY	fiscal year
GDP	gross domestic product
GEM	Global Entrepreneurship Monitor
GFC	global financial crisis
GIDES	Global Index of Digital Entrepreneurship Systems
GST	goods and services tax
H	half
H1–H4	hypotheses 1–4
ICT	information and communication technology
IMF	International Monetary Fund
Lao PDR	Lao People's Democratic Republic
LIBOR	London interbank offered rate
M2	broad money that includes cash and highly liquid accounts
M3	broad money that adds time accounts to M2
MAS	Monetary Authority of Singapore
mb/d	million barrels/day
NFRK	National Fund of the Republic of Kazakhstan
NPL	nonperforming loan
PMI	purchasing mangers' index
PNG	Papua New Guinea
PRC	People's Republic of China
Q	quarter
RBI	Reserve Bank of India
ROK	Republic of Korea
saar	seasonally adjusted annualized rate
US	United States
VAT	value-added tax

ADO 2022 UPDATE—HIGHLIGHTS

Developing Asia's recovery continues, but the outlook is worsening. Economic activity is being supported by the continued relaxation of coronavirus disease (COVID-19) restrictions in many economies, but the impact of the Russian invasion of Ukraine, aggressive monetary tightening in advanced economies, and repeated COVID-19 lockdowns in the People's Republic of China (PRC) are increasingly shaping the region's economic prospects.

Growth forecasts are revised down from the projections made in April in *Asian Development Outlook 2022* to 4.3% from 5.2% for this year and to 4.9% from 5.3% for 2023. Excluding the PRC, the rest of developing Asia is projected to grow by 5.3% in both 2022 and 2023—the first time in more than 3 decades that the rest of developing Asia will grow faster than the PRC.

Price pressures in developing Asia—while remaining lower than elsewhere in the world—are increasing on higher energy and food prices. The regional inflation forecast is raised to 4.5% from 3.7% for 2022 and to 4.0% from 3.1% for 2023.

Several downside risks loom large. A sharp deceleration in global growth, stronger-than-expected monetary policy tightening in advanced economies, the war in Ukraine escalating, a deeper-than-expected deceleration in the PRC, and negative pandemic developments could all dent developing Asia's growth over the forecast horizon.

Sustaining the region's economic growth depends on a vibrant private sector from which dynamic entrepreneurs can emerge to innovate and create many jobs. Dynamic entrepreneurship is examined in this *Update's* theme chapter. Digital entrepreneurship helped keep economies afloat during COVID-19 and it can become a major engine of growth in the post-pandemic world. Yet, with the exception of Singapore and the Republic of Korea, the report's global ranking shows most of the region's economies are lagging behind when it comes to the environment for digital entrepreneurs. Digitalization and a strong rule of law can facilitate innovative entrepreneurship—two areas where policy makers can help create a conducive environment for dynamic entrepreneurs to flourish.

Albert F. Park
Chief Economist
Asian Development Bank

Softening growth amid a darkened global outlook

Mounting headwinds, even as the recovery progresses

- **Developing Asia's recovery continues, but is being slowed by global headwinds.** The Russian invasion of Ukraine continues to affect economies in the region, with supply disruptions and elevated food and energy prices increasing inflationary pressures. Tighter monetary policy in advanced economies is denting global demand and rattling financial markets, and this is adding to the economic fallout from the war in Ukraine.

- **More flexible pandemic policies are allowing activity to expand, but the "zero-COVID" strategy of the People's Republic of China (PRC) is a notable exception.** Easing pandemic restrictions, increasing immunization, falling COVID-19 mortality rates, and the less severe health impact of the Omicron variant are underpinning improved mobility in much of the region. But the PRC remains the big exception because of intermittent but stringent lockdowns to stamp out sporadic outbreaks, in line with its "zero-COVID" strategy.

- **Consumer spending and employment are picking up on reduced mobility restrictions.** Consumption and investment supported the recovery in the first half of 2022, and exports continued adding to growth despite an increasingly challenging external environment. Consumer spending became more broad-based and increasingly rotated from goods to services. Labor market conditions are on the mend, supported by the economic recovery.

- **Headline and core inflation are trending up in developing Asia.** While still below the global average, regional inflation rose to 4.0% in the first half of 2022—higher than pre-pandemic inflation rates—driven by rising prices for food and energy. Core inflation has also been rising in several economies. Although global food prices have abated recently, the continuing war in Ukraine is keeping the costs of imported energy elevated in the region. In response, many governments in developing Asia have taken various policy measures, including subsidies, tax cuts or suspensions, trade restrictions, and price controls.

- **Developing Asia's exports remained strong in the first half of the year, but they are slowing rapidly.** Rising commodity prices supported exports, while global demand for electronics slowed. In the PRC, exports bounced back in June after the lockdown in Shanghai, but they declined in July and August. They also weakened in the Republic of Korea and fell sharply in Taipei,China, both crucial suppliers of inputs to the wider electronics sector. Manufacturing export orders point to a gloomier outlook. They declined in August in seven of the nine regional economies for which data are available, including the PRC and the Republic of Korea, and they plunged in Taipei,China.

- **Tourism is bouncing back in economies that reopened to travelers, and remittances remain healthy.** Tourist arrivals are back to pre-pandemic levels in Maldives. Arrivals continue rising in Armenia, Fiji, Georgia, Nepal, and Singapore, although they remain far below pre-pandemic levels. A rebound in tourism in Sri Lanka was interrupted by the crisis there, and arrivals are still close to zero in most Pacific island economies. Remittances remain healthy in Bangladesh, Pakistan, and the Philippines, which are among developing Asia's largest recipients in absolute terms. Remittances are still healthy in economies where these inflows are large relative to gross domestic product, as they are in the Kyrgyz Republic, Samoa, and Tajikistan.

- **Fiscal improvement continues at a slower pace, while the monetary policy tightening cycle is mounting across developing Asia.** In most economies, budget balances will improve less than initially expected this year and next, as slowing growth reduces tax revenue and governments increase spending to cushion the impact of higher energy and food prices. In contrast to the more gradual fiscal improvement underway across the region, monetary policy tightening is accelerating—there have been more and larger policy rates hikes in the region since April than there were in the first quarter. The tightening cycle should continue into early 2023, given rising inflationary pressures and weakening currencies.

- **Financial conditions deteriorated further on the dimming growth outlook and accelerated monetary tightening.** Currencies depreciated, equity markets retreated, risk premiums widened, and there have been foreign portfolio outflows in most developing Asian economies since April 2022. Financial conditions deteriorated substantially in some markets on economy-specific factors that included heavy debt burdens, worsening macroeconomic fundamentals, and exposure to the economic fallout from the Russian invasion of Ukraine.

- **This *Update* revises down the forecasts for developing Asia made in April to 4.3% from 5.2% for 2022 and to 4.9% from 5.3% for 2023.** Excluding the PRC, the rest of developing Asia is projected to grow by 5.3% in both 2022 and 2023. The revised outlook is shaped by a slowing global economy, the fallout from the war in Ukraine, more aggressive monetary tightening in advanced economies, and lockdowns resulting from the PRC's "zero-COVID" strategy. East Asia and South Asia account for most of the downgrade. East Asia's growth is revised down to 3.2% from 4.7% for 2022, as growth in the PRC will be much weaker than expected earlier. This will be the first time in more than 3 decades that the rest of developing Asia will grow faster than the PRC. Growth in South Asia this year is revised down to 6.5% from 7.0% in the earlier projection and to 6.5% from 7.4% for 2023. This reflects modest downward revisions to India's forecast on higher-than-anticipated inflation and monetary tightening, and Sri Lanka's sharp contraction caused by its sovereign debt and balance-of-payment crises. Growth forecasts are raised for the Caucasus and Central Asia, and the Pacific. The forecast for Southeast Asia remains largely unchanged.

- **The regional inflation forecast is raised to 4.5% from 3.7% for 2022 and to 4.0% from 3.1% for 2023 due to higher energy and food prices.** Inflationary pressures in developing Asia are expected to remain less severe than elsewhere in the world. But headline inflation is expected to accelerate in all subregions, to varying degrees. With recoveries continuing and labor markets improving, monetary authorities in economies where inflation pressures are broadening should push forward with tightening.

- **Risks to the outlook are skewed to the downside.** A sharp deceleration in global growth would severely undermine demand for developing Asia's exports. Stronger-than-expected monetary policy tightening in advanced economies could result in large exchange rate depreciations, financial instability, and balance-of-payment difficulties in economies with vulnerable fundamentals. An escalation of the war in Ukraine and the spillovers of this on global commodity markets remain a threat that could increase inflationary pressures further and trigger slower growth in the region. Other risks are a deeper-than-expected deceleration in the PRC, debt-related fragilities in some economies, food insecurity, geopolitical tensions, and climate change–related disruptions. Negative pandemic developments, such as the emergence of new COVID-19 variants, also remain a risk.

Entrepreneurship in the digital age

Entrepreneurs contribute to economic dynamism

- **Some entrepreneurs are more productive than others.** The defining trait of entrepreneurs is that they start and run businesses. Entrepreneurs are a heterogeneous group, though, ranging from street vendors to game-changing innovators, so their economic contributions are similarly heterogeneous. New analysis of 14,892 businesses younger than 42 months old in 17 Asian Development Bank members[1] suggests that a small group of dynamic entrepreneurs contribute disproportionately to the positive economic impact of entrepreneurship. For example, just 0.4% of the entrepreneurs in the sample account for 46% of the aggregate employment created by these businesses. These dynamic entrepreneurs are often innovators, who are a relatively small minority of entrepreneurs.

- **Innovative entrepreneurs help fuel economic dynamism.** Sustained economic growth depends on a vibrant private sector, and private sector development depends in turn on innovation and the emergence of new businesses—that is, on entrepreneurship. Innovative entrepreneurs generate dynamic competition in which new firms, products, and technologies compete with existing counterparts. Transformative entrepreneurs often play a central role in the introduction of such game-changing products as personal computers and mobile phones. More recently, the scientist-entrepreneur couple Uğur Şahin and Özlem Türeci of BioNTech were instrumental in developing one of the world's first safe and effective COVID-19 vaccines. Yet, despite its large economic potential, entrepreneurship remains a relatively under-researched topic in economics, in part for lack of good data on entrepreneurs—a gap this chapter helps fill.

- **Dynamic entrepreneurs can help sustain economic growth in Asia.** Developing Asia has reached a development stage where the private sector typically assumes a larger role in economic growth. While the government's role remains vital, it is increasingly to provide an enabling environment for private enterprise. Rapid growth has transformed Asia into a predominantly middle-income region where sustaining rapid growth becomes harder than at low income. It is at this stage where innovation becomes critical. In successful economies, such as the Republic of Korea (ROK), visionary entrepreneurs and innovators created world-class companies that contributed greatly to the journey from middle to high income. The ongoing digitalization of economic activity that accelerated during COVID-19 has fortunately opened up a world of entrepreneurial opportunities. Digital entrepreneurship can thus become an engine of growth in the post-pandemic world.

- **Digitalization is a powerful enabler of entrepreneurial resilience.** The global health and economic crisis triggered by COVID-19 highlighted the pivotal role of information and communication technology (ICT) in economic resilience. ICT enabled economies and societies to continue to function under an epidemic unprecedented in modern times. New analysis of 12,990 firms in 32 economies and 28 industries globally from May to September 2020 empirically confirms a significantly positive impact from ICT on entrepreneurial resilience during the pandemic. Compared with entrepreneurs who did not have web pages or social media presence, those that did were significantly more likely to remain open because digitalization enabled them to shift more of their activities online. Digital entrepreneurship thus helped keep economies afloat during the pandemic.

---

[1]   Armenia; Bangladesh; Georgia; Hong Kong, China; India; Indonesia; Kazakhstan; Malaysia; Pakistan; the People's Republic of China; the Philippines; the Republic of Korea; Singapore; Taipei,China; Thailand; Vanuatu; and Viet Nam.

A conducive digital environment promotes entrepreneurship

■ **Digital technology lowers entry barriers to new firms.** ICT reduces the cost of starting a business by facilitating extensive outsourcing of activities and eliminating the need for physical retail space even as it enables new firms to reach customers far and wide at low cost through the internet. Better access to foreign business partners and customers through ICT boosts internationalization and exports. More generally, digitalization improves productivity and efficiency, lowering the cost of economic transactions. Digital technology expands not only the opportunity landscape for entrepreneurs but also the avenues available for pursuing new opportunities.

■ **A new index rates the national environment for digital entrepreneurship.** The Global Index of Digital Entrepreneurship Systems (GIDES), presented in the theme chapter of this volume, measures the quality of the environment for digital entrepreneurs by capturing the degree of digitalization in society and the economy and how effectively it supports the entrepreneurial ecosystem. The index is constructed with eight pillars that capture the diverse elements of the digital entrepreneurship environment: culture, institutions, market conditions, infrastructure, human capital, knowledge, finance, and networking. Significantly, the index allows for a meaningful comparison of the quality of national digital ecosystems across 113 global economies.

■ **Singapore boasts the world's best digital entrepreneurship system.** Singapore has the top GIDES score, 81.3 out of 100, ranking it first among 15 top-tier "leaders" that include, in descending order, the US, Sweden, Denmark, and Switzerland. The next tier comprises 10 "followers," primarily innovation-driven high-income economies such as France, Israel, and the ROK. The next 15 "catchers-up" are a mixed group that includes Chile, the PRC, Italy, and Malaysia. Seven economies are among 32 "laggards," which are mainly upper-middle income, and 10 economies are among 41 "tailenders," which are mostly low and lower-middle income. The first of two observations is the sizable scope for improvement even among leaders, which have an average score of 71.2. The second is the huge gaps that exist between tiers, with the average among followers at 53.8, catchers-up 39.1, laggards 26.0, and tailenders 14.2.

■ **Productive entrepreneurship depends on a conducive digital environment.** New analysis of more than 190,000 entrepreneurs in 14 economies explored the relationship between the national digital environment, measured by GIDES, and firm productivity. For new businesses less than 42 months old, GIDES was significantly and positively linked to two indicators of individual firm productivity: product innovation and expected future job creation. An increase by one standard deviation in GIDES, for example, is associated with a 8.2 percentage point increase in the probability of a new business innovating.

Digital entrepreneurs outperform their nondigital peers

■ **Digital technology is changing the very nature of entrepreneurship.** There are two fundamental consequences of digitalization on entrepreneurial activity. First, digitalization significantly expands the scope of entrepreneurial opportunity. Smartphones, for example, have spawned such a wealth of innovative mobile applications from thousands of independent developers that the smartphone industry is essentially boundless. Second, digitalization facilitates entrepreneurial experimentation, which enables greater innovation. Entrepreneurs can test their ideas very quickly and cheaply by modifying descriptions of their offerings on their web pages and monitoring almost in real time how potential customers react.

■ **Digitalization improves entrepreneurial performance.** In-depth interviews with 685 entrepreneurs in six Southeast Asian countries—Indonesia, Malaysia, the Philippines, Singapore, Thailand, and Viet Nam—assessed how their adoption of digital technology affected their business. Digital tech applications and the digitalization of business activities were both strongly associated with the likelihood of business model experimentation—an indirect contributor to success. More directly, both were positively linked with business profitability and contribution to sustainability. In other words, digitalization helped entrepreneurs not only with their bottom line but also with their social responsibility.

■ **Surveys revealed economy-specific digital contexts in Southeast Asia.** Just as Indonesia, Malaysia, the Philippines, Singapore, Thailand, and Viet Nam vary greatly in their stage of development, interviews with entrepreneurs in the six economies suggest that their entrepreneurial ecosystems differ substantially. Furthermore, digital entrepreneurs have become active in a wide range of diverse industries across the subregion, reflecting the capability of entrepreneurs to leverage digital technology in versatile ways. These industries include food delivery in Indonesia, drone technology in Malaysia, creative enterprise including the arts and media in the Philippines, finance technology in Singapore, health and wellness in Thailand, and education in Viet Nam. Vital contributions from entrepreneurs to Thailand's official campaign to provide online health care during the pandemic confirms the social value added through entrepreneurship.

Sound institutions remain vital for entrepreneurs

■ **Solid institutions create a conducive environment for entrepreneurs.** Institutions define the rules of the game in an economy, both formal and informal, that organize economic relations. Growth-conducive institutions cited in the research literature include strong property rights, honest and effective governments, political stability, reliable legal systems, and open and competitive markets. They reduce the cost of economic transactions, create incentives to invest in human and physical capital, and contribute to more efficient allocation of resources. Intuitively, good institutions are beneficial for entrepreneurial activity because they mitigate the high risk and uncertainty that entrepreneurs face.

■ **A sound institutional environment nurtures productive entrepreneurship.** New evidence documents a link between institutions and entrepreneurship. In recent analysis drawing on more than 230,000 individuals in 15 economies, the theme chapter confirms a strong relationship between national institutional conditions and productivity in individual firms. In particular, strong rule of law, which mitigates the risk and uncertainty that entrepreneurs face, has a strong positive association with the propensity of entrepreneurs to introduce new products. An improvement by one standard deviation in the rule of law was associated with a 5.4% increase in the likelihood of product innovation by businesses less than 42 months old.

■ **Corrupt institutions impose on entrepreneurship one risk too many.** Starting a business requires an individual to assume a lot of risk because many new ventures fail. Corruption deepens risk by potentially reducing returns from successful ventures with the threat that profits may be arbitrarily expropriated. New cross-economy empirical analysis confirms that corruption is significantly associated with lower entrepreneurship. A decrease in corruption by one standard deviation is associated with an in increase in the entry of new entrepreneurs by as much as 10 percentage points.

Policy should target both entrepreneurial hardware and software

- **Policy makers enable entrepreneurship indirectly but importantly.** Entrepreneurship is inherently an individual and private pursuit. Policy makers must realize therefore that they have little direct influence on entrepreneurship—unlike investing in, for example, power plants. What policy makers can do is influence how individuals weigh entrepreneurship against other pursuits by creating an institutional, digital, and broader environment conducive to entrepreneurship. This is especially important for nurturing talented individuals who may establish high-growth firms or "gazelles" that contribute disproportionately to the economy by innovating, exporting, and creating lots of jobs. Such gazelles may later grow into globally recognized brands. Ample experience shows that policy makers cannot pick these winners, but they can give them the right environment to grow.

- **Improving regional digital entrepreneurship ecosystems will take a lot of work.** As noted earlier, the GIDES ranks Singapore the world's best digital environment for entrepreneurs, the ROK in the second tier of followers, and Malaysia and the PRC in the third tier of catchers-up. Another seven measured economies were in the fourth tier of laggards, and 10 were in the fifth tier of tailenders. This reveals plenty of scope for improving the quality of the entrepreneurial climate in the region. The scores of economies across the eight GIDES pillars are relatively balanced, which suggests that a broad policy mix will have a bigger impact than focusing on any single policy area. Economies have very different digital entrepreneurship system profiles, pointing to a need for tailored policies on entrepreneurship and digitalization.

- **Hardware and software need upgrades to catalyze dynamic entrepreneurship.** New analysis presented in the theme chapter provides strong empirical evidence of a significant and positive association between a conducive digital and institutional environment—encompassing a wide range of elements from a high-speed broadband network to strong rule of law—and productive entrepreneurs who innovate, export, and create many jobs. In the region as a whole, the weakest GIDES pillar is "culture and informal institutions." One way to strengthen that pillar is to improve public perceptions of entrepreneurship, for example through education. To conclude, policy makers have plenty of scope to foster a more entrepreneurial Asia full of dynamic entrepreneurs who innovate, create jobs, and propel growth.

GDP growth rate, % per year

	2021	2022		2023	
		April ADO 2022	*September Update*	*April ADO 2022*	*September Update*
Developing Asia	**7.0**	**5.2**	**4.3**	**5.3**	**4.9**
Developing Asia excluding the PRC	**5.9**	**5.5**	**5.3**	**5.8**	**5.3**
Caucasus and Central Asia	**5.7**	**3.6**	**3.9**	**4.0**	**4.2**
Armenia	5.7	2.8	7.0	3.8	4.5
Azerbaijan	5.6	3.7	4.2	2.8	2.8
Georgia	10.4	3.5	7.0	5.0	6.0
Kazakhstan	4.3	3.2	3.0	3.9	3.7
Kyrgyz Republic	3.6	2.0	3.0	2.5	3.5
Tajikistan	9.2	2.0	4.0	3.0	5.0
Turkmenistan	5.0	6.0	5.8	5.8	5.8
Uzbekistan	7.4	4.0	4.0	4.5	5.0
East Asia	**7.7**	**4.7**	**3.2**	**4.5**	**4.2**
Hong Kong, China	6.3	2.0	0.2	3.7	3.7
Mongolia	1.4	2.3	1.7	5.6	4.9
People's Republic of China	8.1	5.0	3.3	4.8	4.5
Republic of Korea	4.1	3.0	2.6	2.6	2.3
Taipei,China	6.6	3.8	3.4	3.0	3.0
South Asia	**8.1**	**7.0**	**6.5**	**7.4**	**6.5**
Afghanistan	...	...	...	...	...
Bangladesh	6.9	6.9	7.2	7.1	6.6
Bhutan	4.1	4.5	4.5	7.5	4.0
India	8.7	7.5	7.0	8.0	7.2
Maldives	37.1	11.0	8.2	12.0	10.4
Nepal	4.2	3.9	5.8	5.0	4.7
Pakistan	5.7	4.0	6.0	4.5	3.5
Sri Lanka	3.3	2.4	−8.8	2.5	−3.3
Southeast Asia	**3.3**	**4.9**	**5.1**	**5.2**	**5.0**
Brunei Darussalam	−1.6	4.2	2.2	3.6	3.6
Cambodia	3.0	5.3	5.3	6.5	6.2
Indonesia	3.7	5.0	5.4	5.2	5.0
Lao People's Democratic Republic	2.3	3.4	2.5	3.7	3.5
Malaysia	3.1	6.0	6.0	5.4	4.7
Myanmar	−5.9	−0.3	2.0	2.6	2.6
Philippines	5.7	6.0	6.5	6.3	6.3
Singapore	7.6	4.3	3.7	3.2	3.0
Thailand	1.5	3.0	2.9	4.5	4.2
Timor-Leste	1.5	2.5	2.3	3.1	3.0
Viet Nam	2.6	6.5	6.5	6.7	6.7
The Pacific	**−1.5**	**3.9**	**4.7**	**5.4**	**5.5**
Cook Islands	−29.1	9.1	10.5	11.2	11.2
Federated States of Micronesia	−1.2	2.2	2.2	4.2	4.1
Fiji	−4.1	7.1	11.7	8.5	8.5
Kiribati	1.5	1.8	1.8	2.3	2.3
Marshall Islands	−3.3	1.2	−1.2	2.2	−0.3
Nauru	1.6	1.0	1.2	2.4	2.2
Niue	...	...	...	...	...
Palau	−17.1	9.4	4.6	18.3	8.8
Papua New Guinea	−0.2	3.4	3.5	4.6	4.9
Samoa	−7.1	0.4	−5.3	2.2	2.0
Solomon Islands	−0.5	−3.0	−4.2	3.0	3.0
Tonga	−2.7	−1.2	−2.0	2.9	3.7
Tuvalu	1.5	3.0	2.5	3.0	2.7
Vanuatu	1.0	1.0	2.0	4.0	4.0

... = unavailable, *ADO = Asian Development Outlook,* GDP = gross domestic product, PRC= People's Republic of China.

Note: Because of the uncertain situation, no data and forecasts are provided for 2021–2023 for Afghanistan.

Inflation, % per year

	2021	2022		2023	
		April ADO 2022	September Update	April ADO 2022	September Update
Developing Asia	**2.5**	**3.7**	**4.5**	**3.1**	**4.0**
Developing Asia excluding the PRC	**4.1**	**5.1**	**6.6**	**4.2**	**5.5**
Caucasus and Central Asia	**8.9**	**8.8**	**11.5**	**7.1**	**8.5**
Armenia	7.2	9.0	8.5	7.5	7.2
Azerbaijan	6.7	7.0	11.5	5.3	7.0
Georgia	9.6	7.0	11.0	4.0	5.0
Kazakhstan	8.0	7.8	11.2	6.4	7.5
Kyrgyz Republic	11.9	15.0	15.0	12.0	12.0
Tajikistan	8.0	15.0	10.0	10.0	9.0
Turkmenistan	12.5	13.0	13.0	10.0	10.5
Uzbekistan	10.7	9.0	12.0	8.0	11.0
East Asia	**1.1**	**2.4**	**2.5**	**2.0**	**2.5**
Hong Kong, China	1.6	2.3	2.0	2.0	2.0
Mongolia	7.1	12.4	14.7	9.3	11.6
People's Republic of China	0.9	2.3	2.3	2.0	2.5
Republic of Korea	2.5	3.2	4.5	2.0	3.0
Taipei,China	2.0	1.9	2.8	1.6	2.0
South Asia	**5.8**	**6.5**	**8.1**	**5.5**	**7.4**
Afghanistan	5.2	...	...	...	...
Bangladesh	5.6	6.0	6.2	5.9	6.7
Bhutan	7.4	7.0	6.5	5.5	5.5
India	5.5	5.8	6.7	5.0	5.8
Maldives	0.5	3.0	3.3	2.5	2.8
Nepal	3.6	6.5	6.3	6.2	6.1
Pakistan	8.9	11.0	12.2	8.5	18.0
Sri Lanka	6.0	13.3	44.8	6.7	18.6
Southeast Asia	**2.0**	**3.7**	**5.2**	**3.1**	**4.1**
Brunei Darussalam	1.7	1.6	3.5	1.0	2.0
Cambodia	2.9	4.7	5.0	2.2	2.2
Indonesia	1.6	3.6	4.6	3.0	5.1
Lao People's Democratic Republic	3.7	5.8	17.0	5.0	4.5
Malaysia	2.5	3.0	2.7	2.5	2.5
Myanmar	3.6	8.0	16.0	8.5	8.5
Philippines	3.9	4.2	5.3	3.5	4.3
Singapore	2.3	3.0	5.5	2.3	2.3
Thailand	1.2	3.3	6.3	2.2	2.7
Timor-Leste	3.8	2.6	7.4	2.7	5.5
Viet Nam	1.8	3.8	3.8	4.0	4.0
The Pacific	**3.1**	**5.9**	**6.2**	**4.7**	**4.8**
Cook Islands	2.2	4.3	4.3	4.0	4.0
Federated States of Micronesia	2.0	4.6	8.8	2.0	4.1
Fiji	0.2	4.5	4.8	4.0	4.2
Kiribati	1.0	5.0	5.0	3.7	3.7
Marshall Islands	1.0	4.1	11.0	4.0	5.5
Nauru	1.2	2.3	2.3	2.2	2.5
Niue	...	...	...	...	...
Palau	0.5	4.3	10.2	4.2	5.0
Papua New Guinea	4.5	6.4	6.5	5.1	5.1
Samoa	−3.0	8.9	8.8	3.2	3.2
Solomon Islands	−0.2	5.0	4.0	4.0	4.0
Tonga	1.4	7.6	8.5	4.2	4.2
Tuvalu	6.7	3.8	7.6	3.3	3.3
Vanuatu	2.3	4.8	4.8	3.2	3.2

... = unavailable, ADO = Asian Development Outlook, GDP = gross domestic product, PRC = People's Republic of China.

Notes: Data on Afghanistan was collected from international sources. Because of the uncertain situation, no forecasts are provided for 2022–2023 for Afghanistan.

1

SOFTENING GROWTH AMID
A DARKENED GLOBAL OUTLOOK

SOFTENING GROWTH AMID A DARKENED GLOBAL OUTLOOK

Developing Asia's economic recovery faces mounting challenges. The Russian invasion of Ukraine has heightened global uncertainty and upended energy and food markets. More aggressive tightening by the Federal Reserve and other central banks is denting global demand and rattling financial markets. And growth in the region's largest economy, the People's Republic of China (PRC), is slowing markedly.

Coronavirus disease (COVID-19) risks have fallen as economies make further progress on vaccination and booster shots. This is leading to more flexible pandemic containment policies in much of developing Asia—except the PRC, which is continuing to follow a zero-COVID strategy. As many economies reopen, domestic consumer spending and investment are increasingly driving growth, supported by recovering tourism and healthy remittances. But export growth is already decelerating due to flagging global demand. Regional central banks are raising their policy rates as inflation has now risen above pre-pandemic levels. This is contributing to tighter financial conditions amid a dimming growth outlook and accelerated monetary tightening by the Fed.

Against this backdrop, developing Asia is now projected to grow more slowly, at 4.3% in 2022 and 4.9% in 2023. For the first time in more than 3 decades, the rest of developing Asia will grow faster than the PRC. Inflation forecasts are revised up—from 3.7% to 4.5% for 2022 and from 3.1% to 4.0% for 2023—on higher energy and food prices. Regional central banks should ensure that they do not fall behind the curve.

Risks to the outlook remain elevated. A sharp deceleration in global growth would severely undermine demand for developing Asia's exports, and stronger-than-expected monetary policy tightening in advanced economies could result in exchange rate depreciations, financial instability, and balance-of-payments difficulties in economies with vulnerable fundamentals. An escalation of the war in Ukraine and its spillovers on global commodity markets would further increase inflationary pressures and slow growth. And a deeper-than-expected deceleration in the PRC— due to recurrent lockdowns or problems in the property sector—would affect not just the PRC but also economies that are closely linked to it via trade and supply chains. Negative COVID-19 developments, such as the emergence of new variants, remain a risk. Other risks include debt-related fragilities in some economies, food insecurity, geopolitical tensions, and climate change–related disruptions.

This section was written by Abdul Abiad, Shiela Camingue-Romance, David Keith De Padua, Jules Hugot, Yothin Jinjarak, Matteo Lanzafame (lead), Nedelyn Magtibay-Ramos, Yuho Myoda, Pilipinas Quising, Irfan Qureshi (colead), Arief Ramayandi, Marcel Schroder, Dennis Sorino, Shu Tian, and Mai Lin Villaruel of the Economic Research and Regional Cooperation Department (ERCD), ADB, Manila, and Emmanuel Alano, Jesson Pagaduan, Rene Cris Rivera, and Michael Timbang, ERCD consultants.

Domestic demand leads the recovery even as inflation rises

Developing Asia's recovery continues, but external challenges and lingering effects from the COVID-19 pandemic are slowing its pace.
The region's economy remains on an expansionary trajectory, even though several hurdles are hindering that progress. The fallout on the global economy from the Russian invasion of Ukraine has intensified, and this is being marked by supply disruptions and elevated food and energy prices stoking inflationary pressures. Tightening monetary policy in the United States and other advanced economies is producing additional headwinds that are buffeting financial markets and denting global demand for developing Asia's exports.[1] Sporadic COVID-19 outbreaks and renewed lockdowns in the PRC have slowed that country's growth momentum, causing negative spillovers on other economies. But despite these headwinds, reopening policies are sustaining the region's recovery.

With the pandemic in check, containment policies remain more flexible and mobility patterns continue normalizing in much of developing Asia.
With new daily COVID-19 cases stabilizing at lower levels, most economies in the region moved toward less stringent containment measures in the first half of 2022 (Figure 1.1.1). Economies gradually lifted limits on business operations and relaxed social distancing rules. Reflecting these developments, domestic mobility picked up, especially where restrictions were substantially lowered (Figure 1.1.2). A notable exception to this pattern is the PRC, which, in line with its commitment to a zero-COVID approach, conducted mass testing and imposed strict lockdowns in Shanghai over April and May, and Chengdu and Shenzhen in September, and implemented severe restrictions in several other cities.

Figure 1.1.1 New COVID-19 cases

A. World and developing Asia

COVID-19 cases have stayed below their peaks, including in developing Asia.

- European Union
- US
- World
- Developing Asia

New cases, 7-day moving average, thousand

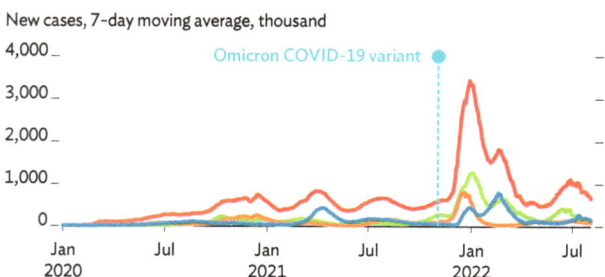

B. Developing Asia subregions

New cases rose more in East Asia than in other subregions in 2022.

- Caucasus and Central Asia
- East Asia
- South Asia
- Southeast Asia
- The Pacific

New cases, 7-day moving average, thousand

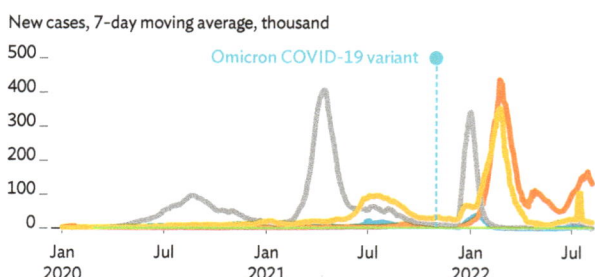

COVID-19 = coronavirus disease, US = United States.
Note: The vertical line indicates the date when the World Health Organization classified Omicron as a variant of concern (26 November 2021).
Source: Our World in Data (accessed 1 September 2022).

---

[1]   Developing Asia in *Asian Development Outlook* reports refers to 46 developing economies in Asia and the Pacific.

Figure 1.1.2 Government COVID-19 stringency index for developing Asia

COVID-19 containment measures are being eased, but not in the PRC.

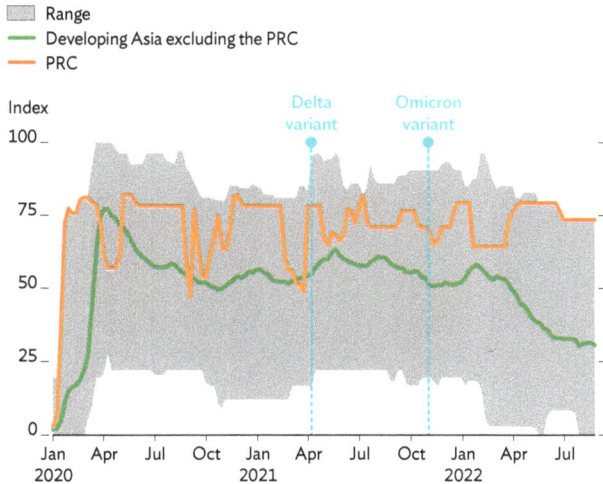

COVID-19 = coronavirus disease, PRC = People's Republic of China.

Notes: The line for developing Asia excluding the PRC plots the average for all economies with data. Vertical lines indicate the dates when the World Health Organization classified Delta as a variant of interest (4 April 2021) and Omicron as a variant of concern (26 November 2021).

Source: CEIC Data Company (accessed 31 August 2022).

The world is in a new pandemic phase of falling COVID-19 fatality rates. Increased vaccination and booster coverage, natural immunity from previous outbreaks, and the Omicron variant's less severe effect on health have resulted in a declining COVID-19 mortality risk, both across developing Asia and other regions. But vaccination coverage remains uneven. As of 30 August, 73.7% of the region's population was fully vaccinated, ahead of the US at 67.4% and almost the same as the European Union (Figure 1.1.3). About 32% of developing Asia's population have had a booster shot, and the share exceeds 70% in Bhutan, Brunei Darussalam, the Republic of Korea (ROK), Singapore, and Taipei,China. A large share of the region's population also has natural immunity after contracting COVID-19. As a result, the case fatality rate—the ratio of confirmed deaths to infections— fell by an average 0.9 percentage points since Omicron was first identified in November 2021 (Figure 1.1.4).

Figure 1.1.3 Vaccinated against COVID-19

Vaccination coverage in developing Asia is on par with the European Union's, although a few economies are lagging behind.

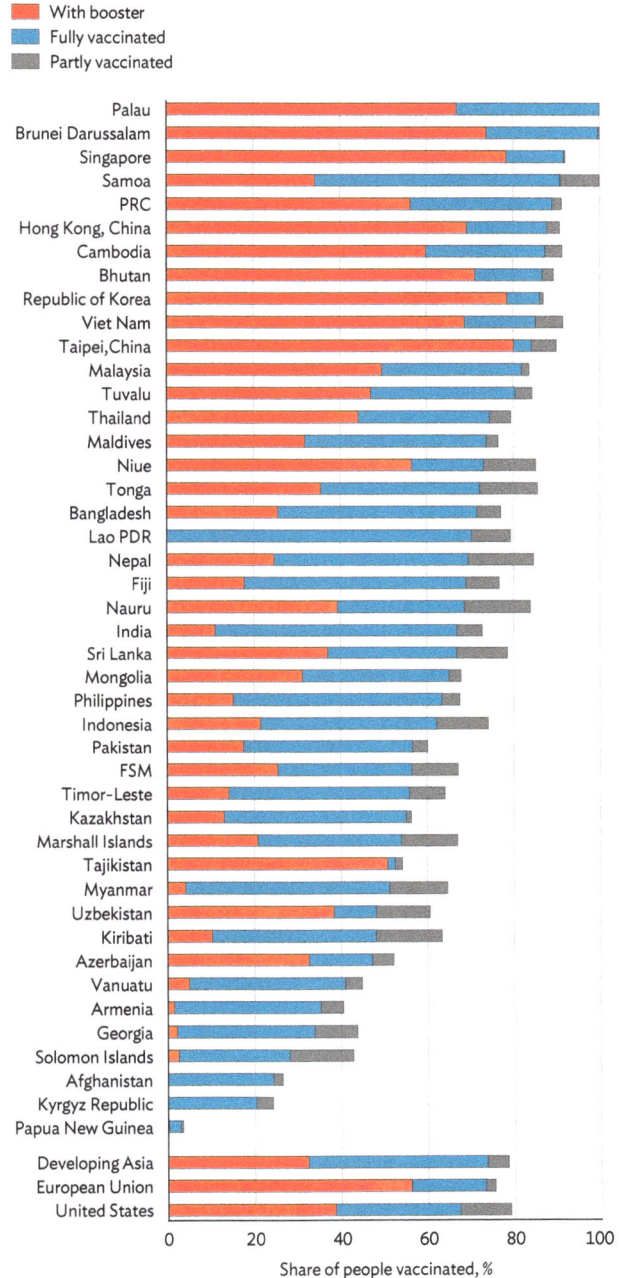

COVID-19 = coronavirus disease, FSM = Federated States of Micronesia, Lao PDR = Lao People's Democratic Republic, PRC = People's Republic of China.

Notes: Fully vaccinated is the total number of people who received all doses prescribed by the vaccination protocol; with booster is the total number of COVID-19 vaccination booster doses administered (i.e., doses administered beyond the number prescribed by the vaccination protocol). Data as of 30 August 2022.

Source: Our World in Data (accessed 1 September 2022).

Figure 1.1.4 COVID-19 case fatality rates

Rates have fallen in developing Asia and other regions.

■ Case fatality rate, 25 November 2021
■ Case fatality rate, 30 August 2022

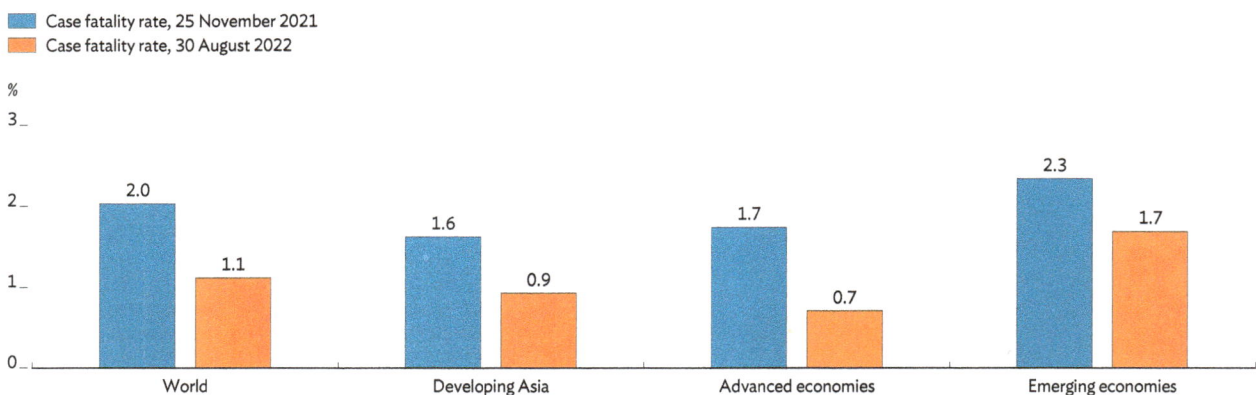

COVID-19 = coronavirus disease.

Notes: Case fatality rate is the ratio of confirmed deaths to infection cases. World Health Organization classified Omicron as a variant of concern on 26 November 2021.

Source: Our World in Data (accessed 1 September 2022).

Reopening and increased mobility led to stronger domestic demand and growth in many developing Asian economies—with some important exceptions. Year-on-year gross domestic product (GDP) growth was higher in the first half of 2022 than in 2021 among most of Southeast Asia's economies with available quarterly data, including Indonesia, Malaysia, the Philippines, and Thailand. The higher growth was led by strengthening domestic demand (Figure 1.1.5, panel A). The contribution of domestic consumption to overall growth rose in these economies as they reopened, marking an important shift from the more export-driven growth in earlier phases of the recovery. The ROK, Singapore, and Taipei,China were less affected by last year's Delta-driven COVID-19 waves and were therefore able to reopen earlier. Domestic demand, particularly investment, already rebounded in 2021, and the first half of 2022 saw GDP growth and domestic demand moderating in these economies. The PRC and Hong Kong, China are important exceptions to the pattern of reopening and strengthening domestic demand. Here, lockdowns from zero-COVID policies led to sharply lower consumption and GDP growth in the first half.

As reopening progresses, the rotation of demand away from goods toward services is gradually taking hold in developing Asia. This mirrors the experience of economies outside the region that opened up earlier. Sectoral growth patterns reflect these demand-side developments, with the contribution of industry remaining positive and growth in services advancing the recoveries of many economies in the region (Figure 1.1.5, panel B).

Labor market dynamics showed continued improvement this year. Unemployment rates in several economies in the region declined further from their pandemic peaks and are now close to pre-pandemic levels (Figure 1.1.6). Strong growth last year closed the gap with pre-pandemic output levels and normalized unemployment rates in the ROK and Taipei,China. In some economies unemployment rates have dropped below their pre-pandemic averages, but this could reflect declines in labor force participation relative to these pre-pandemic averages. This is the case in Armenia and Mongolia, where the labor force participation rate is 4.6 and 1.7 percentage points, below the average for 2015–2019.

Figure 1.1.5 Growth components

A. Demand-side contributions to growth in developing Asian economies

Domestic demand has been strong in many regional economies ...

- Investment
- Consumption
- Net exports
- ○ 2021 GDP growth, year on year
- ● 2022 H1 GDP growth, year on year

Percentage points

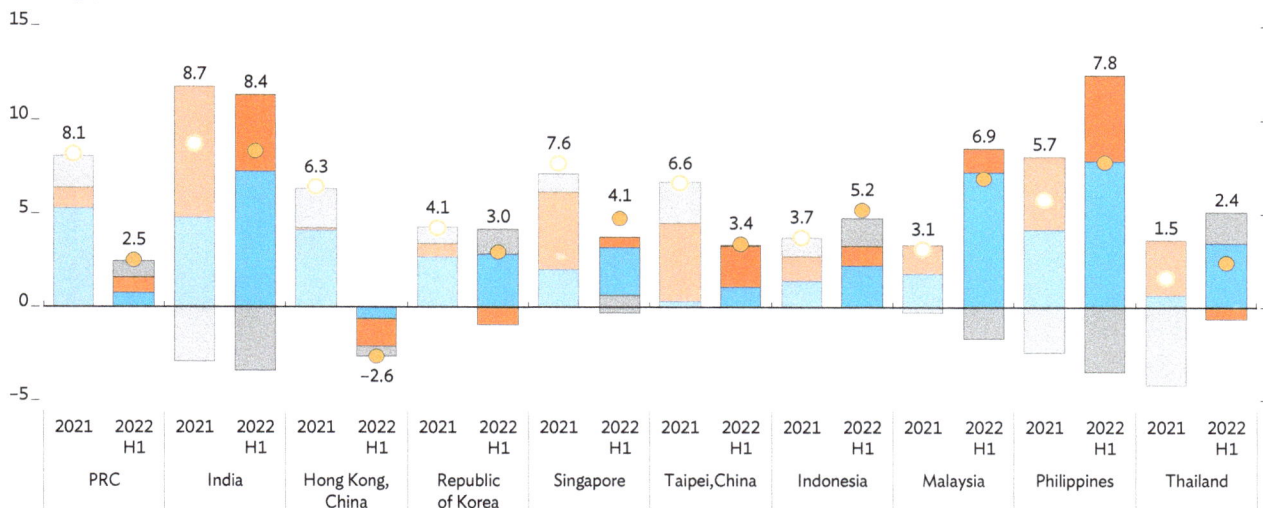

B. Supply-side contributions to growth in developing Asian economies

... and the services sector continues to contribute substantially to growth.

- Agriculture
- Industry
- Services
- ○ 2021 GDP growth, year on year
- ● 2022 H1 GDP growth, year on year

Percentage points

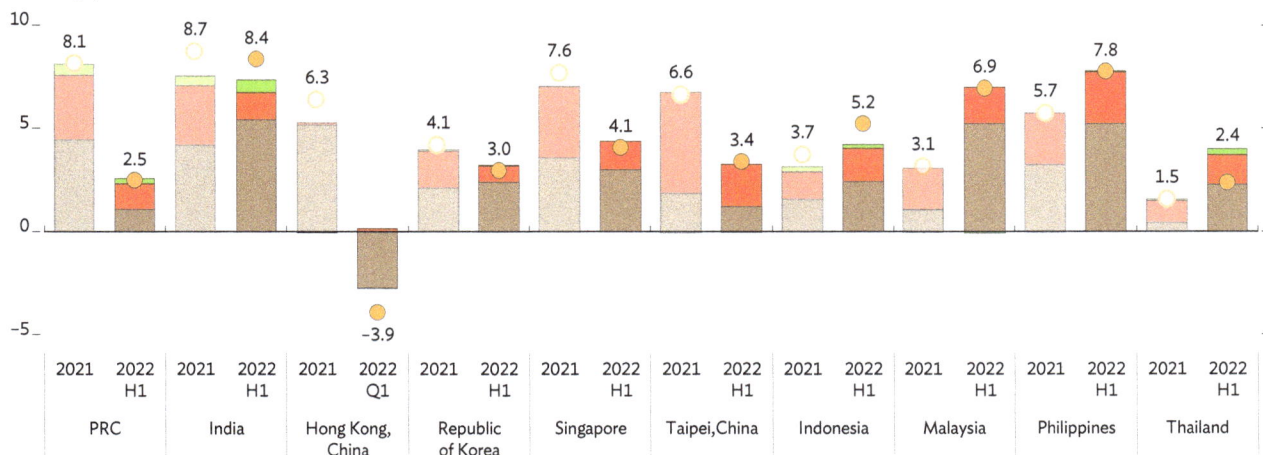

GDP = gross domestic product, H = half, PRC = People's Republic of China, Q = quarter.

Notes: Supply-side contributions to growth may not sum to GDP growth at market prices because they exclude taxes less subsidies on products.
Supply-side contributions to GDP are available only for Q1 2022 for Hong Kong, China by data cut-off.

Source: CEIC Data Company (accessed 1 September 2022).

Figure 1.1.6 Unemployment rates in developing Asian economies

Unemployment rates have declined substantially from their pandemic peaks.

| 2015–2019 average
● Pandemic peak
● June 2022

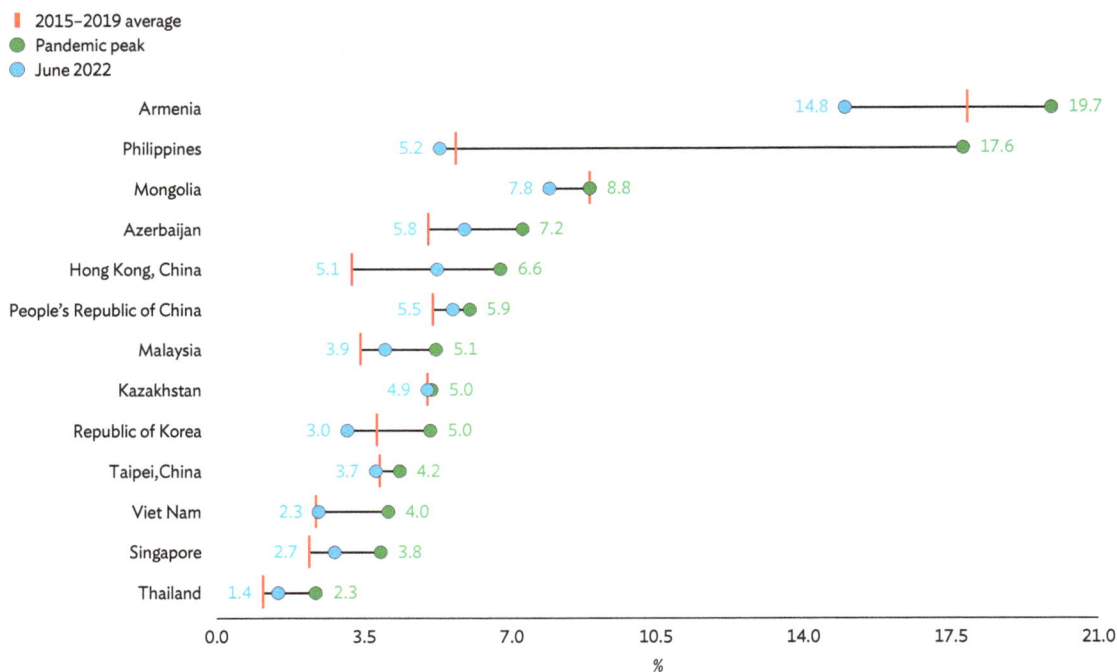

Economy	June 2022	Pandemic peak
Armenia	14.8	19.7
Philippines	5.2	17.6
Mongolia	7.8	8.8
Azerbaijan	5.8	7.2
Hong Kong, China	5.1	6.6
People's Republic of China	5.5	5.9
Malaysia	3.9	5.1
Kazakhstan	4.9	5.0
Republic of Korea	3.0	5.0
Taipei,China	3.7	4.2
Viet Nam	2.3	4.0
Singapore	2.7	3.8
Thailand	1.4	2.3

0.0   3.5   7.0   10.5   14.0   17.5   21.0
%

Notes: Unless otherwise specified, pre-pandemic average refers to the average unemployment rate from 2015 to 2019, while pandemic peak refers to the highest unemployment rate from 2020 to June 2022. Because unemployment rates are defined differently by each economy's statistics agency, comparisons of rates across economies should not be made. The most recent data for the Philippines are from July 2022 and March 2022 for Armenia. The People's Republic of China's pre-pandemic average spans 2017 to 2019.
Source: CEIC Data Company (accessed 8 September 2022).

Leading indicators suggest economic activity in developing Asia has continued to expand since April, with a few exceptions. Purchasing managers' index (PMI) readings for most economies stayed above the 50-point threshold that indicates improvement (Figure 1.1.7). But importantly, PMI readings fell below 50 in the ROK and plummeted in Taipei,China. Given the role of these two economies as global trade bellwethers, this is a strong signal of weakening global demand—as discussed in the next section. The PRC's manufacturing and services PMI recovered in June after 3 months of continuous contraction, as lockdowns were lifted in some major cities. But the manufacturing PMI dipped below 50 again in August, suggesting continued fragility in the PRC's recovery.

Headline inflation in developing Asia is on the rise.
The average inflation rate in the region increased to 5.3% in July from 3.0% in January (Figure 1.1.8).

At this level, price pressures remain more moderate than in advanced economies, including the US and the euro area, and most emerging economies. But the continued rise in inflation this year has pushed the regional rate 2.5 percentage points above the 2015–2019 prepandemic average, which suggests an increasing deviation from more normal price dynamics. The regional aggregate masks significant differences across subregions. In July, the Caucasus and Central Asia had the highest inflation rate, at 13.5%, followed by South Asia, at 10.0% (Figure 1.1.9). Inflation in East Asia was just 3.0%. Even these subregional figures hide differences across economies (Figure 1.1.10). These are due to domestic drivers—including very high inflation in Sri Lanka driven by supply disruptions and foreign currency shortages; fuel subsidy withdrawals in Pakistan; and currency depreciation in the Lao People's Democratic Republic (Lao PDR).

Figure 1.1.7 Purchasing managers' index in developing Asian economies

Manufacturing and services activity continued improving in most economies since April 2022.

Manufacturing PMI, seasonally adjusted

Economy	Jan	Feb	Mar	Apr	May	Jun	Jul	Aug	Sep	Oct	Nov	Dec	Jan	Feb	Mar	Apr	May	Jun	Jul	Aug
India	57.7	57.5	55.4	55.5	50.8	48.1	55.3	52.3	53.7	55.9	57.6	55.5	54.0	54.9	54.0	54.7	54.6	53.9	56.4	56.2
Indonesia	52.2	50.9	53.2	54.6	55.3	53.5	40.1	43.7	52.2	57.2	53.9	53.5	53.7	51.2	51.3	51.9	50.8	50.2	51.3	51.7
Malaysia	48.9	47.7	49.9	53.9	51.3	39.9	40.1	43.4	48.1	52.2	52.3	52.8	50.5	50.9	49.6	51.6	50.1	50.4	50.6	50.3
Philippines	55.5	55.5	55.2	52.0	52.9	53.8	53.4	49.4	53.9	54.0	54.7	54.8	50.0	52.8	53.2	54.3	54.1	53.8	50.8	51.2
PRC	51.5	50.9	50.6	51.9	52.0	51.3	50.3	49.2	50.0	50.6	49.9	50.9	49.1	50.4	48.1	46.0	48.1	51.7	50.4	49.5
Republic of Korea	53.2	55.3	55.3	54.6	53.7	53.9	53.0	51.2	52.4	50.2	50.9	51.9	52.8	53.8	51.2	52.1	51.8	51.3	49.8	47.6
Taipei,China	60.2	60.4	60.8	62.4	62.0	57.6	59.7	58.5	54.7	55.2	54.9	55.5	55.1	54.3	54.1	51.7	50.0	49.8	44.6	42.7
Thailand	49.0	47.2	48.8	50.7	47.8	49.5	48.7	48.3	48.9	50.9	50.6	49.5	51.7	52.5	51.8	51.9	51.9	50.7	52.4	53.7
Viet Nam	51.3	51.6	53.6	54.7	53.1	44.1	45.1	40.2	40.2	52.1	52.2	52.5	53.7	54.3	51.7	51.7	54.7	54.0	51.2	52.7

Services PMI, seasonally adjusted

Economy	Jan	Feb	Mar	Apr	May	Jun	Jul	Aug	Sep	Oct	Nov	Dec	Jan	Feb	Mar	Apr	May	Jun	Jul	Aug
India	52.8	55.3	54.6	54.0	46.4	41.2	45.4	56.7	55.2	58.4	58.1	55.5	51.5	51.8	53.6	57.9	58.8	59.2	55.5	57.2
PRC	52.0	51.5	54.3	56.3	55.1	50.3	54.9	46.7	53.4	53.8	52.1	53.1	51.4	50.2	42.0	36.2	41.4	54.5	55.5	55.0

Whole Economy PMI, seasonally adjusted

Economy	Jan	Feb	Mar	Apr	May	Jun	Jul	Aug	Sep	Oct	Nov	Dec	Jan	Feb	Mar	Apr	May	Jun	Jul	Aug
Hong Kong, China	47.8	50.2	50.5	50.3	52.5	51.4	51.3	53.3	51.7	50.8	52.6	50.8	48.9	42.9	42.0	51.7	54.9	52.4	52.3	51.2
Singapore	52.9	54.9	53.5	51.8	54.4	50.1	56.7	52.1	53.8	52.3	52.0	55.1	54.4	52.5	52.9	56.7	59.4	57.5	58.0	56.0

Delta COVID-19 variant   Omicron COVID-19 variant

COVID-19 = coronavirus disease, PMI = purchasing managers' index, PRC = People's Republic of China, Q = quarter.

Notes: The PMI is an indicator of business activity. Shades of red indicate deterioration (<50), while shades of green indicate improvement (>50).

Source: CEIC Data Company (accessed 7 September 2022).

Figure 1.1.8 Inflation by region

Inflation is trending up and is now well above the 2015–2019 average.

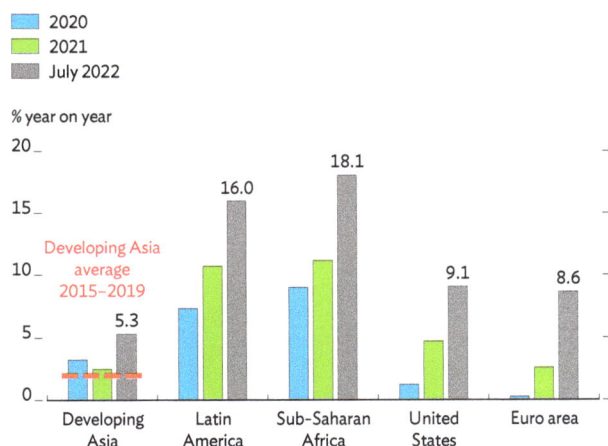

Source: CEIC Data Company (accessed 6 September 2022).

Figure 1.1.9 Inflation in developing Asia by subregion

Inflation was highest in the Caucasus and Central Asia and lowest in East Asia.

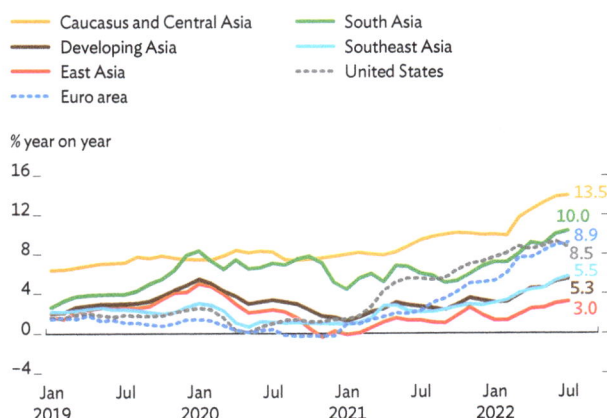

Source: CEIC Data Company (accessed 6 September 2022).

Figure 1.1.10 Monthly inflation in developing Asia

Inflation dynamics differed across economies.

Economy	Dec 2021	Jan 2022	Feb 2022	Mar 2022	Apr 2022	May 2022	Jun 2022	Jul 2022
Central Asia and Caucasus								
Armenia	7.7	7.1	6.5	7.4	8.4	9.0	10.3	9.3
Azerbaijan	12.0	12.4	11.9	12.1	12.9	13.7	14.1	13.7
Georgia	13.9	13.9	13.7	11.8	12.8	13.3	12.8	11.5
Kazakhstan	8.4	8.5	8.7	12.0	13.2	14.0	14.5	15.0
Kyrgyz Republic	11.2	11.2	10.8	13.2	14.5	14.0	13.1	13.8
Tajikistan	8.0	7.8	7.1	7.3	7.3	7.5	8.3	...
Uzbekistan	10.0	9.8	9.7	10.4	10.4	11.0	12.2	12.3
East Asia								
Hong Kong, China	2.4	1.2	1.6	1.7	1.3	1.2	1.8	1.9
Mongolia	13.4	14.6	14.2	14.4	14.4	15.2	16.1	15.7
PRC	1.5	0.9	0.9	1.5	2.1	2.1	2.5	2.7
Republic of Korea	3.7	3.6	3.7	4.1	4.8	5.4	6.0	6.3
Taipei,China	2.6	2.8	2.3	3.3	3.4	3.4	3.6	3.4
South Asia								
Bangladesh	6.1	5.9	6.2	6.2	6.3	7.4	7.6	7.5
India	5.7	6.0	6.1	7.0	7.8	7.0	7.0	6.7
Maldives	0.0	0.2	0.6	1.1	1.2	2.5	5.2	...
Nepal	7.1	5.6	6.0	7.1	7.3	7.9	8.6	8.1
Pakistan	12.3	13.0	12.2	12.7	13.4	13.8	21.3	24.9
Sri Lanka	14.0	16.8	17.5	21.5	33.8	45.3	58.9	66.7
Southeast Asia								
Brunei Darussalam	2.2	2.8	3.2	3.8	3.9	3.8	...	...
Cambodia	3.7	4.1	6.3	7.2	7.3	7.2	7.8	...
Indonesia	1.9	2.2	2.1	2.6	3.5	3.6	4.3	4.9
Lao PDR	5.3	6.2	7.3	8.5	7.3	12.8	23.6	25.6
Malaysia	3.2	2.3	2.2	2.2	2.3	2.8	3.4	4.4
Myanmar	12.6	13.8	14.1	17.3	17.8	...	...	...
Philippines	3.1	3.0	3.0	4.0	4.9	5.4	6.1	6.4
Singapore	4.0	4.0	4.3	5.4	5.4	5.6	6.7	7.0
Thailand	2.2	3.2	5.3	5.7	4.6	7.1	7.7	7.6
Viet Nam	1.8	1.9	1.4	2.4	2.6	2.9	3.4	3.1
The Pacific								
Fiji	3.0	2.7	1.9	4.7	4.7	5.0	5.1	5.2
Papua New Guinea	5.7	...	...	6.9	...	...	...	...
Solomon Islands	2.6	2.0	-1.1	-2.7	1.5	4.3	..	...
Tonga	9.2	8.2	9.0	7.9	9.4	11.2	11.3	13.1
Vanuatu	0.7	...	...	2.7	...	...	...	...

... = not available, Lao PDR = Lao People's Democratic Republic, PRC = People's Republic of China.

Notes: Dark green denotes low inflation; dark red denotes high inflation, both relative to the range of inflation datapoints for all economies from December 2021 to July 2022. The table includes Asian Development Bank developing member economies for which monthly inflation data are available.

Sources: CEIC Data Company (accessed 4 September 2022); Solomon Islands National Statistics Office; Tonga Statistics Department; Vanuatu National Statistics Office.

Figure 1.1.11 Global energy and food prices

Prices of energy products

Oil prices are decreasing on softening global demand, but natural gas prices are surging as the Russian Federation's exports to Europe plunge.

Prices of key agricultural products

Food prices remain high, but have recently fallen from their peaks on sluggish demand and improved crop expectations.

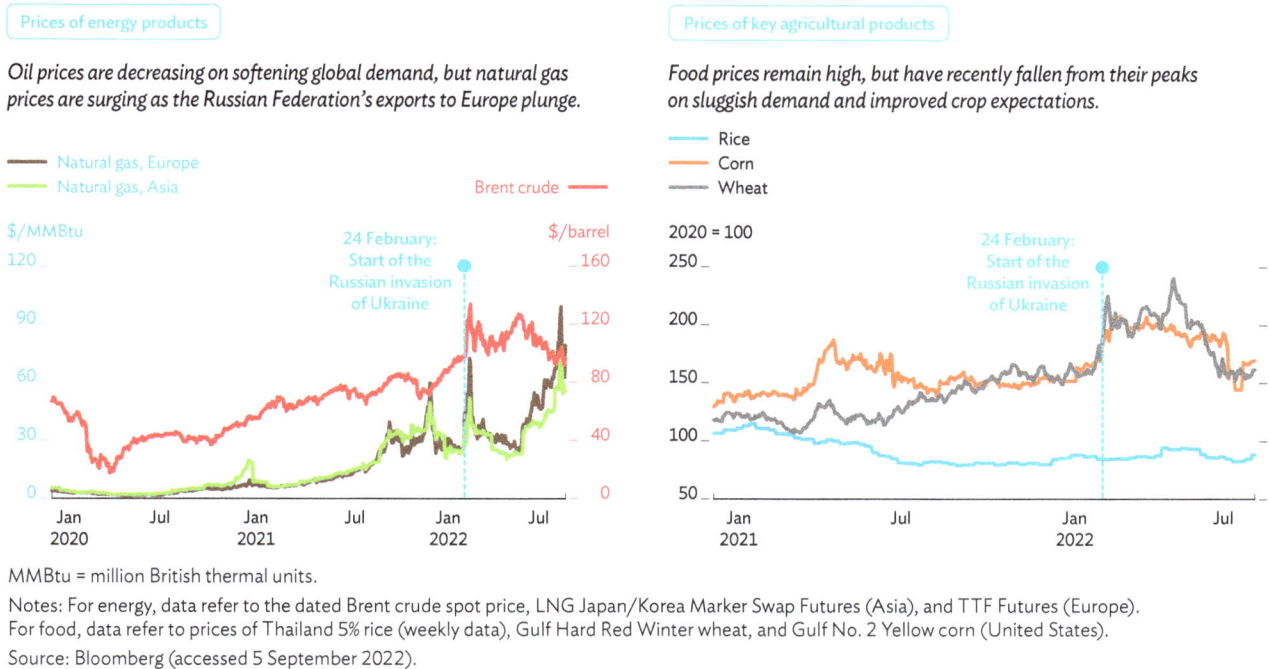

MMBtu = million British thermal units.
Notes: For energy, data refer to the dated Brent crude spot price, LNG Japan/Korea Marker Swap Futures (Asia), and TTF Futures (Europe). For food, data refer to prices of Thailand 5% rice (weekly data), Gulf Hard Red Winter wheat, and Gulf No. 2 Yellow corn (United States).
Source: Bloomberg (accessed 5 September 2022).

Rising food and energy prices contributed to inflation accelerating throughout the region.
Price pressures largely resulted from the rise in global commodity prices and supply chain disruptions that had already started during the pandemic recovery and were exacerbated by the Russian invasion of Ukraine (Figure 1.1.11). The rise in food and energy prices over the past year remains the main driver of the recent rise in inflation (Figure 1.1.12). This is in line with empirical evidence indicating the pass-through from international food and fuel prices to domestic inflation is significant, particularly for food prices (Box 1.1). While global food and energy prices have been decreasing recently, it will take time for these declines to translate into lower domestic prices.

Inflation seems to be broadening on consumer spending on services. Core inflation—which excludes volatile components, such as food and energy—also rose further in many regional economies over January–July 2022, above the average during 2015–2019 and the 2021 level (Figure 1.1.13).

The increase in core inflation was likely driven by the gradual recovery and broadening in consumption demand. Consumers have been adjusting their spending patterns, previously focused on goods, to encompass more services, including high-contact services such as hotel and restaurants, leading to a pickup in services inflation in various economies.

Governments in developing Asia have responded to rising food and energy prices with various policy actions this year. About 70% of the region's economies (32 out of 46) had adopted at least one policy aimed at cushioning the impact of food or energy price increases as of mid-September. These are either new measures (about 67% of the total) or enhancements of policies already in place—for example, extending the measures to a larger share of the population and/or lengthening their duration (Online Appendix Table 1). Out of the 102 policy measures introduced or enhanced in 2022 in the region, 58 targeted food and agriculture-products, and 44 fuel and energy (Figure 1.1.14).

Figure 1.1.12 Contributions to average inflation in developing Asian economies, January to July 2022

Food and energy prices have driven recent inflation in much of the region.

- Food and nonalcoholic beverages
- Energy related
- Other items
- Overall inflation

Percentage points

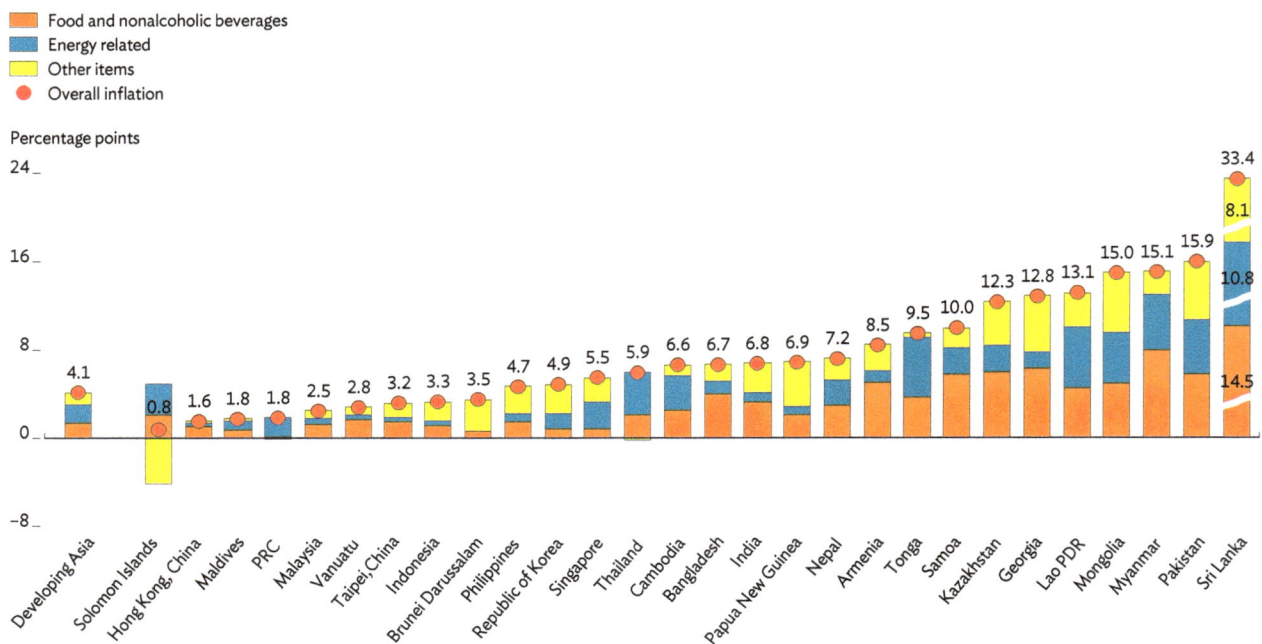

Lao PDR = Lao People's Democratic Republic, PRC = People's Republic of China.

Notes: Data for Cambodia, Malaysia, Maldives, and Tonga are from January to June 2022; for Brunei Darussalam and Solomon Islands up to May; for Myanmar, Papua New Guinea, and Vanuatu up to March. Because of a lack of a more disaggregated breakdown, energy-related consumer prices for most economies include housing, water, and nonfuel transport. Developing Asia is calculated as the weighted average of all the economies covered.

Sources: Asian Development Bank estimates using data from Haver Analytics; CEIC Data Company; national sources (all accessed 29 August 2022).

Figure 1.1.13 Core inflation in developing Asia

Rising and elevated core inflation is above the pre-pandemic average of 2015–2019.

- 2015–2019 average
- 2021
- 2022

%

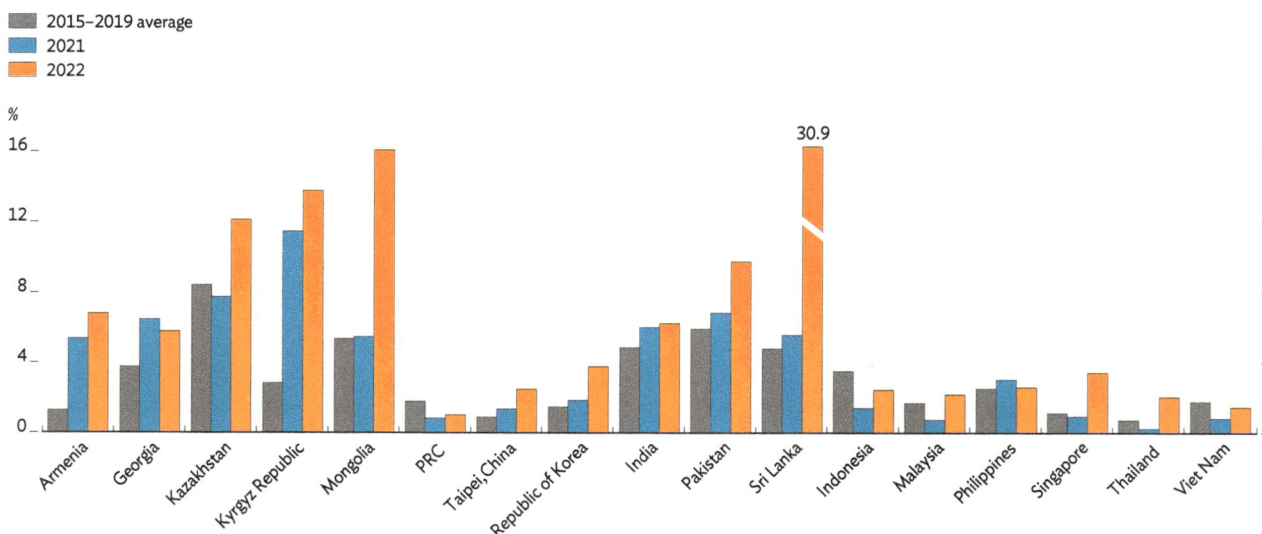

PRC = People's Republic of China.

Notes: 2022 data from January to July, but to June for Mongolia. Pre-pandemic average data for Malaysia and Mongolia from 2016 to 2019.

Source: CEIC Data Company (accessed 18 September 2022).

Figure 1.1.14 Policies aimed at rising food and energy prices in developing Asia, by implementation period

Rising food and energy prices prompted a significant policy response in 2022.

- ☐ Old (since 2021 or earlier)
- ☐ Enhanced old policy (2022)
- ☐ New (2022)

Number of policies

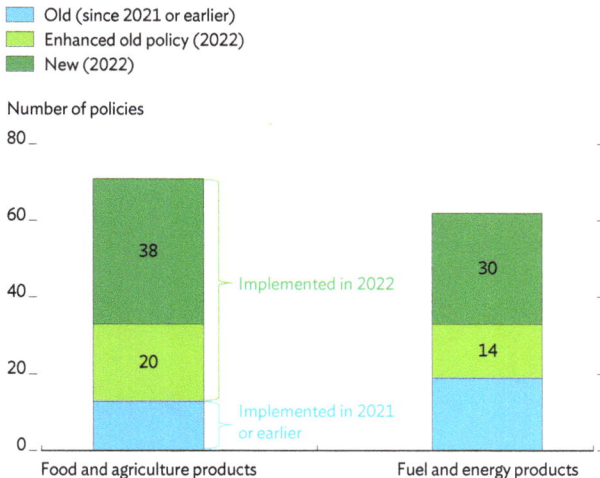

Sources: Asian Development Bank survey of 46 developing Asian economies; Food Export Restrictions Tracker Working Paper 2. International Food Policy Research Institute; D. Laborde and A. Mamun. 2022. Documentation for Food and Fertilizers Export Restriction Tracker: Tracking Export Policy Responses Affecting Global Food Markets during Crisis; national sources and online articles; World Bank. 2022. Food Security Update. 29 July (accessed 9 September 2022).

Most policy measures this year have been subsidies and suspensions or cuts in taxes and duties.
More than half of the policies implemented have been price or direct subsidies, export restrictions, and suspensions or cuts in taxes and duties (Figure 1.1.15, panel A). Price or direct subsidies include cash payments, transfers, discounts, or other forms of targeted funds allocated by the government. Almost 59% of subsidies are directed toward fuel and energy products, while the rest are aimed at food and agriculture (Figure 1.1.15, panel B). Some 60% of authorities reduced or suspended value-added tax on imports and other duties, mostly on fuel and energy products.

Some governments also imposed temporary trade restrictions to safeguard domestic food security. Export restrictions accounted for 20% of the total policy measures adopted this year. These were aimed at boosting the domestic supply of and moderating price increases for food and agricultural products, and included quantitative restrictions on exports as well as outright export bans.

Figure 1.1.15 Policy measures aimed at tackling rising food and energy prices and tighter supply in developing Asia by type, product, and implementation period

Governments increased the use of subsidies, typically the most-used tool to affect food and energy prices.

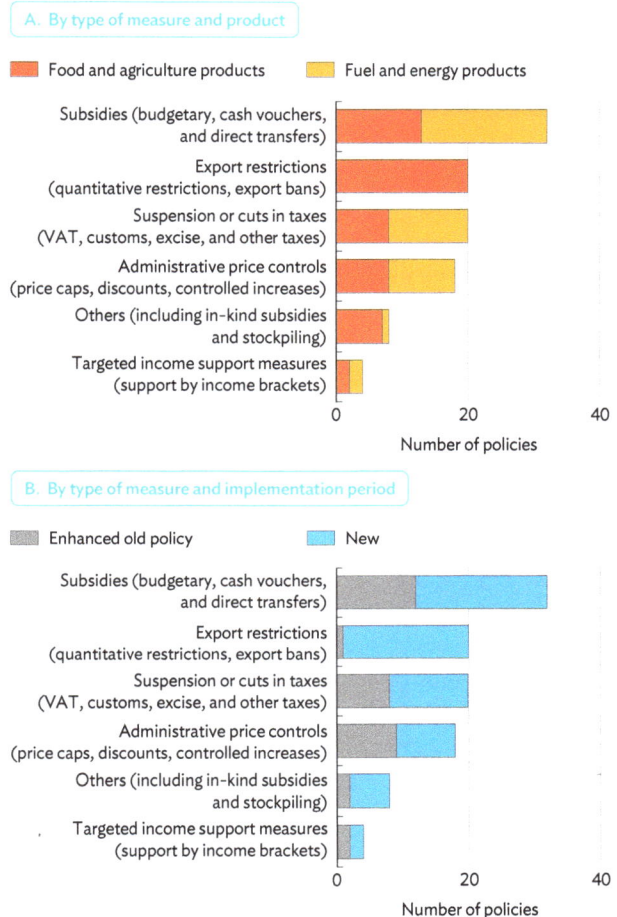

VAT = value-added tax.
Sources: Asian Development Bank survey of 46 developing Asian economies; Food Export Restrictions Tracker Working Paper 2. International Food Policy Research Institute; D. Laborde and A. Mamun. 2022. Documentation for Food and Fertilizers Export Restriction Tracker: Tracking Export Policy Responses Affecting Global Food Markets during Crisis; national sources and online articles; World Bank. 2022. Food Security Update. 29 July (accessed 9 September 2022).

Temporary export bans were imposed in Afghanistan, Azerbaijan, Bangladesh, Georgia, India, Kazakhstan, the Kyrgyz Republic, Malaysia, Pakistan, the PRC, and the ROK. Other measures aimed at supporting domestic food supply include stockpiling of agricultural products and direct purchase from farmers, as well as administrative price controls, which accounted for about 18% of overall measures.

Exports remain healthy, but clouds are gathering

Exports grew in developing Asia in the first half of 2022, but slower than last year. Regional exports grew by 15.1% year on year in nominal terms, down from 23.8% in the same period last year (Figure 1.1.16). Two-thirds of this growth was due to rising prices, as exports increased by only 5.2% in real terms. Nominal exports rose by 13.5% in the PRC, slightly slower than in the rest of the region. For the first time since 2020, this resulted in export growth relative to pre-pandemic levels underperforming in the PRC. Regional exports dipped over March–April on the fall in exports from the PRC, where the lockdown in Shanghai from 14 March to 1 June caused severe disruptions to trade. Redirected shipments to other ports in May and the easing of pandemic restrictions in June led the recovery, although electronics exports did not fully recover. Exports then fell sharply in July and August, erasing all growth since the beginning of the year.

Commodity exports increased on rising global prices following the Russian invasion of Ukraine. This increase in nominal exports benefited the region's exporters of crude oil and natural gas— Azerbaijan, Brunei Darussalam, Indonesia, Kazakhstan, Malaysia, Papua New Guinea, and Turkmenistan (Figures 1.1.17 and 1.1.18). Rising oil prices also supported commodity exports in India and Singapore, which refine crude oil from the Middle East and supply economies eastward, including Indonesia, Malaysia, and the PRC. Rising food prices supported commodity exports in Central Asia, South Asia, and Southeast Asia, including wheat from Kazakhstan; coffee from Timor-Leste, the Lao PDR, and Viet Nam; and palm oil from Indonesia, Papua New Guinea, and Malaysia. Exports of base and precious metals in the Caucasus and Central Asia were supported by prices rising from February to April for these commodities, before they started falling in May. In parallel, nominal exports to the Russian Federation were boosted by the ruble's appreciation since March.

Figure 1.1.16 Nominal exports in developing Asia and advanced economies

Export growth slowed, but remained healthy in developing Asia in H1 2022.

H = half, PRC = People's Republic of China.

Notes: In this figure, developing Asia excluding the PRC comprises Hong Kong, China; India; Indonesia; the Republic of Korea; Malaysia; Pakistan; the Philippines; Singapore; Taipei,China; Thailand; and Viet Nam. Data are seasonally adjusted. The PRC's exports for January and February are averaged to avoid reflecting the timing of the lunar new year holidays.

Sources: CEIC Data Company; CPB World Trade Monitor (both accessed 7 September 2022).

Export growth of manufactured goods is slowing, particularly for electronics. Manufactured goods contributed a modest 1.4 percentage points to regional export growth in the first half of this year in a sample of 12 economies that account for 88% of the region's exports. This is a sharp decrease from the second half of last year, when they contributed 6.9 percentage points. Among manufactured goods, electronics contributed a negative 1.6 percentage points to total export growth in the first half. These declines particularly affected the ROK and Taipei,China, the key suppliers of inputs for wider electronics manufacturing in the region. Electronics exports were more resilient in Southeast Asia, but they did not increase over the first half, suggesting the deceleration is primarily driven by a slowdown in global demand.

Figure 1.1.17 Sector contributions to nominal export growth in developing Asia

Commodity exports picked up, but electronics exports moderated.

Legend:
- Food and beverage
- Electronics
- Other manufacturing
- Mineral fuels
- Other commodities
- Other sectors
- Overall change

% change from same month in 2019

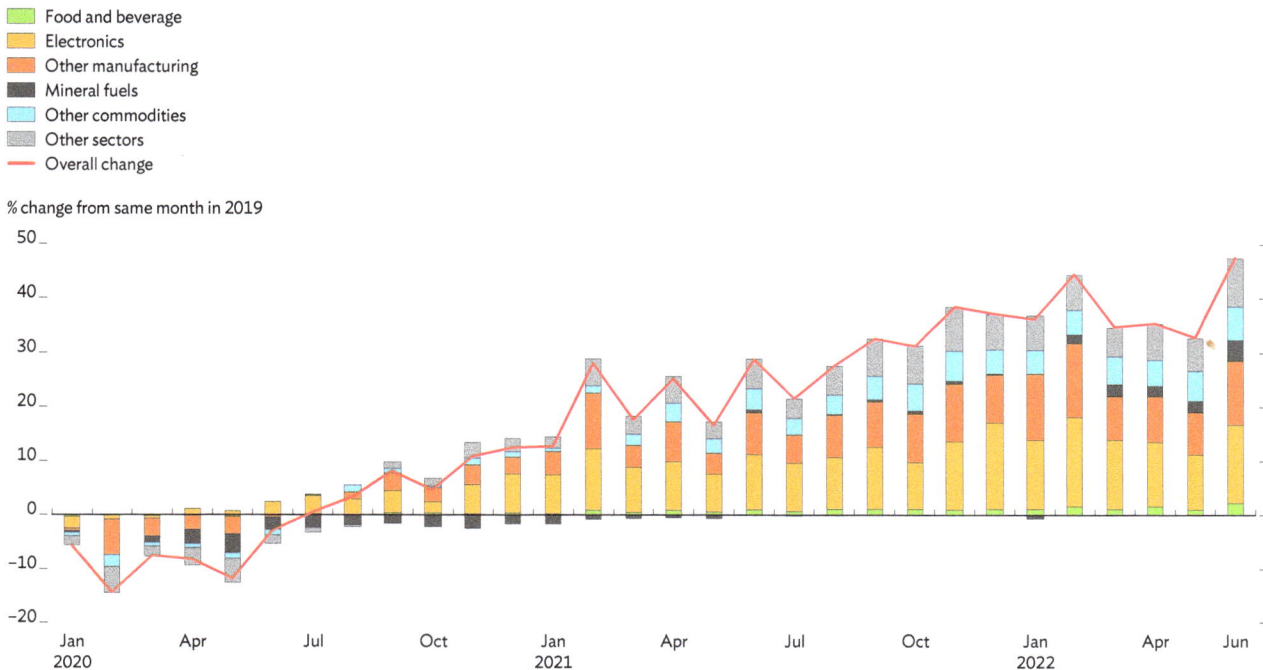

Note: The sample comprises Armenia; Georgia; Hong Kong, China; India; Indonesia; Malaysia; the People's Republic of China; the Republic of Korea; Singapore; Taipei,China; Thailand; and Uzbekistan.
Sources: International Trade Centre. Trade Map; Observatory of Economic Complexity; United Nations Comtrade Database (all accessed 1 September 2022).

Exports of inputs for electronics manufacturing are decelerating sharply. The ROK's exports grew by 13.7% year on year in the first 8 months of 2022, down from 27.6% in the same period last year (Figure 1.1.19). Chip exports contracted by 1.6% in the first half of the year relative to the second half of 2021, with memory chip exports—the ROK's largest export—contracting by 7.3% (Figure 1.1.20). Export growth also decelerated sharply in Taipei,China, at 18.7% in the first 8 months of the year, down from 27.7% in the same period last year. In August alone, exports fell 9.8% from the previous month, declining to their level in August last year. Chip exports still grew in the first half of the year, up 9.7% relative to the second half of 2021, but quarter-on-quarter growth slowed from 7.7% in the first quarter to 3.1% in the second. Overall, the fall in exports of key inputs for downstream electronic manufacturing suggests an upcoming slowdown in exports of final electronic goods in developing Asia.

New manufacturing export orders are weakening in developing Asia. The new export orders index for manufactured goods contracted in August in seven of the nine economies for which the index is available, reflecting a decline in orders relative to the previous month (Figure 1.1.21). The contraction was particularly sharp in Taipei,China—the leading global supplier of semiconductor chips. Export orders also fell in the ROK, the region's key supplier of memory chips. In both economies, the contraction in August follows declines every month since March. Manufacturing export orders remained healthy in India, driven by orders for labor-intensive goods, such as textiles. They also remained healthy in Viet Nam, which has attracted large foreign investments in manufacturing recently. In both economies, robust export orders for manufactured goods partly reflect the diversification of suppliers away from the PRC because of trade tensions with the US.

Figure 1.1.18 Sector contributions to nominal export growth by subregion in developing Asia

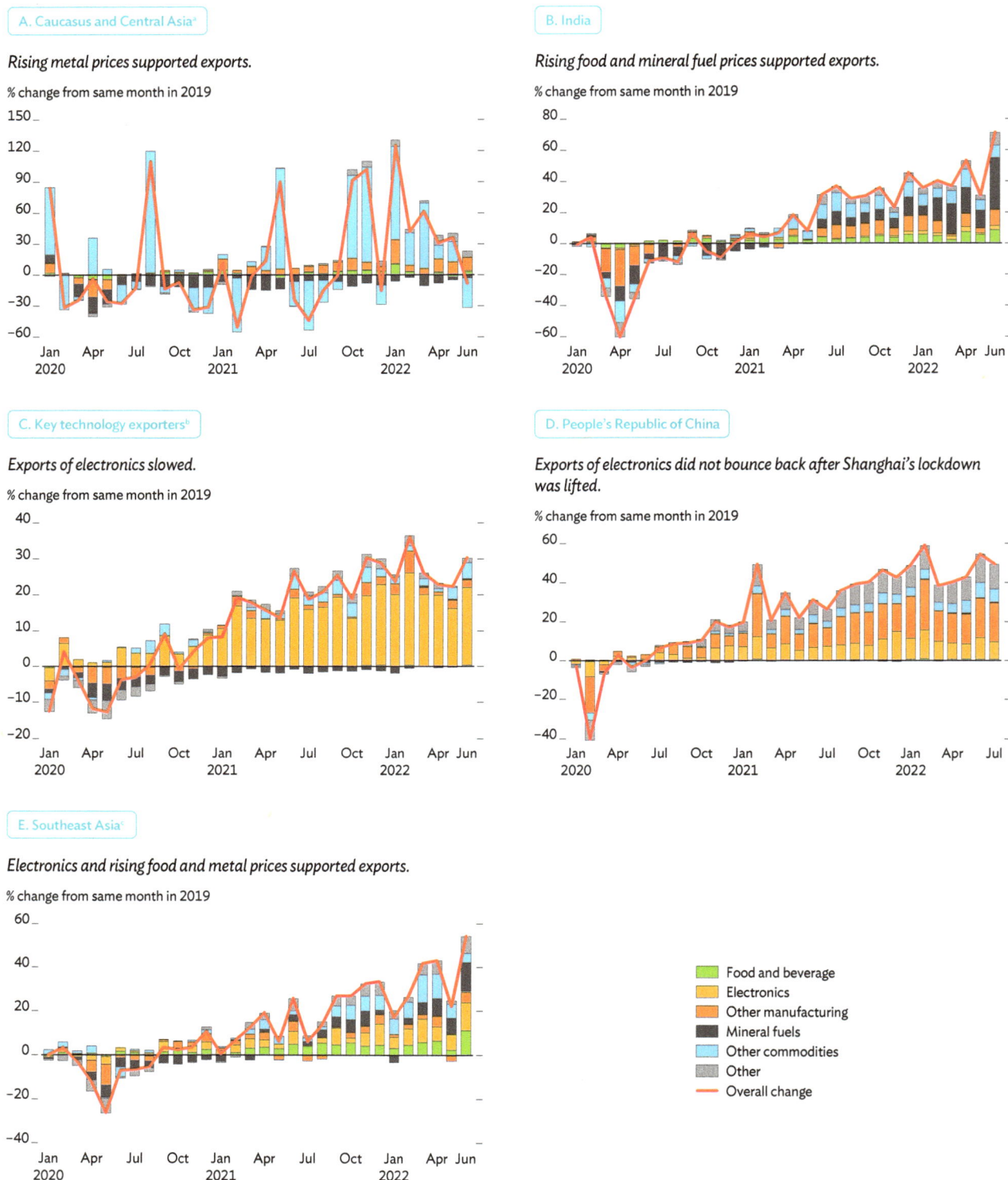

A. Caucasus and Central Asia[a]

Rising metal prices supported exports.

% change from same month in 2019

B. India

Rising food and mineral fuel prices supported exports.

% change from same month in 2019

C. Key technology exporters[b]

Exports of electronics slowed.

% change from same month in 2019

D. People's Republic of China

Exports of electronics did not bounce back after Shanghai's lockdown was lifted.

% change from same month in 2019

E. Southeast Asia[c]

Electronics and rising food and metal prices supported exports.

% change from same month in 2019

Legend:
- Food and beverage
- Electronics
- Other manufacturing
- Mineral fuels
- Other commodities
- Other
- Overall change

[a] Armenia, Georgia, Uzbekistan; [b] Hong Kong, China; Republic of Korea; Singapore; Taipei,China; [c] Indonesia, Malaysia, Thailand.
Sources: International Trade Centre. Trade Map; Observatory of Economic Complexity; United Nations Comtrade Database (all accessed 1 September 2022).

Figure 1.1.19 Nominal exports in developing Asia's key technology exporters

Export growth is slowing in the region's key exporters of electronics inputs.

— Republic of Korea
— Singapore
— Taipei,China

$, 2019 = 100

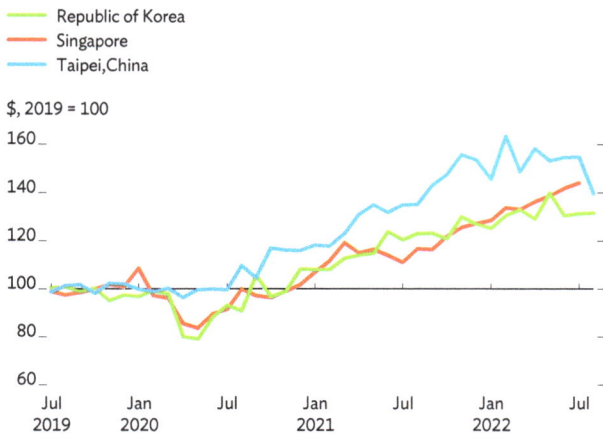

Source: CEIC Data Company (accessed 8 September 2022).

Figure 1.1.20 Chip exports in the Republic of Korea and Taipei,China

The Republic of Korea's chip exports have been stable since Q3 2021; Taipei,China's grew.

$ billion

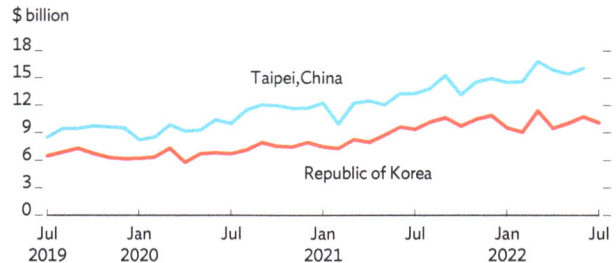

Q = quarter.

Note: Chips correspond to electronic integrated circuits in the Harmonized System classification (code 8542); they include processors and controllers, memory chips, and semiconductor chips.

Sources: International Trade Centre. Trade Map; Observatory of Economic Complexity; United Nations Comtrade Database (all accessed 1 September 2022).

Figure 1.1.21 New manufacturing export orders index for developing Asian economies

Manufacturing export orders are weakening in the region, particularly in the Republic of Korea and Taipei,China, the two leading exporters of electronic inputs.

A. East Asia and India

— India
— People's Republic of China
— Republic of Korea
— Taipei,China

Index

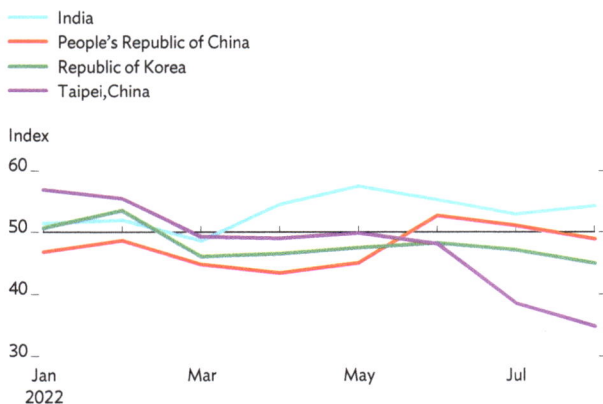

B. Southeast Asia

— Indonesia
— Malaysia
— Philippines
— Thailand
— Viet Nam

Index

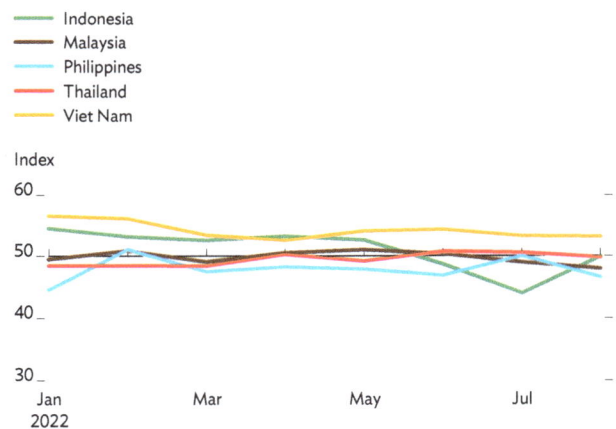

Note: Index over 50 indicates higher orders relative to the previous month.
Sources: IHS Markit; Observatory of Economic Complexity (both accessed 4 September 2022).

The slowdown in exports of manufactured goods eased supply chain constraints. Container shipping rates from East Asia to Europe and the US declined significantly in the first half of 2022, except for a temporary increase in rates caused by the lockdown in Shanghai (Figure 1.1.22). The lower rates over the first half followed sharp increases last year.

Shipping rates within Asia, however, have yet to come down, although they have not risen as much as for East Asia's exports to Europe and the US. As of 26 August, shipping a container from East Asia to the US cost about $7,000, down from $16,000 in January. The drop reflects the slowdown in global demand associated with the rebalancing of expenditure from goods to services in advanced economies.

Figure 1.1.22 Container freight rates

Shipping costs remain high within Asia, but have fallen between Asia and Europe, and Asia and the US.

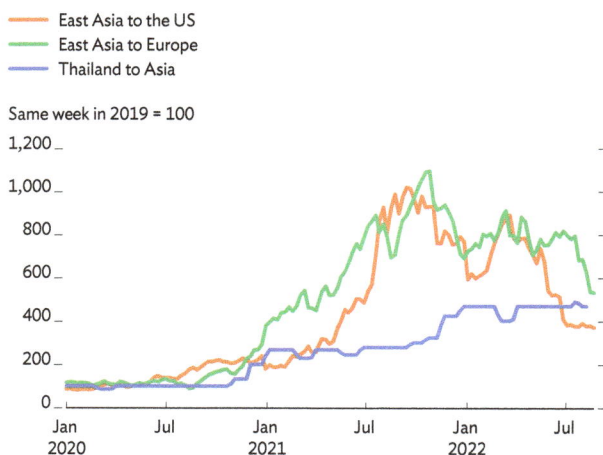

- East Asia to the US
- East Asia to Europe
- Thailand to Asia

Same week in 2019 = 100

US = United States.

Note: Freight rates from Thailand to Asia are the average of freight rates from Thailand to Hong Kong, China; Japan; and Shanghai.

Sources: Freightos Baltic Index; Thai National Shippers' Council (both accessed 31 August 2022).

Figure 1.1.23 Purchasing managers' index of delivery times of suppliers

Delivery times shortened considerably in H1 2022.

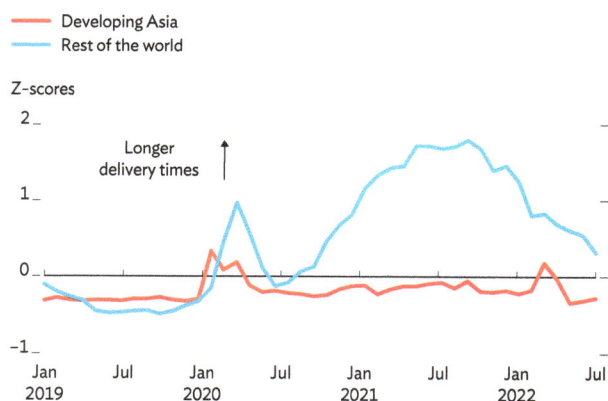

- Developing Asia
- Rest of the world

Z-scores

Longer delivery times

H = half.

Notes: The index measures the number of standard deviations between each supplier's delivery time index in an economy and the mean for the sample with all economies over 2016–2021. Developing Asia is the average of India; Indonesia; Malaysia; the People's Republic of China; the Philippines; the Republic of Korea; Taipei,China; Thailand; and Viet Nam weighted by gross domestic product based on purchasing power parity.

Source: CEIC Data Company (accessed 4 September 2022).

This rebalancing weakened demand for electronics exports from developing Asia. Shorter supplier delivery times also reflect easing supply chain disruptions (Figure 1.1.23).

Tourism has rebounded in 14 regional economies.
This largely reflects the timing and extent of international border reopenings (Figure 1.1.24). Tourist arrivals have fully recovered in Maldives, which was the first economy in the region to relax travel restrictions in July 2020. Arrivals gradually picked up in the first half of 2022 in Armenia, Fiji, Georgia, India, and Nepal, but the increase is still, depending on the destination, 18%–33% below pre-pandemic levels. Arrivals picked up quickly in Cambodia, Indonesia, Malaysia, the Philippines, Singapore, Thailand, and Viet Nam after travel restrictions were relaxed in late 2021 and early 2022. But tourist arrivals to these countries were still down by 58%–75% in June from their pre-pandemic level, in part because of the absence of tourists from the PRC and elsewhere in East Asia. In Sri Lanka, the rebound in tourism that started in September 2021 came to an abrupt halt in April due to the crisis there.

International tourism is still at a standstill in East Asia and most Pacific island economies.
In developing Asia, 60% of economies still require COVID-19 tests—including Tonga and Vanuatu, where tourist arrivals remain close to zero. Travel restrictions are even tighter in nearly a third of economies in developing Asia, including Bhutan; Brunei Darussalam; Hong Kong, China; and the PRC, where tourists are also virtually absent.

Remittances remained healthy in the first quarter (Q1) of 2022. They were above pre-pandemic levels, by 43% in Pakistan, 25% in Bangladesh, and 9% in the Philippines—some of developing Asia's largest recipients of remittances, with inflows exceeding the equivalent of 5% of GDP (Figure 1.1.25). Remittances were also healthy in Armenia, Georgia, Nepal, and Uzbekistan—four economies where they exceed 10% of GDP. But remittances continued falling in Sri Lanka, reaching only 43% of their pre-pandemic level due to parallel exchange rates discouraging migrant workers from sending money through official channels. In Cambodia, remittances remained sluggish because the land border with Thailand only opened in May.

Figure 1.1.24 International tourist arrivals in developing Asian economies

Tourism rebounded in 14 economies, but remains at a standstill in East Asia and most Pacific island economies.

A. Economies where tourism began rebounding in 2020-2021

Armenia	Maldives
Fiji	Nepal
Georgia	Sri Lanka
India	

B. Economies where tourism has rebounded since January 2022

Cambodia	Singapore
Indonesia	Thailand
Malaysia	Viet Nam
Philippines	

C. Economies where tourism has not rebounded

Bhutan	Republic of Korea
Hong Kong, China	Taipei,China
Myanmar	Tonga
Palau	Vanuatu

% change from 2018–2019 monthly average

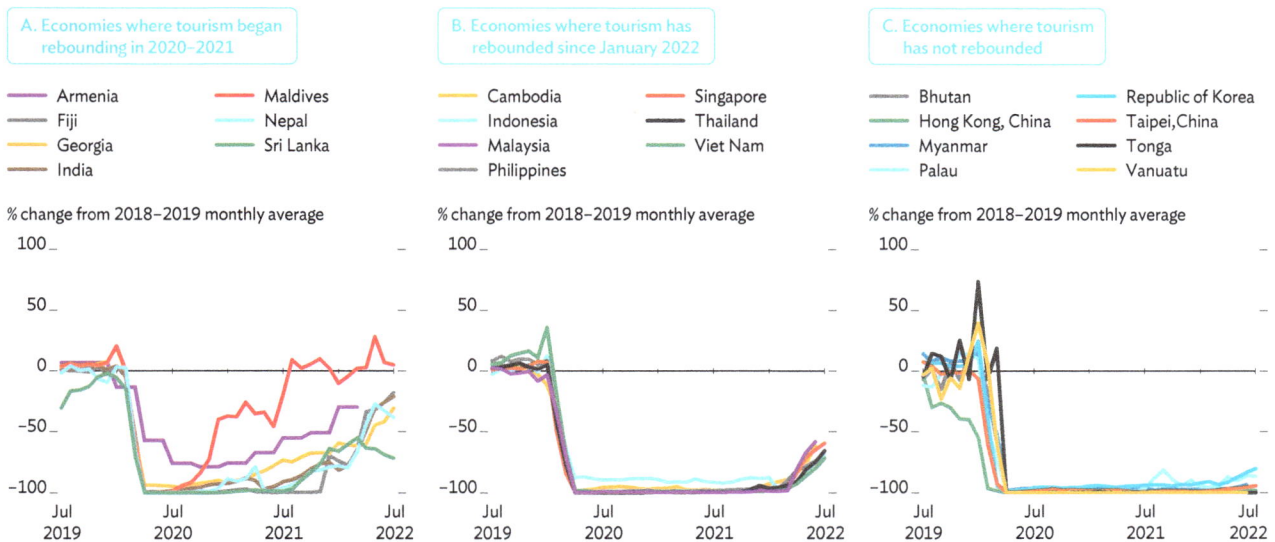

Note: Economies are included in panel A if tourist arrivals in December 2021 exceeded 20% of the 2018–2019 average for the same month, panel B if the latest reading exceeds 20% and the December 2021 reading was below 20%, and panel C if the latest reading is below 20%.
Sources: CEIC Data Company; national sources (all accessed 1 September 2022).

Figure 1.1.25 Remittance growth in developing Asian economies

Economies where remittances were equivalent to 5%–10% of pre-pandemic GDP

Remittances remained strong in Bangladesh and Pakistan in Q1 2022.

- Bangladesh
- Cambodia
- Fiji
- Pakistan
- Philippines
- Sri Lanka

Average of the same quarter in 2018–2019 = 100

Economies where remittances were equivalent to more than 10% of pre-pandemic GDP

Remittances picked up in Armenia, Georgia, and Nepal in Q1 2022.

- Armenia
- Georgia
- Kyrgyz Republic
- Nepal
- Samoa
- Tajikistan
- Uzbekistan

Average of the same quarter in 2018–2019 = 100

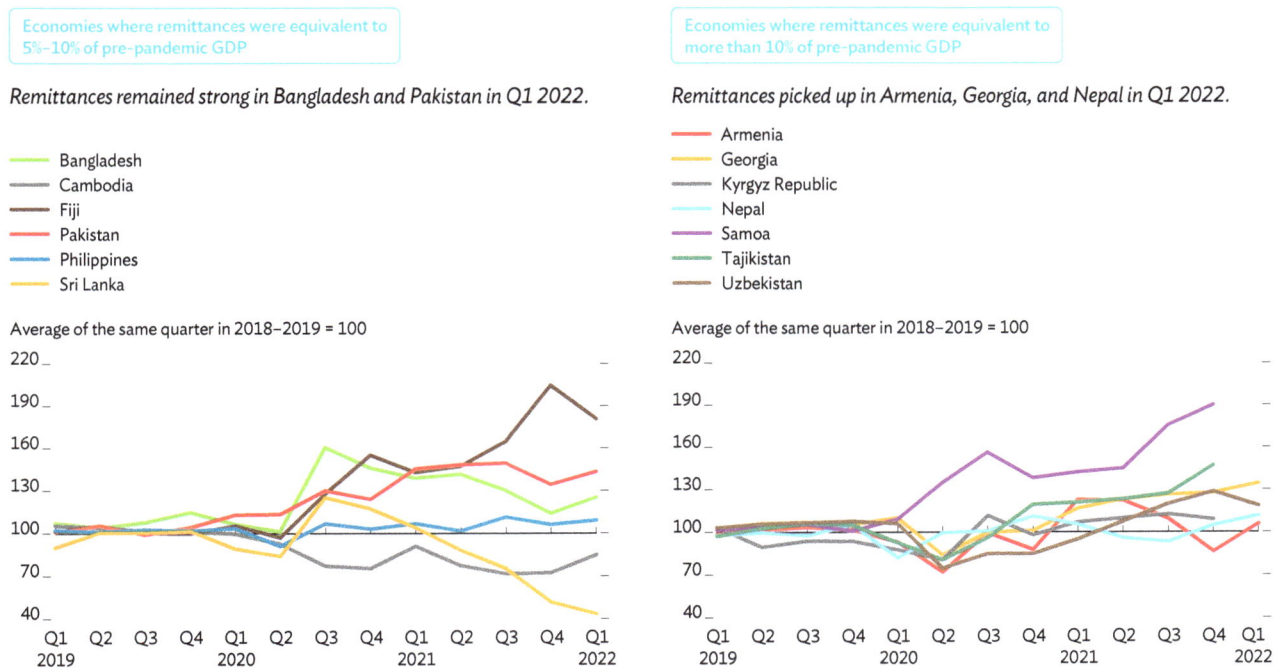

GDP = gross domestic product, Q = quarter.
Sources: CEIC Data Company; International Monetary Fund. Balance of Payments and International Investment Position Statistics; national sources; World Bank. World Development Indicators database (all accessed 1 September 2022).

Fiscal improvement slows as monetary tightening accelerates

Economic policy in developing Asia's economies is adapting to the changing macroeconomic environment of weaker recoveries and higher inflation. Fiscal and monetary policies are set to continue tightening in most economies in the region, but at a different pace than projected in *Asian Development Outlook 2022* (*ADO 2022*) in April. The improvement in fiscal balances will slow as governments increase outlays to help households and businesses deal with elevated food and energy prices (Figure 1.1.14, above)—and softer growth will dent fiscal revenue. Monetary authorities in the region are pressing ahead with the policy tightening cycle on the view that further rate hikes may be needed to stay ahead of the curve, quell inflationary pressures, and address financial stability concerns.

Lower growth and rising public expenditure due to worsening economic conditions will delay improvements in fiscal balances. The weaker growth momentum will be reflected in lower tax revenue, even as automatic stabilizers boost outlays. Governments in the region also face rising debt-servicing costs from higher interest rates, and they are increasing spending to cushion the impact of higher energy and food prices. Because of this, fiscal improvements—defined as rising budget balances as a percentage of GDP—are now expected to be smaller than *ADO 2022's* projections in most cases (Figure 1.1.26). In some economies—including Hong Kong, China; the ROK; and Taipei,China—government budgets are now expected to worsen rather than improve this year.

In the PRC, the fiscal position will deteriorate more than was projected earlier due to lackluster growth in the first half of 2022 and rising government expenditure to support the economy.

Monetary policy tightening is gathering pace in developing Asian economies on rising inflationary pressures, exchange rate depreciations, and financial stability concerns. There were 14 policy rate hikes in Q1, 15 in Q2, and 14 from 1 July to 31 August. The size of these hikes has also increased from an average of 67.1 basis points (bps) in Q1 to 82.5 bps in Q2, before moderating to 34.7 bps from 1 July to 31 August. Policy rates have started rising or have increased further in several economies as central banks take action to curb inflation and safeguard financial stability. Weakening currencies are also prompting monetary authorities to accelerate the hiking cycle because rapid exchange rate depreciations may thwart price stability objectives and monetary policy transmission channels. Monetary tightening in the region is also being driven by the Fed's cumulative 225 bps rate hike since January 2022 and the European Central Bank's 50 bps rate increase in July—the first in 11 years—which are triggering capital outflows from and exchange rate depreciations in the region. In Sri Lanka and, to a lesser extent, Pakistan, this is compounding preexisting macroeconomic vulnerabilities, causing monetary authorities to hike policy rates very aggressively this year—by 950 bps in Sri Lanka and 525 bps in Pakistan (Figure 1.1.27).

Figure 1.1.26 Projected changes in fiscal balances in 2022 and 2023 in developing Asian economies: ADO 2022 Update vs ADO 2022

Budget balances will improve less than previously expected.

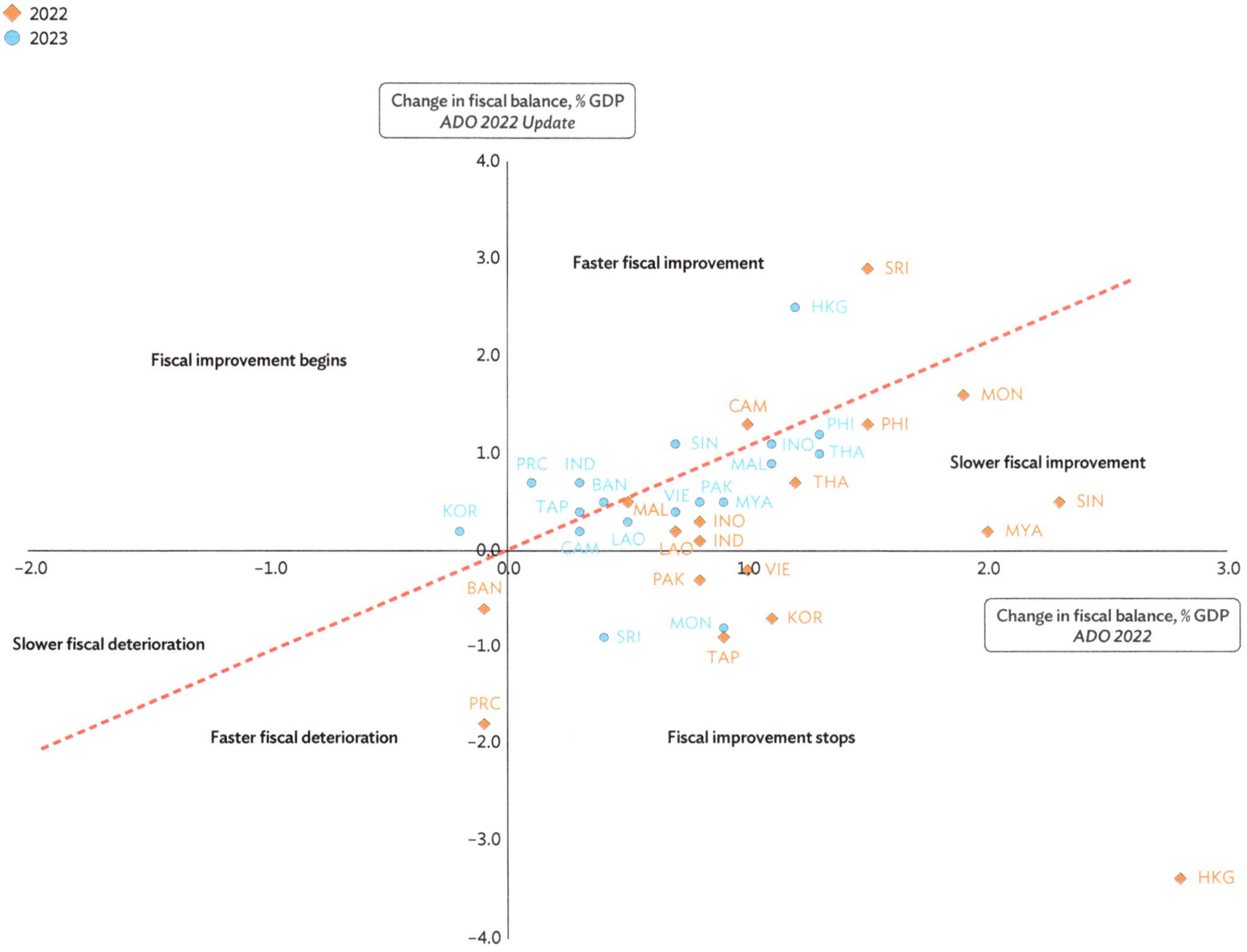

◆ 2022
● 2023

ADO = Asian Development Outlook, BAN = Bangladesh, BRU = Brunei Darussalam, CAM = Cambodia, GDP = gross domestic product, HKG = Hong Kong, China, IND = India, INO = Indonesia, KOR = Republic of Korea, LAO = Lao People's Democratic Republic, MAL = Malaysia, MON = Mongolia, MYA = Myanmar, PAK = Pakistan, PHI = Philippines, PRC = People's Republic of China, SIN = Singapore, SRI = Sri Lanka, TAP = Taipei,China, THA = Thailand, VIE = Viet Nam.

Notes: Fiscal improvement is a positive change in the fiscal balance from the previous year, expressed as a percentage of GDP. Fiscal deterioration is a negative change in the fiscal balance from the previous year, expressed as a percentage of GDP. Fiscal balance, also referred to as government budget balance, is defined in FocusEconomics (2022) and calculated as the difference between a government's revenue (taxes and proceeds from asset sales) and expenditure.

Sources: FocusEconomics. 2022. *Economic Consensus Forecast Reports*. February and August; Asian Development Bank calculations.

Figure 1.1.27 Policy interest rates

Several central banks in developing Asia hiked policy rates in 2022 to curb inflation, cushion falling exchange rates, and safeguard financial stability.

- 2021
- Q1 2022
- Q2 2022
- 1 July to 31 August 2022

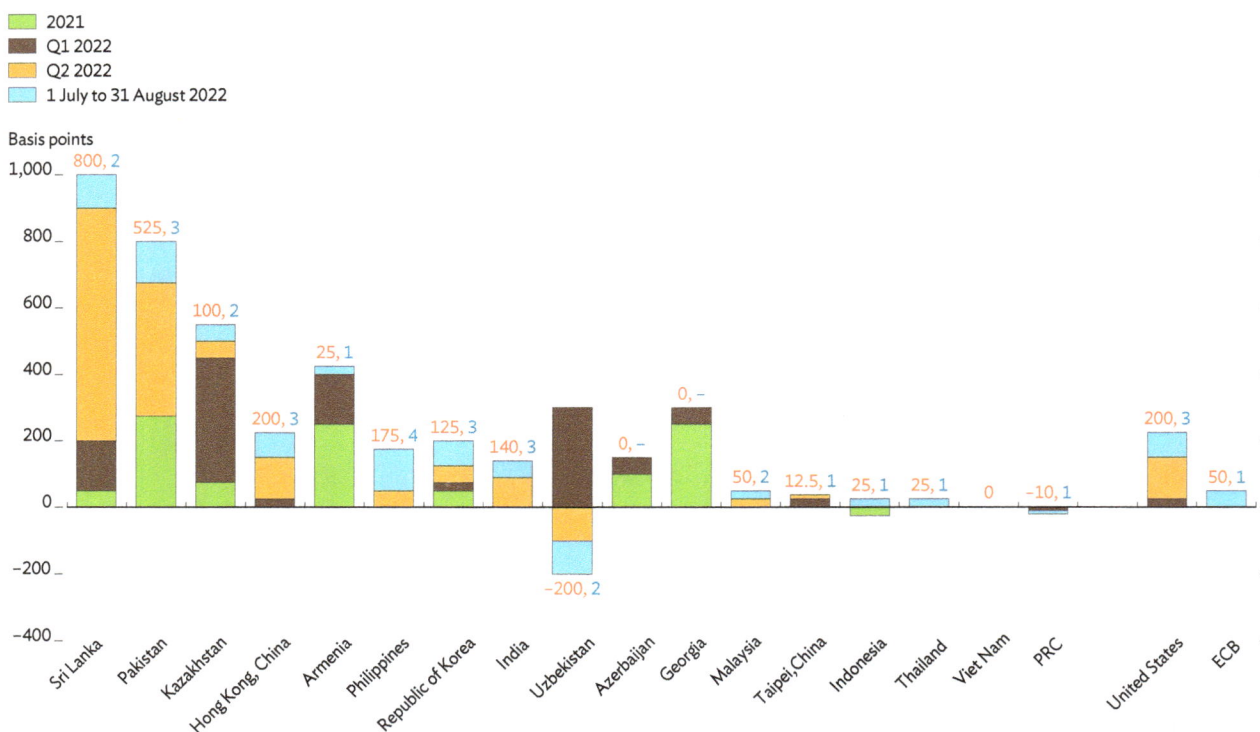

ECB = European Central Bank, PRC = People's Republic of China, Q = quarter.
Note: Numbers in orange are the total change in policy rates (in basis points) from 1 April to 31 August and numbers in blue are the number of interest rate changes from 1 April to 31 August.
Source: Bloomberg (accessed 31 August 2022).

Even though the tightening cycle has progressed, central banks in the region may have to hike policy rates further to tame inflationary pressures.
As expected, inflation increased since April, and real interest rates—constructed as the difference between policy rates and expected inflation—followed suit in many economies, indicating that central banks reacted promptly and adequately to accelerating inflation by raising rates (Figure 1.1.28, panel A).[2]

India, Pakistan, and the Philippines are partial exceptions to this pattern. In these economies real policy rates declined, because policy rates increased by less than the increase in expected inflation. Real interest rates, however, are low or even negative in many economies (Figure 1.1.28, panel B). This suggests that, in the absence of softening price pressures, several central banks in the region may have to tighten policy further to keep inflation in check and prevent possible capital outflows.

[2]   Standard monetary theory suggests that central banks concerned by rising inflation should increase the policy rate (i) more than proportionally for changes in expected inflation (π^e), so as to raise the real interest rate ($r = i - \pi^e$). This will, in turn, reduce aggregate demand and price pressures. To see this, consider a standard Taylor-type rule.

$$i_t = i^* + \beta(\pi_t^e - \pi^*) + \theta(y_t - y^*), \quad (1)$$

where the subscript t refers to time and i^* is the natural rate of interest—that is, the rate of interest consistent with expected inflation equal to the target inflation rate (π^*) and an output gap equal to zero ($y_t = y^*$). Taking the first difference of (1) and assuming the central bank only cares about inflation, so that $\theta = 0$, the following is obtained:

$$\Delta i_t = \beta(\Delta \pi_t^e). \quad (2)$$

Faced with a rise in expected inflation ($\Delta \pi_t^e > 0$), a central bank that aims at keeping inflation close to target will react by increasing the policy rate more than proportionally ($\beta > 1$) so that the real interest rate will increase too—
$\Delta r = \Delta i_t - \Delta \pi^e = (\beta - 1)\Delta \pi^e > 0.$

Figure 1.1.28 Real interest rates in developing Asian economies

With monetary authorities tightening on rising inflation expectations, real interest rates increased—but remain low or negative in many economies.

A. Changes in real interest rates and expected inflation

B. Real interest rates, August 2022

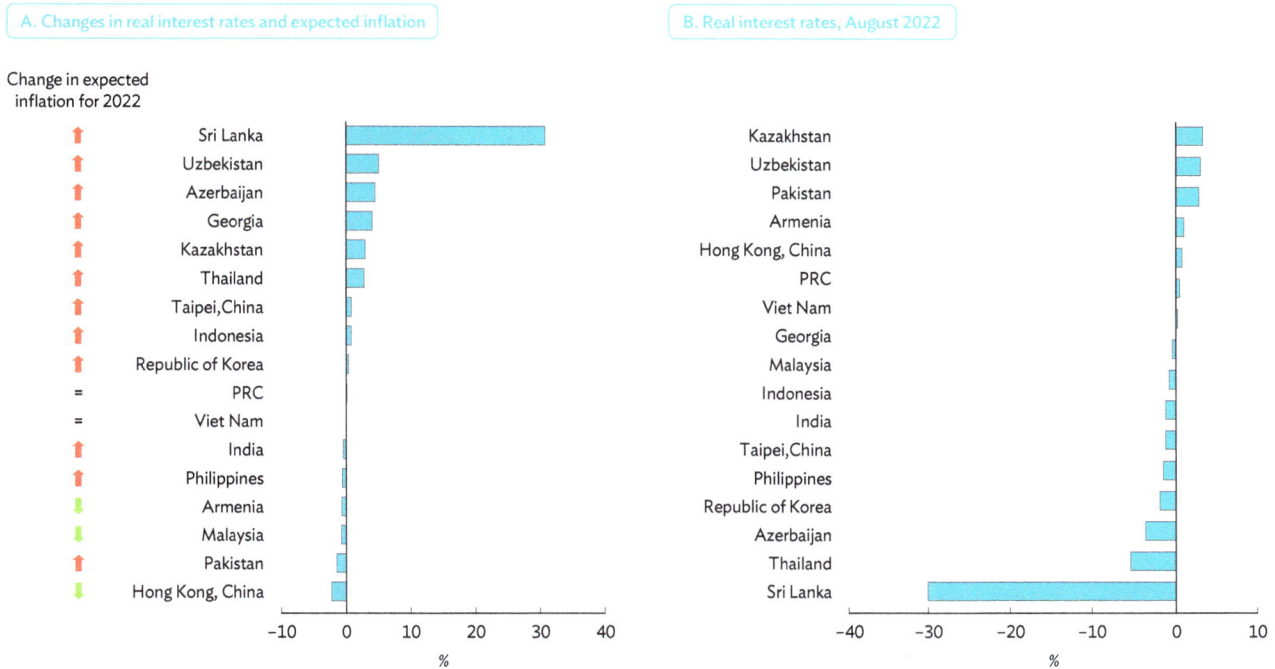

PRC = People's Republic of China.

Notes: Panel A: Change in real interest rates compared to projections in *Asian Development Outlook 2022*. Real interest rates constructed as the difference between policy rates and forecast headline inflation for 2022. Red arrow means forecast headline inflation for 2022 increased compared to projections in *Asian Development Outlook 2022*, green arrow means forecast headline inflation decreased, equals sign means forecast headline inflation did not change. Panel B: Real interest rate is the difference between a policy rate and forecast inflation for 2022 in the September 2022 *Asian Development Outlook Update*.

Sources: Bloomberg; Haver Analytics (both accessed 31 August 2022); and Asian Development Bank calculations.

Financial conditions deteriorated on monetary tightening and moderating growth

Financial conditions in developing Asia have tightened since April. From 1 April to 31 August, the region by and large saw retreating equity markets, widening risk premiums, currency depreciation, and foreign portfolio outflows largely driven by monetary tightening and moderating global growth. The deterioration was especially pronounced in Q2, but financial conditions eased from mid-July to mid-August on optimistic market sentiment, supported by expectations of a milder-than-expected Fed tightening path.

Equity markets in developing Asia retreated, closely tracking expectations over the Fed's tightening path. Inflationary pressures, COVID-19 lockdowns in the PRC, and expectations over Fed tightening shaped the performance of equity markets in developing Asia. From 1 April to 31 August, equities in the region experienced a market value–weighted loss of 5.0% and a 7.2% loss excluding the PRC. While the drop was more pronounced in the rest of the region in Q2, the PRC's equity market recovered on a rally in June triggered by the lifting of Shanghai's lockdown and the introduction of stimulus measures (Figure 1.1.29).

Figure 1.1.29 Equity index performance

Asian equity markets retreated on aggressive monetary tightening and a slower growth outlook, largely tracking expectations of the Federal Reserve's tightening path.

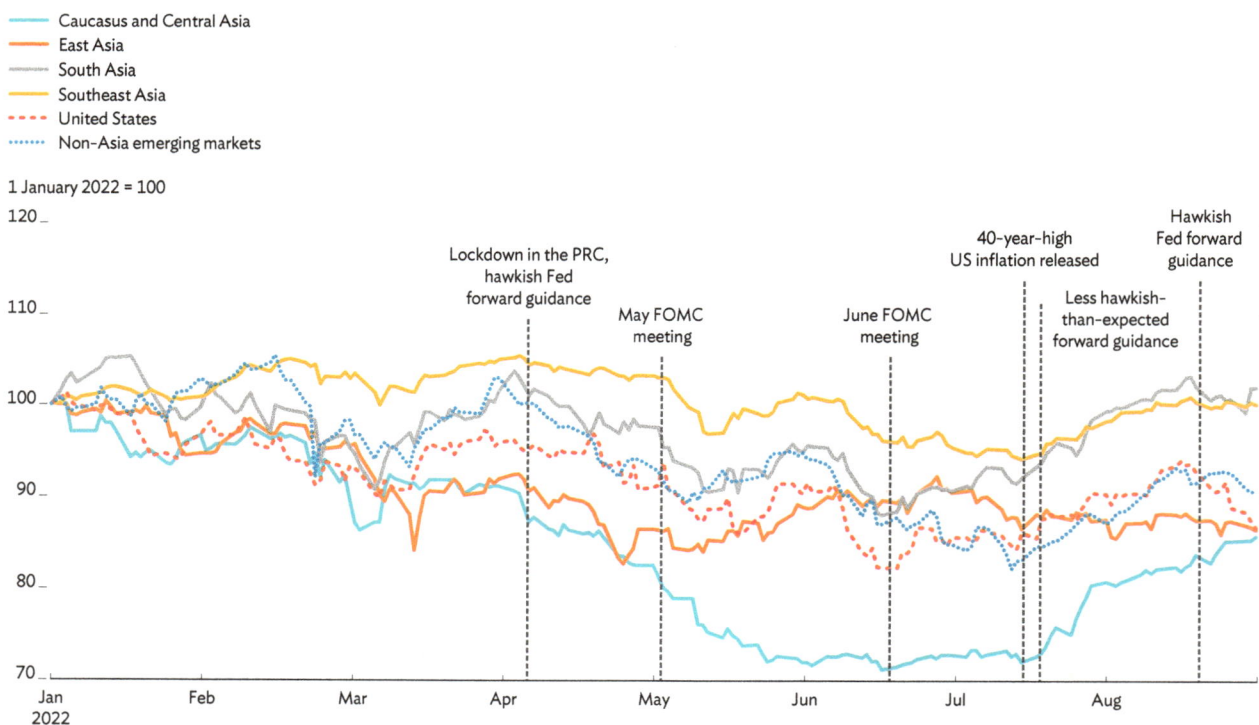

Fed = Federal Reserve, FOMC = Federal Open Market Committee, PRC = People's Republic of China.
Note: Non-Asia emerging markets include Brazil, the Russian Federation, and South Africa.
Sources: Bloomberg; CEIC Data Company (both accessed 1 September 2022).

Market sentiment turned optimistic in July and August, posting a size-weighted average gain of 1.7% excluding the PRC on better-than-expected corporate earnings and a strong labor market in the US, as well as expectations of a less hawkish Fed tightening path. In the PRC, however, stock valuations declined by 5.8% in July and August on a weaker economic outlook.

Rising returns on safe assets and slower growth prospects pushed up risk premiums in developing Asian economies. Risk premiums widened in most economies since April (Figure 1.1.30). Global factors, including accelerated monetary tightening, rising inflation, and negative spillovers from slowing growth in major trade partners, marginally pushed up regional risk premiums by a GDP-weighted average of 4.4 bps from 1 April to 31 August. Premiums widened faster by 14.2 bps in Q2, and then narrowed by 9.9 bps in July and August on improved market sentiment.

Risk premiums co-moved closely across developing Asia's subregions, but market-specific factors drove a wedge between their levels. Higher risk premiums were caused by debt-related financial stress in some South Asian economies and uncertainty over the war in Ukraine in the Caucasus and Central Asia. It is worth noting that major non-Asia emerging markets had larger fluctuations in risk premiums compared to developing Asia.

Currencies in developing Asia have continued weakening since Q2 2022. After depreciating in Q1, Asian currencies weakened further from 1 April to 31 August by 3.4% (or 0.18% in GDP-weighted average terms). The depreciation accelerated in Q2 on a softening growth outlook and a stronger US dollar, before moderating in July and August (Figure 1.1.31). The weakening of Asian currencies appears to reflect to a large extent the strength of the US dollar.

Figure 1.1.30 J. P. Morgan EMBIG stripped spreads in developing Asian economies

Average risk premiums widened in Q2 2022 and narrowed in July and August, tracking investment sentiment over global, regional, and market factors.

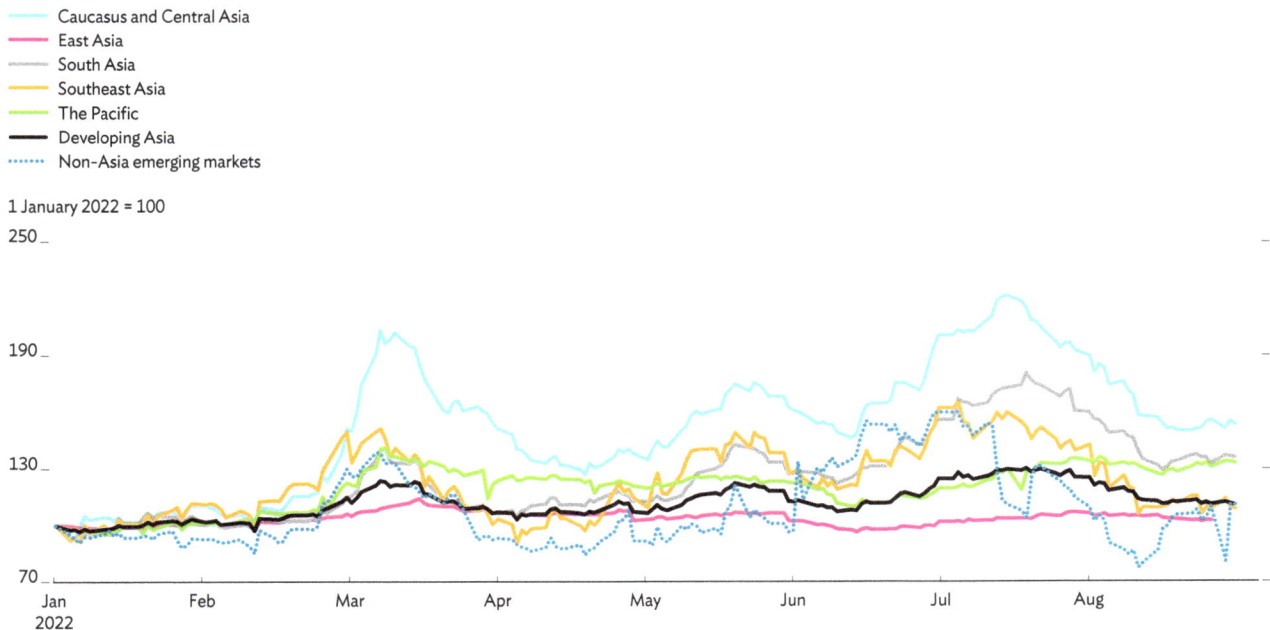

Legend:
- Caucasus and Central Asia
- East Asia
- South Asia
- Southeast Asia
- The Pacific
- Developing Asia
- Non-Asia emerging markets

1 January 2022 = 100

EMBIG = Emerging Markets Bond Index Global, Q = quarter.

Notes: EMBIG is a benchmark index capturing government bond performance in emerging markets. Non-Asia emerging markets include Argentina, Brazil, Mexico, Poland, South Africa, and the Republic of Türkiye.

Source: Bloomberg (accessed 1 September 2022).

Figure 1.1.31 Changes in nominal exchange rates against the US dollar and real effective exchange rates in developing Asian economies

Currencies continued to depreciate on rising growth headwinds and the strong US dollar.

- Q1 2022
- Q2 2022
- 1 July to 31 August 2022
- ◆ REER January–June 2022

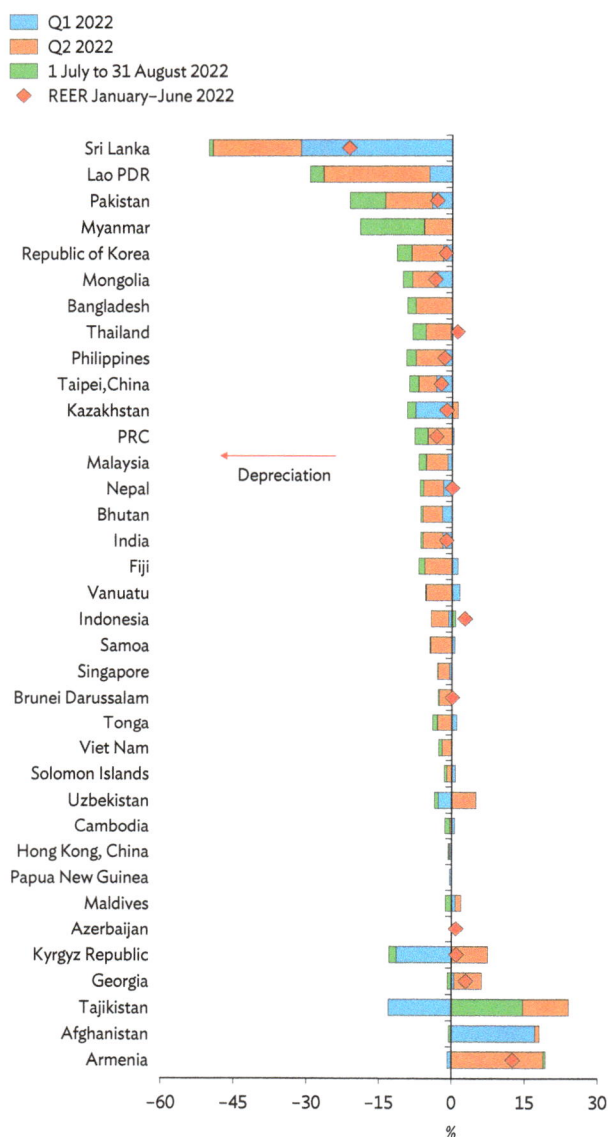

Sri Lanka
Lao PDR
Pakistan
Myanmar
Republic of Korea
Mongolia
Bangladesh
Thailand
Philippines
Taipei,China
Kazakhstan
PRC
Malaysia   ← Depreciation
Nepal
Bhutan
India
Fiji
Vanuatu
Indonesia
Samoa
Singapore
Brunei Darussalam
Tonga
Viet Nam
Solomon Islands
Uzbekistan
Cambodia
Hong Kong, China
Papua New Guinea
Maldives
Azerbaijan
Kyrgyz Republic
Georgia
Tajikistan
Afghanistan
Armenia

-60   -45   -30   -15   0   15   30
%

Lao PDR = Lao People's Democratic Republic, PRC = People's Republic of China, Q = quarter, REER = real effective exchange rate, US = United States.

Notes: Negative values indicate currency depreciation against the US dollar and positive values indicate currency appreciation against the US dollar. Real effective exchange rate indicates an economy's international competitiveness compared to trade partners.

Source: Bloomberg (accessed 1 September 2022).

During the first half of 2022, for markets with available data, real effective exchange rates in developing Asia depreciated by a milder average 0.7% (0.1% GDP-weighted) against a basket of major trade partners' currencies compared to an average depreciation of 5.4% (0.3%) against the US dollar (Figure 1.1.31). These averages, however, hide some differences across economies. Because of worsening debt-related financial stress, the currencies of the Lao PDR, Pakistan, and Sri Lanka fell sharply. In contrast, exchange rates in several economies in the Caucasus and Central Asia appreciated, mirroring a strengthening ruble (e.g., Tajikistan) and labor and capital inflows from the Russian Federation boosting economic activity (e.g., Armenia and Georgia).

Foreign portfolio outflows continued in Q2 2022, but turned to inflows in July and August.
A weakening growth outlook and the acceleration of monetary tightening, both globally and in developing Asia, led to net foreign portfolio outflows of $23.1 billion from the region from 1 April to 25 August (Figure 1.1.32). The PRC bucked the negative trend, with portfolio inflows of $14.4 billion in Q2 on the lifting of lockdowns in major cities and stimulus measures, while in the rest of developing Asia outflows increased to $43.7 billion from Q1's $31.2 billion. In contrast, the PRC had $2.7 billion outflows from 1 July to 25 August as its economic outlook worsened, while the rest of the region had portfolio inflows of $9.0 billion.

Foreign direct investment into developing Asia remained robust in Q1 2022 on solid medium- and long-term economic fundamentals. Despite short-term headwinds causing portfolio outflows in Q1, FDI to the region rose to $205.8 billion in the quarter, up 15.0% year on year and 10.8% from Q4 2021, largely driven by higher inflows to East Asia (Figure 1.1.33). These inflows are higher than typical pre-pandemic levels. Average quarterly FDI flows from Q1 2020 to Q1 2022 rose to $162.7 billion, nearly 30% higher than the $125.2 billion from Q1 2018 to Q4 2019. The share of greenfield FDI in total FDI, however, has declined since the start of the pandemic and remains subdued—with a quarterly average of only $33.8 billion in 2020–2021, down from $75.5 billion in 2018–2019. The share of greenfield FDI from non-Asia investors has remained fairly stable.

Figure 1.1.32 Portfolio flows to developing Asian economies

Net outflows excluding the PRC continued in Q2 2022, but turned to net inflows in July and August on optimistic sentiment.

- Developing Asia
- Developing Asia excluding the PRC
- People's Republic of China

$ billion, 3-week moving average

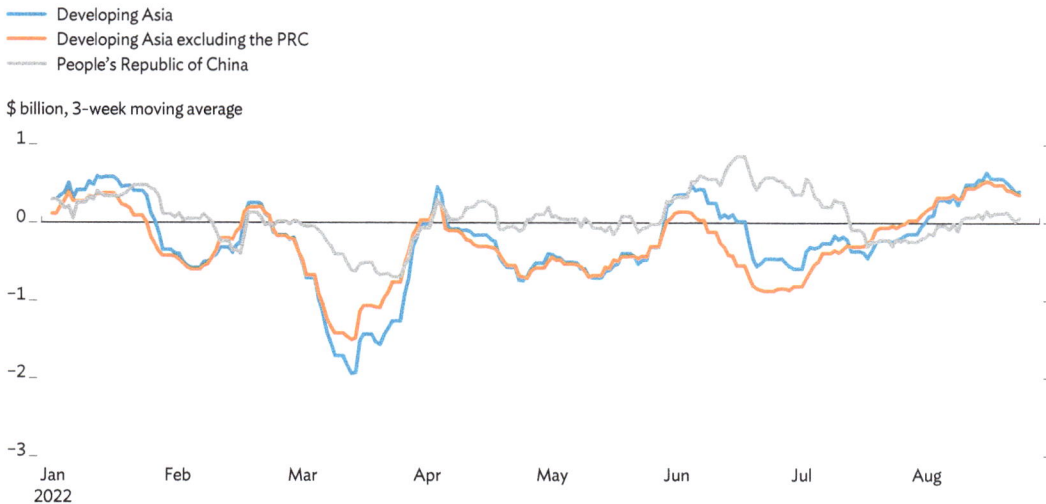

PRC = People's Republic of China, Q = quarter.

Source: Institute of International Finance (accessed 29 August 2022).

Figure 1.1.33 FDI to developing Asian subregions

FDI is above pre-pandemic levels, but the share of greenfield FDI is below.

- Caucasus and Central Asia
- East Asia
- South Asia
- Southeast Asia
- The Pacific

Greenfield FDI to developing Asia, % of total FDI

Non-developing Asia greenfield FDI to developing Asia, % of total greenfield FDI

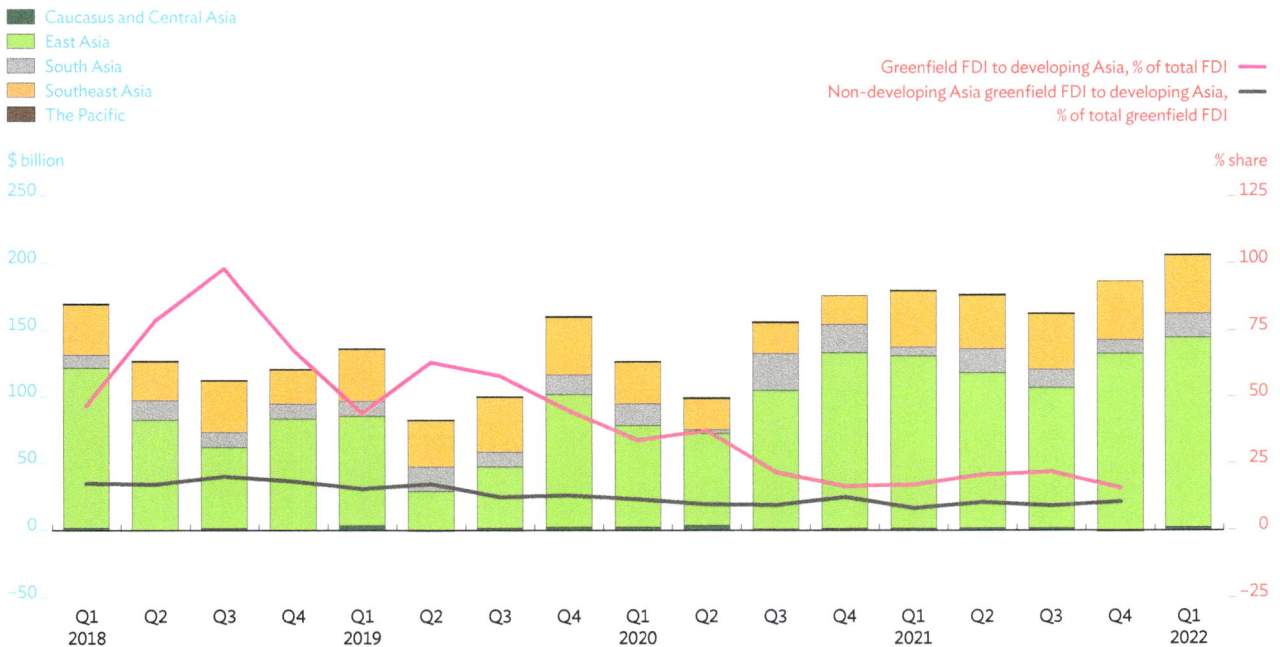

FDI = foreign direct investment, Q = quarter.

Note: Greenfield FDI collected by fDi Markets from company announcements.

Sources: FDI data from the International Monetary Fund using Haver Analytics (accessed 24 August 2022); greenfield FDI from Asian Development Bank. *Asian Economic Integration Report* FDI database, which is based on data from fDi Markets; *Financial Times*.

Developing Asia's outlook dims

Global demand is expected to soften as monetary policy tightens. The major advanced economies are forecast to grow slower than envisioned in *ADO 2022*, at 1.9% in 2022 and 1.0% in 2023 (Annex Table A.1). High inflation prompted central banks in the US and the euro area to aggressively tighten monetary policy, weakening aggregate demand in these economies. The baseline assumes inflation in the US will decline gradually after peaking in June, but inflation will continue to edge higher in the euro area for the coming months. Monetary policy tightening is expected to continue, resulting in lower demand for exports from developing Asia—the US and the euro area absorbed about 29% of the region's total merchandise exports in 2021. Growth in the US is expected to slowly resume in the second half of 2022, while GDP in the euro area is projected to contract in Q3 and Q4 before gradually expanding in 2023.

This *Update* revises down the forecasts for GDP growth for developing Asia to 4.3% for 2022 from the earlier 5.2% projection and to 4.9% from 5.3% for 2023. The revision reflects the worsening outlook for the global economy, although changes in the growth forecasts vary across subregions (Figure 1.1.34 and Table 1.1.1). The downward revision is driven largely by lower forecasts for growth in East Asia, particularly the PRC because of its size. This year will be the first time in more than 3 decades that the rest of developing Asia will grow faster than the PRC: the last time was in 1990, when growth slowed to 3.9% while GDP in the rest of the region expanded by 6.9%. Excluding the PRC, the rest of developing Asia is projected to grow by 5.3% in 2022 and in 2023.

Weaker economic prospects in East Asia and South Asia will drag down regional growth. This *Update* revises down the forecast for East Asia's growth this year to 3.2% from the earlier 4.7% and to 4.2% from 4.5% for 2023. Corrections to the growth forecasts for the PRC are behind the downward revisions to East Asia's projected growth for this year and next. The PRC's economy is now expected to expand by 3.3% in 2022 rather than the 5.0% forecast earlier as the lockdowns from the zero-COVID strategy, problems in the property sector, and weaker external demand continue weighing on economic activity (Figure 1.1.35).

Figure 1.1.34 GDP growth forecasts for developing Asian subregions

Growth is forecast to weaken in East Asia and South Asia, but strengthen in other subregions.

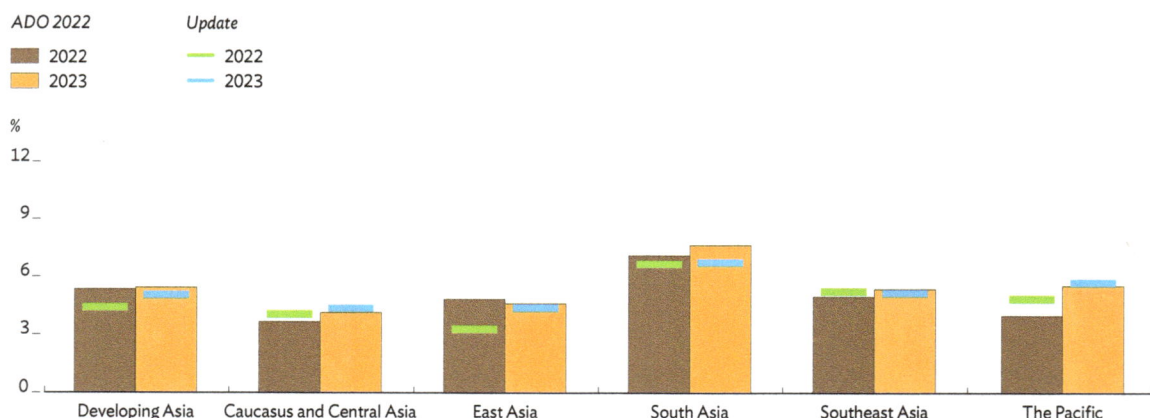

ADO = Asian Development Outlook.
Source: ADO database.

Table 1.1.1 GDP growth in developing Asia, % per year

For the first time in 3 decades, the PRC will grow less than the rest of developing Asia.

Economy	2021	2022 ADO 2022	2022 Update	2023 ADO 2022	2023 Update
Developing Asia	7.0	5.2	4.3	5.3	4.9
Developing Asia excluding the PRC	5.9	5.5	5.3	5.8	5.3
Caucasus and Central Asia	5.7	3.6	3.9	4.0	4.2
Armenia	5.7	2.8	7.0	3.8	4.5
Azerbaijan	5.6	3.7	4.2	2.8	2.8
Georgia	10.4	3.5	7.0	5.0	6.0
Kazakhstan	4.3	3.2	3.0	3.9	3.7
Kyrgyz Republic	3.6	2.0	3.0	2.5	3.5
Tajikistan	9.2	2.0	4.0	3.0	5.0
Turkmenistan	5.0	6.0	5.8	5.8	5.8
Uzbekistan	7.4	4.0	4.0	4.5	5.0
East Asia	7.7	4.7	3.2	4.5	4.2
Hong Kong, China	6.3	2.0	0.2	3.7	3.7
Mongolia	1.4	2.3	1.7	5.6	4.9
People's Republic of China	8.1	5.0	3.3	4.8	4.5
Republic of Korea	4.1	3.0	2.6	2.6	2.3
Taipei,China	6.6	3.8	3.4	3.0	3.0
South Asia	8.1	7.0	6.5	7.4	6.5
Afghanistan	...	...	...	...	...
Bangladesh	6.9	6.9	7.2	7.1	6.6
Bhutan	4.1	4.5	4.5	7.5	4.0
India	8.7	7.5	7.0	8.0	7.2
Maldives	37.1	11.0	8.2	12.0	10.4
Nepal	4.2	3.9	5.8	5.0	4.7
Pakistan	5.7	4.0	6.0	4.5	3.5
Sri Lanka	3.3	2.4	-8.8	2.5	-3.3
Southeast Asia	3.3	4.9	5.1	5.2	5.0
Brunei Darussalam	-1.6	4.2	2.2	3.6	3.6
Cambodia	3.0	5.3	5.3	6.5	6.2
Indonesia	3.7	5.0	5.4	5.2	5.0
Lao People's Democratic Republic	2.3	3.4	2.5	3.7	3.5
Malaysia	3.1	6.0	6.0	5.4	4.7
Myanmar	-5.9	-0.3	2.0	2.6	2.6
Philippines	5.7	6.0	6.5	6.3	6.3
Singapore	7.6	4.3	3.7	3.2	3.0
Thailand	1.5	3.0	2.9	4.5	4.2
Timor-Leste	1.5	2.5	2.3	3.1	3.0
Viet Nam	2.6	6.5	6.5	6.7	6.7
The Pacific	-1.5	3.9	4.7	5.4	5.5
Cook Islands	-29.1	9.1	10.5	11.2	11.2
Federated States of Micronesia	-1.2	2.2	2.2	4.2	4.1
Fiji	-4.1	7.1	11.7	8.5	8.5
Kiribati	1.5	1.8	1.8	2.3	2.3
Marshall Islands	-3.3	1.2	-1.2	2.2	-0.3
Nauru	1.6	1.0	1.2	2.4	2.2
Niue	...	...	...	...	...
Palau	-17.1	9.4	4.6	18.3	8.8
Papua New Guinea	-0.2	3.4	3.5	4.6	4.9
Samoa	-7.1	0.4	-5.3	2.2	2.0
Solomon Islands	-0.5	-3.0	-4.2	3.0	3.0
Tonga	-2.7	-1.2	-2.0	2.9	3.7
Tuvalu	1.5	3.0	2.5	3.0	2.7
Vanuatu	1.0	1.0	2.0	4.0	4.0

... = not available, ADO = Asian Development Outlook, PRC = People's Republic of China.
Note: Because of the uncertain situation, no data and forecasts are provided for 2021–2023 for Afghanistan.
Source: ADO database.

The 2023 growth forecast for the PRC is revised down to 4.5% from 4.8% due to deteriorating external demand continuing to dampen investment in manufacturing. The forecasts for growth in South Asia are revised down to 6.5% for 2022 from 7.0% and to 6.5% from 7.4% for 2023. The new forecasts are mainly because of a modest downward revision to India's projected growth due to higher-than-anticipated inflation and monetary tightening, and Sri Lanka's sharp contraction as its economic crisis deepens.

Growth in Southeast Asia in 2022 will be slightly higher than earlier forecast. The subregional economy is projected to grow by 5.1% this year, up from *ADO 2022*'s 4.9% projection. Higher growth forecasts for Indonesia, Myanmar, and the Philippines are almost entirely offset by downward revisions for Singapore and Thailand. Robust domestic demand is benefiting Indonesia and the Philippines, while higher global commodity prices and dimmer global economic prospects are denting consumer and business sentiment in Singapore and Thailand. The forecast for 2023 growth in Southeast Asia is revised down slightly, to 5.0% from 5.2%, on expectations of weaker global demand (Figure 1.1.34).

Faster growth is expected this year and next in the Pacific and the Caucasus and Central Asia. The forecast for growth in the Pacific subregion is revised up to 4.7% from 3.9% for 2022 and to 5.5% from 5.4% for 2023. The brighter outlook is mainly due to a stronger-than-expected recovery in tourism in Fiji—the subregion's second-largest economy— as the easing of travel restrictions attracts tourists from especially Australia, New Zealand, and North America. In some smaller Pacific island economies, including Palau and Samoa, growth is being revised down substantially because of the delayed recovery in tourism (Figure 1.1.35). The Caucasus and Central Asia subregion is forecast to grow by 3.9% this year, up from the earlier 3.6% projection, as growth in some economies in the subregion benefits from certain economic impacts of the Russian invasion of Ukraine. For example, money transfers from the sanctioned Russian Federation to Armenia and Georgia are rising sharply as Russian businesses relocate their bases to these countries. And Azerbaijan's hydrocarbon exports are increasing because of tight supply caused by the war.

Figure 1.1.35 Changes to GDP growth forecasts from *ADO 2022*

Revisions vary across and within subregions.

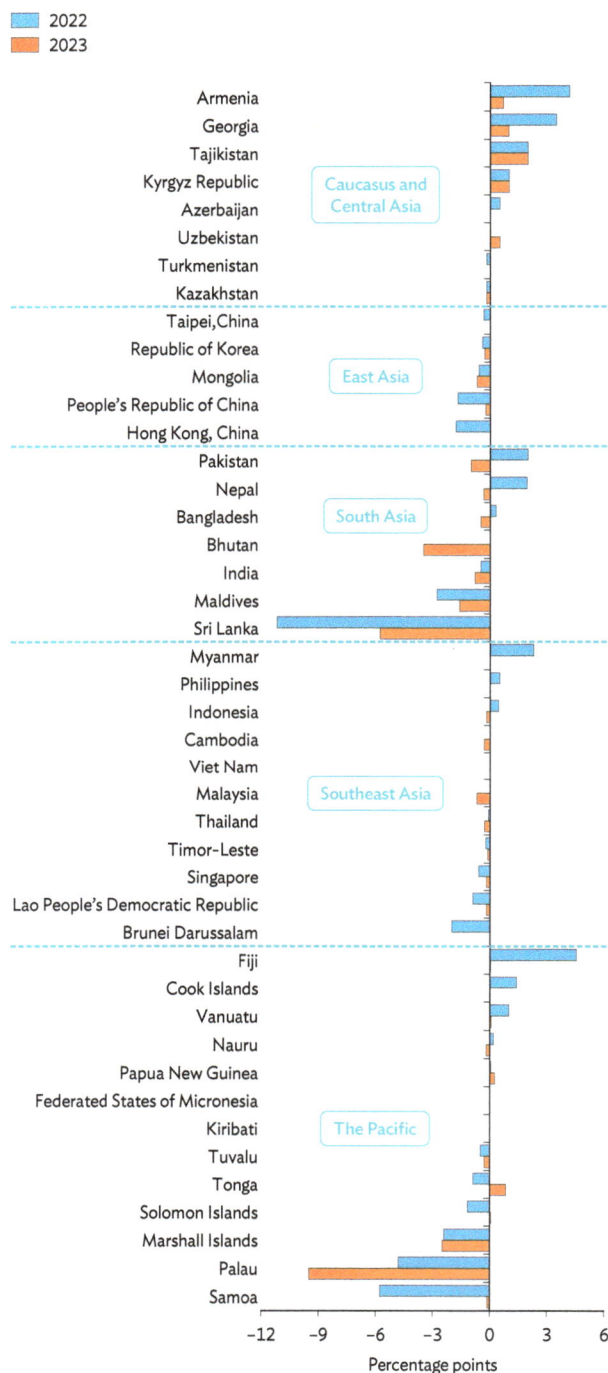

ADO = Asian Development Outlook.
Source: ADO database.

Higher food and energy costs push up inflation

Despite developing Asia's slow recovery, the region's inflation rate will rise on higher energy and food prices. This *Update* revises up the forecasts for regional inflation to 4.5% for 2022 from the earlier 3.7% projection and to 4.0% from 3.1% for 2023 (Figure 1.1.36). Inflationary pressures in developing Asia this year are expected to remain less severe than elsewhere in the world. Headline inflation is forecast to accelerate in all subregions, but more slowly in East Asia and the Pacific. With recoveries continuing and labor markets improving, monetary authorities in economies where inflation pressures are broadening should push forward with tightening.

Expected declines in global commodity prices will slow inflation in 2023. After another large increase this year, international commodity prices are expected to ease next year. Global oil prices will decline, with the average Brent crude spot price forecast falling from $106/barrel this year to $95 next year (Annex Table A.1). According to the World Bank's 26 April 2022 Commodities Price Forecast, global food

prices are expected to decline in 2023 on easing supply chain disruptions. These trends of lower international commodity prices will ease inflationary pressures in developing Asia and other regions next year.

Inflation forecasts are substantially revised up for South Asia and the Caucasus and Central Asia. Inflation in South Asia is projected to rise to 8.1% in 2022 from the earlier 6.5% projection and to 7.4% from 5.5% for 2023. The upward revisions mainly reflect surging global commodity prices accelerating inflation in India, Pakistan, and Sri Lanka (Figure 1.1.37). Shrinking food supply in Sri Lanka and the removal of energy subsidies in Pakistan are affecting the inflation outlook for these economies. The forecast for average inflation in 2022 in the Caucasus and Central Asia is raised to 11.5% from the earlier 8.8% projection and to 8.5% from 7.1% for 2023. Elevated food and energy prices point to higher inflation across the subregion, except for Armenia and Tajikistan, where monetary policy tightening and exchange rate appreciations have helped to damp inflation in the first half of this year.

Figure 1.1.36 Inflation forecast

Revised up across developing Asia subregions mainly due to higher food and fuel prices.

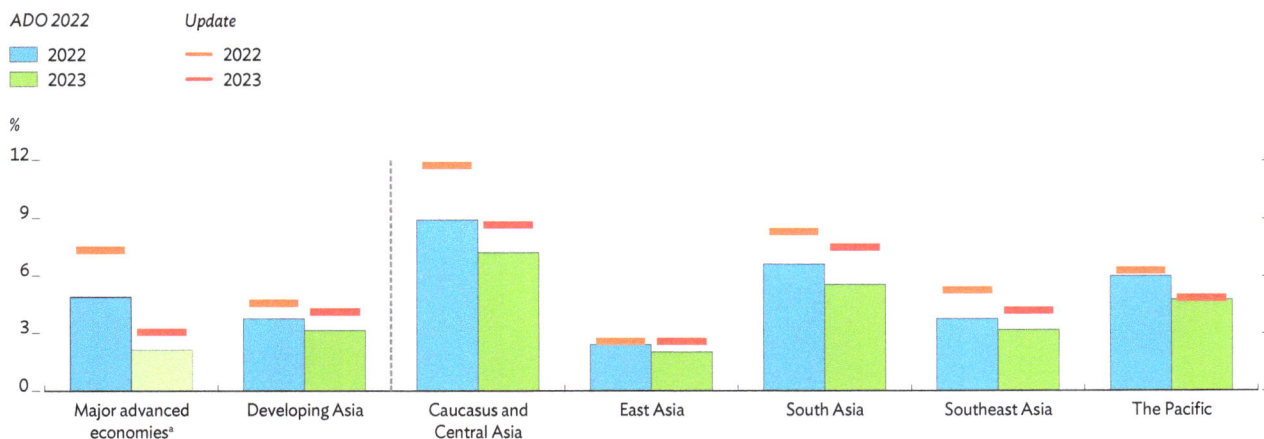

ADO = Asian Development Outlook.
[a] Major advanced economies comprise the United States, euro area, and Japan.
Source: ADO database.

Inflation will also increase substantially in Southeast Asia. The subregion's inflation forecast for 2022 is revised up to 5.2% from the earlier 3.7% projection and to 4.1% from 3.1% for 2023 on the impact of higher food and energy prices, especially in Indonesia, Thailand, and the Philippines, as well as the subregion's other larger economies. Rising import prices because of exchange rate depreciations against the US dollar are also clouding the subregion's inflation outlook, especially in the Lao PDR, Myanmar, and other smaller economies. Malaysia is the exception to both these trends. Here, price controls and subsidies on oil and basic food products led to a downward revision to the inflation forecast for 2022.

The revisions to the inflation forecasts for East Asia and the Pacific are more moderate than for the other subregions. Average inflation in East Asia is forecast at 2.5% in 2022, slightly higher than the earlier 2.4% projection. The forecast for 2023, however, is revised up to 2.5% from 2.0%. This is driven mainly by the PRC. Although the country's 2022 inflation forecast is unchanged, the forecast for 2023 is revised up to 2.5% on expectations of higher food prices. The forecasts for the subregion's other economies are revised up on higher global commodity prices—except for Hong Kong, China, where inflation in 2022 will be lower than earlier expected due to additional energy subsidies and subdued domestic demand. The Pacific will see a mild acceleration in inflation on higher-than-expected global commodity prices, but the effect of this will be moderated by only slight revisions to the forecasts for Fiji and Papua New Guinea (Figure 1.1.37).

Figure 1.1.37 Changes to inflation forecasts from *ADO 2022*

Inflationary pressures are higher in the larger economies of the Caucasus and Central Asia and South Asia.

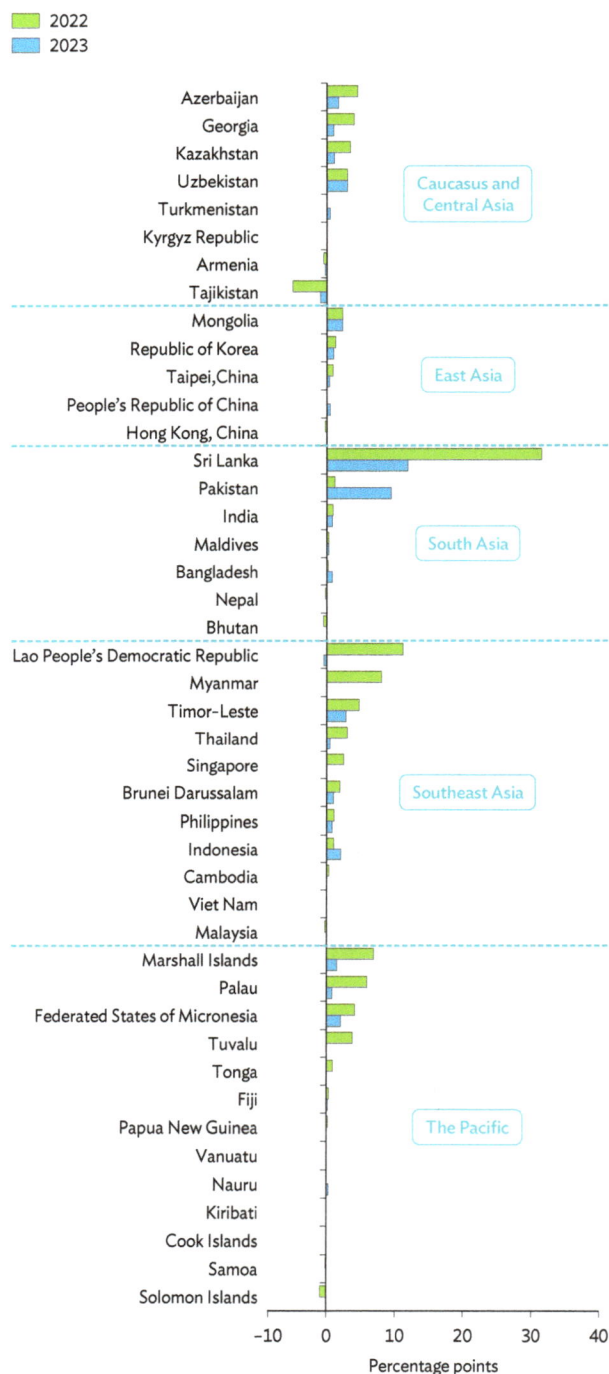

ADO = Asian Development Outlook.
Source: ADO database.

Developing Asia's current account will remain in surplus

The region's current account will remain in surplus, at a forecast of 0.7% of GDP in 2022 and 2023.
Relative to the projections made in *ADO 2022*, current accounts will worsen in South Asia and Southeast Asia, remain more or less the same in East Asia and the Pacific, and improve substantially in the Caucasus and Central Asia (Figure 1.1.38). Over the forecast horizon, slower growth rates in the major advanced economies will temper demand for developing Asia's exports. Imports are expected to rise in line with the progress of economic recoveries and weaker exchange rates in many economies in the region. The current accounts of economies with high import reliance will also suffer, especially when coupled with exchange rate depreciations. Balances, however, will improve in commodity-exporting economies and those benefitting from an influx of capital.

Current account balances will worsen in South Asia and Southeast Asia. South Asia's current account deficit will widen further than the earlier projection. Wider current account deficits are expected in Bangladesh, India, and Pakistan on a combination of higher trade deficits and lower remittances (Figure 1.1.39). Sri Lanka's deficit will narrow on severe shortages of foreign exchange, which have led to sharply lower imports. Southeast Asia's current account surplus will narrow substantially on weaker-than-expected export demand and higher import prices. Current accounts in Thailand and Viet Nam are now projected to turn into deficits this year, and the deficit in the Philippines will widen. Timor-Leste's deficit will narrow substantially due to higher commodity exports and healthy remittances flows.

Figure 1.1.38 Current account balances in developing Asian subregions

Current accounts will improve in commodity-exporting economies, but worsen in those highly dependent on imports.

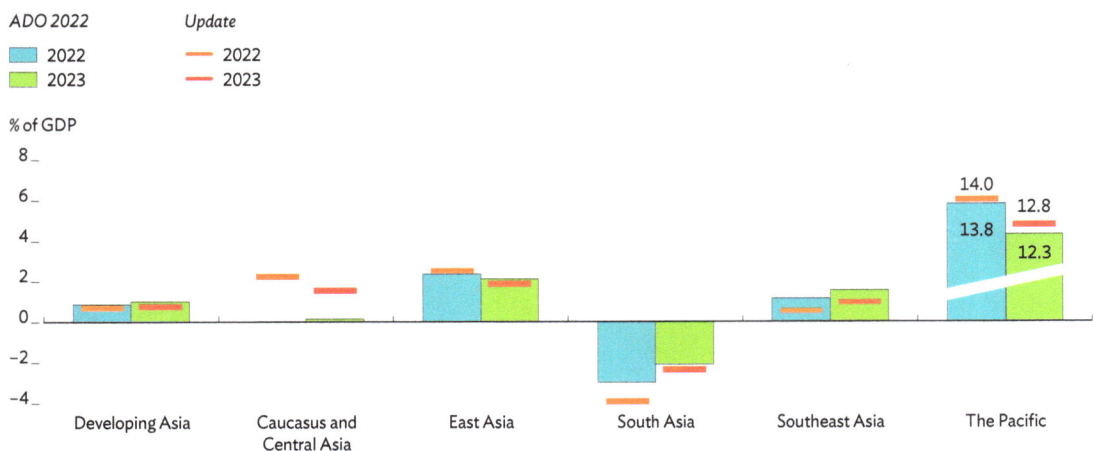

ADO = Asian Development Outlook, GDP = gross domestic product.
Source: *ADO* database.

The current accounts of the East Asia and the Pacific subregions will remain in surplus.
East Asia's current account is largely determined by the PRC's, which will improve this year as exports pick up after being disrupted by widespread COVID-19 lockdowns in April. Even so, this *Update* slightly revises down the forecast for East Asia's current account surplus for 2023 from the earlier projection because exports from the PRC, the ROK, and Taipei,China will slow on weaker global demand. The current account surplus in the Pacific subregion will be slightly higher than earlier projected, due mainly to a stronger rebound in Papua New Guinea's commodity exports, higher tourism receipts in Fiji, and stronger exports from Vanuatu. This will outweigh the worsening forecasts for the current account balances of the smaller economies, keeping the subregion in surplus.

The current account surplus of the Caucasus and Central Asia will increase substantially. This *Update* forecasts the surplus rising to the equivalent of 2.2% of GDP in 2022 from *ADO 2022*'s projected balance of zero and to 1.5% from 0.2% in 2023. Improved current account conditions are projected for five out of the subregion's eight economies. The current accounts of Azerbaijan, Kazakhstan, and Turkmenistan will benefit from higher oil and gas exports. Deficits in Georgia and Uzbekistan will be narrower due to increased inward money transfers. But Armenia's deficit will be wider due to higher imports (Figure 1.1.39).

Figure 1.1.39 Changes in current account balance forecasts from *ADO 2022*

Balances in developing Asian subregions will be driven by trends in their larger economies.

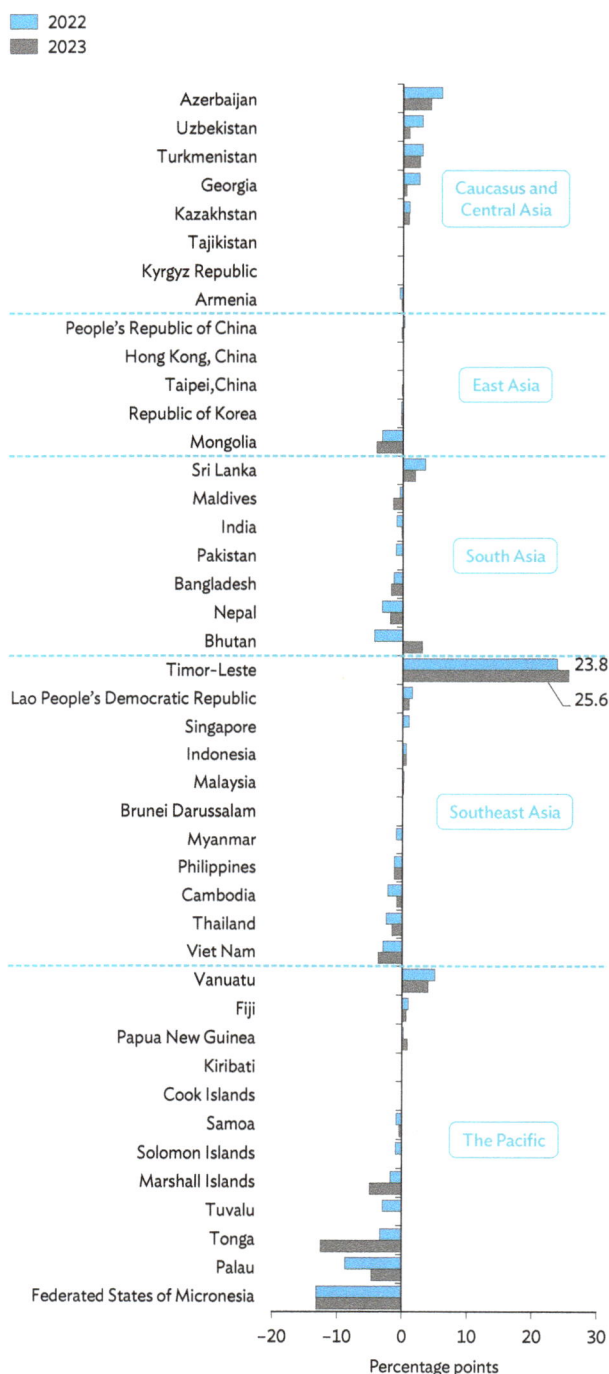

ADO = Asian Development Outlook.
Source: ADO database.

Global headwinds gathering pace

Developing Asia's outlook comes with significant downside risks, including sharper-than-expected monetary policy tightening in advanced economies. Sustained inflationary pressures could trigger more aggressive monetary policy tightening than expected in the US and other major economies. A quantitative scenario suggests the impact of such an event would be significant. Assuming that the Fed hikes the policy rate by an additional 150 bps compared with this *Update's* baseline between now and Q2 2023, model simulations suggest that business and household sentiment will deteriorate, global equity prices will fall by 15%–20%, and advanced economies will go into recession next year (Figure 1.1.40). For developing Asia, one of the key transmission channels is dampened export prospects which, under the model, slows growth by 1.3 percentage points compared with the baseline forecast. Outward-oriented economies in East Asia would be hit hard, with the subregion's growth falling by 1.8 percentage points below the baseline. Inflation in developing Asia would unwind by about 0.3 percentage points below the baseline as supply chain pressures ease, oil prices fall, and global growth slows. Not quantified in the scenario is the possibility that economies with more vulnerable fundamentals may suffer financial instability and pressure on their currencies, which would raise the cost of external debt servicing and worsen balance-of-payments difficulties.

An escalation of the war in Ukraine and its spillovers on global commodity markets remain a threat. The fallout from the war could become heavier now that a large part of the international community has hardened its stance against Russian aggression, as exemplified by the European Union's decision to ban seaborne imports of Russian oil by the end of this year.

A heavier fallout from the war could translate into heightened inflationary pressures, further monetary tightening, and ultimately slower growth in developing Asia and other regions. As analyzed in the *Asian Development Outlook Supplement* in July, should oil prices spike to $200/barrel, growth in developing Asia would fall by about 1.4 percentage points below the baseline this year and 0.7 percentage points next year. Headline inflation would surge well above the baseline, to 6.1% in 2022 and 4.2% in 2023.

Negative pandemic developments remain a risk. Renewed COVID-19 outbreaks in the PRC amid its zero-COVID policy could trigger lockdowns in several cities, resulting in a sharp fall in consumption in the PRC and heightened supply chain disruptions that push up input costs globally. If this happens, model simulations suggest that growth in developing Asia this year would drop by an estimated 1.8 percentage points below the baseline, driven by a sharp fall of 2.8 percentage points in East Asia (Figure 1.1.41). Although increased immunization has reduced the severity of COVID-19, the emergence of new, vaccine-evading variants cannot be ruled out—and with it, the risk that economies around the world may once again have to resort to more stringent containment measures to keep the pandemic in check. Under this scenario, growth in the other subregions next year would take a big hit: 1.9 percentage points below the baseline in the Caucasus and Central Asia, 1.6 points in Southeast Asia, 1.2 points in South Asia, and 1.1 points in the Pacific. Because of lower domestic and external demand, inflation across all subregions would decelerate—and fastest in the Caucasus and Central Asia, at 2.2 percentage points below the baseline.

Economy-specific risks will require close monitoring and could exacerbate scarring from the pandemic. Rising food insecurity, geopolitical tensions, and climate change-related disruptions are among the additional risks that can affect developing Asia's economies to varying degrees. High debt burdens can heighten the potential impact of these risks, and—as a source of significant vulnerability in some cases—threaten recoveries. If one or more of the downside scenarios just discussed happens or high-debt fragilities lead to a crisis, the impact on growth in developing Asia could go from nontrivial to substantial. Given still incomplete recoveries, an additional negative shock would likely further deepen the scarring from COVID-19. These risks add renewed urgency to raise the resilience of economies in developing Asia. One key element in this is fostering new sources of growth, including private sector innovation and entrepreneurship—the topic of this *Update*'s theme chapter.

Figure 1.1.40 Impact of sharper-than-expected monetary tightening in advanced economies, difference from *ADOU 2022* baseline

Growth in developing Asia would slow following a fall in external demand due to recessions in advanced economies.

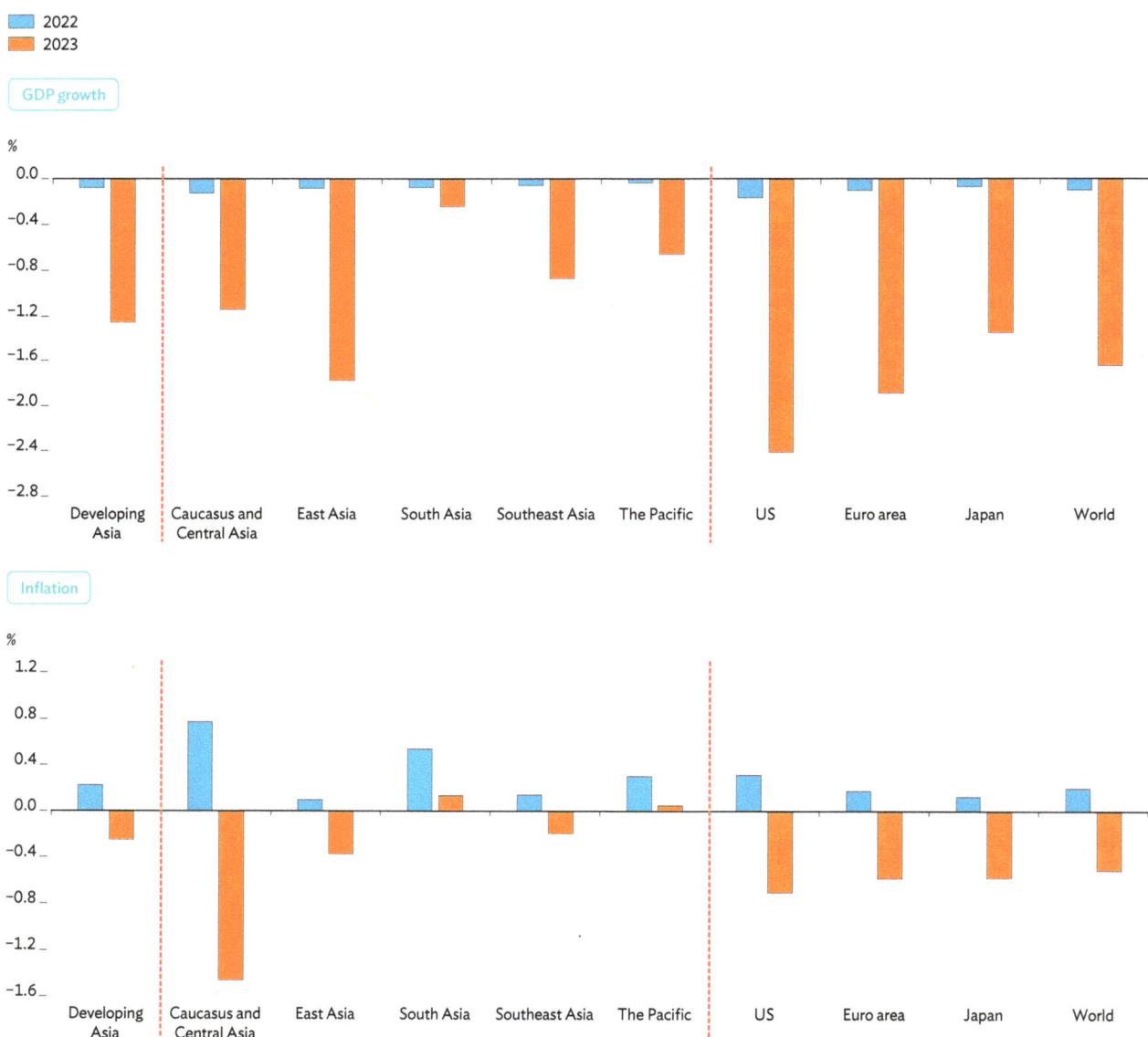

ADOU = Asian Development Outlook Update, GDP = gross domestic product, US = United States.
Sources: Oxford Economics; Asian Development Bank estimates.

Figure 1.1.41 Impact of negative pandemic developments, difference from *ADOU 2022*

Renewed lockdowns in the PRC and the emergence of new COVID-19 variants would worsen the economic outlook across developing Asia.

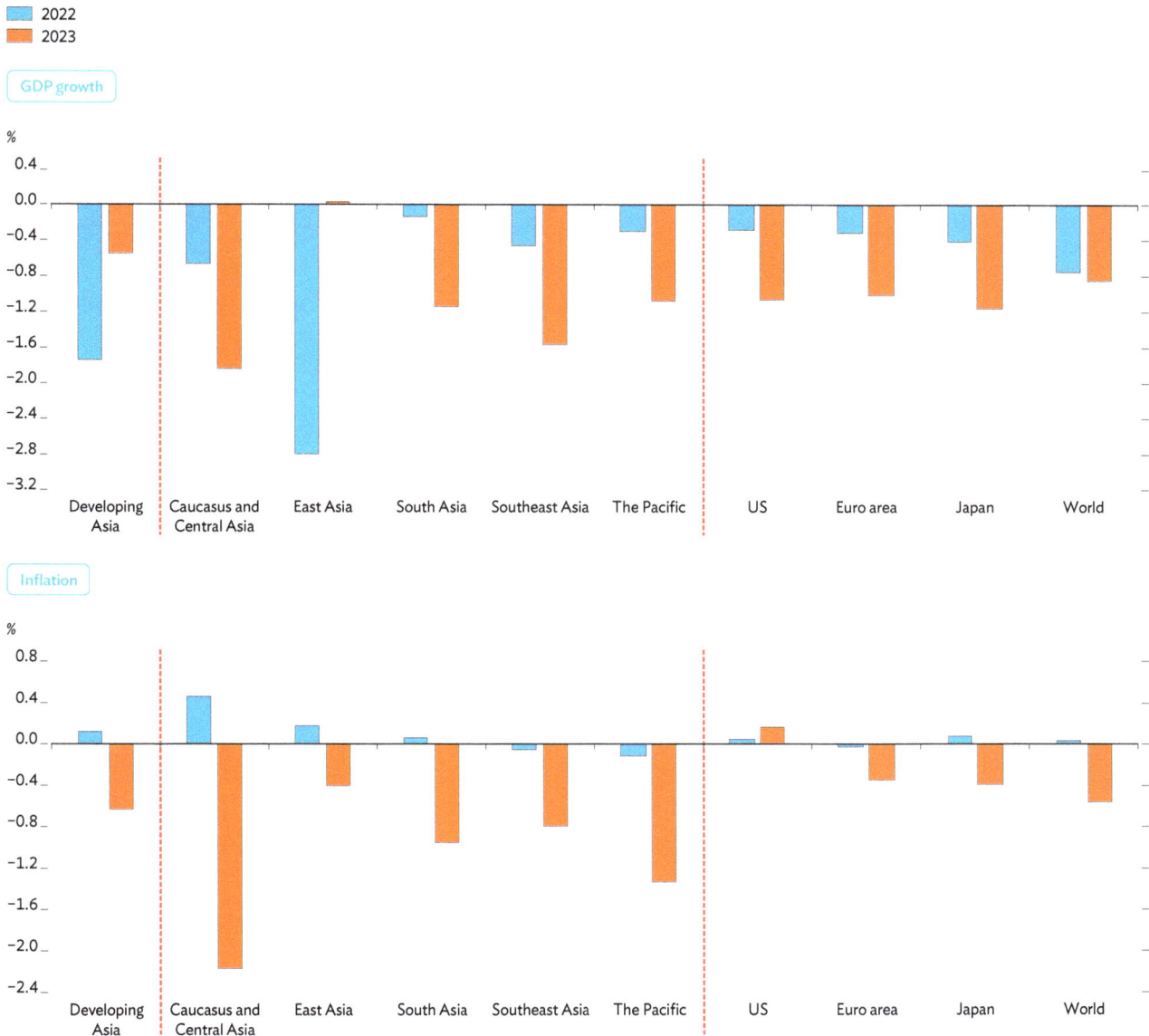

■ 2022
■ 2023

GDP growth

Inflation

ADOU = *Asian Development Outlook Update*, COVID-19 = coronavirus disease, GDP = gross domestic product, PRC = People's Republic of China, US = United States.

Sources: Oxford Economics; Asian Development Bank estimates.

Box 1.1 Estimates of pass-through from global commodity prices to inflation in developing Asia and across the world

Energy and food prices have contributed to mounting inflationary pressures in most of the world this year. Although the dynamics of aggregate prices vary across economies, inflationary pressures continue to build globally. This trend raises three key questions for policy makers and monetary authorities: To what extent do increasing global commodity prices translate into higher domestic headline inflation? Is the impact different for food and fuel prices? And are the effects homogenous across economies?

The pass-through from global commodity prices to inflation is investigated using panel vector autoregression techniques. Relying on quarterly data for a panel of 106 advanced and emerging economies, covering the first quarter of 1990 to the second quarter of 2021, this box provides estimates of the pass-through effect of changes in global food and fuel prices on domestic inflation. The empirical approach makes use of panel vector autoregression techniques (Abrigo and Love 2016). Global food and fuel inflation are included as exogenous variables so that impulse-response functions can be generated to identify the impact of a change in these exogenous variables on inflation. These functions isolate the effects of an exogenous change in one variable— either international food or fuel prices—on domestic inflation, while keeping all else constant.

The impact of international food and fuel price shocks is positive and significant, but varies across different groups of economies. The pass-through is found positive and significant for advanced economies and for developing Asia. The relative importance of international food and fuel price shocks also differs substantially. In advanced economies, a percentage point increase in food prices raises the average domestic price level by 0.07 percentage points after 5 years (panel A in the figure), but by four times this amount (0.28 percentage points) in developing Asia (panel C). The estimate for international fuel prices in advanced economies is 0.06 percentage points (panel B), twice as large as the 0.03 percentage points estimate in developing Asia (panel D). Some 51% of the pass-through from global food prices and 53% of the pass-through from global fuel prices occurs in the first year. In the current context, global fuel prices

as measured by the World Energy Index increased by 104.8% year on year in August 2022, and global food prices by 5.9%.[a] This suggests that—keeping all else constant—the increase in global fuel and food prices would add a cumulative 4.8 percentage points to domestic inflation in developing Asia, on average, over a 5-year horizon, with 2.5 percentage points coming in the first year. Two-thirds of the impact comes from fuel and one-third from food.

The extent of pass-through likely differs from economy to economy. Estimates for the panel of emerging and developing economies do not return statistically significant results, suggesting substantial heterogeneity in the degree of pass-through across economies within this group.[b] These differences in pass-throughs are likely to depend on a number of structural characteristics, such as the weight of food and energy in economies' consumer baskets, whether an economy is a net oil exporter, and whether there are policy measures, such as subsidies or price controls, aimed at cushioning the impact of commodity price shocks (Online Appendix Table 1).

The impact of rising commodity prices is persistent and calls for close monitoring. The findings offer at least two important insights for policy makers in developing Asia. First, the pass-through of commodity price shocks in the region is persistent and non-negligible, with a substantial impact in the first year and additional effects on price pressures for up to 5 years, particularly for food prices. These results suggest that shocks to commodity prices can generate second-round effects on headline inflation through different transmission channels. Second, the evidence of cross-economy heterogeneity in pass-through estimates (Lanzafame et al. forthcoming) indicates that, to be effective, policies should be tailored to economy-specific contexts and characteristics (Qureshi and Liaqat 2020). Structural characteristics and policy frameworks must be considered as they may affect the inflationary impact of commodity price shocks (Gelos and Ustyugova 2017).

Central banks face complex challenges when dealing with commodity price shocks. Higher inflation associated with increases in commodity prices worsens the trade-off between the two policy targets of price stability and sustained

continued on next page

Box 1.1 *Continued*

Response of inflation to a 1% increase in food and fuel prices

The impact of international food and fuel price shocks is positive, statistically significant and economically meaningful, and varies across different groups of economies.

A. Advanced economies international food price pass-through

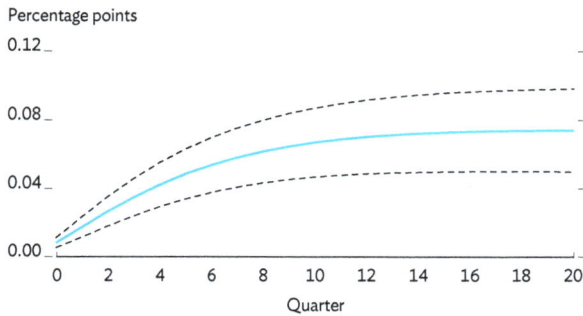

Percentage points

B. Advanced economies international fuel price pass-through

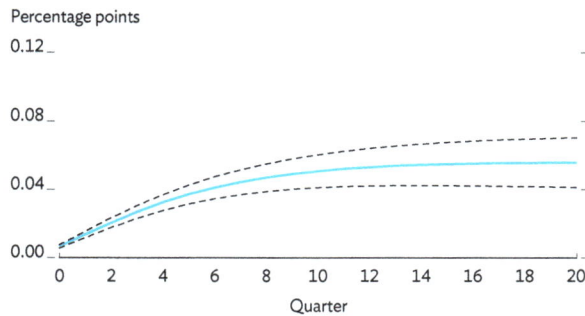

Percentage points

C. Developing Asian economies international food price pass-through

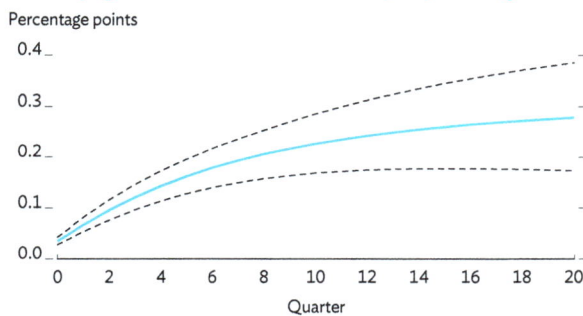

Percentage points

D. Developing Asian economies international fuel price pass-through

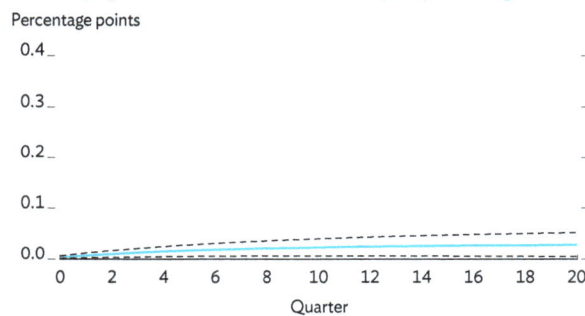

Percentage points

Notes: Cumulative impulse responses with 90% confidence bands in dashed lines are reported. Impulse response functions are generated using a sample of 34 advanced economies, 72 emerging and developing economies, and 18 Asian Development Bank developing member economies from the first quarter of 1990 to the second quarter of 2021. The size of the shock is a 1% increase in food and fuel prices, and horizontal axes refer to time in quarters. The international fuel price index used includes crude oil, natural gas, coal and propane price indices; the international food price index used includes cereal, vegetable oils, meat, seafood, sugar, and other food price indices.

Source: Asian Development Bank calculations using data from Haver Analytics (accessed 30 June 2022).

economic growth. Because growth in developing Asia is slowing while price pressures are rising, the complexity of these challenges is manifest in most of the region's economies. Central banks in the region should continue to remain vigilant and act promptly to forestall persistent rises in inflation, which could not only jeopardize the objective of price stability but also, ultimately, slow the economic recovery from the COVID-19 pandemic.

[a]   Despite recently declining substantially from their peaks this year, international food prices remain elevated, at 32% above January 2020 levels.

[b]   Indeed, when the sample of emerging and developing economies is split into different geographical groupings, the results change substantially. Food pass-through estimates are positive and significant for developing Asia, the Middle East and Central Asia, and sub-Saharan Africa,

but not for emerging and developing Europe. Energy pass-through estimates are significant only for developing Asia. See Lanzafame et al., forthcoming.

References:
Abrigo, M. and I. Love. 2016. Estimation of Panel Vector Autoregression in Stata. *Stata Journal* 16(3).

Gelos, G. and Y. Ustyugova. 2017. Inflation Responses to Commodity Price Shocks—How and Why Do Countries Differ? *Journal of International Money and Finance* 72.

Lanzafame, M., I. Qureshi, A. Ramayandi, R. Rivera, and M. Timbang. Forthcoming. *Commodity Prices and Inflation Pass-Through.* Asian Development Bank.

Qureshi, I. and Z. Liaqat. 2020. The Long-Term Consequences of External Debt: Revisiting the Evidence and Inspecting the Mechanism Using Panel VARs. *Journal of Macroeconomics* 63.

Growth in major advanced economies losing steam on the uphill

Growth in the major advanced economies of the United States, euro area, and Japan in 2022 and 2023 is revised down. The aggregate forecasts for growth for 2022 are lowered to 1.9% for 2022 and to 1.0% for 2023 from the projections in *Asian Development Outlook 2022 (ADO 2022)* (Table A.1). Higher-than-expected inflation in the US, at 9.1% year on year (yoy) in June, is eroding purchasing power and has forced the Federal Reserve onto a more aggressive path of rate hikes than was previously assumed. High inflation in the euro area, at 8.9% yoy in July, prompted the European Central Bank to tighten more aggressively even though economic activity is being undermined by subdued confidence and tighter energy and commodity supply following the Russian invasion of Ukraine. Japan's recovery will be held back by weaker exports due to continued supply chain disruptions, particularly in automobile manufacturing, and the delayed resumption of foreign tourist arrivals.

Table A.1 Baseline assumptions on the international economy

Growth forecasts for major advanced economies are adjusted downward as the US and the euro area tighten monetary policy to tame inflation.

	2021	2022		2023	
		April ADO 2022	*September Update*	*April ADO 2022*	*September Update*
GDP growth, %					
Major advanced economies[a]	5.0	3.5	1.9	2.4	1.0
United States	5.7	3.9	1.6	2.3	1.0
Euro area	5.2	3.3	2.5	2.6	0.7
Japan	1.7	2.7	1.4	1.8	1.6
Prices and inflation					
Brent crude spot prices, average, $/barrel	70.44	107.00	106.00	93.00	95.00
Consumer price index inflation, major advanced economies' average, %	3.3	4.8	7.2	2.1	3.0
Interest rates					
United States federal funds rate, average, %	0.1	0.5	1.5	1.3	3.6
European Central Bank refinancing rate, average, %	0.0	0.0	0.6	0.5	1.8
Bank of Japan overnight call rate, average, %	0.0	0.0	0.0	0.0	0.0
$ Libor, %[b]	0.1	0.5	1.5	1.3	3.6

ADO = Asian Development Outlook, GDP = gross domestic product, US = United States.

[a] Average growth rates are weighted by GDP purchasing power parity.

[b] Average London Interbank Offered Rate quotations on 1-month loans.

Sources: Bloomberg; CEIC Data Company; Haver Analytics; International Monetary Fund. *World Economic Outlook Update July 2022* (all accessed 1 September 2022); Asian Development Bank estimates.

This annex was written by Jules Hugot, Matteo Lanzafame, Nedelyn Magtibay-Ramos, Yuho Myoda, Pilipinas Quising, Irfan Qureshi, Arief Ramayandi, Marcel Schroder, and Dennis Sorino of the Economic Research and Regional Cooperation Department (ERCD), ADB, Manila, and Michael Timbang and Jesson Pagaduan, consultants, ERCD.

Recent developments in the major advanced economies

United States

The economy grappled with two consecutive quarters of GDP contractions over the first half of 2022. GDP declined by 1.6% in seasonally adjusted annualized terms in the first quarter (Q1) and 0.6% in Q2 (Figure A.1). The outbreak of the Omicron COVID-19 variant resulted in restrictions and disruptions that limited consumption in the first half. Investment in Q2 fell by 13.2%, particularly retail trade inventories. The consumption of goods contracted, but this was offset by services consumption that continued to increase, particularly food and accommodation, and health care. Government spending fell as several federal programs tapered off. Net trade helped boost the economy by contributing 1.4 percentage points to gross domestic product (GDP) growth. Exports rebounded by 17.6%, but imports were up by only 2.8%.

Fixed investment in Q2 contracted on stagnating industrial production and negative growth in home sales. But still strong indicators from the Institute for Supply Management composite purchasing managers' index (PMI) suggest investment will recover somewhat in Q3. The PMI has consistently stayed above 55.0 since January (above 50.0 indicates expansion). Although the manufacturing PMI fell to 53.0 in June from 56.1 in May—and remained at about that level in July and August—this was offset by relative resilience in the nonmanufacturing PMI, at about 57.0 in July and August. The gradual improvement in retail sales in April–July came mainly from surging prices. But high inflation is still a concern, particularly with core inflation remaining way above its historical average. Consumer confidence fell in May, June, and July, bringing this indicator to its lowest level since February 2021, before rebounding somewhat in August.

Earnings in the US continue to grow as the labor market remains robust. The unemployment rate fell to 3.5% in July after staying at 3.6% since March, but it rose to 3.7% in August. However, this rate of unemployment remains below the non-accelerating inflation rate of unemployment, estimated at 4.4% in both 2022 and 2023, and may therefore contribute to inflationary pressures. Inflation remains high, at 8.5%

Figure A.1 Demand-side contributions to growth, United States

Growth faltered in H1 2022 due to weaker spending on consumption and investment.

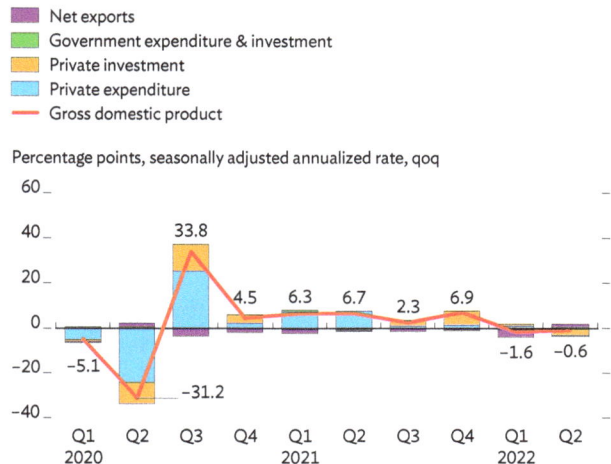

- Net exports
- Government expenditure & investment
- Private investment
- Private expenditure
- Gross domestic product

Percentage points, seasonally adjusted annualized rate, qoq

H = half, Q = quarter, qoq = quarter on quarter.
Sources: United States Department of Commerce. Bureau of Economic Analysis; Haver Analytics (both accessed 5 September 2022).

Figure A.2 Inflation and federal funds rate, United States

The Federal Reserve went hawkish to curb inflationary pressures.

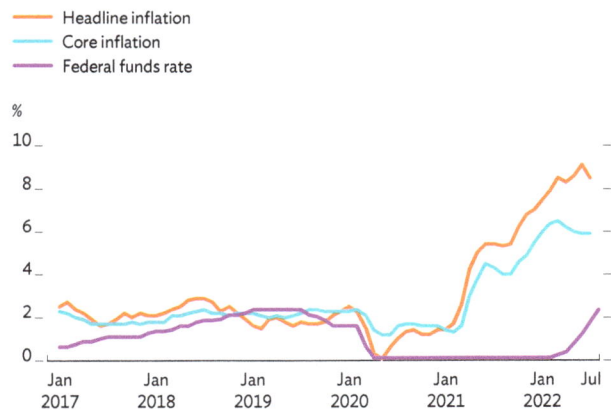

- Headline inflation
- Core inflation
- Federal funds rate

Source: Haver Analytics (accessed 5 September 2022).

in July after 9.1% in June, and is still mainly driven by high food and energy prices. Core inflation, at 5.9% in July, remained elevated and was much higher than the historical average (Figure A.2). Services inflation continues to edge up, mainly on higher rental costs. To curb inflation, the Federal Reserve increased again the federal funds rate by 75 basis points (bps) in July after a hike of 75 bps in June, bringing the policy rate to a range of 2.3%–2.5%.

Inflation will likely remain elevated this year at a forecast 8.0% due to continuing pressure from high commodity prices, before it moderates to a projected 3.2% in 2023. The federal funds rate is expected to increase further to ease demand-driven inflationary pressures.

Even with continued high inflation and faster-than-expected Fed tightening, the probability of a recession in the US remains fairly low at present. This is supported by recession indicators monitored by the National Bureau of Economic Research that include nonfarm payrolls, industrial production, real personal income less transfers, and real manufacturing and trade sales, which still point to continued expansion (Figure A.3). But growth in the US will weaken this year, with the forecast revised down to 1.6% from *ADO 2022*'s 3.9% projection. Growth is expected to moderate to 1.0% in 2023. The downward revision reflects a much more aggressive tightening by the Fed—in response to higher-than-expected inflation—than was assumed earlier.

Euro area

Growth in the euro area accelerated to a seasonally adjusted annualized rate (saar) of 2.8% in Q2 (Figure A.4). This was achieved despite the mounting economic fallout from the Russian invasion of Ukraine. Preliminary data indicate the pick-up in economic activity was driven by services and tourism, which benefited from COVID-19 restrictions being relaxed further. Support for economic activity also came from European Union (EU) Recovery and Resilience Facility funds. But growth in some EU economies is expected to have been dampened by weaker industrial activity because of surging energy costs and supply disruptions caused by the impact of COVID-19 lockdowns in the People's Republic of China (PRC). Q2 GDP in Spain rose by 4.6% saar (6.3% yoy), in Italy by 4.2% saar (4.6% yoy), and in France by 2.1% saar (4.2% yoy). But Germany's economy contracted by 0.1% saar on weaker private spending and falling net trade.

Leading indicators at the beginning of Q3 are consistent with a rapidly deteriorating outlook, reflecting fears of a recession in the euro area. All components of the economic sentiment indicator—consumer confidence, industry, services, retail trade, and construction—have worsened, with the index plummeting to a 17-month low of 99 in July, below its

Figure A.3 National Bureau of Economic Research recession indicators, United States

The NBER's closely watched indicators still point to expansion.

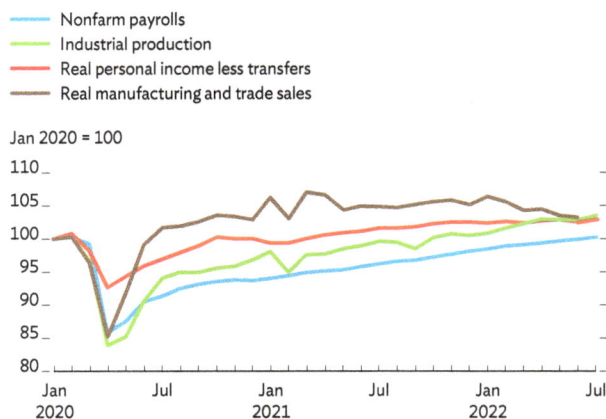

NBER = National Bureau of Economic Research.
Source: Haver Analytics (accessed 5 September 2022).

Figure A.4 Demand-side contributions to growth, euro area

Growth picked up in Q2 2022, buoyed by further reopening from eased COVID-19 restrictions.

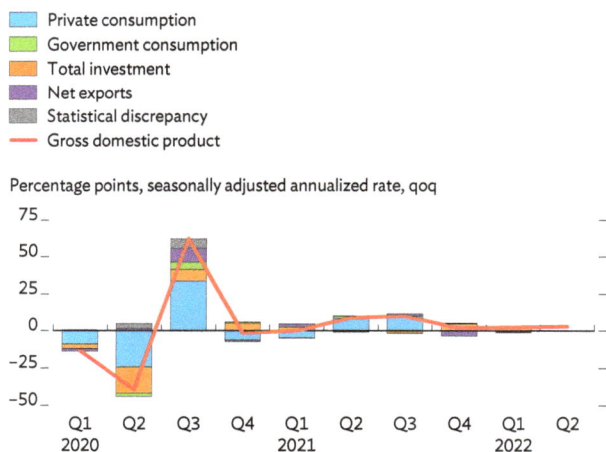

COVID-19 = coronavirus disease, Q = quarter, qoq = quarter on quarter.
Source: Haver Analytics (accessed 31 July 2022).

long-term average of 100. The composite PMI fell into contractionary territory, dropping to 49.9 in July from 52.0 in June as output and new orders fell for the first time since COVID-19 lockdowns in February 2021 (Figure A.5). Manufacturing nosedived: the manufacturing output index dropped to a 26-month low of 46.1 in July. The services PMI remained expansionary, albeit falling to a 15-month low of 50.6 in July.

Figure A.5 Economic sentiment and purchasing managers' indexes, euro area

Leading indicators in Q3 2022 deteriorated on fears of a looming recession.

— PMI composite   — Economic sentiment

Index   Long-term average = 100, seasonally adjusted

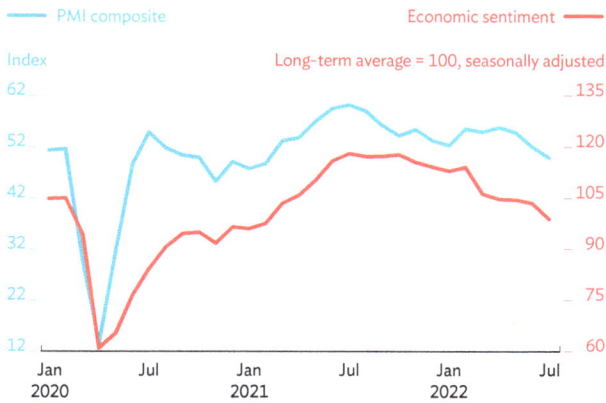

PMI = purchasing managers' index, Q = quarter.

Sources: CEIC Data Company; Haver Analytics (both accessed 10 August 2022).

This *Update* revises down the growth forecasts for the euro area to 2.5% for 2022 and to 0.7% for 2023. This year's seemingly strong growth, however, reflects a carryover effect of 2 percentage points from 2021 that will overshadow 2022's subdued growth dynamics. Growth is expected to cool this year and next on softening domestic and external demand, pessimism over the Russian invasion of Ukraine, high inflation, and worsening liquidity conditions. Eased COVID-19 pandemic restrictions will continue to support demand for the rest of this year. But private consumption will remain weak as household incomes suffer from high inflation and rising debt service costs due to tightening monetary policy translating into slower credit growth and higher interest rates. Economies heavily dependent on gas imports from the Russian Federation could be severely affected by the EU's proposed plan for rationing gas in Q4. Estimates suggest the plan's full implementation could result in GDP losses of up to 2 percentage points in Germany and Italy. Despite these growing headwinds, recovering tourism, tighter labor markets, and further disbursements of EU funds will help sustain economic activity.

The inflation forecast for the euro area is substantially revised up, to 7.9% for 2022 and 3.5% for 2023. Sharply higher energy prices, supply disruptions, and rising core inflation will continue shaping price dynamics. Headline inflation increased to 8.6% in June and to 8.9% in July, the highest rate since records began in January 1997, primarily driven by soaring energy and food prices (Figure A.6). Core inflation also edged up, from 4.6% in June to a record high of 5.0% in July. With inflation accelerating faster than expected, the European Central Bank hiked interest rates by 50 bps in July and approved the Transmission Protection Instrument. This is aimed at ensuring the efficient transmission of monetary policy via secondary market purchases of securities issued in jurisdictions experiencing deteriorating financing conditions. Despite the worsening growth outlook, the European Central Bank is expected to press ahead with an aggressive tightening cycle over the next 12 months to curb inflationary pressures.

Figure A.6 Headline and core inflation, euro area

Consumer prices reached record highs on sharply higher energy price pressures.

▨ Headline inflation
— Core inflation

%

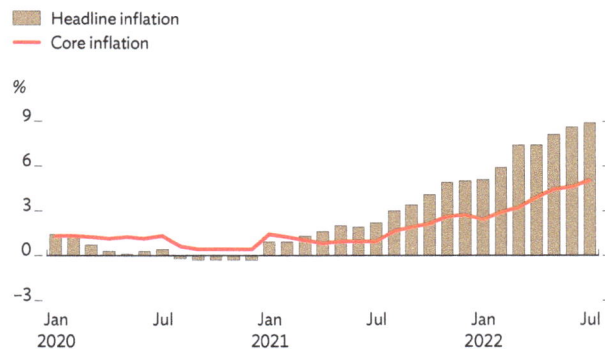

Source: Haver Analytics (accessed 31 July 2022).

The outlook is still subject to significant downside risks. An escalation in the war in Ukraine and particularly a worsening political standoff between the EU and the Russian Federation could further disrupt energy supply and derail the euro area's recovery. The war could also result in energy and food prices remaining higher for longer than expected, thus keeping inflation elevated and weighing on growth. Tighter monetary policy and liquidity conditions, and renewed stress in sovereign bond markets, also pose downside risks.

Japan

The economy in Q2 grew by 2.2%, the third consecutive quarter of positive growth. Spending on consumer services recovered robustly after COVID-19 mobility restrictions were lifted in late March. A significant increase in spending on semi-durable goods and services, including clothing, travel, and eating out, led the Q2 recovery, especially during the holiday weeks from April to May (Figure A.7). Private nonresidential investment grew for the first time in 2 quarters, supported by improved corporate earnings. Software investment led the growth. Private inventory investment fell sharply, dragging headline GDP. Q2 exports grew only moderately, partly due to the economic impact of lockdowns in the PRC. Net exports were barely positive in the quarter. Headline GDP is still below pre-pandemic 2019's level.

Consumer price inflation was above 2.0% yoy from April to June; the core consumer price in index in July was at 2.4% yoy. The upward pressure on prices was primarily because of higher import prices caused by the war in Ukraine and the yen's depreciation against the US dollar caused by the widening interest rate gap between Japan and the US. Even though inflation in Japan is still much lower than elsewhere in the world, this is the first time in almost 14 years that it has risen by at least 2%—excluding the consumption tax-driven inflation from April 2014 to March 2015. Prices in the broader categories of goods, including general food items, accelerated in Q2 (Figure A.8).

This *Update* revises down the forecasts for growth to 1.4% for 2022 from the earlier 2.7% projection and to 1.6% from 1.8% for 2023. A steady recovery in private consumption will drive growth in the second half. Services consumption, such as travel and eating out, will continue to pick up strongly throughout the vacation seasons. Exports are expected to recover in the near term, but the strength of this recovery will be weaker than expected due to continuing supply chain disruptions, particularly in automobile manufacturing, and the stalled resumption of tourism from abroad. Accelerating inflation and weak wage growth will weigh on consumer confidence, especially among lower-income groups, and adversely affect consumer spending.

Figure A.7 Demand-side contributions to growth, Japan

Private consumption remains robust, but the recovery in net exports is slow.

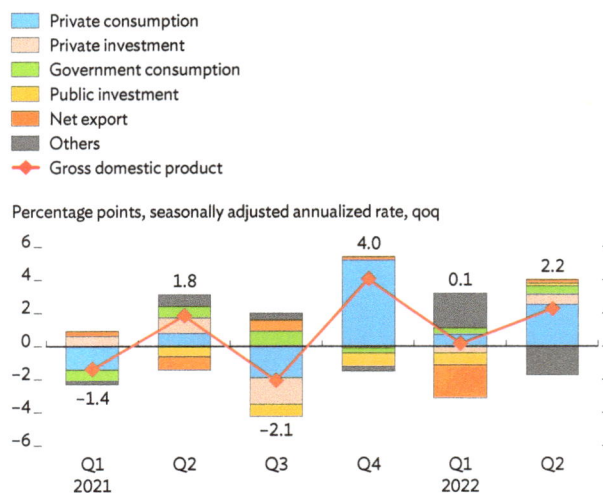

Q = quarter, qoq = quarter on quarter.
Source: Cabinet Office Japan (accessed 15 August 2022).

Figure A.8 Consumer Price Index, Japan

Elevated commodity prices have started to be passed through to broader CPI components.

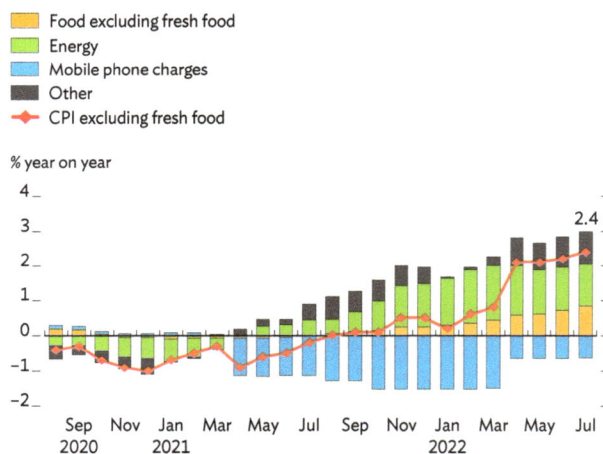

CPI = consumer price index.
Source: CEIC Data Company (accessed 19 August 2022).

Inflation is forecast rising to 2.1% in 2022, far higher than the earlier 1.3% projection, and to 0.8% from 0.5% in 2023. Elevated input prices have started to partially pass through to downstream goods and services (Figure A.9). Firms are expected to raise prices further to cover rising input prices toward the end of this year. This will accelerate inflation, which is forecast to average close to 3% over the second half.

Figure A.9 Final demand-intermediate demand price indexes, Japan

Inflationary pressures are rising even for downstream intermediate goods and final goods.

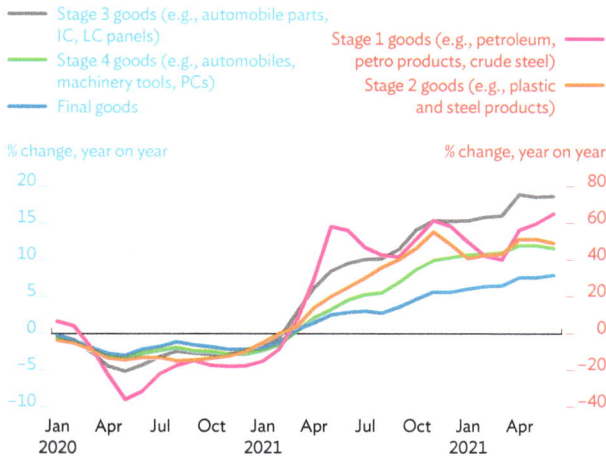

─── Stage 3 goods (e.g., automobile parts, IC, LC panels)
─── Stage 4 goods (e.g., automobiles, machinery tools, PCs)
─── Final goods
─── Stage 1 goods (e.g., petroleum, petro products, crude steel)
─── Stage 2 goods (e.g., plastic and steel products)

IC = integrated circuits, LC = liquid crystal, PC = personal computers.
Source: Bank of Japan (accessed 31 July 2022).

Next year's deceleration in inflation will come from the effects of higher commodity prices and the yen's sharp depreciation gradually fading. Because the inflation rate is unlikely to stay above 2%, the Bank of Japan is not expected to change its monetary policy significantly during the forecast horizon.

The risks to the outlook are generally balanced.
Upside risks include accelerating the restart of nuclear power plants, normalizing international travel, and a coming fiscal stimulus package. If well-targeted, the fiscal package—which will include extensive relief measures against inflation—could support the economic recovery by mitigating any deterioration in consumer confidence. Restarting the suspended nuclear plants will immediately decrease Japan's high dependence on fossil fuels, which will stabilize soaring domestic energy prices and improve the trade balance. A major downside risk is the Bank of Japan's premature exit from its current monetary policy. A possible acceleration in global monetary tightening may accelerate the yen's depreciation and domestic inflation, increasing public pressure on the central bank to follow the suit. A premature exit may depress investment by reinforcing low inflation expectations. Even a modest rise in interest rates will significantly increase the government's debt service costs, which would considerably limit the fiscal space.

Recent developments and outlook in nearby economies

Australia

The recovery continues with moderate growth, supported by domestic demand and exports.
Growth increased to 3.6% saar in Q2 2022 from 2.9% in Q1 (Figure A.10). Consumption and net exports were the largest contributors to growth, adding 3.9 percentage points each. Exports, up 23.7%, surged after two consecutive quarters of contraction. Fixed investment contributed 0.1 percentage points; private investment contracted by 6.0% and public investment grew by 25.8%. The low unemployment rate, at 3.4% seasonally adjusted in July (almost a 5-decade low), continued to support consumer spending, up by 16.5% seasonally adjusted in July.

Figure A.10 Demand-side contributions to growth, Australia

Growth remained robust in H1 2022.

▢ Consumption
▢ Gross fixed capital formation
▢ Changes in inventories
▢ Net exports
─── Gross domestic product

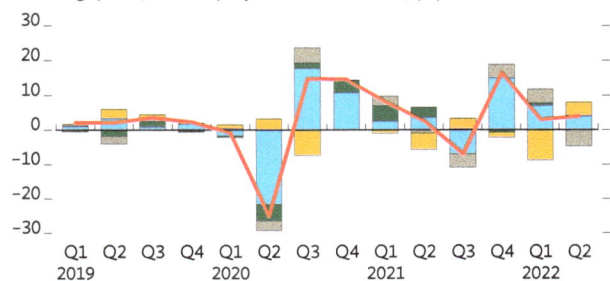

Q = quarter, qoq = quarter on quarter.
Source: CEIC Data Company (accessed 7 September 2022).

The economy will expand at a solid pace this year and next, but higher inflation weighs on the outlook. Accumulated savings, favorable labor market dynamics, the reopening of borders, and strong external demand for commodities will buoy growth. Still, pessimism is building over rising inflation and higher interest rates. The Q2 inflation rate, at 6.1%, was the highest in over 20 years and well above the Reserve Bank of Australia's 2.0%–3.0% target.

The consumer sentiment index in March fell below the 100-point threshold indicating optimism and reached a 2-year low of 81.2 in August. The Reserve Bank Board increased the cash rate by 50 bps to 2.35% at its 6 September meeting and hinted at further tightening to tame inflationary pressures. Risks to the outlook include sustained inflation, the effect of the Russian invasion of Ukraine on prices, and the PRC's COVID-19 trajectory. Consensus Forecasts, as of 5 September 2022, had GDP growing by 3.9% in 2022 and 2.3% in 2023.

New Zealand

Growth lost momentum on tighter COVID-19 restrictions amid the spread of the Omicron variant. The economy contracted by 0.3% saar in Q1 2022 mainly on a slump in exports that depressed GDP growth by 12.6 percentage points (Figure A.11). Growth is expected to rebound in Q2 on a recovery in electronic card transactions and the reopening of borders. Visitor arrivals in the first half of 2022 were up by 65.9% from the same period in 2021. Headline inflation surged to 7.3% in Q2, above the Reserve Bank of New Zealand's 1%–3% target and the highest in almost 32 years. Because of this and ongoing supply chain disruptions, business and consumer sentiment remained pessimistic.

Figure A.11 Demand-side contributions to growth, New Zealand

The economy contracted in Q1 2022, pulled down by falling exports.

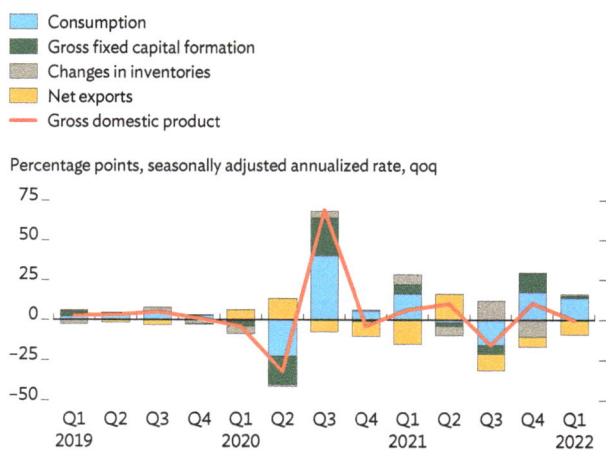

Percentage points, seasonally adjusted annualized rate, qoq

Q = quarter, qoq = quarter on quarter.
Source: CEIC Data Company (accessed 15 August 2022).

The business confidence index improved to −47.8 in August from −56.7 in July; the consumer confidence index rose to 81.9 in July from 80.5 in June. The unemployment rate in Q1, at 3.2%, was at its lowest in 35 years, although it ticked up to 3.3% in Q2.

The growth outlook has moderated because of higher interest rates and energy prices. In response to looming inflation, the Monetary Policy Committee increased the official cash rate by 50 bps to 3.0% at its August 2022 meeting. Growth will be supported by accrued savings and improved tourism due to easing COVID-19 restrictions. The downside risks are sustained supply disruptions and rising energy prices due to the economic impact of the Russian invasion of Ukraine. Consensus Forecasts, as of 5 September 2022, had GDP growing by 2.0% in 2022 and 1.9% in 2023.

Russian Federation

International sanctions following the invasion of Ukraine pushed the Russian economy into recession. GDP was down by 4.9% yoy in June. Domestic demand, down by 9.6% in the same month, was particularly hard hit by soaring inflation and declining real wages. Industrial output declined in June—albeit by a moderate 1.8% as soaring commodity prices somewhat offset declines in consumer goods manufacturing.

The Russian Federation has withstood sanctions better than expected. As of 30 August, Consensus Forecasts expected the economy to contract by 6.6% in 2022 after projecting a 10.0% contraction in April, with the forecast contractions continuously narrowing since April. The country successfully diverted oil exports from Europe to Asia and domestic demand has held up better than expected. A rapid increase in interest rates and the ruble's appreciation on a record-high trade surplus (Figure A.12) helped contain inflation—at 15.9% in June after it hit a 20-year high of 17.8% in April. As a result, the Central Bank of the Russian Federation was able to cut its key interest rate to 8% in July—below its level before the invasion of Ukraine. Large fiscal stimulus by the government also helped contain the recession; measures included a 10% raise in civil service salaries and pensions.

Figure A.12 Ruble–US dollar exchange rate and trade balance, Russian Federation

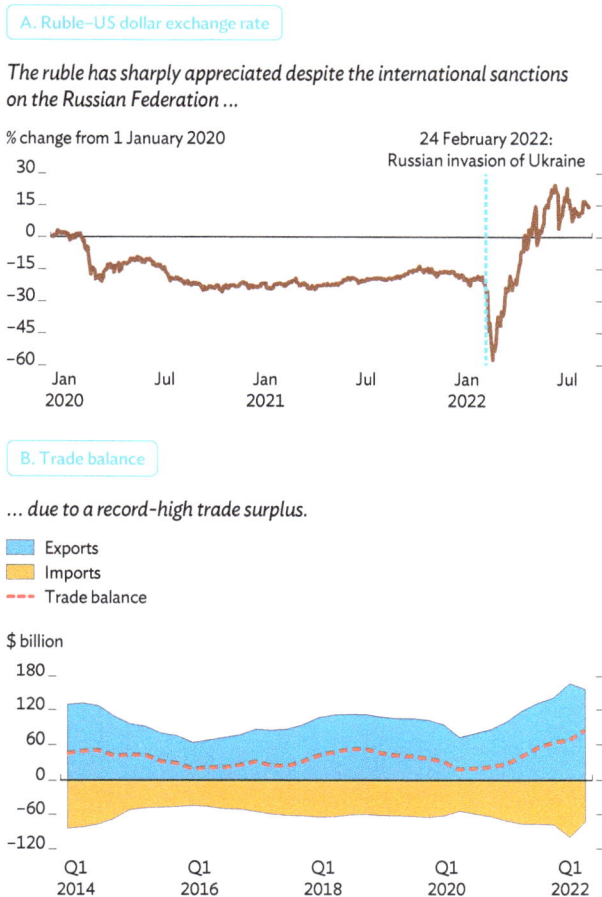

A. Ruble–US dollar exchange rate

The ruble has sharply appreciated despite the international sanctions on the Russian Federation ...

B. Trade balance

... due to a record-high trade surplus.

Q = quarter, US = United States.
Sources: CEIC Data Company; Haver Analytics (both accessed 30 August 2022).

The medium- and long-term forecasts for the Russian Federation are increasingly gloomy.

As of 30 August, Consensus Forecasts expected the economy to contract by 2.7% in 2023, a sharp worsening from the projected contraction of 0.7% in April (Figure A.13). The impact of sanctions will take effect more gradually than expected due to large inventories accumulated before the invasion of Ukraine and the several-year life cycle of most machinery, especially in industry and transport. Sanctions will be expanded in 2023 by the EU's sixth package of sanctions that includes a ban on seaborne imports of Russian oil. The package also includes a ban on EU operators insuring or financing the transport of Russian oil to third countries, which will hamper exports to Asia.

Figure A.13 Consensus Economics GDP forecasts relative to 2021, Russian Federation

The impact of the sanctions is expected to be delayed and slightly milder than originally expected.

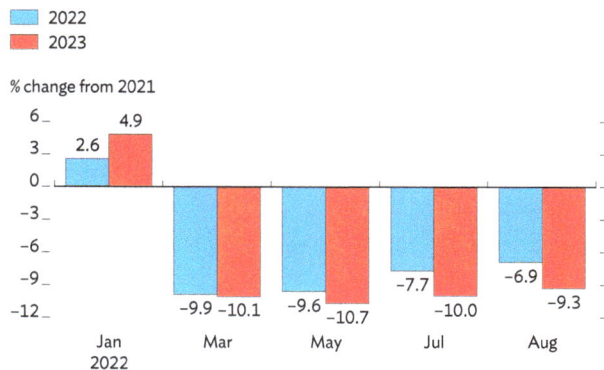

GDP = gross domestic product.
Note: The dates on the horizontal axis are those when each forecast for 2022 and 2023 was made.
Source: Consensus Economics (accessed 30 August 2022).

This, together with increased global oil output and slower global growth, will reduce income from oil exports. The sanctions also threaten longer-term growth prospects. The withdrawal of foreign companies has translated into an exodus of foreign capital and will affect domestic productivity. And the Russian Federation's default on its foreign debt payments in June will raise future borrowing costs.

Oil prices

Brent crude oil spot prices averaged $98.60/barrel in August, 9.5% lower month on month, but 40.8% higher year on year. Crude oil prices rose sharply in the first half of June, reaching their highest level since March, as oil demand forecasts improved amid tight global oil supply. But crude oil prices have since fallen as the macroeconomic outlook deteriorated and recession fears weighed on market sentiment. The Russian Federation's strong oil output in the face of sanctions, as well as the EU softening its Russian oil sanctions, also pushed down prices, with Brent crude spot prices falling by more than $30 since reaching a high of $127.18/barrel in June (Figure A.14). In the final week of August, Brent crude traded from $95.71 to $104.17.

Figure A.14 Brent crude oil spot prices

Prices are down from recent peaks.

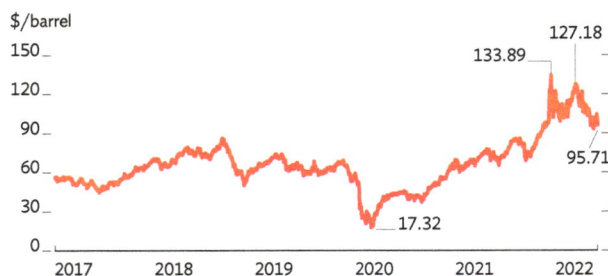

Source: Bloomberg (accessed 1 September 2022).

Despite the recent dip, crude oil prices remain elevated as the oil market continues to be tight due to low global inventories. In the first half of 2022, global oil production was estimated to be slightly higher than global oil consumption. The International Energy Agency, however, reports that global oil inventories remain critically low, with recent additions concentrated in the PRC due to lower demand because of COVID-19 lockdowns. Industry oil stocks held by Organisation for Economic Co-operation and Development countries, at nearly 300 million barrels, is about 10% below their 5-year average. In August, the International Energy Agency predicted that global oil consumption would rise by 2.1 million barrels a day (mb/d) to 99.7 mb/d in 2022 and another 2.1 mb/d to reach 101.8 mb/d in 2023. In 2022, the global oil supply is expected to average 100.1 mb/d before peaking at 101.1 mb/d in 2023.

Fears of a global slowdown, monetary policy tightening, and weaker demand in the PRC are putting downward pressure on oil prices. COVID-19 outbreaks in the PRC and the resulting pandemic restrictions reduced the PRC's oil consumption in Q2 2022. Some restrictions on business activities and mobility are expected to persist into Q3.

Despite the numerous challenges that the global economy faces, the global manufacturing and services PMIs have performed fairly well so far, staying above the 50-point threshold. This, combined with the protracted war in Ukraine, supply constraints, and recovering domestic and international travel as economies continue to reopen, is putting upward pressure on oil prices. US oil production has increased, but at a much slower rate. As of 2 September, the number of oil rigs has increased this year to 596, up 51.3% from 394 at 3 September 2021. But oil production increased by only 5% in the first 8 months of 2022 compared to the same period last year. And because of years of underinvestment and occasional political conflicts in oil-producing countries, the Organization of the Petroleum Exporting Countries Plus has only added about half of the agreed-upon output per month.

Given all these factors, Brent crude oil prices are forecast to average $106/barrel in 2022 and $95 in 2023 (Figure A.15). Oil prices are expected to remain volatile, and prices could swing quickly in either direction as the market continuously reassesses the prospects of demand for fuel slowing because of constrained supply.

Figure A.15 Oil price forecast

Oil prices are forecast falling in 2022 and 2023.

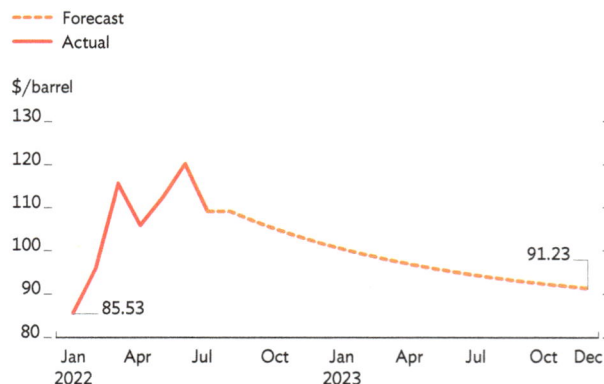

Sources: Bloomberg (accessed 27 July 2022); Asian Development Bank estimates.

2

ENTREPRENEURSHIP IN THE DIGITAL AGE

ENTREPRENEURSHIP IN THE DIGITAL AGE

The defining trait of entrepreneurs is that they start and run businesses. Dynamic entrepreneurs can help sustain economic growth in Asia. Developing Asia has reached a development stage where the private sector typically assumes a larger role in economic growth. The ongoing digitalization of economic activity that accelerated during coronavirus disease (COVID-19) has reduced the cost of starting a business and opened up a world of entrepreneurial opportunities. Digital entrepreneurship can thus become an engine of growth in the post-pandemic world.

The newly developed Global Index of Digital Entrepreneurship Systems (GIDES) measures the quality of an economy's environment for digital entrepreneurs. Significantly, the index allows meaningful comparisons across 113 global economies. It ranks Singapore in first place globally, and the Republic of Korea, Malaysia, and the People's Republic of China also score well. However, most Asian Development Bank (ADB) developing member economies lag far behind, suggesting plenty of scope for improvement. New analysis confirms the importance of a conducive environment in fostering dynamic entrepreneurs who innovate and create a lot of jobs. Further, a survey of 685 entrepreneurs across Southeast Asia indicates that digital entrepreneurs outperform their non-digital peers.

Digitalization facilitates entrepreneurship but cannot reduce the risk and uncertainty inherent in starting a new business, which entails a high likelihood of failure. Intuitively, sound institutions such as strong property rights mitigate the high risk and uncertainty that entrepreneurs face. New analysis of 230,000 individuals in 15 economies supports a strong positive association between a conducive institutional environment, especially strong rule of law, and dynamic entrepreneurship. Evidence also indicates that entrepreneurship tends to be more vibrant in less corrupt economies.

Policy makers cannot pick innovative entrepreneurs but they can go a long way toward creating the right environment for them to grow. They can contribute such conducive hardware as high-speed broadband networks and such software as reliable legal systems. Policy makers have plenty of scope to foster a more entrepreneurial Asia full of dynamic entrepreneurs who innovate, create jobs, and propel growth.

This chapter was written by Donghyun Park, Yothin Jinjarak, Cynthia Castillejos-Petalcorin, Gemma Estrada, Yuho Myoda, Pilipinas Quising, and Shu Tian. It draws on background papers and notes listed at the end of the chapter. The authors thank Heili Bravo for administrative support and Emmanuel Alano for research support. Strategic advice was provided by Erkko Autio, Kun Fu, and Willem Smit. Guidance from Albert Park, Joseph E. Zveglich, Jr., and Abdul Abiad is gratefully acknowledged. Arndt Husar and Yoonee Jeong provided valuable suggestions on digitalization. All other contributions are listed in the Acknowledgments section of this volume.

Entrepreneurs contribute to economic dynamism

Entrepreneurship, or the initiative to start and run a business, is vital to economic growth and development. Entrepreneurs contribute greatly to innovation, and they are central to the dynamic competition that drives modern economies through what economist Joseph Schumpeter called "creative destruction." Innovative entrepreneurs are the principal agents of the never-ending Schumpeterian process of new products, services, technologies, firms, and industries replacing existing products, services, technologies, firms, and industries. Behind the constant emergence of new companies with new technologies and new products are visionary, game-changing, risk-taking entrepreneurs such as Lee Byung-Chul of Samsung, Jack Ma of Alibaba, or N. R. Narayana Murthy of Infosys. Competition forces even mundane, ordinary entrepreneurs to innovate. Furthermore, multitudes of common entrepreneurs serve the economy in other significant ways, most notably by creating multitudes of jobs. The contribution of entrepreneurship to the economy therefore comes not only from transformational entrepreneurs.

Despite its significant contribution to innovation and economic growth, entrepreneurship is relatively under-researched. This is partly for lack of data until recent years, when the Global Entrepreneurship Monitor and other entrepreneurship databases were developed. More broadly, the lack of research and appreciation reflects the innate difficulty of quantifying entrepreneurship and the factors that motivate people to become entrepreneurs. Furthermore, entrepreneurship is challenging to explain as a rational endeavor because most new businesses fail. Yet another possible reason why economists have tended to neglect entrepreneurship is its tremendous diversity. Entrepreneurs range from street food vendors to transformational innovators such as Elon Musk, making it difficult to clearly conceptualize entrepreneurship (Box 2.1.1).

While mundane entrepreneurs contribute a lot to the economy by, for instance, creating jobs, game-changing entrepreneurs contribute disproportionately to innovation, productivity growth, and economic dynamism.

Transformational entrepreneurs are often the first to take risks and seize unrecognized opportunities despite the low probability of success. Bold, visionary, creative entrepreneurs think outside of the box to create new products, services, and industries. Entrepreneurs are adept at commercializing new technology into products and services that are useful for consumers. Commercially successful applications of the internet such as Flipkart, Grab, or Tencent are good examples. While the public sector played a big role in the development of basic internet technology, entrepreneurs were responsible for the bulk of its myriad commercial applications. In addition to products that consumers find useful, entrepreneurs create products that address humanity's most urgent challenges. One prominent example is the COVID-19 vaccine produced by the German biotech startup BioNTech, founded by two innovative entrepreneurs, Uğur Şahin and Özlem Türeci (Box 2.1.2). By fostering knowledge spillover and radical innovation, innovative entrepreneurs contribute greatly to economic growth, employment creation, productivity, and social welfare in economies of all income and development levels (Kritikos 2014). Everyday entrepreneurs and innovative entrepreneurs cannot always be clearly distinguished, as a creative street food vendor who invents uniquely delicious dishes, for example, may become an influential restauranteur. Nevertheless, a relatively small group of highly productive entrepreneurs account for the lion's share of the entrepreneurship contribution to the economy.

The vital role of entrepreneurship in economic growth and development is a powerful motive for delving into entrepreneurship in developing Asia, especially considering how thinly the topic has been researched (Alano and Quising 2022a). Entrepreneurship holds the key to the emergence and development of a vibrant private sector, an indispensable ingredient of sustained growth.

The advent of digital entrepreneurship in recent years means that now is an especially opportune time to analyze why individuals start new businesses. Information and communication technology (ICT), or digital technology, has dramatically reduced the cost of starting a business by minimizing the need for brick-and-mortar stores and other physical facilities (Alano and Quising 2022b). More fundamentally, ICT reduces information and communication costs and thus promotes productivity. Specific benefits to entrepreneurs include expansion of market access at low cost, better coordination with other players, and ready exposure to new innovative ideas. Furthermore, digital technology contributed greatly to entrepreneurial resilience during COVID-19. By lowering barriers to entry into an industry, ICT can foster inclusive growth and development. Importantly, ICT can open up entrepreneurial opportunities for women and the poor. Standing in the way of this promise, however, is a digital divide that erects a major barrier to ICT-enabled entrepreneurship. Further, good digital infrastructure alone does not automatically invigorate entrepreneurship.

Digital technology is not a panacea for a lack of entrepreneurship, because multiple factors influence entrepreneurial activity in a society. To become an entrepreneur is fundamentally an individual decision. Talented individuals who become game-changing innovative entrepreneurs typically have plenty of opportunities to work highly paid jobs. Their decision to court risk by starting their own business instead is shaped by their values but also by social norms, formal and informal institutions, and the overall business environment (Baumol and Strom 2007; Acs, Desaid, and Hessels 2008). The same is true of everyday entrepreneurs. The enabling entrepreneurial ecosystem constantly evolves. In recent years, organizational innovations such as venture accelerators and crowdfunding have improved the entrepreneurial climate.

Technological innovations such as the emergence of 5G broadband also affect the climate. While it is difficult to pin down why some individuals start a business while others do not, what is certain is that the decision to become an entrepreneur is inherently a complex, multidimensional process.

This theme chapter explores the issue of entrepreneurship in developing Asia. Entrepreneurship has contributed substantially to the economic dynamism of the world's fastest-growing region. The remarkable transformation of the People's Republic of China (PRC) was enabled by unleashing a tsunami of entrepreneurship and private enterprise growth since market reform in 1978. Similarly, India owes more recent growth acceleration partly to more vibrant entrepreneurial activity, most notably in ICT. Still missing, though, is a more comprehensive and systematic analysis of entrepreneurship in developing Asia.

This chapter seeks to fill the gap. It delves into entrepreneurship in general and the more recent phenomenon of digital or ICT-enabled entrepreneurship. ICT reduces the cost of starting a new business, notably by eliminating the need for costly physical stores and making it possible to reach large numbers of potential customers at low cost. This should make ICT a catalyst for entrepreneurship. Furthermore, online shopping or e-commerce helped keep many businesses afloat during COVID-19 and thus contributed greatly to economic resilience (ADB 2021). Asia is home to a thriving digital economy underpinned by digital entrepreneurs such as Jack Ma of Alibaba. In this context, another major contribution of this study is to present in-depth analysis of digital entrepreneurship in Asia and the Pacific.

The chapter explores the following key research questions: (i) What are the key drivers of entrepreneurship in Asia and globally? (ii) What are the salient barriers to entrepreneurship? (iii) What is the role of policy in promoting entrepreneurial activity? While entrepreneurship remains a relatively under-researched topic, it has a growing empirical literature (Myoda and Castillejos-Petalcorin 2022a). In particular, more researchers are looking into the determinants of entrepreneurship (Roman, Bilan, and Ciumas 2018). More literature now explores the link between entrepreneurship and institutional factors.

Chowdhury, Terjesen, and Audretsch (2015), for instance, found that institutional factors such as property rights, freedom from corruption, and fewer procedures for starting new businesses to be significantly and positively related to the emergence of new firms. Other studies that find a positive link include ADB (2020) and Arin et al. (2015).

This study adds to the literature by delving into the determinants of entrepreneurship in a more systematic and comprehensive manner. In particular, analysis explicitly recognizes that a relatively small group of innovative entrepreneurs are disproportionately more productive. The link between the quality of a country's institutional and digital environment and the quality of its entrepreneurship is empirically analyzed using a large, updated dataset. In addition, the study develops a new database based on in-depth interviews of 685 entrepreneurs in six Southeast Asian countries.

Another significant contribution is the construction of an internationally comparable index of digital entrepreneurship that allows countries to benchmark their entrepreneurial ecosystems against other countries. The index identifies the relative strengths and weaknesses of each country's entrepreneurial ecosystem.

Evidence points to the key role of the institutional and digital environment. New analysis in the chapter provides strong empirical support for a positive and significant relationship between a sound institutional environment and high-quality entrepreneurship. Results from economies in developing Asia indicate that better-quality institutions go hand in hand with mobilizing entrepreneurs who innovate, export, and create many jobs. Specific policy options include easing the cost of business registration, strengthening the rule of law, and fostering financial development. In addition, policy makers can promote high-quality entrepreneurship by enhancing the environment for digital entrepreneurs. This includes both the hardware of digital technology infrastructure and the software of ICT skills and societal perceptions of entrepreneurship.

Some entrepreneurs are more productive than others

The notion that entrepreneurship benefits growth is intuitively plausible. To test the relationship between entrepreneurship and GDP growth, Kim et al. (2022) recently reported on new cross-country analysis that found opportunity-driven entrepreneurship to have a positive impact on growth in developing economies where manufacturing is more prevalent, but necessity-driven entrepreneurship to have a positive impact where services are more prevalent. The study did not, however, yield evidence of a positive general link between economic growth and total entrepreneurship (Box 2.1.3).

Other empirical analysis provides some evidence that entrepreneurship is associated with economic growth, though the evidence is limited and qualified. One possible explanation is that a small group of highly successful entrepreneurs contribute disproportionately to positive economic outcomes. These entrepreneurs set up fast-growing new firms known in the industry as "gazelles," which account for the lion's share of entrepreneurial innovation, output, and job creation (ADB 2020). In this section, analysis sifts through firm-level data from 17 ADB developing member economies for which data are available.[1] The data confirm that not all entrepreneurs are created equal when it comes to their contribution to the economy.

Table 2.1.1 shows the employment size of baby businesses at the time of the interview. Of the baby businesses, 51.0% qualified as micro businesses that employed at most two employees including their owner-manager(s). Of the established businesses, the corresponding share was almost the same: 51.2% of the sample total. In contrast, entrepreneurial businesses with 250 or more employees represented only 0.4% of both baby businesses and established businesses in the sample.

In both age groups, the number of firms belonging to the smallest employment size category was over 100-fold larger than that of the firms belonging to the largest employment size category.

---

[1]   Armenia; Bangladesh; Georgia; Hong Kong, China; India; Indonesia; Kazakhstan; Malaysia; Pakistan; the People's Republic of China; the Philippines; the Republic of Korea; Singapore; Taipei,China; Thailand; Vanuatu; and Viet Nam.

Table 2.1.1 Current employment in baby businesses

A small group of dynamic entrepreneurs accounts for a disproportionate share of jobs created by new businesses.

Firm size	Firms	%	Total employees	%
1–2	7,602	51.0	10,888	8.2
3–9	5,900	39.6	25,695	19.5
10–49	1,169	7.8	20,240	15.3
50–249	166	1.1	14,401	10.9
250+	55	0.4	60,785	46.0
Total	**14,892**	**100.0**	**132,009**	**100.0**

Notes: Baby businesses are no older than 42 months old.
The sample is in Asian Development Bank developing member economies, listed in Autio and Fu (2022a).
Source: Autio and Fu 2022a.

However, the contributions of these two categories to total employment generated by baby and established businesses were dramatically different. Whereas micro businesses generated 8.2% of total employment by baby businesses and 7.7% by established businesses, baby and established businesses with over 250 employees generated over 45% of the total employment in both samples.[2] Put another way, the firm-level employment potential of a new entrepreneurial business that grows to the largest employment size category is roughly 600 times that of a typical micro business.

It is interesting that the share of both the smallest and largest employment categories is practically the same among baby and established businesses—the dividing line between them 42 months in business. Also, the portion of firms falling into three middle-employment categories (3–9 employees, 10–49 employees, and 50–249 employees) were also virtually the same among baby and established businesses. So was the average number of employees per business: 8.9 employees per baby business and 9.2 employees per established business. For exports and product innovation, two other indicators of firm productivity, the pattern resembles that of job creation, with a relatively small number of firms accounting for a disproportionate share of exports and product innovation (Autio and Fu 2022a).

Digitalization is a powerful enabler of entrepreneurial resilience

ICT played a key role in the resilience of entrepreneurs and firms during COVID-19. In the face of unprecedented mobility restrictions, the internet enabled entrepreneurs to go online to sell their products, communicate with their workers, and meet their business partners. In this way, digital technology significantly cushioned the severe adverse impact of the pandemic on entrepreneurial activity. Indeed it served as a lifeline for many entrepreneurs who would have gone out of business without the internet. Retailers who had to shut down their stores under lockdown turned to online orders for sales and revenue. Similarly, restauranteurs who had to close their dining rooms relied on online orders for takeout or home delivery to keep their business going. Furthermore, while COVID-19 posed a daunting challenge to most businesses, digital technology opened up new business opportunities. More precisely, the pandemic and the need to minimize personal contact fueled a huge surge in demand for e-commerce.

Against this background, Vo, Le, and Park (2022) empirically examined the impact of ICT on entrepreneurial resilience during COVID-19. It may seem obvious that ICT helped many entrepreneurs continue their businesses operations in the face of this monumental health and economic crisis, but the study delved into the data to test this intuition with rigorous analysis. It used firm-level data from World Bank Enterprise Surveys, a primary advantage of which is comparability using a wide range of variables across a large number of economies. To better identify the role of digital technology during COVID-19 period, surveys covered two broadly defined data periods: pre-2020 and 2020. Pre-2020 uses the latest data available from 2016 to 2019, before the pandemic, that shed light on a broad range of business environment topics, including access to finance, corruption, infrastructure, crime, competition, and firm-performance measures. In 2020, the Enterprise Analysis Unit of the World Bank collected information on exactly the same firm sample to gain insights into the various firm-level impacts of the COVID-19 pandemic.

---

2   Data excluded businesses with more than 2,000 employees to avoid distortion from outliers.

The study used the first round of this follow-up survey, which covers the greatest number of economies and provides information on the immediate impact of the pandemic shock. Most importantly, it successfully merged the 2020 follow-up data with the baseline pre-2020 data. The merged cross-sectional sample consists of 12,990 unique firms interviewed from 5 May to 30 September 2020, covering 32 economies and 28 industries as counted by the International Standard Industrial Classification of All Economic Activities.

Confirming that digital technology is strongly associated with entrepreneurial resilience during COVID-19, empirical analysis found that website ownership significantly mitigated the adverse impact of the crisis on almost all firm performance measures (Box 2.1.4).

Dynamic entrepreneurs can help sustain growth in Asia

In addition to economic dynamism and resilience, many entrepreneurs contribute to sustainable development by enhancing environmental protection (Kim and Castillejos-Petalcorin 2022) and gender equity (Castillejos-Petalcorin and Kim 2022). Myoda (2022) reported abundant examples of indigenous sustainable entrepreneurship in poorer countries. Kenyan entrepreneur Disimus Kisilu, for instance, developed affordable and green mobile cold storage units powered by renewal energy, thereby greatly helping smallholder farmers. By economically empowering women, female entrepreneurship fosters gender equality—as, for example, enterprises led by women tend to have narrower gender pay gaps (Pham and Tan 2022a). Vietnamese entrepreneur Van Vu is an example of a highly successful female entrepreneur. Her startup Elsa Speak, which leverages big data and artificial intelligence to improve speech recognition technology, has become one of the world's top five English learning apps, with more than 10 million users in more than 100 economies.

With profits from Elsa Speak, Van Vu founded Vietseeds, a nonprofit organization that supports education for poor girls in Viet Nam. In addition to financial assistance, Vietseeds provides training and mentoring programs for its beneficiaries. The growing role of entrepreneurs in sustainable development is epitomized by the recent emergence of a new breed of social entrepreneurs who explicitly seek to serve a social purpose (Habaradas 2022a).

To conclude, dynamic entrepreneurs—the relatively small group of innovative entrepreneurs—can help sustain growth in Asia. They have contributed significantly to regional growth in the past, and their contribution is likely to grow even larger going forward. This is because many economies in developing Asia have reached a development stage where the private sector typically assumes a larger role in economic growth. While the government's role remains vital, it is increasingly to provide an enabling environment for private enterprise. Rapid growth has transformed Asia into a predominantly middle-income region, in which sustaining rapid growth becomes harder than at low income. Visionary entrepreneurs like Lee Byung-Chul and Jung Ju-Young created world-class companies, Samsung and Hyundai, which contributed greatly to the rare and widely admired journey undertaken by the Republic of Korea (ROK) from middle to high income. Furthermore, the digitalization of economic activity, which accelerated during COVID-19, has opened up a world of entrepreneurial opportunity by reducing the cost of starting a business. Digital entrepreneurship can thus become an engine of growth in the wake of COVID-19.

The next section delves into the relationship between an economy's environment for digital entrepreneurship and the dynamic digital entrepreneurs who innovate, export, and create many jobs.

Box 2.1.1 Entrepreneurs driven by opportunity versus necessity

Entrepreneurship is highly heterogeneous and encompasses a wide range of activities. It is conceptually useful to distinguish individuals who become entrepreneurs out of sheer economic necessity from those who start a new business to capitalize on profit opportunities from innovative ideas. The distinction is not always clear cut, nor does it come close to capturing the full spectrum of entrepreneurial activity.

Nevertheless, the distinction is found in the Global Entrepreneurship Monitor, one of the most widely used sources of entrepreneurship data. The key indicator of country-level entrepreneurial activity is "total early-stage entrepreneurial activity," or the percentage of the working-age population who are "nascent," or actively involved in starting a

new business, or else new entrepreneurs and young business owners already running a new business that is less than 42 months old. This total consists of "opportunity-driven early-stage entrepreneurial activity," the percentage of individuals involved in early-stage entrepreneurial activity who claim to be purely or partly driven by opportunity, and "necessity-driven early-stage entrepreneurial activity," the percentage of individuals involved in early-stage entrepreneurial activity who claim to be driven by necessity, having no better choice for work.

Reference:
Kim, J. et al. 2022. *Entrepreneurship and Economic Growth: A Cross-Sectional Analysis Perspective.* Asian Development Bank.

Box 2.1.2 Innovative entrepreneurs create COVID-19 vaccine

At the forefront of the development of the Pfizer–BioNTech vaccine, one of the world's first safe and effective COVID-19 vaccines, is the husband-and-wife entrepreneurial team of Uğur Şahin and Özlem Türeci. They are the chief executive officer and the chief medical officer, respectively, of Biopharmaceutical New Technologies or BioNTech (Castillejos-Petalcorin 2022). The German biotech firm was founded in 2008 by the two scientists turned entrepreneurs. For decades, BioNTech used its proprietary messenger RNA (mRNA) technology as a novel immunotherapy for cancer and other diseases. mRNA technology was considered too risky for large pharmaceutical companies to use in mass production.

When COVID-19 emerged in January 2020 and caused a global pandemic, the cofounders of BioNTech devoted the company's resources—and leveraged 2 decades of cancer research—to swiftly develop a vaccine to fight the novel virus SARS-CoV-2. The project was called Project Lightspeed. The entrepreneurial couple knew that their mRNA technology had the potential to provide protection from the virus. By focusing their firm's resources on vaccine development, they were able to develop a safe and effective COVID-19 vaccine in months.

While the rapid development of the BioNTech Comirnaty vaccine was a remarkable scientific achievement, major obstacles stood in the way of commercialization. Above all, the vaccine had to be stored at a temperature between –90°C and –60°C. Other challenges to bringing the vaccine to patients included large-scale production, logistics, supply chain coordination, financing, and complying with regulations. While the vaccine was still being developed, the cofounders reached out to regulators, investors, manufacturers, and experts on cold chain management to ensure cold temperature storage and transportation.

BioNTech received a significant dose of venture capital and, to compensate for its low production capacity, teamed up with Pfizer. BioNTech and Pfizer collaborated to manufacture the vaccine in large quantities in record time. Combining BioNTech's technological expertise and Pfizer's stellar track record in vaccine development, mass production, and delivery, the companies were able to deliver a billion doses of the vaccine in a few months. The Comirnaty vaccine was shown to be 95% effective in clinical trials, and it has saved millions of lives around the world.

continued on next page

Box 2.1.2 *Continued*

BioNTech revenue and employees, 2017–2021

The innovative biotech startup has experienced a sharp increase in revenue and staff strength.

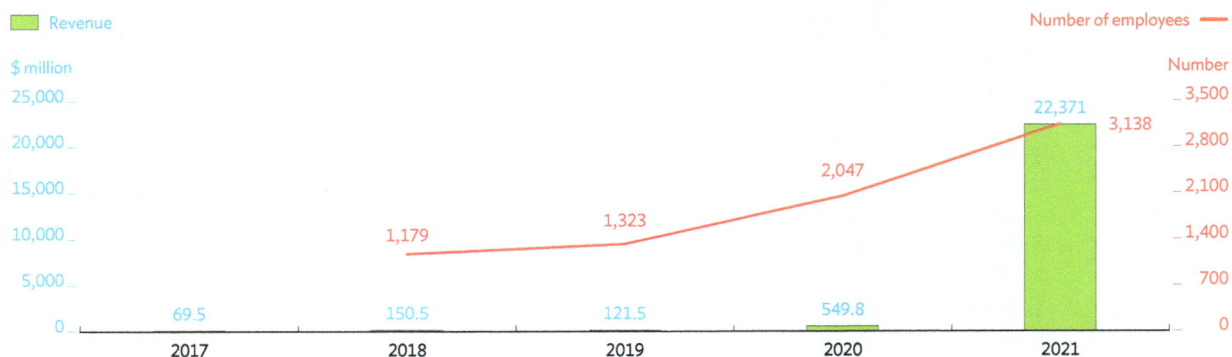

Sources: BioNTech financial reports, various years. https://investors.biontech.de.

Entrepreneurial success has followed the development of the COVID-19 vaccine. BioNTech revenue exploded from $151 million in 2018 to $22.4 billion in 2021 (box figure). BioNtech has announced plans to use the vaccine windfall to fund the development of new cancer drugs and new vaccines for other diseases, as a way to contribute to society. In addition, in February 2022, it unveiled mobile vaccine production units called BioNTainers to be deployed on a nonprofit basis across Africa and other developing regions.

The units can produce 50 million doses per year (Pancevski 2002). BioNTech's central role in COVID-19 vaccine development highlights the contributions possible from dynamic entrepreneurs who think outside of the box to address even the biggest and most urgent global challenges.

References:
Castillejos-Petalcorin, C. 2022. *High-Valued Social Entrepreneurs: BioNTech and the Ocean Cleanup.* Asian Development Bank.
Pancevski, B. 2022. BioNTech Unveils Mobile COVID-19 Factories for Developing World. *The Wall Street Journal.* 16 February.

Box 2.1.3 Manufacturing is more conducive for opportunity-driven entrepreneurship

To test the relationship between entrepreneurship and GDP growth, Kim et al. (2022) deployed in new cross-country analysis a standard growth model that included a number of control variables that can influence growth and are widely used in the literature. The dependent variable is GDP growth, and the key independent variables are three measures of entrepreneurship: total early-stage entrepreneurship, opportunity-driven early-stage entrepreneurship, and necessity-driven early-stage entrepreneurship. To address possible feedback or endogeneity in the relationship between entrepreneurship activity rates and economic growth, analysis includes lagged entrepreneurship activity rates and their interactions.

Analysis did not yield evidence of a positive general link between economic growth and total entrepreneurship. However, evidence points to the importance of distinguishing between different types of entrepreneurship and between advanced versus developing economies.

This is plausible given the immense heterogeneity of entrepreneurial activity. Interestingly and significantly, opportunity-driven entrepreneurship has a positive impact on growth in developing economies where manufacturing is more prevalent, but necessity-driven entrepreneurship has a positive impact when services are more prevalent (box table). Intuitively, technological breakthroughs present opportunities for innovative manufacturing entrepreneurs but less so for service entrepreneurs, who adapt only gradually to new technologies (Andrews 2022). The effects are economically significant. For instance, an increase in opportunity-driven entrepreneurship from the mean level in developing economies to the mean level in advanced economies, together with a standard deviation increase in the share of manufacturing in the GDP of developing economies, is associated in developing economies with 0.41% increase in annual GDP per capita.

Estimation results for GDP growth per capita in developing economies

Opportunity-driven entrepreneurship has a positive impact on economic growth in developing economies where manufacturing is relatively important.

Variables	Model 1 (TEA)	Model 2 (NEA)	Model 3 (OEA)
L.GDP per capita growth (annual %)	−0.05 (0.06)	−0.001 (0.04)	−0.02 (0.05)
L.Total early-stage entrepreneurial activity (TEA)	0.21 (0.30)		
L.Necessity-driven early-stage entrepreneurship activity (NEA)		−0.49 (0.27)	
L.Opportunity-driven early-stage entrepreneurship activity (OEA)			0.30 (0.27)
L.NEA * Services, value added		0.0101* (0.004)	
L.OEA * Manufacturing, value added			0.005* (0.002)
Number of observations	214	214	214
R^2	0.2040	0.2350	0.2410
adj. R^2	0.1730	0.2050	0.2120

* = statistically significant at 10%, ** = at 5%, *** = at 1%, ( ) = robust standard error, GDP = gross domestic product, L. = lag length of 1.
Source: Kim et al. 2022.

References:
Andrews, M. J. et al. (eds). 2022. *The Role of Innovation and Entrepreneurship in Economic Growth.* University of Chicago Press. https://www.nber.org/books-and-chapters/role-innovation-and-entrepreneurship-economic-growth.
Kim, J. et al. 2022. *Entrepreneurship and Economic Growth: A Cross-Sectional Analysis Perspective.* Asian Development Bank.

Box 2.1.4 Websites help entrepreneurs weather COVID-19

To analyze the impact of information and communication technology on entrepreneurial resilience during COVID-19, ownership of a website or social media page was used as a proxy for capability to do business online (Vo, Le, and Park 2022). Without access to online infrastructure such as a website, it is difficult for a firm to shift its activities and workforce online. The study experimented with three econometric models based on the nature of the dependent variable: (i) a linear regression model for continuous variables, (ii) a probit model for binary variables, and (iii) an ordered probit model for ordered-categorical variables.

Empirical analysis confirmed that digital technology is strongly associated with entrepreneurial resilience during COVID-19. Website ownership significantly mitigated the adverse impact of the crisis on almost all firm performance measures. The box table shows that firms with websites or social media pages were 2.9% less likely to suffer permanent closure than firms without such online presence, 3.7% less likely to suffer temporary closures, and thus 6.6% more likely to remain open. Among those that were currently open at the time of the survey or had temporarily closed, the probability of pandemic-induced closure was 7.1% lower for website owners.

Additional analysis found that website owners suffered less temporary closure than nonowners by 0.9 weeks and enjoyed higher sales by 7.7 percentage points. Website owners were 6.1% less likely to see their weekly work hours reduced, 4.8% more likely to see them unchanged, and 1.3% more likely to see them increase. As a result, their production capacity utilization was 2.5 percentage points higher. Finally, the share of workers that were furloughed was 3.2 percentage points lower in firms with websites. Differences in workers quitting or being laid off due to the pandemic were not significant.

Analysis estimated the impact of website ownership on several mechanism variables. Compared with nonowners, website owners were 5.3% more likely to start or increase their online business activities and 8.8% more likely to facilitate remote work arrangements. The share of online sales was 1.6 percentage points higher for website owners, and the share of remote workers 1.3 points higher.

Adopting an online business model significantly reduced the probability of temporary closure by 21.3% and of reduced sales by 10.4%, and increased the probability of unchanged sales by 5.8% and of increased sales by 4.5%. While remote work arrangements did not significantly affect the number of temporary workers or the share of workers who quit or were laid off, working remotely did reduce the share of furloughed workers by a significant 3.4 percentage points.

Effects of website ownership on business closure during COVID-19

Entrepreneurs with websites were less likely to close during the pandemic.

Dependent variable	Model	Marginal effect of website ownership
Probability of permanent closure	Ordered probit	−2.88*** (0.65)
Probability of temporary closure	Ordered probit	−3.69*** (0.79)
Probability of remaining open	Ordered probit	6.57*** (1.40)
If currently open or temporarily closed, probability of temporary closure	Probit	−7.08*** (2.20)

* = statistically significant at 10%, ** = at 5%, *** = at 1%, ( ) = robust standard error.

Notes: (i) There are two groups of control variables: (a) firm characteristics, including share of permanent, full-time production workers in unskilled jobs, growth rate of annual sales, firm size, firm age, firm ownership type, the type of main market for main product; and (b) country and industry-level factors, including daily economic support index, daily growth rate of new COVID-19 cases per million people, and sector type. (ii) The results for probit and ordered probit models are average marginal effects and are multiplied by 100. These are the changes in the probability of a firm closing its business when it owns a website.

Source: Vo, Le, and Park 2022.

Reference:
Vo, L. H., T. Le, and D. Park. 2022. *Digital Divide Decoded: Can E-Commerce and Remote Workforce Enhance Enterprise Resilience in the COVID-19 Era?* Asian Development Bank.

A conducive digital environment promotes entrepreneurship

The digital economy was already large and growing well before COVID-19, but the pandemic has accelerated its expansion. Indeed, digital activities such as online shopping, working from home, and Zoom meetings kept economies and societies afloat despite unprecedented mobility restrictions imposed during the global crisis. Digital entrepreneurship is part and parcel of the growing digitalization of the economy. ICT was instrumental to resilience in the entire economy and among individual entrepreneurs. Figure 2.2.1 illustrates just some of the many ways in which ICT and digitalization facilitates entrepreneurial activity. Entrepreneurs who had to close their stores during lockdowns relied on online orders to keep operating. They were also able to meet their suppliers and other business partners and discuss business on videoconferencing apps. Furthermore, ICT enables entrepreneurs to outsource many activities.

Even well before the onset of COVID-19, the combination of digital technology and entrepreneurship gave rise to a new breed of entrepreneur: the digital entrepreneur who creates a business on the internet and sells services or products online without investing in a physical presence. Not having to invest in costly offline facilities helps explain why ICT substantially reduces the cost of starting a business. In addition, the internet allows the entrepreneur to connect with large numbers of potential customers at low cost. By extension, the internet enables entrepreneurs to expand to foreign countries affordably (Lee, Vu, and Park 2022). Adopting ICT in back-office and other business functions can also reduce other costs of doing business. The potential of ICT to significantly reduce the cost of entrepreneurship suggests that digitalization can give a big boost to entrepreneurial activity.

Figure 2.2.1 How information and communication technology and digitalization help entrepreneurs

ICT promotes entrepreneurial activity in a wide range of avenues.

ICT = information and communication technology.
Source: Asian Development Bank.

The intensification of digitalization since COVID-19 is yet another reason to explore the relationship between digital technology and entrepreneurship, as in this section.

Digital framework conditions

In addition to the intrinsic quality of entrepreneurs' resources, the allocation of resources to entrepreneurship may be influenced by country entrepreneurial framework conditions (EFCs) (Levie and Autio 2008). EFCs are country factors that condition the allocation and appropriation of returns on economic activity such as entrepreneurial opportunity pursuit (de Soto 2000). Examples of EFCs include regulations that govern the creation of new firms (Djankov et al. 2002a; Klapper, Laeven, and Rajan 2006), employment regulations (Botero et al. 2004), and the quality of the country's political and economic institutions, such as the rule of law (Djankov et al. 2003), which may either enhance or undermine the appropriation of economic returns to fund investment in entrepreneurial opportunity pursuit (Autio and Fu 2015; Autio, Fu, and Levie 2019; Djankov et al. 2002b).

This section examines a specific category of EFC: a country's digital framework conditions for entrepreneurship (DFCs). In recent decades, countries' digital infrastructure (e.g., for telecommunications, the internet, and the digital resources accessible therein) have grown to become increasingly important regulators of economic activity (Tilson, Lyytinen, and Sørensen 2010; Yoo et al. 2012). As economic and societal activities become increasingly digitalized,[3] this development enables new ways of organizing economic activities for the discovery, creation, delivery, and capture of economic value. Because of the potency of Moore's Law, which states that computing power at a given cost doubles every 18 months, business firms are being supplied with a virtual explosion of opportunities to harness digital technology and infrastructure in novel ways to create and capture value.

This explosion of digital capability has fueled a wealth of opportunities to innovate business models, or to rethink how businesses organize their daily operations to create, deliver, and capture economic value. The bulk of these opportunities are being exploited by new, entrepreneurial businesses (Autio et al. 2018a; Thomas, Sharapov, and Autio 2018). Other visible manifestations of the transformative impact of digitalization on the economy include the emergence of the platform economy, platform ecosystems, and innovation ecosystems as important ways to organize collective action to jointly produce value (Van Alstyne, Parker, and Choudary 2016).

Given the importance of digitalization as an enabler of innovative entrepreneurial activity, it is surprising that there has been little research to explore associations between country DFCs and the quality of a country's entrepreneurial dynamic (Autio et al. 2018a). This report undertakes such exploration. Specifically, advances in digital technology and infrastructure are expected to help improve the quality of the country's entrepreneurship by making third-person entrepreneurial opportunities more easily accessible to those individuals and teams whose human and other resources are valuable and have a high opportunity cost in time and resources. This is because digitalization reduces the opportunity cost of resource allocation toward entrepreneurial opportunity pursuit for the following five reasons.

Freely accessible digital technology and infrastructure should lower the cost of opportunity pursuit by allowing entrepreneurs to forego expensive privately held shop space in favor of freely accessible resources on the digital commons (Dulong De Rosnay and Stalder 2020). Because digitalization enables the efficient creation and coordination of novel value-creating combinations, it opens up attractive entrepreneurial opportunities that established incumbent firms may have difficulty addressing due to their investment in legacy business models (Autio et al. 2018a). Digital infrastructure reduces the cost of internationalization and scaling up, thereby extending the upside potential of entrepreneurial opportunity pursuit (Mograbyan and Autio 2021).

---

[3]   Digitalization is the implementation of digital technologies in economic and societal processes to the extent that they become infrastructural.

By enabling extensive outsourcing of activities, digital technology and infrastructure help lower the cost of entrepreneurial entry (Bardhan, Whitaker, and Mithas 2006). Digital technologies also help enable low-cost experimentation with alternative value offerings, thereby reducing the downside potential of entrepreneurial opportunity pursuit (Andries, Debackere, and Van Looy 2013; Kerr, Nanda, and Rhodes-Kropf 2014).

The quality of the national environment for digital entrepreneurs can differ substantially from country to country. To objectively measure and assess the state of the national digital entrepreneurship ecosystem, this study presents a new set of indicators codified as the Global Index of Digital Entrepreneurial Systems (GIDES).

Global Index of Digital Entrepreneurship Systems: an index comparing digital entrepreneurship systems across economies

GIDES adapts the calculation method of the European Index of Digital Entrepreneurship Systems (Autio et al. 2018b, 2019, and 2020) and extends its scope to cover more world regions. The primary focus of the index is on the national digital entrepreneurship systems of 21 economies in developing Asia. In addition, GIDES includes 92 economies in other world regions for benchmarking purposes.

GIDES 2021 captures general, systemic, and digital financial conditions at the economy level. Its methodology builds on the Systems of Entrepreneurship Theory (Acs, Autio, and Szerb 2014) and provides a way to profile an economy's digital entrepreneurship systems. An important feature of GIDES methodology is an algorithm called the penalty of bottleneck, which helps pinpoint the elements of digital entrepreneurship systems that are most likely to hold back system performance. GIDES policy portfolio optimization analysis helps policy makers target policy actions to elements of the digital entrepreneurship system most likely to improve their performance.

GIDES builds on two central premises. First, it recognizes that entrepreneurship is highly heterogeneous, ranging from low-productivity self-employment (e.g., street vendors) to knowledge-intensive services (e.g., legal and financial services), and taking in manufacturing, digital start-ups, and the development and commercialization of research-intensive high-technology products and services. It follows that the productivity potential of entrepreneurs, defined as their ability to contribute to total factor productivity in their economies, can also vary tremendously. From an economic development perspective, the quality of an economy's entrepreneurial dynamic (and not so much the number of self-employed individuals) should therefore be a central consideration. Second, GIDES assumes that national EFCs can play an important role in influencing the quality of entrepreneurial resource allocation dynamic, or the ability of this dynamic to channel resources such as human, social, financial capital and other resources to highly productive uses.

Ultimately, the launch of any given entrepreneurial business is triggered by a decision of an individual or a team of individuals to allocate their human, social, and financial capital to the pursuit of a perceived entrepreneurial opportunity. When making this decision, the individual or team has to weigh trade-offs between alternative career pursuits. For individuals to decide to allocate their human, social, and financial capital to the pursuit of an entrepreneurial opportunity, they need to see this opportunity as promising to provide a higher return on this capital allocation than what they might expect to receive from alternative occupational pursuits. Simply put, if the entrepreneur stumbles upon a high-quality opportunity, he or she will make more money by pursuing this opportunity than by pursuing alternative career options, and the entrepreneur will continue working on the business. If the opportunity turns out less profitable than expected, the entrepreneur will soon drop the effort and turn to other pursuits.

The net result of a well-functioning entrepreneurial dynamic should therefore translate into a positive contribution to the economy's total factor productivity. GIDES assumes that EFCs are important regulators of the trade-offs individuals face when deciding between entrepreneurship and alternative occupational pursuits. It considers both non-digitalized and digitalized versions of its general and systemic EFCs, the digitalized versions of which are called DFCs.

To successfully enhance the ability of the national entrepreneurial dynamic to allocate resources to highly productive uses, it is important to have high-quality and informative EFC data. GIDES is designed to provide such data in the hope that policy makers and researchers will find it a useful resource to inform entrepreneurship policy design (Box 2.2.1).

The results of GIDES 2021 analysis, shown in Table 2.2.1, rank 113 economies and place them in five categories: leaders, followers, catchers-up, laggards, and tailenders. ADB developing member economies are shown in bold. Singapore featured the world's best digital entrepreneurship system in 2021, followed by the United States, Sweden, Denmark, and Switzerland. The leaders include 15 economies, most of them European. The 15 follower economies are also predominantly European but include the ROK. The 15 catchers-up are a mixed group that includes Malaysia and the PRC. The laggards comprise 32 economies, mostly upper-middle income and including 7 economies, and the tailenders 41 economies, primarily lower-middle and low income and including 10 economies. In summary, while a few economies currently perform well, most offer ample room to improve their digital entrepreneurship system.

Table 2.2.1 Global Index of Digital Entrepreneurship Systems 2021 scores

The quality of the national environment for digital entrepreneurs is generally better in more developed economies.

Economy	Stand-up system		Start-up system		Scale-up system		GIDES	
	Score	Rank	Score	Rank	Score	Rank	Score	Rank
Leaders	**71.4**		**72.4**		**69.9**		**71.2**	
Singapore	**79.8**	**2**	**83.6**	**1**	**80.4**	**1**	**81.3**	**1**
United States	79.9	1	79.3	4	79.7	2	79.7	2
Sweden	78.3	4	82.3	2	78.2	3	79.6	3
Denmark	79.4	3	79.6	3	77.5	4	78.8	4
Switzerland	77.1	5	77.0	6	76.7	5	76.9	5
Netherlands	76.3	6	75.0	7	75.3	6	75.6	6
Finland	72.1	7	77.2	5	70.6	7	73.3	7
Norway	71.7	8	70.8	9	67.1	10	69.9	8
Luxembourg	69.1	10	71.8	8	67.8	9	69.6	9
United Kingdom	70.0	9	68.8	10	68.1	8	69.0	10
New Zealand	67.9	11	65.1	12	63.1	12	65.3	11
Germany	63.1	13	67.3	11	63.6	11	64.7	12
Canada	63.4	12	63.6	13	61.2	13	62.7	13
Australia	63.0	14	61.7	15	59.3	15	61.3	14
Austria	59.2	15	62.6	14	59.8	14	60.5	15
Followers	**52.9**		**55.1**		**53.2**		**53.8**	
Israel	55.4	19	60.6	16	58.3	17	58.1	16
Ireland	57.7	16	59.5	18	56.1	19	57.8	17
Belgium	55.8	18	57.8	19	56.2	18	56.6	18
Estonia	56.2	17	59.6	17	52.4	22	56.1	19
Japan	53.2	21	54.8	21	59.0	16	55.7	20
United Arab Emirates	54.9	20	52.3	23	55.7	21	54.3	21
Republic of Korea	**51.6**	**22**	**54.9**	**20**	**55.9**	**20**	**54.1**	**22**
France	48.3	24	53.2	22	49.4	23	50.3	23
Malta	50.0	23	51.4	24	45.3	24	48.9	24
Spain	46.0	25	47.2	25	44.0	27	45.7	25

continued on next page

Table 2.2.1 *Continued*

Economy	Stand-up system		Start-up system		Scale-up system		GIDES	
	Score	Rank	Score	Rank	Score	Rank	Score	Rank
Catchers-up	**39.2**		**39.4**		**38.7**		**39.1**	
Czech Republic	44.0	27	46.1	26	44.4	25	44.8	26
Malaysia	**43.1**	**28**	**41.7**	**29**	**44.3**	**26**	**43.1**	**27**
Slovenia	41.1	29	44.1	27	39.8	30	41.7	28
Bahrain	44.2	26	39.1	34	41.1	29	41.5	29
Saudi Arabia	41.0	30	39.7	32	41.3	28	40.7	30
Lithuania	39.6	32	42.0	28	39.6	31	40.4	31
Italy	39.0	33	41.5	30	38.6	32	39.7	32
Cyprus	39.6	31	41.3	31	36.5	36	39.2	33
Latvia	37.9	35	39.7	33	37.7	33	38.4	34
Portugal	38.0	34	38.3	35	35.8	38	37.4	35
Qatar	37.9	36	34.1	41	37.6	34	36.5	36
Slovak Republic	36.5	37	37.4	37	35.6	40	36.5	37
Poland	35.4	39	37.6	36	35.8	39	36.2	38
People's Republic of China	**34.8**	**40**	**34.1**	**40**	**37.1**	**35**	**35.3**	**39**
Chile	36.5	38	33.4	42	36.0	37	35.3	40
Laggards	**26.1**		**25.7**		**26.3**		**26.0**	
Russian Federation	32.3	43	34.5	39	33.3	42	33.4	41
Hungary	31.9	44	35.5	38	32.6	43	33.3	42
Kuwait	34.3	41	30.4	44	34.1	41	33.0	43
Costa Rica	32.8	42	27.8	50	30.7	44	30.4	44
Croatia	29.1	47	32.6	43	28.4	48	30.0	45
Bulgaria	28.6	49	29.8	45	29.3	45	29.2	46
Mauritius	30.1	45	27.5	52	28.8	46	28.8	47
Uruguay	29.6	46	27.7	51	28.1	50	28.5	48
Romania	27.4	52	29.4	47	28.2	49	28.3	49
Georgia	**28.7**	**48**	**28.8**	**48**	**27.6**	**52**	**28.3**	**50**
Oman	28.0	50	27.4	53	28.5	47	28.0	51
Kazakhstan	**27.6**	**51**	**26.6**	**58**	**28.0**	**51**	**27.4**	**52**
Greece	26.6	54	29.8	46	25.6	60	27.3	53
Republic of Türkiye	26.8	53	26.6	56	27.4	53	26.9	54
Ukraine	25.9	57	27.3	54	25.8	58	26.3	55
Montenegro	25.7	58	26.9	55	26.2	57	26.3	56
Serbia	24.9	60	28.1	49	25.2	61	26.1	57
Armenia	**25.6**	**59**	**26.6**	**57**	**25.8**	**59**	**26.0**	**58**
Thailand	**25.9**	**55**	**24.4**	**59**	**27.3**	**54**	**25.9**	**59**
Azerbaijan	**25.9**	**56**	**23.5**	**60**	**27.0**	**55**	**25.5**	**60**
South Africa	24.3	62	22.4	62	26.8	56	24.5	61
North Macedonia	24.8	61	23.3	61	24.6	62	24.2	62
Viet Nam	**22.9**	**63**	**21.8**	**65**	**24.5**	**63**	**23.1**	**63**
Brazil	22.6	64	21.7	66	23.6	64	22.7	64
Jordan	22.2	67	22.1	63	22.9	65	22.4	65
Argentina	22.3	66	22.0	64	22.1	67	22.2	66
Colombia	22.2	68	20.9	68	22.8	66	21.9	67
Moldova	21.5	70	21.5	67	20.5	72	21.2	68
Mexico	20.2	72	20.4	69	21.8	70	20.8	69
Panama	21.5	69	19.5	73	20.2	74	20.4	70
Indonesia	**22.4**	**65**	**16.8**	**82**	**22.0**	**69**	**20.4**	**71**
Namibia	20.4	71	18.5	76	21.3	71	20.1	72

continued on next page

Table 2.2.1 *Continued*

Economy	Stand-up system		Start-up system		Scale-up system		GIDES	
	Score	Rank	Score	Rank	Score	Rank	Score	Rank
Tailenders	**14.3**		**13.6**		**14.8**		**14.2**	
Egypt	19.4	76	18.0	78	22.1	68	19.8	73
Morocco	19.7	73	19.0	75	20.3	73	19.7	74
India	**19.0**	**78**	**19.7**	**71**	**20.2**	**75**	**19.6**	**75**
Lebanon	19.4	75	19.9	70	19.3	78	19.5	76
Tunisia	19.2	77	19.6	72	19.5	77	19.4	77
Bosnia and Herzegovina	19.5	74	19.3	74	19.0	79	19.3	78
Philippines	**18.5**	**79**	**16.9**	**81**	**20.1**	**76**	**18.5**	**79**
Peru	17.9	83	17.7	79	17.8	83	17.8	80
Dominican Republic	17.9	81	16.2	85	18.7	81	17.6	81
Sri Lanka	**17.9**	**80**	**16.7**	**83**	**17.9**	**82**	**17.5**	**82**
Kenya	17.9	82	15.5	86	18.8	80	17.4	83
Mongolia	**17.1**	**85**	**18.2**	**77**	**16.4**	**86**	**17.2**	**84**
Botswana	17.0	87	16.4	84	17.5	84	17.0	85
Albania	17.1	84	17.0	80	16.0	88	16.7	86
Ecuador	17.0	86	14.8	90	16.7	85	16.2	87
Kyrgyz Republic	**15.1**	**90**	**15.0**	**87**	**15.5**	**90**	**15.2**	**88**
Rwanda	14.8	91	14.9	88	15.9	89	15.2	89
Paraguay	15.5	88	13.9	91	15.2	91	14.9	90
Ghana	15.2	89	13.4	92	16.0	87	14.9	91
Algeria	14.2	93	14.8	89	15.1	92	14.7	92
Honduras	14.5	92	13.2	93	13.9	94	13.8	93
Guatemala	13.8	94	10.9	100	13.9	93	12.9	94
Tajikistan	**13.2**	**95**	**12.4**	**95**	**12.8**	**99**	**12.8**	**95**
Bangladesh	**12.4**	**98**	**11.9**	**96**	**13.3**	**95**	**12.5**	**96**
Pakistan	**12.0**	**100**	**11.7**	**97**	**13.3**	**96**	**12.3**	**97**
Senegal	12.9	96	10.4	105	13.1	97	12.2	98
Bolivia	12.6	97	11.5	99	12.1	105	12.1	99
El Salvador	12.4	99	10.7	102	13.0	98	12.1	100
Cambodia	**11.9**	**101**	**11.7**	**98**	**12.3**	**103**	**12.0**	**101**
Nigeria	11.3	103	10.9	101	12.5	101	11.6	102
Zimbabwe	10.7	108	12.6	94	11.5	109	11.6	103
Nepal	**11.8**	**102**	**10.4**	**104**	**12.2**	**104**	**11.5**	**104**
Benin	10.7	107	10.6	103	12.3	102	11.2	105
Tanzania	10.7	106	9.4	107	12.6	100	10.9	106
Uganda	11.0	105	9.7	106	11.8	106	10.8	107
Zambia	11.3	104	9.2	108	11.6	107	10.7	108
Cameroon	10.3	109	8.8	109	11.4	110	10.2	109
Mali	10.0	110	7.9	112	11.5	108	9.8	110
Madagascar	8.3	112	7.8	113	9.5	111	8.5	111
Burkina Faso	8.8	111	8.7	110	7.6	113	8.4	112
Mozambique	7.8	113	8.1	111	8.1	112	8.0	113
Average	**32.0**		**31.9**		**32.0**		**31.9**	

GIDES = Global Index of Digital Entrepreneurship Systems.

Notes:

(1) Overall GIDES scores range from 0 to 100. Economies in developing Asia are in **bold** letters.

(2) Stand up, start up, and scale up refers to the three different stages of the entrepreneurial journey. Stand up is early stage, start up is the middle stage, and scale up is the later stage.

Source: Autio et al. 2022a.

Digital framework conditions and individual entrepreneurship dynamics: some empirical evidence

This section analyzes the link between national digital frameworks and individual entrepreneurial productivity. Figure 2.2.2 illustrates the conceptual relationship between the two, drawing on several datasets for analysis. As explained above, publicly available data from the GEM dataset is used for data on entrepreneurial attitudes, activities, and aspirations by individuals in selected ADB developing member economies (Reynolds et al. 2005). GEM data is used for all economies for which this data are available for any or all of the years 2010–2019, and for which sufficient data are also available to characterize an economy's DFCs. In total, 14 economies met these criteria.

For empirical analysis, the GEM dataset covers 190,515 unweighted interviews of working-age individuals, 16–65 years old, in the following 14 economies: Armenia, Bangladesh, Georgia, India, Indonesia, Kazakhstan, Malaysia, Pakistan, the Philippines, the PRC, Singapore, the ROK, Thailand, and Viet Nam. Pooling the data for each economy achieved a sample that was clustered across 14 economies. Table 2.2.2 shows the numbers of baby businesses less than 42 months old in the pooled sample.

For analysis, individual GEM data on entrepreneurial activities were combined with national data such as population and GDP data from the World Bank and digital condition data from GIDES, as explained above.

Table 2.2.2 Number of baby businesses in each sample economy

The sample consists of 13,532 baby businesses in 14 economies.

ADB economies	Baby businesses	% of total
People's Republic of China	2,884	21.3
Indonesia	2,773	20.5
Thailand	2,159	16.0
Viet Nam	1,146	8.5
India	1,130	8.4
Republic of Korea	970	7.2
Philippines	623	4.6
Malaysia	609	4.5
Kazakhstan	328	2.4
Singapore	307	2.3
Pakistan	195	1.4
Armenia	144	1.1
Bangladesh	133	1.0
Georgia	131	1.0
Total	**13,532**	**100.0**

ADB = Asian Development Bank.
Source: Autio and Fu 2022a.

Figure 2.2.2 National digital framework conditions and individual entrepreneurship

Digital environment affects the productivity of its entrepreneurs.

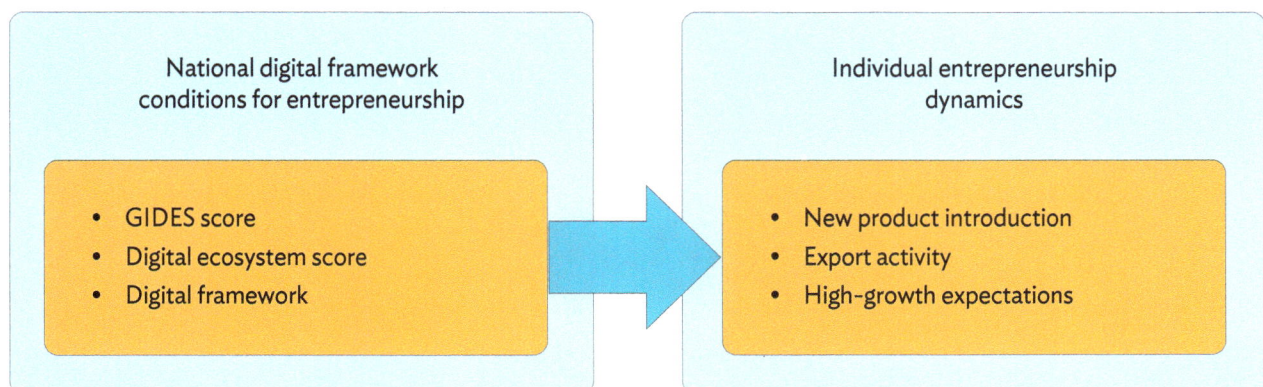

National digital framework conditions for entrepreneurship
- GIDES score
- Digital ecosystem score
- Digital framework

Individual entrepreneurship dynamics
- New product introduction
- Export activity
- High-growth expectations

GIDES = Global Index of Digital Entrepreneurship Systems.
Source: Asian Development Bank.

Variables

Below is a list of dependent and independent variables, including variables of interest and control variables, used in the empirical analysis. The dependent variables are three indicators of entrepreneur productivity potential. The independent variables of interest are three indicators of an economy's DFCs. Finally, several control variables are included because they also affect entrepreneurial productivity.

To assess the impact of an economy's DFCs on the quality of its entrepreneurial dynamic, three dependent variables were measured using the GEM data. Export orientation was measured by a dummy variable that took value 1 if the entrepreneurial business had any customers living outside of the country and 0 otherwise. High-growth expectation was measured by a dummy variable 1 if the entrepreneurial business expected to employ at least 20 employees within 5 years and 0 otherwise. New product introduction was measured by a dummy variable 1 if at least some customers of the entrepreneurial business considered the firm's product or service to be new to them and 0 otherwise.

Three alternative measures were adopted to capture DFCs. All three variables were measured using data from GIDES 2021, a composite indicator that captures the quality of an economy's DFCs. The GIDES score is the average of both general and systemic framework conditions. General framework conditions consist of four pillars: (i) culture and informal institutions; (ii) formal institutions, regulation, and taxation; (iii) market conditions; and (iv) physical infrastructure. Systemic framework conditions reflect resources with direct effects on the entrepreneurial dynamic. It consists of four pillars—(i) human capital, (ii) knowledge creation and dissemination, (iii) finance, and (iv) networking and support—which are assessed at three different stages of entrepreneurship development: stand-up, start-up, and scale-up. Analysis also experiments with two alternative, narrower measures of DFCs: digital entrepreneurship score and digital conditions (Figure 2.2.3).

In addition to DFCs, a number of other variables can affect the productivity potential of entrepreneurs, requiring control for different factors at both the individual and the national level.

Figure 2.2.3 Global Index of Digital Entrepreneurship Systems, digital ecosystem score, and digital conditions

All three indicators of national digital environment are based on GIDES.

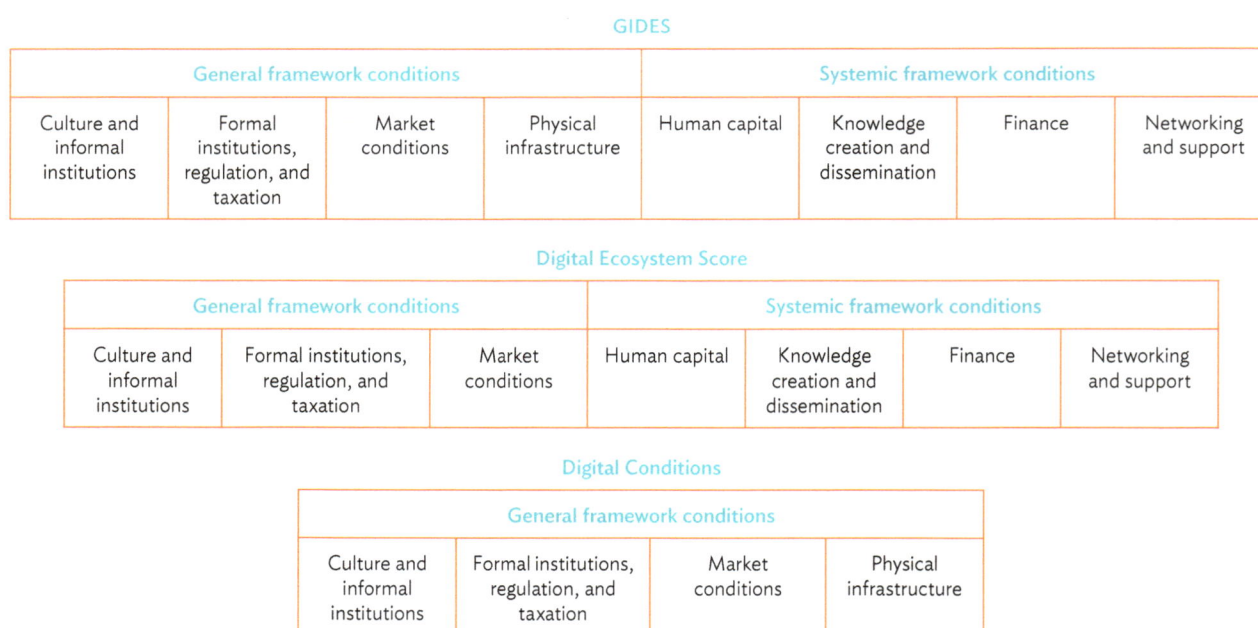

GIDES

General framework conditions				Systemic framework conditions			
Culture and informal institutions	Formal institutions, regulation, and taxation	Market conditions	Physical infrastructure	Human capital	Knowledge creation and dissemination	Finance	Networking and support

Digital Ecosystem Score

General framework conditions			Systemic framework conditions			
Culture and informal institutions	Formal institutions, regulation, and taxation	Market conditions	Human capital	Knowledge creation and dissemination	Finance	Networking and support

Digital Conditions

General framework conditions			
Culture and informal institutions	Formal institutions, regulation, and taxation	Market conditions	Physical infrastructure

GIDES = Global Index of Digital Entrepreneurship Systems.
Source: Autio and Fu 2022a.

At the individual level, analysis controlled the entrepreneur's demographical characteristics: age, gender, household income, education, fear of failure, and entrepreneurial self-efficacy. At the economy level, it controlled for the rate of business formation within an economy each year, the population size and population growth, GDP per capita, GDP growth and key institutional factors such as business registration costs, number of procedures to start a business, minimum paid-in capital for business registration, and financial development conditions. It also controlled for time fixed effects by including year dummies in the analysis. Box 2.2.2 describes the econometric methodology used for empirical analysis.

Empirical findings

Here are the key findings of empirical analysis. Box 2.2.3 shows the estimation of the effects of DFCs on product innovation in baby businesses. The results for the control variables are not reported here but are consistent with economic intuition. The full sets of results are available in Autio and Fu (2022a). For baby businesses, all three measures of DFCs—GIDES, digital ecosystem, and digital conditions—have positive and significant associations with both new product introduction and high-growth expectations. The results for exports were not significant.

Empirical analysis supports a positive association between the quality of an economy's DFCs and product innovation and employment growth by its entrepreneurial businesses. Economies with stronger DFCs had entrepreneurial businesses that innovated more and aspired to increase their number of employees more rapidly. These statistical associations were quite large, even with potential selection bias eliminated. A one standard-deviation increase in the quality of an economy's digital condition is associated with an increase in the probability of its entrepreneurial baby businesses reporting product innovation by 10.1%.

In summary, analysis has uncovered quite significant positive associations between the quality of an economy's DFCs and the productivity potential of its entrepreneurial businesses in a set of economies. This is an important finding as no previous studies are known to have explored this particular association and because of the transformative impact that digital technology and infrastructure have on how economic activity is organized. Besides innovation and employment generation, the quality of DFCs can affect other important dimensions of entrepreneurial performance.

The vital role of digital technology in keeping entrepreneurs afloat during COVID-19 suggests that resilience under large economic shocks is one such dimension. The next section takes a closer look at the link between entrepreneurial digitalization and entrepreneurial performance by sifting through a new database compiled from interviews of 685 entrepreneurs in six Southeast Asian economies.

Box 2.2.1 What is GIDES 2021?

The Global Index of Digital Entrepreneurship Systems (GIDES) 2021 covers 113 economies and relies on 103 different indicators to capture the quality of each economy's digital framework conditions for entrepreneurship (DFCs). The primary focus of the index is upon 21 developing members of the Asian Development Bank, but it also covers 92 economies in other regions to benchmark results.

GIDES is designed to capture the digitalization of society and economy. Digital technology is ubiquitous and thus infrastructural, allowing digital devices to connect to it almost anywhere. As digital components can be added to almost any device, ubiquitous digital connectivity means that digital technology is able to permeate almost any function or component of society and thereby digitalize it.

The index is composed of eight pillars, each of which captures conditions relevant to entrepreneurship. For each pillar, a corresponding digital weight is calculated to capture an economy's relevant digital conditions for that pillar—for each a non-digital version and a digitally weighted or digitalized version. The non-digitalized versions of the eight pillars are called EFCs, and the digitalized versions DFCs. GIDES is then calculated as the bottleneck-corrected average of the eight DFCs to reflect the state of an economy's digital entrepreneurship system.

GIDES scores range from 0 to 100. The economy's EFCs—as captured in the eight pillars of the index—are divided into general framework conditions and systemic framework conditions. For each of these, a non-digitalized and a digitalized version is calculated:

- General framework conditions describe the economy's general context of entrepreneurship in terms of (i) culture and informal institutions; (ii) formal institutions, regulation, and taxation; (iii) market conditions; and (iv) physical infrastructure. Each framework condition is then digitalized with a corresponding digital weight.

- Systemic framework conditions describe the economy's resource provision for entrepreneurship in terms of (i) human capital, (ii) knowledge creation and dissemination, (iii) finance, and (iv) networking and support. These resource conditions directly connect with different stages of the entrepreneurial process: entrepreneurial stand-up, start-up, and scale-up stages. Each framework condition is then digitalized with a corresponding digital weight.

An economy's digital entrepreneurship system is described by its general and systemic framework conditions, as captured in the eight GIDES pillars. General framework conditions regulate how the economy's systemic framework conditions can facilitate different stages of the entrepreneurial process, which together define the national entrepreneurial dynamic. An economy's overall GIDES score is the bottleneck-corrected average of the digitalized versions of its general and systemic framework conditions.

An earlier use of the GIDES methodology, the European Index of Digital Entrepreneurship Systems (EIDES) was developed as part of a 3-year research project in 2018–2020 for the European Commission's Joint Research Centre. EIDES was the first attempt to measure both physical and digital conditions for entrepreneurial stand-up, start-up, and scale-up businesses in the 27 member countries of the European Union and in the United Kingdom. As an evolution of EIDES, GIDES has the same index structure, but its indicator set has been adjusted according to data availability.

Reference:
Autio, E. et al. 2022a. *Asian Index of Digital Entrepreneurship Systems 2021.* Asian Development Bank.

Box 2.2.2 Empirical approach for testing the relationship between country digital framework conditions and entrepreneur productivity potential

Cross-level analyses of country effects on individual entrepreneurial behavior estimated the effect of country digital framework conditions (DFCs) on the quality of the country's entrepreneurial dynamic at the individual level. Due to the nested nature of the dataset, with individuals nested within each economy, analysis adopted multilevel modeling techniques to estimate proposed relationships.

Before the analysis, potential sample selection issues were investigated. Analysis focuses on high-quality entrepreneurs and their businesses with high productivity potential. High-potential entrepreneurs are defined as those who introduce product and service innovations, export, and/or aspire for high employment growth. These attributes can be observed in only those individuals who self-select as new or established entrepreneurs. There may be unobserved attributes that first prompt the individual to pursue entrepreneurial opportunities and subsequently drive high-quality entrepreneurial outcomes after entry. The presence of potential unobserved heterogeneity may obscure the effect of DFCs on the quality of individual entrepreneurial businesses. To control for potential bias from unobserved heterogeneity, analysis adopted a two-stage Heckman selection model (Heckman 1979).

In the first stage, analysis estimated the probability that a given individual self-selects as an early-stage entrepreneur or an established business owner in the dataset. This first step was estimated as a function of the individual's gender, age, household income, education, fear of failure, familiarity with other entrepreneurs, and entrepreneurial self-efficacy, as well as of population size, population growth,

gross domestic product (GDP) per capita, GDP growth, business registration costs, number of procedures to start a business, minimum paid-in capital for business registration, financial development conditions, and country DFCs. In the second stage of the Heckman model, analysis used the error residual (referred to as the "inverse Mills ratio") of the first-stage estimation to control for unobserved heterogeneity when estimating the impact of DFCs on the quality of entrepreneurial businesses, on the condition that an individual had identified as an early-stage entrepreneur in the sample. To facilitate model identification, familiarity with other entrepreneurs was excluded from the second-stage outcome model. This step reduces the possible effect of self-selection bias in the analysis.

Analysis specified and tested a set of two-level models with random intercepts, which allowed both individual factors and country factors to affect the likelihood of product innovation and export and the employment growth aspirations of individual entrepreneurs, accounting for variation in these outcomes across economies. Maximum likelihood algorithms were used to fit the models. In the regression models, continuous independent variables were all standardized to have a mean of 0 and a standard deviation of 1 to increase comparability in estimated coefficients.

References:
Autio, E. and K. Fu. 2022a. *Digital Framework Conditions and the Productivity Potential of a Country's Entrepreneurial Dynamic: A Study of Selected ADB Member Economies.* Asian Development Bank.
Heckman, J. J. 1979. Sample Selection Bias as a Specification Error. *Econometrica* 47(1).

Box 2.2.3 Digital environment and entrepreneur productivity: empirical findings

Box table 1 reports results from empirical analysis of the link between national digital framework conditions and the productivity of individual entrepreneurs.

Note that the coefficients in logistic regressions are in the form of log odds. That is, regression coefficients imply that a one-unit increase in an independent variable is associated with a change in the log of the odds ratio indicated by the coefficient: $\log(p/1-p)$ or $\text{logit}(p)$. (p) is the probability of "success" (dependent variable takes value 1), such as an entrepreneurial venture that exports, introduces product innovations, or exhibits high-growth aspirations. $(1-p)$ is the probability of failing to do so (dependent variable taking value 0). For example, the coefficient of GIDES 0.381 in box table 1 means that a one-standard deviation increase in GIDES is associated with 0.381 change in the log of the odds ratio.

The result can be understood better in terms of percentage change. Analysis calculated the average marginal effects of the key explanatory variables by taking the average value of the predicted effects evaluated at each observation and reported the significant marginal effects in box table 2. It shows the average marginal effects for digital framework variables that had a statistically significant association with product innovation in baby businesses. For instance, a one standard-deviation increase in digital conditions was associated with an increase in the probability of a baby business engaging in product innovation by 10.1 percentage points—i.e., the average marginal effect was 0.101. The results for high-growth expectations, which are not reported here, also indicate an association of sizable magnitude. That is, the association between DFCs and the productivity potential of the economy's entrepreneurial resource allocation dynamic is not only statistically significant but also large in absolute terms.

1 Effects of digital framework conditions on new product introduction by baby businesses

The national digital environment is positively and significantly associated with innovation by entrepreneurs.

Variable	Model 1	Model 2	Model 3
	New product introduction by baby businesses		
GIDES	0.381* (0.122)		
Digital ecosystem		0.387* (0.126)	
Digital condition			0.474** (0.144)
Pseudo R^2	0.1904	0.1904	0.1905
Observations	11,741	11,741	11,741

* $p < 0.01$, ** $p < 0.001$, ( ) = standard error, GIDES = Global Index of Digital Entrepreneurship Systems.
Source: Autio and Fu 2022a.

2 Average marginal effects of digital framework conditions on product innovation by baby businesses

The association between the national digital environment and entrepreneurial innovation is significant not only statistically but also economically.

New product introduction by baby businesses	Average marginal effects	Std. Err.
GIDES	0.082**	0.026
Digital ecosystem	0.083*	0.027
Digital condition	0.101**	0.03

* $p < 0.01$, ** $p < 0.001$, GIDES = Global Index of Digital Entrepreneurship Systems.
Source: Autio and Fu 2022a.

Reference:
Autio, E. and K. Fu. 2022a. *Digital Framework Conditions and the Productivity Potential of a Country's Entrepreneurial Dynamic: A Study of Selected ADB Member Economies.* Asian Development Bank.

Digital entrepreneurs outperform their nondigital peers

The previous section explored the relationship between digitalization and entrepreneurship. Empirical analysis revealed that country digital framework conditions had significant and positive impacts on individual entrepreneurs' productive potential, proxied by product innovation, exports, and job creation. This section takes a deeper dive into the nexus between digitalization and entrepreneurship by delving into exactly how adopting digital technology helps entrepreneurs in six member countries of the Association of Southeast Asian Nations (ASEAN-6): Indonesia, Malaysia, the Philippines, Singapore, Thailand, and Viet Nam. Analysis does not look at the impact of country conditions but rather the impact of the entrepreneurs' own digitalization actions. The six countries vary a lot in terms of income and development stage, but all have significant numbers of entrepreneurs who use digital technology in various ways. Empirical analysis was informed by an interview survey of 685 entrepreneurs across ASEAN-6 to build a database. Empirical evidence strongly supports the notion that entrepreneurs' adoption of digital technology improves their business performance and contribution to United Nations Sustainable Development Goals.

Introduction

Advances in digital technology in recent decades have precipitated a major structural transformation in the organization of society and the economy. Ubiquitous digital connectivity has enabled economic and societal processes to be increasingly reorganized to take advantage of digital technology. This process has also transformed the context within which entrepreneurs discover and pursue entrepreneurial opportunities and compete against established firms (Nambisan 2017). Arguably the most important characteristic of digital technology is how it enables business model innovation with radical rethinking of how entrepreneurial businesses organize to create and deliver customer value and capture this value as business profit (Bouwman, Nikou, and De Reuver 2019; Massa and Tucci 2013; Rachinger et al. 2019). This is a particularly important opportunity driver for entrepreneurs, as established businesses tend to focus on optimizing their existing business models, which may hamper their ability to take advantage of the latest digital opportunities (Autio et al. 2018a). Yet, surprisingly little is known about how entrepreneurial businesses' adoption of digital technology affects their performance. This report explores such performance effects using a six-country survey of digital entrepreneurial businesses.

Although the importance of digitalization and its impact on entrepreneurship through business model innovation are widely recognized (Autio et al. 2018a), surprisingly little is known about the effects on firm performance of the adoption of a business model using digital technology (Bouwman, Nikou, and De Reuver 2019). It is widely appreciated that digitalization has a transformative effect on entrepreneurial opportunity landscapes and on optimal modes of entrepreneurial opportunity pursuit. Due to digitalization, entrepreneurial activities have become less constrained by spatial, temporal, and sectoral boundaries (Nambisan 2017). The digitally induced lifting of conventional constraints limiting entrepreneurial agency means that entrepreneurial opportunity pursuit has become a viable occupational option for more people than ever before. At the same time, and largely for the same reasons, effective means of pursuing entrepreneurial opportunities have been transformed, with entrepreneurs increasingly adopting innovation techniques and practices originally pioneered elsewhere, such as design thinking, design sprints, growth hacking, and agile development (Contigiani and Levinthal 2019; Bocken and Snihur 2020). More broadly, digital technology has fundamentally changed the nature of entrepreneurship (Box 2.3.1).

Such ideas have prompted a novel, iterative approach to entrepreneurial opportunity discovery and validation, often referred to as "lean entrepreneurship" (Blank 2013; Ries 2011). The lean entrepreneurship approach builds on the insight that entrepreneurial opportunities seldom appear readily formed in the market, ready to be exploited by entrepreneurs. Instead, opportunities need to be gradually created and shaped through entrepreneurial experiments by which the entrepreneur tests ideas and hunches, discarding those that do not work and retaining those that receive supportive feedback (Camuffo et al. 2019; Dimov 2016; Romme and Reymen 2018). In the boundaryless and interconnected digital world, steady-state, independently existing and objectively discoverable market opportunities have become a rarity, and entrepreneurs are better off harnessing digital technology for an iterative process of opportunity development.

This narrative rests on two important assumptions: first, that the adoption of digital technology enables entrepreneurs to experiment more effectively, and second, that validated ideas are operationalized through their incorporation in the firm's business model, or its operational architecture for the discovery, creation, delivery, and capture of customer value. These assumptions imply that both the adoption of digital technology in itself and iterative experimentation using them on the firm's business model should constitute important drivers of entrepreneurial firm performance in the digital age. If entrepreneurs shape and pursue opportunities more effectively through iterative experimentation, and if that experimentation is enhanced by the adoption of digital technology, both should support more effective opportunity development and therefore enhance the performance of entrepreneurial businesses.

However, these assumptions have seldom been subjected to direct empirical test, and, with rare exceptions, the few tests that have been conducted have mostly taken place in high-income Western economies (Bouwman, Nikou, and De Reuver 2019; Camuffo et al. 2019; Ferreira, Fernandes, and Ferreira 2019; Liu, Liu, and Gu 2021).

Evidence regarding the impact of digitalization on entrepreneurial performance remains scarce in general and in particular for emerging economies.

This is an important gap because emerging economies arguably stand to benefit the most from digitalization, as it offers the opportunity of catching up by leapfrogging over steps conventionally required to advance economic development (Michelle 2009; Xiong et al. 2021).

The current study addresses this gap through an interview survey of digital entrepreneurs in ASEAN-6: Indonesia, Malaysia, the Philippines, Singapore, Thailand, and Viet Nam. In a project sponsored and coordinated by the Asian Development Bank and conducted in collaboration with research teams in six leading academic institutions in the six countries, the study identified and interviewed a population of 685 digital entrepreneurs, focusing in particular on their adoption of digital technology in their business models and their business model experimentation, and exploring the implications of these processes on their business performance and their performance in terms of conforming to and advancing the United Nations' Sustainable Development Goals.

Regarding sustainability performance, research sought to capture any effect of firm digitalization and business model experimentation on three dimensions of business sustainability: environmental sustainability, social sustainability, and stakeholder welfare. Among survey statements designed to measure different aspects of business sustainability performance, nine measured environmental sustainability, six social sustainability, and six stakeholder welfare.

Novel operationalizations of business digitalization and business model experimentation were designed to test mediating relationships between digitalization, business model experimentation, and business and sustainability performance. Empirical analysis revealed that entrepreneurial businesses' adoption of digital technology is a potent enabler of business model experimentation, which is in turn a potent driver of business and sustainability performance. Analysis also showed that the adoption of digital technology exercises a strong direct effect on business and sustainability performance in addition to its mediating effect through business model experimentation, revealing that digital technology has broad performance implications for entrepreneurial businesses.

Digitalization, business model experimentation, and entrepreneurial performance: a conceptual model and empirical analysis

This study presents a new conceptual model of how digitalization, business model experimentation, and entrepreneurial performance are related, as illustrated in Figure 2.3.1. Digitalization affects entrepreneurial performance both directly and indirectly via business model experimentation. The model builds on the premise that digitalization is an infrastructural process that shapes the context in which all economic actors conduct their business. This means that the impact of digitalization is not limited only to a specific category of digital businesses. Instead, the inferences encapsulated in the model should apply to any type of business firm, regardless of sector. Four hypotheses are elaborated below.

First, entrepreneurial businesses' adoption of digital technology is expected to drive business model experimentation in those businesses. Digital technology is Turing technology in that it can be flexibly reprogrammed to perform different functions at low cost. Low-cost reprogrammability, which can take the simple form of modifying a firm's web page, makes it cheaper to experiment with alternative value offerings.

Furthermore, digitalization reduces asset specificity and enables the outsourcing of business activities that previously had to be built through in-house capability development (Afuah 2003; Mani, Barua, and Whinston 2010; Whitaker, Mithas, and Krishnan 2010). By outsourcing, firms contract out activities previously performed in house. Although the outsourcing of manufacturing has been a well-established and researched trend since the early 1990s, business process outsourcing started to gather momentum only in this millennium, as functional service providers have become more sophisticated and multinational enterprises have become more adept at standardizing their business processes (Davenport 2005; Jean, Sinkovics, and Cavusgil 2010; Karmarkar 2004; Lahiri and Kedia 2011; Lewin and Volberda 2011).

Increasingly accessible to new and small ventures, these trends afford internationalizing ventures with greater flexibility when organizing their international operations. A particularly notable trend is the standardization of offshoring services, as software-as-a-service applications are increasingly available for internationalizing new ventures: notably, Basecamp or Trello for distributed project management, Infusionsoft for customer e-mail management, or Freshbooks for accounting services (Di Gregorio, Musteen, and Thomas 2008). These developments enable new entrepreneurial businesses considerable latitude when configuring their business operations for value creation, delivery, and capture, including experimenting with alternative business models.

Figure 2.3.1 Digitalization, business model experimentation, and entrepreneurial performance

Business model digitalization affects performance both directly and indirectly via business model experimentation.

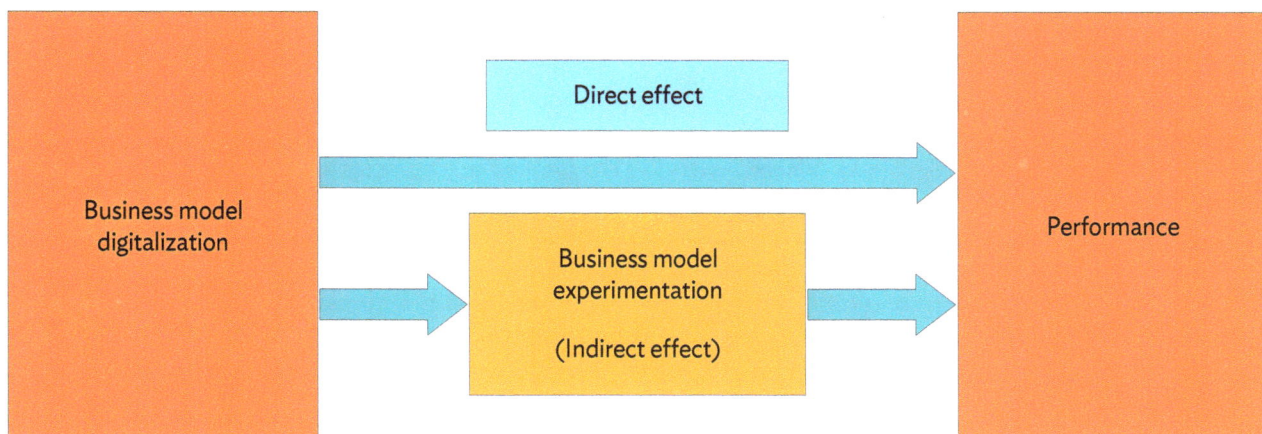

Source: Asian Development Bank.

Analysis therefore predicts that greater adoption of digital technology by entrepreneurial businesses accompanies greater propensity for business model experimentation.

Second, business model experimentation is expected to be associated with enhanced business performance. With digitalization, boundaries between products and services become increasingly blurred, enabling other operators to connect with them and potentially combine them with their own offerings—an activity that is quite common in digital platform ecosystems. A general trend toward coevolutionary creation of entrepreneurial opportunities increasingly replaces conventional modes of entrepreneurial opportunity pursuit that were based on the discovery of independent entrepreneurial opportunities within static market conditions. With platformization, economic activities reorganize around platform ecosystems characterized by nonhierarchical relationships, as opposed to the pre-defined, one-to-one supplier contracts that characterize conventional supply chains.

As organic structures, platform ecosystems emphasize mutual adjustment. Digital technology allows entrepreneurial businesses to experiment flexibly with different kinds of organizational arrangements for value creation, delivery, and capture. The low cost of experimentation enables entrepreneurial businesses to discover quickly which business models work and to discard those that do not. As business models define a firm's activity architecture for value creation, delivery, and capture, analysis predicts that greater intensity of business model experimentation to goes hand-in-hand with better business performance.

While business performance is expected to be the overriding goal of entrepreneurial businesses, a noteworthy trend is toward a stakeholder orientation, by which entrepreneurial and established businesses alike have begun to emphasize their responsibilities to society and the natural environment alongside their responsibilities to their immediate shareholders. The increasing adoption of such stakeholder thinking, as opposed to the more narrow shareholder thinking, means that, when new businesses optimize their activity systems, they may have more goals in mind than simply increasing economic profitability.

Alongside business performance, entrepreneurial businesses are increasingly aware of their responsibilities to the natural environment, their social communities, and their various stakeholders. Thus, when entrepreneurial businesses experiment to enhance their business performance, they will likely seek as well to optimize their impact on their natural and social environments and their stakeholders at large. Analysis therefore predicts that greater intensity of business model experimentation is associated with better sustainability performance.

Finally, analysis predicts that at least some of the impact of digital technology adoption on business and sustainability performance is mediated through the facilitating impact of digital technology on business model experimentation.

Box 2.3.2 elaborates on how survey interviews of entrepreneurs were conducted to build a database for empirical analysis.

Empirical findings

The following are results after empirically testing the study's conceptual hypotheses (H1–H4) about the relationship between the adoption of digital technology, business model innovation, and financial and sustainability performance in ASEAN-6 entrepreneurs: Digital technology adoption enables business model experimentation (H1). Business model experimentation drives business performance (H2). Business model experimentation drives sustainability performance (H3). Business model experimentation mediates the impact of digital technology adoption on business and sustainability performance (H4).

Table 2.3.1 confirms the basic effect of digital technology on business model experimentation: Greater reliance on mobile and web applications was strongly associated with the likelihood of the business introducing nontrivial changes in its business model over the past 12 months. Similarly, the reliance of the business on industrial internet applications was strongly associated with the introduction of nontrivial changes in the firm's business model over the past 12 months. Both of these associations were consistent with hypothesis H1.

Table 2.3.1 Influence of reliance on digital technology applications on business model experimentation

Reliance on digital technology applications is strongly associated with business model experimentation.

Business model experimentation	Coefficient	Standard error
Reliance on mobile and web applications	0.1148*	0.040
Reliance on industrial internet applications	0.1715**	0.040

* = p<0.01, ** = p<0.001.

Notes: Based on 681 observations and 1-tailed test of statistical significance. The controls are firm age, number of full-time employees, and country fixed effects (dummy variables).

Source: Autio et al. 2022b.

The effects of digitalization of different aspects of the firm's business model are shown in Table 2.3.2. It shows separately the direct effects of each digitalization variable: internal activities, marketing and sales, products and services, and partnerships. As can be seen in the table, all digitalization variables exhibited strong and statistically significant effects on business model experimentation, and greater digitalization in firm activities was associated with greater likelihood of nontrivial business model changes during the past 12 months. These findings further reinforce support for H1.

Table 2.3.2 Effect of digital technology application in a firm's business model and business model experimentation

Digitalization of a wide range of business activities is strongly associated with business model experimentation.

Business model experimentation				
Digitalization variables	Model 1	Model 2	Model 3	Model 4
Digitalization of internal activities	0.1395*			
Digitalization of marketing and sales		0.1707*		
Digitalization of products and services			0.1930*	
Digitalization of partnerships				0.2823*

* = p<0.001.

Notes: Based on 681 observations and 1-tailed test of statistical significance. The controls are firm age, number of full-time employees, and country fixed effects (dummy variables).

Source: Autio et al. 2022b.

Analysis next considered the effects of digitalization variables on performance. Table 2.3.3 shows how business reliance on mobile and web applications, and on industrial internet applications, affected sustainability performance and business performance. The direct effect column shows only direct effects of predictor variables on performance.

Table 2.3.3 Effects of reliance on digital technology on sustainability and business performance

Reliance on digital technology is positively associated with sustainability and business performance, and some of this effect is mediated via business model experimentation.

	Direct effect	Indirect effect	Total effect	% mediated
Social sustainability				
Business model experimentation	0.2163***		0.2163***	
Reliance on mobile and web applications	0.0489	0.0248**	0.0737***	33.7
Reliance on industrial internet applications	0.0946**	0.0371***	0.1317***	28.2
Business performance compared to peers				
Business model experimentation	0.1295***		0.1295***	
Reliance on mobile and web applications	0.1020**	0.0149*	0.1168***	12.7
Reliance on industrial internet applications	0.0843*	0.0222**	0.1066***	20.8

* = p<0.05, ** = p<0.01, *** = p<0.001.

Notes: Based on 2-tailed tests of statistical significance. Controls are firm age, number of full-time employees, and country fixed effects (dummy variables).

Source: Autio et al. 2022b.

The indirect effect column shows only how reliance on digital applications affected performance as mediated through its effect on business model experimentation. The total effect column shows combined direct and mediated effects. The % mediated column shows the proportion of independent variable effects that were mediated through their effect on business model experimentation. For simplicity, it shows only the effects of one sustainability performance indicator, namely social sustainability, and one business performance indicator, namely average performance against peers, which is based on sales growth, profitability, number of customers, development of new products and services, and operational efficiency. Results for the other sustainability performance indicators and business performance indicators and for control variables are available in Autio et al. (2022b).

Although not a causal analysis, the results presented in Table 2.3.3 are very consistent with key hypotheses: (i) Business model experimentation is an important driver of both business and sustainability performance, and (ii) firm reliance on digital technology applications is an important enabler of business model experimentation.

The table further shows that, in addition to this mediating effect, digital technology applications are even more strongly associated with performance impact through their direct association with the performance outcome variables.

Analysis considered the digitalization of various activities in firm business models and its potential relationship to performance, both directly and through the mediation of business model experimentation. Due to the complexity of the models relative to sample size, and to relatively strong intercorrelations among digitalization variables, Table 2.3.4 shows only individual path effects for each of the digitalization variables, separately and not as a group.

Analysis of the association between business model digitalization and business and sustainability performance consistently supports the general theoretical framework set out to be tested in this study: Greater degrees of business model digitalization accompany greater business and sustainability performance, either directly or through their facilitation of business model experimentation.

Table 2.3.4 Effects of activity digitalization on sustainability and business performance

Digitalization of a wide range of business activities is positively associated with sustainability and business performance, and some of this effect is mediated via business model experimentation.

	Direct effect	Indirect effect	Total effect	% mediated
Social sustainability				
Business model experimentation	0.1975**		0.1975**	
Digitalization of internal activities	0.2690**	0.0276**	0.2965**	9.3
Digitalization of marketing and sales	0.2965**	0.0319**	0.3284**	9.7
Digitalization of product and service	0.1861**	0.0383**	0.2245**	17.1
Digitalization of partnerships	0.2345**	0.0471**	0.2816**	16.7
Business performance compared to peers				
Business model experimentation	0.1098**		0.1098**	
Digitalization of internal activities	0.2904**	0.0153*	0.3057**	5.0
Digitalization of marketing and sales	0.2487**	0.0187*	0.2674**	7.0
Digitalization of product and service	0.1111*	0.0249*	0.1360**	18.3
Digitalization of partnerships	0.1373**	0.0311*	0.1684**	18.5

* = $p < 0.01$, ** = $p < 0.001$.

Notes: Based on 2-tailed tests of statistical significance. Controls are firm age, number of full-time employees, and country fixed effects (dummy variables).

Source: Autio et al. 2022b.

Total effects are both statistically highly significant and consequential in practice. The overarching message is that investment in digitalization benefits entrepreneurial businesses, and it also benefits society at large by enhancing entrepreneurial businesses' benefits to environmental and social sustainability and stakeholder welfare. As a general conclusion, therefore, empirical data strongly and consistently support the theoretical hypotheses.

Digital entrepreneurship in ASEAN-6: a comparative analysis

Survey interviews of digital entrepreneurs enabled comparative analysis of digital entrepreneurship and its impact on entrepreneurial performance in ASEAN-6: Indonesia, Malaysia, the Philippines, Singapore, Thailand, and Viet Nam. Of particular interest are two key dimensions of entrepreneurial digitalization: (i) the application of digital technology in business and business model experimentation, and (ii) three indicators of entrepreneurial performance: (a) the number of new products and services in the past 12 months, (b) financial and operational performance, and (c) sustainability.

Singapore's digital entrepreneurs demonstrated the most business model experimentation in ASEAN-6 in the past 12 months (Figure 2.3.2). Singapore's digital entrepreneurs responded to a range of challenges posed by COVID-19 much more quickly than their peers in the other ASEAN-6 countries. The application of digital technology includes implementing digital technology through internal activities, marketing, sales and customer interactions, products and services, and partnerships. Digital entrepreneurs in Indonesia and Malaysia exhibit a high degree of digitalization in internal activities and in products and services. Digital entrepreneurs in the Philippines lead in marketing, sales, and customer interactions.

Thai entrepreneurs outperformed their ASEAN peers in sustainability (Figure 2.3.3). Thai businesses often go out of their way, beyond minimum legal requirements, to ensure environmental sustainability, recruiting capable talent to work on sustainability issues.

Figure 2.3.2 Business model changes

Singaporean entrepreneurs led the way in business model experimentation.

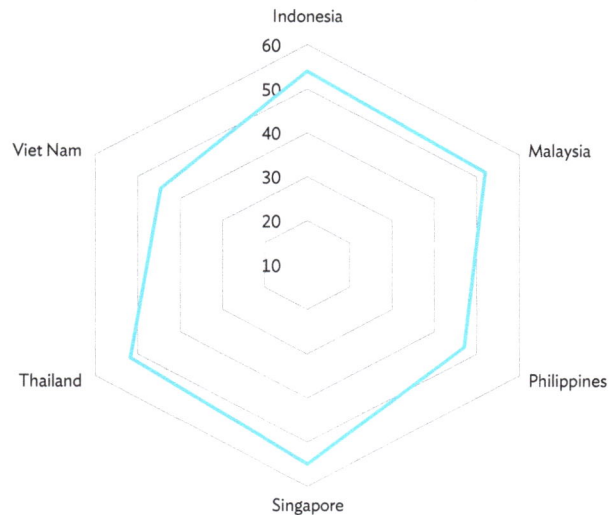

Notes: Index scores range from 0 to 100. Business model changes are shifts in targeted customers, in sales and marketing operations, and how products and services are produced and delivered.
Source: Chiyachantana and Prasarnphanich 2022.

Figure 2.3.3 Sustainability

Thai entrepreneurs performed the best on sustainability.

- Internal environment sustainability
- External environment sustainability
- Social sustainability
- Stakeholders welfare

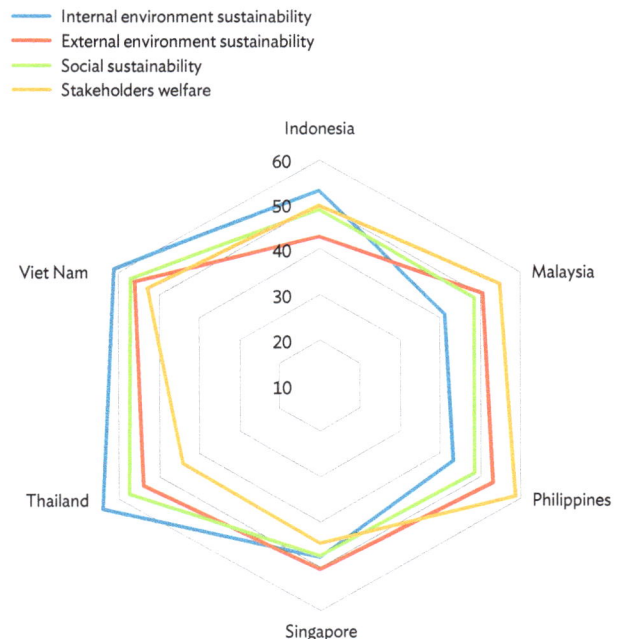

Notes: Index score range from 0–100. Sustainability means including environmental, social, and governance goals as integral parts of the business model to attract investors who value positive social impacts.
Source: Chiyachantana and Prasarnphanich 2022.

Digital entrepreneurs in Indonesia, Malaysia, and Viet Nam put significant effort into innovating products and services. Finally, Indonesian digital entrepreneurs performed the best in all three aspects of business performance: financial and operational aspects and performance compared to peers.

Several significant findings emerge from comparative analysis of digital entrepreneurship in ASEAN-6. First, substantial variation exists in how digital entrepreneurs in ASEAN-6 use digital technology in business. Second, digital entrepreneurs' ability to adapt to the adverse impacts of the pandemic in a relatively short time is strong evidence of their dynamism and resilience. Entrepreneurial mindsets and capabilities, empowered by digitalized business models, are key to turning crises into opportunities, appropriately adapting their products and services, and continuing to create economic value. Third, sustainability can be successfully integrated into the business model and attract investors who value social goals.

ASEAN-6 entrepreneurs leverage digital technology in a wide range of industries

Digital entrepreneurs have become active in a wide range of diverse industries across ASEAN-6, reflecting the capability of the region's entrepreneurs to leverage digital technology in versatile ways. The rapid growth of food delivery services in Indonesia reflects the confluence of three major trends—fast-growing consumption of prepared food, improved internet access, and large numbers of motorcycles as courier vehicles (Muftiadi 2022a, 2022b). The segment's growth has been dominated by three big digital platform companies: Gofood, Grabfood, and Shopee. Notwithstanding the large shadows cast by these three, new food delivery start-ups can serve niche markets with their own platforms. Examples of such start-ups include e-Fisheries (fish products) and Saudagar Buah Indonesia (fruits), which operate only in a few major cities. The start-ups have the option of simultaneously using the existing platforms of the three giants. The key takeaway from the Indonesian food industry is that even markets dominated by large digital platforms offer opportunities to start-ups.

Over the past 25 years, building Malaysia's entrepreneurial ecosystem has been a combined project of government and private sector actors. In the government, federal bodies like the Ministry of Entrepreneur Development and Cooperatives have supported the creation of new start-ups from ideation to funding and beyond (Smit et al. 2022). At the same time, private actors like angel investors organized through the Malaysia Business Angel Network and ScaleUp Malaysia, supplemented by networks of corporate innovation and coworking hubs, have operated intensive incubation and accelerator programs, such as 1337 Ventures, to provide to entrepreneurs peer-to-peer support. Malaysia has recently witnessed the rise of a dynamic drone industry, which depends on high-tech digital technology. Most notably, Aerodyne, founded in 2014, is present in 35 economies and has 500 employees. While the government's role has been limited so far, it is expected to play a bigger role in the future, primarily by creating a more conducive milieu for drone environments.

Creative industries are prominent in the economy in the Philippines (Habaradas 2022b). They combine the creation, production, and commercialization of intangible and cultural content, including visual arts and crafts and audio-visual and interactive media. Interestingly, the degree of digitalization in Philippine creative industries is fairly high, as many creative entrepreneurs have their own websites—and some have their own internet applications. A big motivation for entrepreneurs' adoption of digital technology is to cope with the increasing complexity of business operations and better keep track of finances, customer relationships, inventory, and logistics. There is a great deal of variation in the digital practices of entrepreneurs, with digitalization integral to the business models of some entrepreneurs but not others.

Singapore has one of the world's best digital entrepreneurial ecosystems due to the government's proactive role in creating a favorable overall business environment for entrepreneurs (Chiyachantana 2022). In particular, the government invests heavily in infrastructure, including digital technology infrastructure such as broadband. In addition, it provides financial and other support to businesses of all sizes to strengthening their human resources. Furthermore, Singapore is one of the world's most globalized economies and actively embraces new technology as a key engine of economic and social progress. As Singapore is a global financial center with an advanced financial sector, entrepreneurs at all stages of business development are able to access finance from a wide range of sources, from bank loans and private funds to angel investors and venture capitalists. Fintech, a digital component of the country's financial sector, has gained further momentum since the COVID-19 outbreak. The key lesson from the Singaporean experience is that the government can support the best digital entrepreneurs by providing them with conducive infrastructure, an ample pool of skilled workers, and an efficient legal and regulatory environment.

As in Malaysia, Thailand's entrepreneurial ecosystem is the result of close interplay between the government and the private sector (Prasarnphanich 2022a). Thailand has a government agency dedicated to promoting digital entrepreneurship, the Digital Economy Promotion Agency, which is one of three government agencies to support start-ups, but investment in start-ups is nevertheless led by the private sector. A unique feature of the Thai ecosystem is the large role played by conglomerates such as Siam Cement Group in start-up investment. Other private funding sources include venture capitalists, private incubators, and accelerators. Universities, for their part, have set up university business incubators to provide workspaces, equipment, mentoring services, and administrative support to assist start-ups launched by students, professors, university personnel, and alumni. Another interesting feature is the key role of networks and peer support groups through which entrepreneurs in a specific industry share knowledge about their experiences with different business models. A good example is the Thai Animation and Computer Graphics Association. Digital health care has emerged as a promising opportunity for entrepreneurs in recent years. During COVID-19, vital contributions from entrepreneurs to Thailand's official campaign to provide online health care highlight the potential contribution of entrepreneurship to social goals (Box 2.3.3).

The entrepreneurial ecosystem of Viet Nam is less developed those of the five other ASEAN-6 countries (Pham and Tan 2022b). However, cultural support for entrepreneurial activity is one notable strength, featuring broad societal recognition of the vital role of entrepreneurship in economic growth and a generally positive public image for entrepreneurs. In addition, business opportunities abound in Viet Nam's fast-growing economy, and the government is investing heavily in ICT infrastructure. By far the biggest weakness of Viet Nam's digital entrepreneurial ecosystem is lack of human capital. In particular, digital entrepreneurs need to strengthen their knowledge and skills to become more innovative. Educational reform that encourages independent and critical thinking holds the key to producing a larger pool of innovative entrepreneurs. Training in soft skills and greater focus on business ethics are other reform needs. Finally, online education is growing but still in its early stages, with digitalization largely limited to internal activities.

Digitalization has a powerful effect on the nature of entrepreneurship. Analysis here of a new database informed by interviews of 685 entrepreneurs in ASEAN-6 points to a strong positive association between a firm's digitalization and its business and sustainability performance. Analysis in the previous section suggested a positive link between a conducive national environment for digital entrepreneurship and entrepreneur innovation. While such evidence confirms that digitalization can be a potent engine of entrepreneurship, unlocking entrepreneurial dynamism also requires sound institutions. This is because good institutions can mitigate the risk and uncertainty intrinsic and central to entrepreneurialism.

The next section empirically explores the connection between country institutional environments and individual dynamic entrepreneurship.

Box 2.3.1 The impact of digital technology on the nature of entrepreneurship

Digitalization has two fundamental consequences on entrepreneurial activity. First, it expands the scope of entrepreneurial opportunities by blurring various boundaries that divide products, services, and industries and by redefining entrepreneurial opportunities themselves (Nambisan 2017). With smartphones, for example, mobile app stores host innovative applications developed by thousands of independent developers. Another example is running shoes equipped with motion sensors that can be connected to a smartwatch, enabling the automatic sharing of run routes in online running communities, and perhaps even the creation of new life insurance products that charge lower premiums for individuals who are more physically active. Entrepreneurial opportunities themselves are growing less bounded through digitalization. Digitalization blurs clean separation between products and markets by reorganizing economic activities around platform ecosystems, which makes opportunity creation more important vis-à-vis opportunity discovery (Alvarez and Barney 2007). With digitalization, opportunity creation becomes a collaborative process, as hierarchically independent actors test ideas and learn from one another.

Second, the facilitating effect of digitalization on entrepreneurial experimentation has contributed to the emergence of the lean entrepreneurship heuristic. Because of reprogrammability, digital technology can be cheaply and flexibly modified to test alternative product and service versions and different collaborative arrangements.

Entrepreneurs can test different ideas very quickly and almost without cost by modifying their descriptions of their value offerings on their web pages and monitoring the reactions of potential customers almost in real time. Social media platforms can be harnessed for quick feedback, and their data analytics can be flexibly harnessed to identify market niches that would have been impossible to identify and service before the digital era. The lean entrepreneurship heuristic is therefore a product of an increasingly collaborative mode of opportunity creation facilitated by the migration of economic activity toward platform ecosystems, on the one hand, and, on the other, by greater ease, speed, and flexibility of entrepreneurial experimentation with different value offerings and organizational arrangements.

References:
Alvarez, S. A. and J. Barney. 2007. Discovery and Creation: Alternative Theories of Entrepreneurial Action. *Strategic Entrepreneurship Journal* 1(1–2).
Nambisan, S. 2017. Digital Entrepreneurship: Toward a Digital Technology Perspective of Entrepreneurship. *Entrepreneurship Theory and Practice* 41(6).

Box 2.3.2 Sample, data collection, and questionnaire design

A theoretical model was tested with a questionnaire interview survey of 685 digital entrepreneurial businesses in six Southeast Asian countries: Indonesia, Malaysia, the Philippines, Singapore, Thailand, and Viet Nam. A "digital entrepreneurial business" was defined as an independent firm owner-managed by an entrepreneur or team of entrepreneurs and applying digital technology in its business model. The digital technology criterion was defined quite loosely to avoid confining analysis to the narrow digital sector alone. Analysis intended to capture instead the phenomenon of digitalization more broadly and its effect on new start-up firms in any sector or industry—an approach consistent with the hypothesis that digitalization is an Infrastructural process that affects all sectors of society and the economy. The intention, too, was to sample modern start-ups that were more likely to have been exposed to the digital start-up culture and compete with innovative business models and related offerings.

In identifying start-ups that belonged to the population of interest, several techniques were used. When possible, start-ups were catalogued by tracking tenants of new venture accelerators and coworking spaces. Use was made, where available, of membership lists of national start-up and software business associations and the like. Policy agencies working with start-up companies were consulted for references, as were the business press and start-up events. These leads were followed up by a snowballing technique, under which identified start-ups were asked to name similar companies.

In each country, a team of researchers led by a reputed academic in a highly regarded university was in charge of identifying the target population and collecting data. All data were collected by means of a primarily closed-format interview questionnaire that included some open-ended questions. Trained interviewers, typically candidates for business masters degrees, conducted interviews. The interviewers had the purpose of the research explained to them and were walked through the entire questionnaire to ensure that they understood exactly what kind of data were sought.

The COVID-19 situation required that interviews be carried out over Zoom or by telephone. Interview records were then compiled and harmonized centrally before analysis.

The study's two lead authors composed the interview questionnaire in English and finalized it in video meetings with all teams attending. The questionnaires were translated into local languages and then translated back into English to check translation accuracy. The English-language questionnaire is available from Autio et al. (2022b). The questionnaire was composed in five sections: (i) background of the business and entrepreneur, (ii) description of the business, (iii) business model and digitalization, (iv) sustainability performance, and (v) business performance. Likert-style statement scales were designed to capture qualitative constructs, which comprised the main independent and outcome variables surveyed.

The main control variables in the questionnaire were (i) the age of the business in years (using the question: "What year did your company start doing business?"); (ii) employee size specified as number of full-time equivalents employed by the business; and (iii) country dummies that indicate the home country of the business.

The main independent variables in the questionnaire were (i) reliance on digital technology in the business as captured in two scales, (ii) the application of digital technology in the firm's business model in four scales, and (iii) business model experimentation. Reliance on digital technology was measured with 12 items that queried business reliance on different digital technologies. The application of digital technology in the firm's business model queried how the businesses used digital technology in different aspects of their business model. Consistent with the literature, a business model was defined as the firm's architecture of activities for the creation, delivery, and capture of customer value. Scale composition for the business model experimentation variable is shown in the box table.

continued on next page

Box 2.3.2 *Continued*

Business model experimentation: scale composition

Over the past 12 months, have you changed any of the following elements of your business model? (1 = no change .. 5 = complete rethink)

Scale	Items
Business model experimentation	Our target customers and customer segment
	Our sales and marketing operations
	How we interact with our customers
	How we make and deliver our products and services
	Our partnerships (i.e., who we work with—other than suppliers)
	Our suppliers
	Our products and services
	What activities we do ourselves and what activities our partners do
	How we generate revenue (e.g., how we charge for our products)
	What business opportunities we address
	Our entire business model—i.e., how our company does business and organizes its operations

Source: Asian Development Bank.

The study produced two sets of outcome variables, or firm performance variables: business performance and sustainability performance. Business performance sought to capture any effects from firm digitalization on sales growth, profitability, number of customers, operational efficiency, the development of new products and services, and ability to cope with the pandemic crisis, as mediated by the firm's digitally enhanced ability to experiment with and adjust its business model to take the best possible advantage of the business opportunity.

Sustainability performance sought to capture any effect of firm digitalization and business model experimentation on three dimensions: environmental sustainability, social sustainability, and stakeholder welfare.

Reference:
Autio, E. et al. 2022b. *Adoption of Digital Technologies, Business Model Innovation, and Financial and Sustainability Performance in Startup Firms.* Asian Development Bank.

Box 2.3.3 Mobilizing digital entrepreneurs to deliver public health services during COVID-19

The future of digital entrepreneurship in Thailand is promising, especially in health care. This study has confirmed the vital role entrepreneurs play as enablers of economic resilience. Thailand demonstrated an exciting form of public–private partnership in the fight against COVID-19. A digital entrepreneurial community called Pedthaisupai, which translates as Thai Ducks Fighting the Crisis, is a group of Thai tech start-ups that pulled together their various digital solutions on a voluntary basis and worked with the Medical Council of Thailand to apply their technological innovation and capabilities to support workflow in government field hospitals and for medical staff combating the pandemic. The digital entrepreneurs worked together as a community and joined hands with the Government of Thailand to rethink the delivery of public health-care services in the COVID-19 crisis.

The application of digital solutions from various industries was orchestrated end to end for the entire health-care journey, such as patient data and contact information collection, bed booking, communication between patients and staff, patient case management, a dashboard for field hospital management, and vaccine queuing management. This entrepreneurial community engagement highlights the critical role digital entrepreneurs play in helping Thailand manage the health-care crisis and lead economic recovery (box figure). Two insights and related policy implications can be drawn from this collaborative phenomenon, as follow.

Promoting cross-sector collaboration. Digital entrepreneurship can cross industry boundaries. The digital health industry is not necessarily confined to players directly targeting this segment.

Figure from Facebook illustrating joint Pedthaisupai anti-pandemic efforts in Thailand

Start-ups join the government in Thailand's fight against COVID-19.

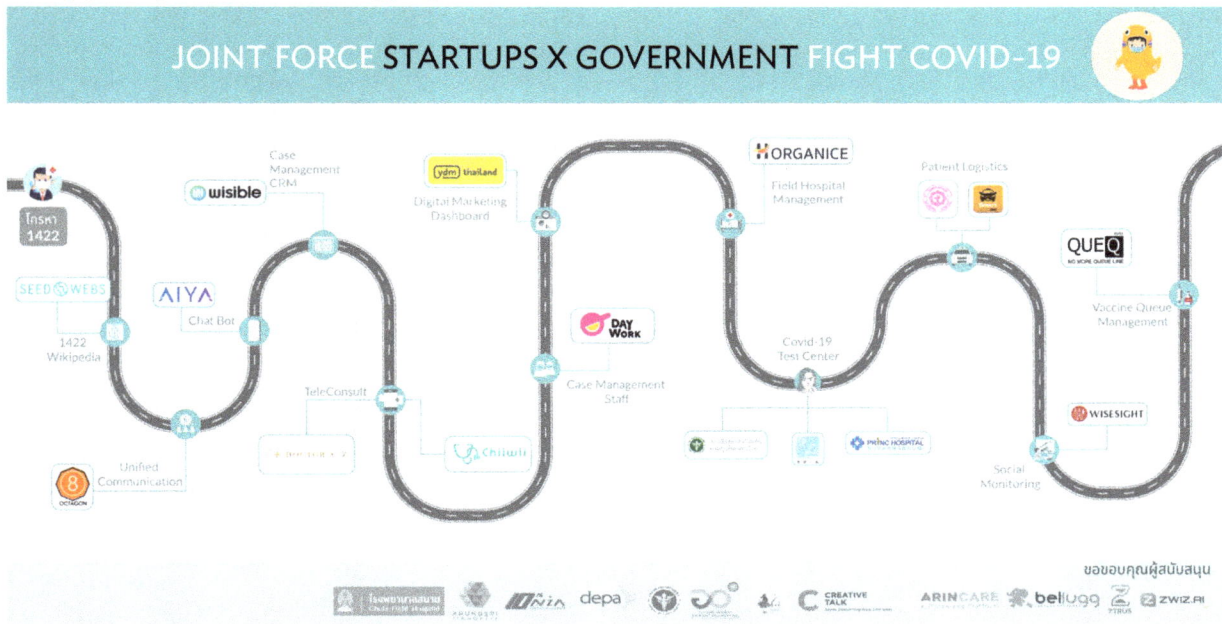

Source: https://www.facebook.com/pedthaisupai/.

continued on next page

Box 2.3.3 *Continued*

Pressured by the pandemic crisis, start-ups in other sectors have found opportunities to apply their digital technologies, products, and services to the health-care industry. QueQ, an app originally designed for retail, proved to be rapidly deployed in other fields, in this case in health care to manage vaccine queues. Similarly, Wisible adapted its business-to-business customer relationship management solution to tracking patient cases in field hospitals. Horganice's rental apartment and dormitory management solution was deployed to book beds in field hospitals. YDM Thailand reconfigured its digital marketing platform to provide a dashboard for health facilities that shows the number of patients in and out, occupancy rates, and the number of patients based on their treatment period, to inform the daily and strategic decisions of medical staff.

As digitalization blurs product and industry boundaries, it opens opportunities for innovative combinations that straddle boundaries. Cross-sector collaboration can expand markets and resource pools. Thus, engaging entrepreneurship communities and cross-fertilizing across sectors should be promoted. Promoting cross-sector networking and collaboration can reveal synergies between start-ups and innovate business models with even more significant positive impacts for all stakeholders. Governments and other stakeholders can provide financial and other incentives, supporting programs, or partnership matching for entrepreneurs to help them look beyond the single sector and adapt or pivot their business models to serve others. Coworking spaces, associations and councils, and innovation districts can pull together solution seekers and providers across industries.

Specifically, a health-care innovation district can incorporate players and stakeholders that may not directly involve the health-care industry but relate to the lifestyle behaviors of consumers seeking well-being products and services.

The role of digital entrepreneurs in driving social missions. It is evident that social missions drove digital entrepreneurs together to address public health-care service delivery. That digital start-ups volunteered to collaborate on managing the COVID-19 crisis suggests that social missions can similarly mobilize digital entrepreneurs to help the economy recover. The adaptability of their existing products and services arises mainly from the combination of entrepreneurial mindsets and digital assets, allowing them to quickly sense opportunities, reconfigure their operations and digital assets, and experiment in new environments. Stakeholders can therefore leverage digital entrepreneurs for social impact and create platforms to tap into their social-oriented collaborative potential. In addition, the cultivation of entrepreneurship mindsets is best served through education. Through education systems, governments and relevant agencies can promote the development of entrepreneurial skills such as opportunity recognition, action orientation, experimentation, teamwork, and collaboration.

Reference:
Prasarnphanich, P. M. 2022b. *Engaging Digital Entrepreneurs for Thailand's Public Health Service Delivery.* Asian Development Bank.

Sound institutions remain vital for entrepreneurs

Digitalization facilitates entrepreneurship but does not mitigate the inherent riskiness and uncertainty of starting a new business, which entails a high likelihood of failure. Given the high risk and uncertainty of entrepreneurship, it is natural to ask what drives an individual to become an entrepreneur. For talented individuals, alternatives can be highly profitable, such as a well-paid job in a large multinational corporation. Yet some individuals choose the risky path of starting a business over the relative security of paid employment. Indeed, many successful entrepreneurs quit secure, well-paid jobs to strike out on their own.

Since entrepreneurship is fundamentally an individual choice and activity, it can be explained by individual attributes. Some individuals become entrepreneurs because they want to be their own boss, others do it to become rich, and yet others take the plunge because they have creative ideas they want to transform into reality. In short, the complex and multifaceted decision to become an entrepreneur is ultimately an individual decision. It depends heavily, however, on the individual's environment. Some may have the benefit of personal or social safety nets that allow them to get back on their feet after a new business fails. Some societies' norms and values may be such that business failure is not stigmatized, and failure is widely accepted as a normal cost of business.

This section analyzes one key dimension of the entrepreneur's environment: institutions, or the formal and informal rules that govern social, political, and economic relations. Institutions such as contracts and contract enforcement, a common commercial code, and arrangements governing the availability of information reduce the cost of economic transactions. Intuitively, institutions can have a big effect on entrepreneurship because they set the rules of the game for economic activity. The most dramatic example is centrally planned economies.

In those economies, entrepreneurial activity waxes and wanes depending on how tightly the government restricts private enterprise. More generally, conducive institutions include strong property rights, honest and effective governments, political stability, reliable legal systems, and open and competitive markets. They promote entrepreneurial activity by reducing the cost of economic transactions, creating incentives to invest in human and physical capital, and contributing to more efficient allocation of resources. Above all, sound institutions facilitate entrepreneurship by mitigating its intrinsic risk and uncertainty.

Sound institutions create a conducive environment for entrepreneurs

An economy's institutional framework conditions, or the conditions that determine the quality of its institutional framework, have been recognized as important determinants of the quality of an economy's entrepreneurial dynamic, or the process by which individuals channel resources toward economic uses through the creation of new businesses (Acs, Szerb, and Autio 2014; Hwang and Powell 2005; Levie et al. 2014; Troilo 2011). Figure 2.4.1 illustrates the relationship between an economy's institutions and individual entrepreneurial productivity. An economy's institutional framework conditions and the quality of its institutions—its culture, social norms, laws and regulations, rates of corruption, rule of law—influence not only who starts new businesses but also what choices the business is likely to make once started (Autio and Acs 2010; Levie and Autio 2011). By influencing what kinds of individuals decide to start a new business—e.g., ones with high human and social capital versus those with less—and what ambitions they set for the new business once started, an economy's institutional framework conditions directly influence the quality of resources allocated through its entrepreneurial dynamic and, therefore, the ability of its entrepreneurs to contribute to the country's productivity (Acs, Autio, and Szerb 2014). Yet, relatively little research exists on the effect of country institutional framework conditions on individual entrepreneurial behavior, especially in Asia (Autio and Fu 2015).

This section examines institutional framework conditions in selected Asian economies and their effect on the quality of individual activity. In so doing, it adds to the few such analyses conducted in this region (Autio and Fu 2015; Autio, Fu, and Levie 2019). It extends previous analyses by expanding the number of years covered and by considering a novel set of institutional framework conditions. In addition to new firm start-up procedures explored previously (the number of procedures required to start a new business, cost of business registration, and paid-in minimum capital), it explores a set of framework conditions that are not known to have been previously studied in the context of emerging economies in Asia: the strength of the rule of law, and the stage of financial development.

It analyzes their effects on three indicators of new business productivity potential: (i) product innovation activity, (ii) exports, and (iii) high growth expectations. Analysis uses a dataset on individual entrepreneurial activity drawn from Global Entrepreneurship Monitor data and combines it with country data on the institutional framework conditions enumerated above.

Effect of institutional conditions on productive entrepreneurship

"Productive entrepreneurship" refers to entrepreneurial self-employment that allocates human capital, social capital, and financial resources toward uses that, on balance, contribute positively to total factor productivity in a country. Not all new businesses do this, and entrepreneurial activity contributes only when it allocates a given resource to its most efficient use in the economy. As a case in point, the highest rates of self-employment in the world are in low-income economies such as Peru and Zambia. This is because they are unable to generate sufficient high-quality employment that would allocate the country's human, social, and financial capital to highly productive uses.

Figure 2.4.1 Institutions and individual entrepreneurship

Institutions affect the productivity of individual entrepreneurs.

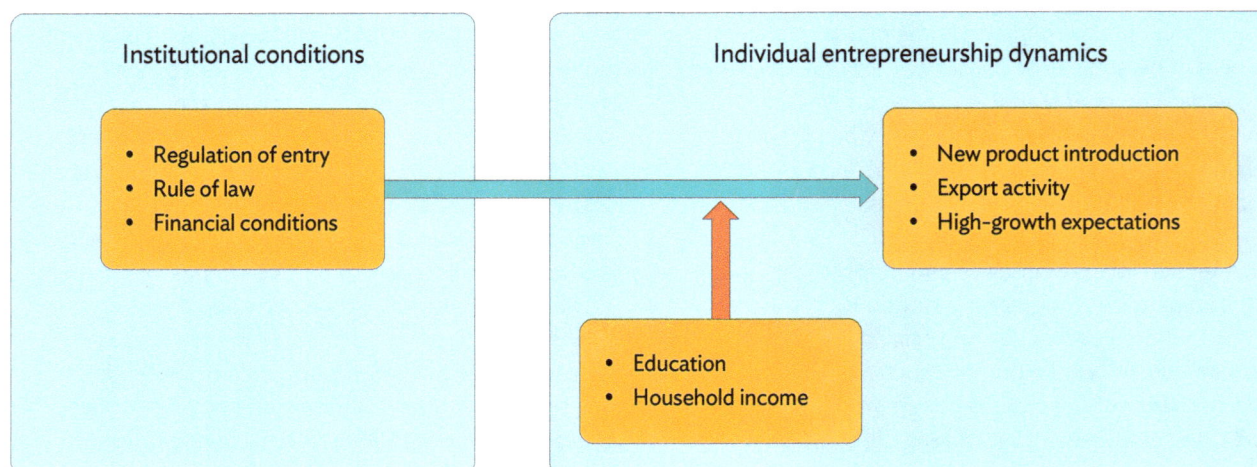

Institutional conditions

- Regulation of entry
- Rule of law
- Financial conditions

Individual entrepreneurship dynamics

- New product introduction
- Export activity
- High-growth expectations

- Education
- Household income

Source: Asian Development Bank.

The current study provisionally assumes that three sets of institutional framework conditions can be particularly influential in regulating the quality of entrepreneurship: (i) regulations on new business entry (Djankov et al. 2002a; Klapper, Laeven, and Rajan 2006), (ii) rule of law (Djankov 2003; Hartog, Stel, and Storey 2010; Levie and Autio 2011), and (iii) a country's financial institutions (Klapper and Love 2010). This section elaborates on each.

Regulation of entry and the productivity potential of new entrepreneurial businesses

Regulations concerning the creation of new businesses can influence the quality of new businesses in a country (Klapper, Laeven, and Rajan 2006). Onerous regulations can keep an individual from starting a business by making registration difficult, lengthy, and expensive. Further, the deterring effect of onerous registration procedures may be particularly acute for individuals who face high trade-offs in the allocation of their human, social, and financial capital. Individuals with high human and social capital have access to higher-quality and more lucrative employment opportunities than do individuals with low human and social capital. As individuals with high human and social capital have plenty of attractive employment opportunities available to them, they are likely to be particularly sensitive to onerous entry regulations. Such regulations may induce other prospective entrepreneurs to avoid registering their business and operate informally (Autio and Fu 2012, 2015; Djankov et al. 2002b). As firms operating in the informal sector may enjoy advantages over registered new businesses by, for example, avoiding taxes and licensing costs, a high prevalence of informality may inhibit the entry and growth aspirations of high-quality formal-sector entrepreneurs (Autio, Fu, and Levie 2019). Suppressed entry by individuals with high human and social capital reduces the productivity potential of new entrepreneurial businesses because human and social capital are important drivers of innovation and growth in new businesses (Autio and Acs 2010; Davidsson and Honig 2003).

Rule of law and productivity potential in new entrepreneurial businesses

The quality of legal institutions in a country is expected to determine to a large extent the productivity potential of entrepreneur-driven resource allocation. As human, social, and financial capital are invested with the expectation of subsequent return on investment, new business creation always carries a degree of risk (Armour and Cumming 2008; Eckhardt and Shane 2003; Seung-Hyun, Peng, and Barney 2007; Thomas 2000). The higher the investment, and the longer the delay between investment and subsequent return—caused, for example, by the time required for product research and development to bear fruit—the more sensitive prospective entrepreneurs will be to this risk. In economies with poor rule of law as expressed in, for example, the strength of its property right protection and the prevalence of corruption, individuals with high human and social capital will be particularly aware of such risks, as will individuals who need to invest substantial amounts to develop the value offering of the new business (Djankov et al. 2003; Levie and Autio 2011). Meanwhile, individuals with low human and social capital will be less likely to develop innovative value offerings and thereby minimize their financial capital investment early on.

Financial conditions and productivity potential in new entrepreneurial businesses

Finally, an economy's financial conditions—specifically, the availability of funds for new entrepreneurial businesses—will have a positive impact of the productivity potential of its entrepreneurial resource allocation dynamic. To develop distinctive value offerings, new ventures typically need to invest time and money. Innovative outputs require investment to develop them, which requires funding. While some prospective entrepreneurs can rely upon their own financial reserves to develop innovative outputs, many have no such financial resources. As a rule, the more distinctive the outputs that the new firm wants to develop, the more time and financial resources it will require. As outputs tend to distinctive in line with being innovative, it is reasonable to expect that new entrepreneurial businesses that require more financial investment will also exhibit higher productivity potential.

Taken together, these intuitions suggest that economies with less burdensome entry regulations, stronger rule of law, and higher financial development will produce more highly productive entrepreneurs who innovate, export, and create many new jobs.

Institutional conditions and individual entrepreneurial dynamics: an empirical analysis

Analysis emphasized the effect of institutional framework conditions on the productivity potential of new individual businesses. In particular, regulation of new business entry, rule of law, and financial conditions can be expected to influence the productivity potential of individual entrepreneurs. To validate this intuitive conjecture, analysis needs to combine data describing country institutional conditions for entrepreneurship with individual data on entrepreneurial activity and aspirations. Box 2.4.1 describes the data and econometric methodology used for empirical analysis.

Analysis examined the influence of institutional conditions on the productivity potential of new entrepreneurial businesses. Because productivity cannot be directly measured, proxies were used to indicate firm performance: product innovation by the firm, on the assumption that innovative products add more value; export activity, on the assumption that more efficiently produced outputs will be competitive beyond national borders; and the firm's employment growth expectations, on the assumption that more efficient firms will be able to outcompete less efficient ones, which should heighten growth expectations. All three measures of firm productivity potential were taken from the GEM dataset. Box 2.4.2 defines the variables.

Empirical findings

Table 2.4.1 shows the results of institutional framework conditions on product innovation by baby businesses. Results for control variables are not reported here but are largely consistent with economic intuition. Full results are available in Autio and Fu (2022b). In Table 2.4.1, Model 1 tests influence from entry regulations on product innovation by baby businesses.

Table 2.4.1 Effects of institutional conditions on product innovation by baby businesses

Institutions, in particular strong rule of law, are strongly associated with entrepreneurial innovation.

	Model 1	Model 2
	New product introduction by baby businesses	
Number of procedures	0.195+	0.262*
	(0.115)	(0.115)
Registration cost	−0.230*	−0.190*
	(0.091)	(0.085)
Minimum paid-in capital	−0.055	−0.042
	(0.108)	(0.109)
Rule of law	0.230**	0.251***
	(0.075)	(0.070)
Financial development	0.179+	
	(0.102)	
Private credit ratio		0.224*
		(0.103)
Pseudo-R^2	0.1891	0.1892
Observations	14,076	14,076

+ = $p < 0.10$, * = $p < 0.05$, ** = $p < 0.01$, *** = $p < 0.001$, ( ) = robust standard errors.
Source: Autio and Fu 2022b.

Among different entry regulations, the cost of registration is shown as a significant influence, with higher cost of registering a new business associated, as expected, with lower product innovation by baby businesses. Business registration procedures seemed to have marginally positive association with baby business product innovation.

Model 1 of Table 2.4.1 also tests the effect of an economy's rule of law and financial development conditions on product innovation by baby businesses. Results show that rule of law has a strong positive association with product innovation by baby businesses, consistent with intuition: The stronger the rule of law, the more likely that entrepreneurial businesses introduce products that are new to at least some of their customers. Economies with stronger rule of law have entrepreneurs who engage in more product innovation. Similarly, a positive association holds between an economy's financial development and the propensity of baby businesses to introduce innovative products.

Model 2 in Table 2.4.1 tests the same set of relationships by using an alternative variable for financial development conditions: the private credit ratio. Private credit ratios exhibited strong positive association with product innovation by baby businesses. Findings for Doing Business indicators and the rule of law remained largely the same as reported above. Combined, these results suggest that stronger rule of law was statistically associated with higher productivity potential in a country's entrepreneurial resource allocation dynamic. Intuitively, strong rule of law attracts individuals with high human capital to start new businesses and encourages them to innovate products (Hypothesis 2). Similarly, wider availability of financial resources for private businesses should be associated with greater supply of entrepreneurs who are more likely to innovate (Hypothesis 3). Empirical observations were consistent with these intuitions.

Table 2.4.2 shows the average marginal effects of explanatory variables that exhibited statistically significant association with product innovation by baby businesses. One standard-deviation increase in registration cost reduced the likelihood of baby business product innovation by 4.1 percentage points. One standard-deviation increase in rule of law was associated with a 5.4% increase in the likelihood of product innovation by baby businesses.

Also empirically analyzed were associations of institutional conditions with two other proxy indicators of entrepreneurial firm productivity potential: export activity and high employment growth expectations. The results, available in Autio and Fu (2022b), were largely consistent with results for product innovation. Evidence indicates that institutional conditions—

entry regulations, rule of law, and financial framework conditions—exhibit a statistically significant positive association with the productivity potential of an economy's entrepreneurial dynamic. Associations are especially strong for rule of law. The key takeaway from this analysis is that a country's institutional framework conditions are strongly associated with the propensity of its entrepreneurs to engage in activities associated with high productivity potential at the firm level: product innovation and exports. Analysis of average marginal effects showed the associations not trivial, as one standard-deviation improvement in an economy's institutional framework conditions was associated with an increase of up to 6% in entrepreneur productivity potential. Corroborating these findings, new cross-country analysis showed corruption negatively associated with entrepreneurship, as detailed below.

Further analysis of how entrepreneur income and education attainment moderated the impact of country institutional framework conditions on productivity potential revealed interesting nuance. Summarizing the results, improvements in financial framework conditions were more strongly associated with increases in the productivity potential of less advantaged entrepreneurs—those less educated or with lower household income. These moderation effects may signal that not all institutional framework conditions operate in the same way or affect all entrepreneurs in the same ways. These insights may help target policy to improve a country's institutional framework conditions to foster productive entrepreneurship.

Table 2.4.2 Average marginal effects of institutional variables on product innovation

The association between national institutional environment and entrepreneurial innovation is not only statistically significant but also economically significant.

Product innovation by baby businesses	Average marginal effect	Standard error	Z
Number of procedures	0.057*	0.025	2.30
Registration cost, % per capita income	−0.041*	0.018	−2.25
Rule of law	0.054**	0.015	3.67
Financial development	0.039+	0.022	1.76
Private credit ratio	0.048*	0.02	2.18

+ = p<0.10, * = p<0.05, ** = p<0.001.

Source: Autio and Fu 2022b.

Does corruption discourage entrepreneurship?

Theoretically, the direction of the relationship between corruption and entrepreneurship is unclear because there are plausible grounds for both positive and negative relationship. In highly regulated economies, corruption can boost entrepreneurship by mitigating the detrimental effects of regulation, especially when excessive—that is, by greasing the wheels of entrepreneurship. On the other hand, corruption can toss sand in the gears of entrepreneurship as the fruits of entrepreneurial activity are arbitrarily confiscated by authorities in the absence of bribes, especially in institutionally weak developing economies. The prevalence of corruption may thus reduce the reward from taking risks, which is a defining feature of entrepreneurship, and thus deter entrepreneurship.

Whether corruption benefits or harms entrepreneurship is thus an empirical issue. However, empirical evidence is mixed and inconclusive. Using cross-country analysis, Dutta and Sobel (2016) found that corruption hurt entrepreneurship even under a bad business environment. However, Dreher and Gassebner (2013) found evidence supporting the wheel-greasing hypothesis with corruption facilitating firm entry in highly regulated economies. Yet another studies, notably Berdiev and Saunoris (2018), showed corruption having both positive and negative effects on entrepreneurship—positive in the formal sector but negative in the informal.

Park and Shin (2022) revisited the relationship between corruption and entrepreneurship by using a sample that included as many economies as possible and making the sample period as long as possible. The number of economies was 61 and the sample period from 2007 to 2017. While the study focused on the role of corruption, it included five other determinants of entrepreneurship that are widely used in the literature. Two proxies are widely used for entrepreneurship in empirical studies. The first is nascent entrepreneurship, collected from GEM, which defines it as the percentage of all respondents aged 18–64 who are involved in a nascent business.

The second is entry rate, calculated using data from World Bank Group Entrepreneurship Survey and defined as the number of new firms divided by the number of currently registered businesses in the previous year.

For the full sample period from 2007 to 2017, analysis found better control of corruption positively associated with entrepreneurship. The evidence is stronger when entry rate is used as the proxy for entrepreneurship. Findings are preserved when other determinants of entrepreneurship are added. Dividing the sample period into two subperiods of 2007–2012 and 2012–2017 does not qualitatively affect the results. Additional findings are that population size, a proxy for market size, is positively associated with entrepreneurship but corporate income tax rate is negatively associated.

An important caveat in interpreting this evidence is that corruption may not be exogenous. That is, although corruption may influence entrepreneurship, entrepreneurship may also influence corruption, making causality difficult to establish (Figure 2.4.2). In economies where entrepreneurship is weak, for instance, entrepreneurs tend to depend on political connections to make a profit rather than on their own efforts, thereby fostering corruption. Lack of entrepreneurship can foster corruption because individuals with limited entrepreneurial skills gain business by cultivating politicians and bureaucrats. Conversely, vibrant entrepreneurship weakens corruption because entrepreneurs compete with each other by creating new businesses instead of fostering political connections. Therefore, it is important to find appropriate instrumental variables that can be employed to eliminate potential estimation bias.

A major contribution of the present study is that it tackles the endogeneity issue by employing instrumental variable regressions. Legal origins can serve as instrumental variables for corruption. Since the seminal studies of La Porta et al. (1998, 1999), a number of researchers found that the historical origins of a country's laws highly correlated with institutions and hence were available as an instrument. The reason is that legal origins are largely exogenous in many economies where legal traditions are rooted in foreign conquest and colonization.

Figure 2.4.2 Two-way causality between corruption and entrepreneurship

Corruption and entrepreneurship may affect each other.

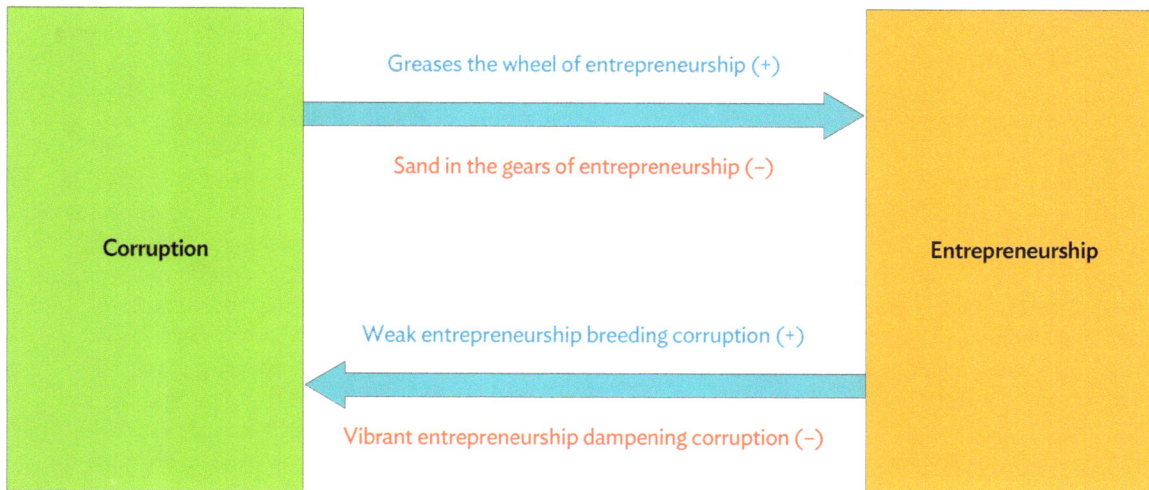

Greases the wheel of entrepreneurship (+)

Sand in the gears of entrepreneurship (–)

Corruption

Entrepreneurship

Weak entrepreneurship breeding corruption (+)

Vibrant entrepreneurship dampening corruption (–)

Source: Asian Development Bank.

Subsequent papers thus use legal origins as instruments for corruption. Using the instrumental variable method does not materially affect the estimated relationship between corruption and entrepreneurship, which suggests that the results are robust. Population size remains positively associated with entrepreneurship, and raising corporate taxes negatively associated. Full results are available in Park and Shin (2022).

Empirical analysis in this section reconfirms the vital role sound institutions play in promoting entrepreneurial activity. Of particular importance is strong rule of law, which mitigates the high risk and uncertainty that entrepreneurs inevitably face.

The two preceding sections provided compelling evidence that digital technology and digitalization can be powerful drivers of entrepreneurship. Hence, the challenge facing developing Asia's policy makers is to create a conducive digital and institutional environment for entrepreneurs to flourish.

The next section discusses some policy options to achieve a more entrepreneurial Asia.

Box 2.4.1 Data and empirical approach for analysis of the relationship between institutional conditions and individual entrepreneurial productivity

Autio and Fu (2022a) test the conjecture that regulation of new business entry, rule of law, and financial conditions influence the productivity potential of individual entrepreneurs, using data drawn from multiple sources. The primary dataset is from the Global Entrepreneurship Monitor (Reynolds, Bosma, and Autio 2005). GEM is an annual survey that tracks individual entrepreneurial attitudes, activities, and aspirations in participating economies. Its dataset is informed by interviews with at least 2,000 individuals per country. GEM applies harmonized data collection methods across the participating economies (Reynolds, Bosma, and Autio 2005). Over 70% of the data were collected by telephone surveys, which were complemented by face-to-face interviews using multistage randomized cluster sampling. The current study used GEM data from 2006 to 2019 on all Asian Development Bank developing member economies for which they were available and combined them with data from other sources, such as World Bank Doing Business surveys, population and GDP data, and Worldwide Governance Indicators. The theoretical model was tested by combining GEM data with relevant country descriptors of institutional framework conditions that described their framework conditions for new business registration, the rule of law, and the availability of financing for new entrepreneurial businesses.

For empirical analysis, the GEM dataset has 232,984 unweighted interviews of working-age individuals aged 16–65 years in the following 15 developing member economies: Armenia; Bangladesh; the People's Republic of China; Georgia; India; Indonesia; Kazakhstan; Malaysia; Pakistan; the Philippines; Singapore; Hong Kong, China; the Republic of Korea; Thailand; and Viet Nam.

GEM defines entrepreneurship as any attempt by individuals to create a new business, including self-employment (Reynolds, Bosma, and Autio 2005). An individual is a "new entrepreneur" if an owner-manager of a new business that has paid salaries to at least some employees, including its owner-manager, for 3–42 months. In the current report, businesses started by new entrepreneurs are called "baby businesses." Analyses samples only baby businesses, excluding those older than 42 months old and nascent entrepreneurs, who under the GEM definition are still trying to start a new business but have not paid salaries to anyone for longer than 3 months. This ensures that analytical focus is on new entrepreneurial businesses in operation.

Cross-level analyses of country effects on individual entrepreneurial behavior were conducted to estimate the effect of institutional conditions on the quality of its entrepreneurial resource allocation dynamic. The data were hierarchical in that individuals were nested within each economy. To account for observations within an economy being potentially dependent on each other and to factor in individual and economy-wide impacts simultaneously, multilevel modelling techniques were employed to estimate the proposed hypotheses.

To control for individuals self-selecting for entrepreneurship, a two-stage Heckman selection model was adopted (Heckman 1979). The first-stage selection model estimated the probability of an individual qualifying as an early-stage entrepreneur or an established business owner as a function of individual demographics that are commonly associated with entrepreneurial entry—such as age, education, household income, fear of failure, familiarity with other entrepreneurs, and entrepreneurial self-efficacy—and controlled for population size, population growth, GDP per capita, GDP growth, and the institutional variables measuring ease of doing business, rule of law, and financial development conditions. The second-stage model, or the outcome model, estimated the impact of the economy's institutional framework conditions on the productivity potential of its entrepreneurial businesses, controlling for any unobserved heterogeneity in the self-selection of entrepreneurs (using the Inverse Mills Ratio computed from the first-stage model) and for age, gender, education, household income, fear of failure, rate of established businesses, GDP per capita, GDP growth, and population size. To facilitate model identification, the variable measuring familiarity with other entrepreneurs was excluded from the second-stage outcome model.

Econometric models were specified as two-level models with random intercepts, which accounted for variation in outcome variables across the economies every year. Model specification allowed both individual

continued on next page

Box 2.4.1 *Continued*

and national variables to affect the prevalence of product innovation, export activity, and employment growth expectations of individual entrepreneurs, using maximum likelihood algorithms to fit the models. In regression models, continuous independent variables were all standardized to have a mean of 0 and a standard deviation of 1, for better comparability in estimated coefficients.

References:

Autio, E. and K. Fu. 2022a. *Country-Level Institutional Conditions and Individual-Level Entrepreneurship Dynamics.* Asian Development Bank.

Heckman, J. J. 1979. Sample Selection Bias as a Specification Error. *Econometrica* 47(1).

Reynolds, P. D., N. Bosma, and E. Autio. 2005. Global Entrepreneurship Monitor: Data Collection Design and Implementation 1998–2003. *Small Business Economics* 24(3).

Box 2.4.2 Measurement of the variables used in empirical analysis

To tease out how institutional conditions affect individual entrepreneurial dynamics, new product introduction was measured by a dummy variable that took value 1 if at least some customers of the firm considered the firm's product or service to be new, or not previously available in the market. The variable took value 0 if none of the firms' customers considered their product or service new. Export activity was measured by a dummy variable that took value 1 if the firm had customers who lived outside of the country and 0 otherwise. High-growth expectations were measured by a dummy variable that took value 1 if the business expected to employ more than 20 employees in 5 years' time and 0 otherwise.

Proxies of an economy's institutional conditions were taken from several different sources. Entry regulations had three measures: (i) The number of procedures required to register and launch a new business proxied the difficulty of launching a new business in the country. (ii) The cost of new business registration measured the cost of new firm registration process. (iii) The required minimum paid-in capital for new business registration measured the financial capital requirement for new business registration. Both costs were calculated as percentages of GDP per capita in purchasing power parity terms.

The strength of an economy's rule of law was measured with a multicomponent variable formed using principal component analysis. The two components were property rights protection and control of corruption. Property rights protection captures the ability of individuals to accumulate private property secured by laws that are fully enforced by the state. Control of corruption captures perceptions of the extent to which public power is exercised for private gain, including both petty and grand corruption, and the capture of state power by elites and private interests.[a] The quality of an economy's financial framework conditions were proxied with two variables: financial development and private credit ratio.

Financial development was measured using the International Monetary Fund's Financial Development Indicator Database. This is an aggregate of nine indexes that assess the development of an economy's financial institutions and financial markets. An alternative measure also adopted for financial development was the private credit ratio, which is the ratio of domestic credit to the private sector relative to GDP (Arcand, Berkes, and Panizza 2012).

Control variables applied at both individual and country levels of analysis. Controls at the individual level were entrepreneur demographic characteristics: age, gender, household income, education, fear of failure, and entrepreneurial self-efficacy. At the economy level, they were the rate of business formation within an economy each year, country population size and growth, GDP per capita, and GDP growth. Time fixed effects were controlled by including year dummies in the analysis.

[a] These two components loaded on a single factor with Eigen value over 1. The value of Cronbach alpha was 0.94, suggesting high internal consistency and reliability.

Reference:

Arcand, M., M. Berkes, and U. Panizza. 2012. *Too Much Finance?* International Monetary Fund.

Policy should target both entrepreneurial hardware and software

Analysis in this theme chapter suggests that the primary role of the government in facilitating digital and other entrepreneurship is to create an environment conducive to entrepreneurial activity. Just as the government is not good at picking winners and losers through an activist industrial policy, it is not good at picking which start-ups are likely to become unicorns, or innovative firms that contribute greatly to the economy. This does not rule out a major role for government in promoting entrepreneurship, as there are plenty of policy levers available.

This report earlier surveyed the importance of institutions—such as ease of registering a new business and property rights protection—in encouraging entrepreneurial activity. Given the inherently risky nature of starting your own business, a sound institutional environment that reduces uncertainty can give a potential entrepreneur the confidence to take the plunge. Good physical and digital infrastructure reduces the cost of doing business. A sound educational system that hones creative minds is essential to securing a large pool of innovative entrepreneurs. These are just a few examples of how governments can prepare the ground for a vibrant ecosystem that enables entrepreneurs to flourish.

Analysis demonstrated earlier that entrepreneurship can contribute significantly to economic growth and development. Entrepreneurs can also help humankind tackle the most salient challenges posed by the United Nations Sustainable Development Goals, such as environmental protection, with their think-outside-of-the-box ingenuity. Their economic and social potential explains why many governments of developing economies prioritize entrepreneurship, as shown above in ASEAN-6.

GIDES 2021: Key takeaways for 21 ADB developing member economies

A necessary first step for policy makers as they grapple with the challenge of fostering entrepreneurship is to get an idea of where their economies stand and what policy areas need the most attention. To this end, ADB developed a set of systematic indicators, the Global Index of Digital Entrepreneurship Systems (GIDES), which was discussed in the second section of this chapter. GIDES objectively assesses and compares the state of entrepreneurship across economies. Analysis included all 21 ADB developing member economies for which complete data was available (Table 2.5.1).

GIDES ranked Singapore by far the top performer in the region, its score of 81.3 out of 100 also ranking it the best performer globally. But Singapore is the only Asian economy in the "leaders," the top group of economies. The ROK ranks second in the region but is a "follower," the second group, ranked 22nd globally. GIDES ranks two economies in developing Asia, Malaysia and the PRC, in the third group, the "catchers-up." The next seven Asian economies on the list, from Georgia to Indonesia, are among the "laggards," the fourth group, and the last 10 economies, from India to Nepal, are "tailenders," the fifth and last group with the weakest digital entrepreneurship systems.

The gap between the best and worst performers in the region is vast, with 69.8 points—more than two-thirds of the scale—separating Singapore and Nepal. Singapore's strongest pillars are human capital, financing, and culture and informal institutions, and its lowest score is in market conditions. Singapore's digital entrepreneurship system is very balanced, outperforming pillar averages among leaders.

Table 2.5.1 GIDES scores of the 21 ADB member economies included in the index

Most economies have relatively weak digital entrepreneurship systems.

Economy	GIDES 2021 score out of 100	GIDES 2021 rank in 113 economies	GIDES 2021 classification
Singapore	81.3	1	Leader
Republic of Korea	54.1	22	Follower
Malaysia	43.1	27	Catcher-up
People's Republic of China	35.3	39	Catcher-up
Georgia	28.3	50	Laggard
Kazakhstan	27.4	52	Laggard
Armenia	26.0	58	Laggard
Thailand	25.9	59	Laggard
Azerbaijan	25.5	60	Laggard
Viet Nam	23.1	63	Laggard
Indonesia	20.4	71	Laggard
India	19.6	75	Tailender
Philippines	18.5	79	Tailender
Sri Lanka	17.5	82	Tailender
Mongolia	17.2	84	Tailender
Kyrgyz Republic	15.2	88	Tailender
Tajikistan	12.8	95	Tailender
Bangladesh	12.5	96	Tailender
Pakistan	12.3	97	Tailender
Cambodia	12.0	101	Tailender
Nepal	11.5	104	Tailender

ADB = Asian Development Bank, GIDES = Global Index of Digital Entrepreneurship Systems.
Source: Autio et al. 2022a.

Looking solely at Singapore's non-digitalized entrepreneurship system (pillar values without digital weights), it is strong in the same pillars, but its entrepreneurship system shows some weaknesses in networking and support. The digital entrepreneurship system in Nepal, the weakest performer, is hampered by its culture and informal institutions, human capital, and market conditions. Nepal scores well below the average for the 21 economies for all pillars. As they have very different digital entrepreneurship system profiles, each needs to tailor its own policies for digitalization and entrepreneurship to address the identified bottlenecks and thereby improve system performance.

The Asia group scored highest on average for physical infrastructure (Figure 2.5.1, red line). This was the only pillar in which the group reached the average pillar score of the 113 economies globally (blue line). This indicates that countries in the region generally have high-quality digital infrastructure and the basic physical infrastructure required to support it. The regional average was worst for culture and informal institutions, where it scored a third below the global average. This suggests that cultural support for digitally enabled entrepreneurship—or how people view entrepreneurs' status and career choice, how corruption in the economy affects this view, and how widely digitalization is accepted—is generally low in the region. However, there is considerable variation across the region in this regard. Overall, the scores of Asian economies were relatively balanced across all GIDES components, suggesting that a broad policy mix is likely to have a greater impact on performance than focusing on a single policy.

Figure 2.5.1 Regional GIDES pillars, non-digitalized and digitalized component averages

Developing Asia scores highest on physical infrastructure and lowest on culture and informal institutions.

- Average normalized entrepreneurial score
- Average normalized digital ecosystem score
- Average GIDES pillar score among Asian 21
- Average GIDES pillar score among global 113

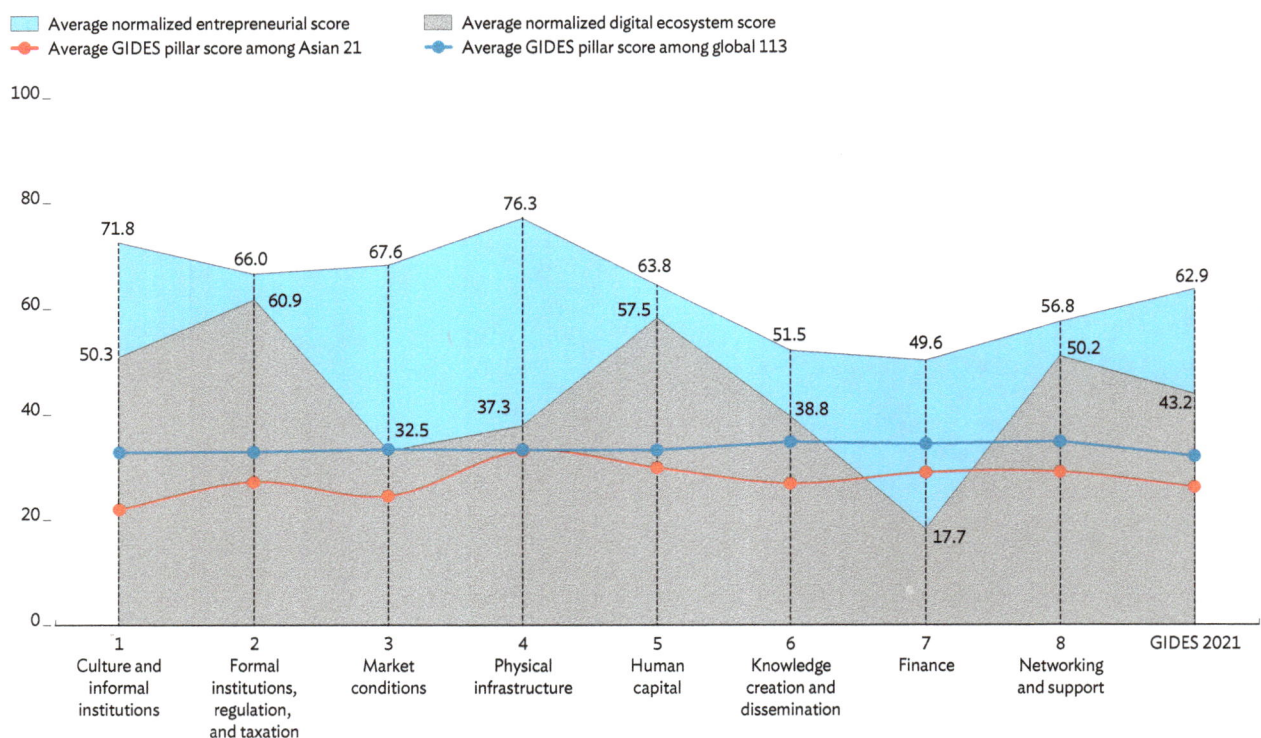

GIDES = Global Index of Digital Entrepreneurship Systems.
Source: Autio et al. 2022a.

Discount digital weighting and focus on framework conditions for the whole entrepreneurial ecosystem, and Asia's strongest pillar is physical infrastructure, with an average score of 76.3. Basic infrastructure is thus generally available in all economies. There is, however, significant variation between economies in the quality of digital infrastructure, with an average score of only 37.3. The weakest Asian pillar is finance at 49.6, as few alternative financing opportunities are available in the region to support entrepreneurs with high potential.

Digital components alone show the same group bottleneck in financing. This means that the adoption rate of novel digital financing opportunities is still low in most economies in the region, with the exception of Singapore. The region performs well in formal institutions, regulation, and taxation, the digital part of this pillar revealing strong government commitment to digitalization through, for example, e-government and data protection.

There is, of course, considerable heterogeneity in pillar scores across economies. Table 2.5.2 shows all eight pillar scores for the developing Asia group and includes two benchmarks: average pillar scores for the leaders with the most advanced digital entrepreneurial ecosystems and average pillar scores for the 21 economies in developing Asia. The last two columns in the table identify the most and least favorable pillar scores for each economy.

Figure 2.5.2 illustrates how policy makers can use GIDES scores to inform their entrepreneurship policy. It compares the eight pillar scores of three selected economies: Malaysia, the ROK, and Thailand. If Malaysian policy makers want to benchmark using the ROK, the figure can inform them of the biggest gaps between the two countries, and it can similarly inform Thai policy makers benchmarking Malaysia.

Table 2.5.2 Pillar values for the 21 economies in developing Asia

Economies in developing Asia tend to perform worst in knowledge and institutions and best in physical infrastructure.

Economy	Pillars								Least favorable pillar	Most favorable pillar
	1	2	3	4	5	6	7	8		
Singapore	97.2	85.7	61.6	74.8	100.0	82.0	100.0	83.8	3	5 and 7
Republic of Korea	55.6	40.7	70.3	61.3	66.4	50.4	50.7	61.6	2	3
Malaysia	46.7	45.6	43.4	32.2	58.5	40.5	40.9	48.9	4	5
People's Republic of China	25.6	33.4	61.1	51.4	32.0	27.6	39.2	30.3	1	3
Georgia	28.5	59.3	18.8	32.0	20.1	22.0	37.3	22.6	3	2
Kazakhstan	37.9	27.8	25.8	36.0	41.1	25.0	25.4	18.9	8	5
Armenia	27.6	28.5	19.4	25.0	32.1	28.9	27.6	24.1	3	5
Thailand	18.3	22.4	27.5	33.4	25.0	23.8	32.2	31.5	1	4
Azerbaijan	39.9	31.2	17.1	28.2	40.7	26.1	15.4	23.5	7	5
Viet Nam	11.6	19.5	31.2	40.8	24.4	22.7	20.7	24.9	1	4
Indonesia	10.4	22.1	14.7	24.0	29.0	22.3	22.0	30.4	1	8
India	5.3	26.4	19.8	32.4	23.1	20.8	20.1	23.0	1	4
Philippines	8.0	16.2	19.3	19.2	21.5	24.4	18.0	30.9	1	8
Sri Lanka	3.0	14.4	8.7	50.3	13.4	23.8	21.7	24.1	1	4
Mongolia	8.4	12.4	16.1	22.4	16.1	18.2	30.2	21.4	1	7
Kyrgyz Republic	11.5	12.1	10.9	18.8	21.4	16.9	17.0	17.0	3	5
Tajikistan	3.7	15.6	8.5	2.9	22.7	19.7	18.6	19.4	4	5
Bangladesh	2.1	10.0	7.8	32.1	8.5	14.5	20.1	14.6	1	4
Pakistan	4.9	13.9	9.1	26.5	6.0	15.9	14.2	16.0	1	4
Cambodia	4.0	14.4	8.8	18.5	9.4	13.1	13.1	20.0	1	8
Nepal	3.1	11.6	7.6	22.7	7.4	17.5	14.5	13.6	1	4
Developing Asia average	21.6	26.8	24.2	32.6	29.5	26.5	28.5	28.6	1	4
Leaders' average	85.2	85.6	71.9	61.9	73.8	76.9	70.7	75.6		

1 = culture and informal institutions, 2 = formal institutions, regulation, and taxation, 3 = market conditions, 4 = physical infrastructure, 5 = human capital, 6 = knowledge creation and dissemination, 7 = finance, 8 = networking and support.

Source: Autio et al. 2022a.

Policy options for an entrepreneurial Asia

Analysis presented in this chapter supports policy lessons for developing Asia as it grapples with the challenge of facilitating entrepreneurship. Private sector development is indispensable to sustained economic growth, and vibrant entrepreneurship is indispensable to a dynamic private sector. While fostering entrepreneurship may be a common goal across the region, its constituent economies have highly diverse entrepreneurship and digital entrepreneurship systems in terms of their nature and quality.

As such, the obvious first policy implication is that no one-size-fits-all policy for advancing entrepreneurship is appropriate across this heterogeneous region. It is unrealistic to expect that major barriers to entrepreneurship will be the same in, for example, the ROK and Nepal. A large digital divide between these two economies suggests that digital infrastructure is much more conducive to digital entrepreneurial activity in the ROK than in Nepal. More generally, the preceding GIDES analysis, and the analysis of ASEAN-6 economies earlier in this chapter, revealed that different economies have different strengths and bottlenecks in their general and digital entrepreneurship systems.

Figure 2.5.2 Eight pillar scores of the Republic of Korea, Malaysia, and Thailand

GIDES allows economies to benchmark their entrepreneurship systems against peers.

— Republic of Korea
— Malaysia
— Thailand

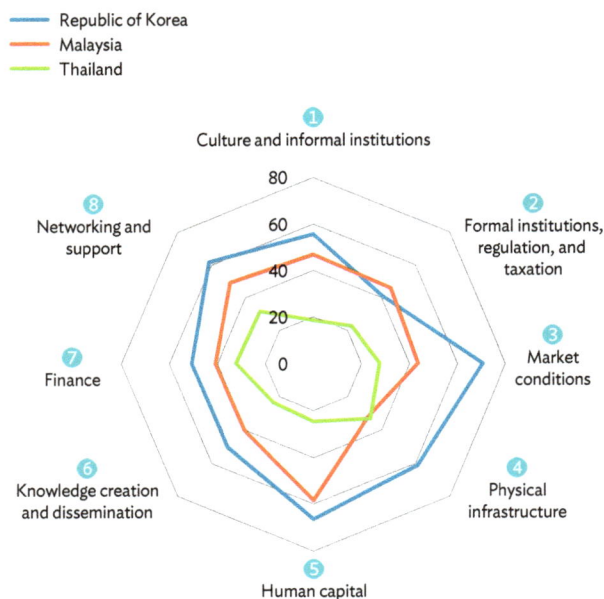

GIDES = Global Index of Digital Entrepreneurship Systems.
Note: Possible index scores are 0–100.
Source: Autio et al 2022a.

What is a relative strength for one economy may be a relative bottleneck for another. As such, the optimal policy mix will differ across economies.

While GIDES analysis underlines the importance of tailoring entrepreneurship policy to each economy's circumstances, it also points to a couple commonalities across the region. Developing Asia's scores are relatively balanced across all GIDES components, suggesting that a broad policy mix is likely to have a greater impact on performance than focusing on a single policy area. Related to this, policy makers must pay attention to both digital and non-digital components of the entrepreneurship system. Developing Asia as a whole performs worst in culture and informal institutions, which implies that people generally have a poor opinion of entrepreneurs in terms of status and career choice. Stressing the positive role of entrepreneurship in general education curricula can create a cultural environment more conducive to entrepreneurialism, as can specific policies such as incentivizing universities to encourage entrepreneurship among students through, for example, university business incubators, as in Thailand.

The first section of this chapter detailed a great deal of heterogeneity in new firm populations in terms of their ability to scale, internationalize, and innovate toward contributing to economic productivity. The important message for policy here is that one-size-fits-all policies may not be very effective in nurturing the productivity potential of new firms. Targeted policies would likely be more effective but raise the difficult question of how to identify and nurture potential winners—a task that governments are not so equipped to undertake (Autio and Rannikko 2017). However, instead of trying to pick winners, governments can enhance the productivity potential of the entrepreneurial dynamic in other ways. One better approach for governments is to influence the trade-offs of an entrepreneurial career choice to make the entrepreneurial option more attractive to individuals with high human, social, and financial capital. This can be done by improving national framework conditions for entrepreneurship (Acs, Autio, and Szerb 2014).

An increasingly important dimension of national framework conditions for entrepreneurship, especially under COVID-19, is the digital environment. Digitalization has transformed entrepreneurship in many ways. ICT creates a plethora of new business opportunities for entrepreneurs by enabling them to reach a large number of consumers, experiment with their business models, and network with their peers at low cost. Empirical analysis in the second section of this chapter indicates that the impact of national digital framework conditions on the quality of digital entrepreneurship is not only significant but large. While there is a lot of variation across developing Asia, the hardware of digital infrastructure—telecommunications and internet infrastructure and the digital resources accessible therein—tend to be relatively strong. Of course, those economies with weak hardware should invest in their telecommunications and internet infrastructure, but a common regionwide policy challenge is to strengthen digital entrepreneurship infrastructure software. This is not limited to changing the culture and societal perceptions of entrepreneurship and incorporating entrepreneurship into education. It includes strengthening the legal and institutional infrastructure to adapt to the fast-evolving digital economy.

While only a few economies have made significant progress in legally regulating digital markets, it is imperative for laws and policies to strengthen competition in them, which are often winner-take-all in nature and thus vulnerable to anticompetitive abuse (Xin and Lee 2022). The World Economic Forum's most recent survey on the adaptability and progress of countries' digital legal frameworks suggests that even advanced economies with well-developed digital infrastructure, such as the ROK, must adapt their legal frameworks to promote a more vibrant, competitive digital business environment. More generally, digitally underdeveloped economies tend to have legal frameworks that adapt too slowly to rapidly evolving digital business models (Figure 2.5.3). According to Quising and Ramayandi (2022), only 34 of 60 economies in Asia and the Pacific currently legislate data protection, 6 have draft legislation, 16 have no legislation, and 4 have no available information. For e-transactions, 50 economies legislate, 3 have draft legislation, 2 have no legislation, and 5 have no data.

While digitalization facilitates entrepreneurial activity, good institutions, in particular strong rule of law, remain vital to entrepreneurship. In tandem with growing recognition of the central role of institutions in economic growth is growing recognition that institutions can strongly affect entrepreneurial activity. Empirical analysis of the link between country institutions and firm productivity in this chapter confirmed that a country's institutional framework conditions have a strong and consistent effect on entrepreneurs' propensity to engage in activities associated with high firm productivity potential: product innovation and export activity. Furthermore, analysis found that those with less corruption enjoyed more entrepreneurial activity. The obvious policy implication is that policy makers intent on encouraging entrepreneurship would do well to reduce the risk and uncertainty facing entrepreneurs by strengthening the institutional environment, notably by strengthening property rights protection.

Given the potentially large positive economic impact of entrepreneurship, governments may consider subsidies, tax incentives, and other fiscal support for entrepreneurs. However, in a review of the empirical literature, Myoda and Castillejos-Petalcorin (2022b) found only limited support, at best, for using fiscal incentives to boost entrepreneurship. Fiscal interventions targeting start-ups and other smaller enterprises can be justified only in specific areas. Even then, quantifying the necessary scale of intervention and predicting how firms respond to incentives are fraught with uncertainty. Further, empirical evidence on the relationship between tax policy and entrepreneurial activity is mixed. The effect of fiscal support varies significantly depending on institutional and cultural factors. Therefore, fiscal incentives per se do not guarantee a tangible stimulus to entrepreneurial activity, but they can complement efforts to improve the business environment for entrepreneurs.

To conclude, catalyzing dynamic entrepreneurship in Asia and the Pacific requires good hardware and software. New analysis presented here provides strong empirical evidence that a conducive digital and institutional environment—notably high-speed broadband network and strong rule of law—positively and significantly affects productive entrepreneurs who innovate, export, and create many jobs. For the region as a whole, the weakest GIDES pillar is culture and informal institutions. One way to strengthen the pillar is to improve public perceptions of entrepreneurship, notably through education. Where the local entrepreneurial ecosystem is underdeveloped, policy makers can help kickstart mentoring, networking, and collaboration among entrepreneurs by, for example, helping to form start-up associations (Box 2.5.1). More generally, policy makers can significantly improve the entrepreneurial climate through such indirect and low-cost interventions.

More broadly, the central role of developing Asia's policy makers in fostering a more entrepreneurial and economically dynamic region is to create a conducive environment for entrepreneurial activity. Entrepreneurship is an inherently individual pursuit because it is ultimately a personal decision to start and run your own business, rather than work for a company or the government.

Figure 2.5.3 Legal framework adaptability to digital business models

Digitally underdeveloped economies have weak legal systems for digital entrepreneurship.

Legal framework adaptability score, 2019

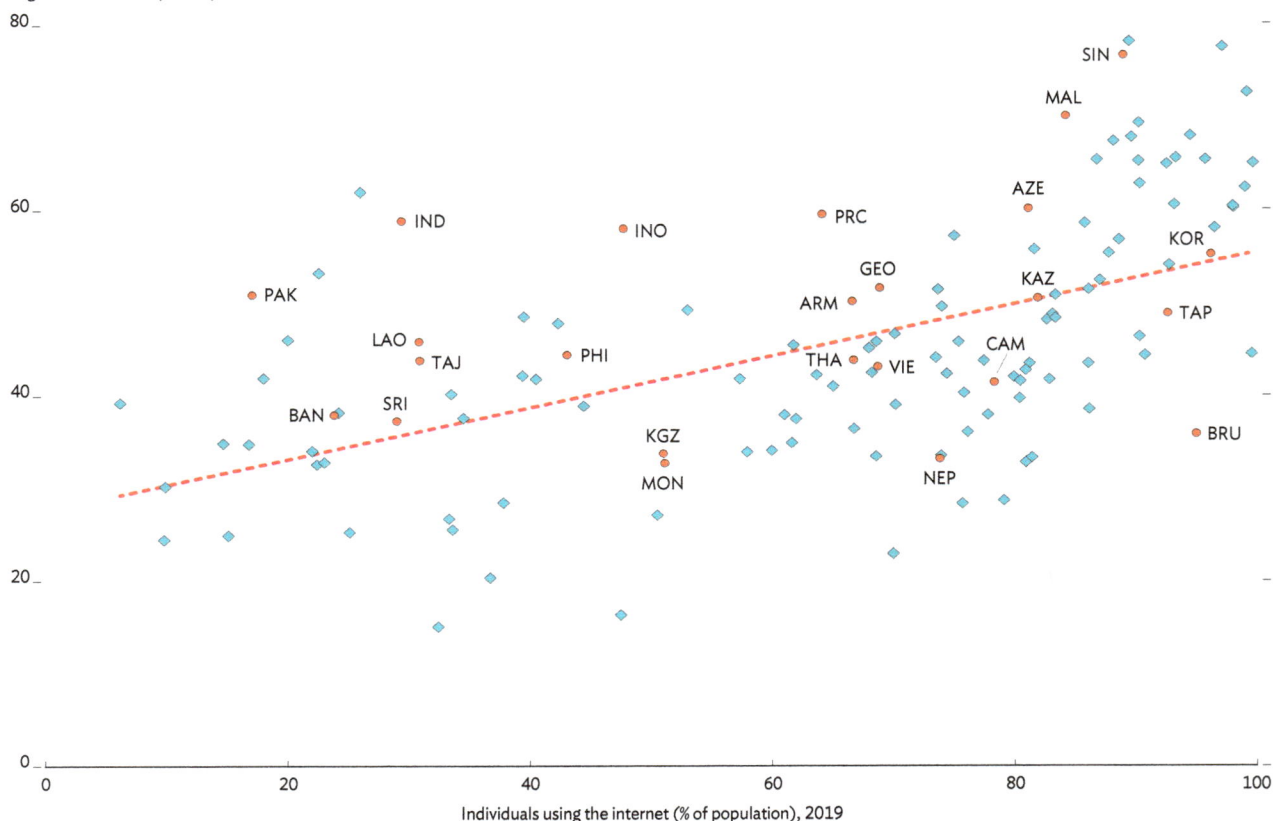

ARM = Armenia, AZE = Azerbaijan, BAN = Bangladesh, BRU = Brunei Darussalam, CAM = Cambodia, GEO = Georgia, IND = India, INO = Indonesia, KAZ = Kazakhstan, KGZ = Kyrgyz Republic, KOR = Republic of Korea, LAO = Lao People's Democratic Republic, MAL = Malaysia, MON = Mongolia, NEP = Nepal, PAK = Pakistan, PHI = Philippines, PRC = People's Republic of China, SIN = Singapore, SRI = Sri Lanka, TAJ = Tajikistan, TAP = Taipei,China, THA = Thailand, VIE = Viet Nam.

Notes: Scores derived from responses to the survey question: "In your economy, how fast is the legal framework adapting to digital business models (e.g., e-commerce, sharing economy, fintech, etc.)?" [1 = not fast at all; 7 = very fast]. The score is from 0 to 100.

Source: Quising and Ramayandi 2022.

Policy makers must realize that their direct influence on entrepreneurship is limited and indirect, unlike building power plants or public health clinics. What they can do is influence trade-offs for the individual between entrepreneurship and other pursuits by creating a conducive institutional, digital, and overall environment for entrepreneurship. It is especially important that policy makers alter the trade-off for talented and creative individuals whose start-ups may blossom into gazelles that contribute disproportionately to productivity growth—a new Apple or Samsung.

In light of intrinsic risk in entrepreneurship, it is not surprising that sound institutions that mitigate economic risk and uncertainty—especially strong rule of law—are significant determinants of entrepreneurship. Finally, physical infrastructure, including digital technology infrastructure, is a necessary but insufficient condition for digital entrepreneurship. Favorable cultural, institutional, and legal infrastructure matters just as much.

Box 2.5.1 Entrepreneurs are the best mentors for potential entrepreneurs

The rise of tech start-ups has been aided by the parallel creation of incubator programs to support entrepreneurs who attempt to commercialize innovative ideas—and possibly create the next Grab, Gojek, or Google.

These programs nurture entrepreneurship by providing advice, information, and networking opportunities that help a start-up produce a prototype of a product, file a patent, secure funding, and so on. Assistance is provided by the manager of the incubator, trainers who deliver courses, guest speakers, and mentors. Current ADB research on tech start-ups in several Asian economies found that an effective incubator must engage high-quality people in these four roles.

The manager of the incubator is most effective if she or he has business experience. While this may seem obvious, it is often not the case. Incubators sponsored by governments often employ civil servants without any business experience, and some university incubators are run by academics. Furthermore, some trainers engaged by government and university incubators often lack real-world business experience. Speakers who provide one-off talks are more effective if they are successful entrepreneurs. Incubators set up by corporations tend to be more effective because they use their own staff or hire people with business experience.

The advice and training offered by incubators without strong business links suffer from three weaknesses: (i) the ideas are too theoretical and tidy, meaning that they do not provide practical, actionable insights; (ii) support is often not specific to a particular sector and thus does not teach the start-up how to address challenges specific to it; and (iii) assistance does not account for the current lifecycle stage of the start-up.

To conclude, a critical attribute of a good incubator is the ability to provide quality mentors. One-on-one mentoring can give the start-up concrete directions on how to organize its business model, form a team, and negotiate the "valley of death," during which costs are incurred without yet a revenue stream. Mentors with no business experience or from different industries are unlikely to be effective and may even be disadvantageous. Unfortunately, incubators often find it difficult to find good mentors. Successful entrepreneurs often lack time to mentor. However, they are more likely to come forward if remunerated by the incubator or start-up, or possibly receive a tax break or subsidy from the government.

Reference:
Vanderberg, P. and A. Hampel Milagrosa. 2022. *The Challenges of Providing Quality Advice and Mentorship through Incubators.* Asian Development Bank.

Background Papers

Autio, E. and K. Fu. 2022a. *Digital Framework Conditions and the Productivity Potential of a Country's Entrepreneurial Dynamic: A Study of Selected ADB Member Economies.* Asian Development Bank.

———. 2022b. *Country-Level Institutional Conditions and Individual-Level Entrepreneurship Dynamics.* Asian Development Bank.

Autio, E. et al. 2022a. *Asian Index of Digital Entrepreneurship Systems 2021.* Asian Development Bank.

———. 2022b. *Adoption of Digital Technologies, Business Model Innovation, and Financial and Sustainability Performance in Startup Firms.* Asian Development Bank.

Chiyachantana, C. 2022. *Digital Entrepreneurship in Asia for Economic Resilience and Post-Pandemic Recovery: Country Report—Singapore.* Asian Development Bank.

Habaradas, R. 2022a. *Digital Entrepreneurship in Asia for Economic Resilience and Post-Pandemic Recovery: Country Report—Philippines.* Asian Development Bank.

Kim, J. et al. 2022. *Entrepreneurship and Economic Growth: A Cross-Sectional Analysis Perspective.* Asian Development Bank.

Lee, K., T. P. Vu, and D. Park. 2022. *Digitalization of Value Chains in the Apparel Industry: Implications for Small and Medium-Sized Enterprises and Startups.* Asian Development Bank.

Muftiandi, A. 2022a. *Digital Entrepreneurship in Food Delivery in Industry in Indonesia.* Asian Development Bank.

Park, D. and K. Shin. 2022. *Does Corruption Discourage Entrepreneurship?* Asian Development Bank.

Pham, Q. M. and L. P. Tan. 2022b. *Digital Entrepreneurship: Viet Nam.* Asian Development Bank.

Prasarnphanich, P. M. 2022a. *Thailand's Digital Entrepreneurship and Digital Health and Wellness.* Asian Development Bank.

Smit, W. et al. 2022. *Digital Entrepreneurship in Asia for Economic Resilience and Post-Pandemic Recovery: Country Report—Malaysia.* Asian Development Bank.

Vo, L. H., T. Le, and D. Park. 2022. *Digital Divide Decoded: Can E-Commerce and Remote Workforce Enhance Enterprise Resilience in the COVID-19 Era?* Asian Development Bank.

Xin, S. and K. Lee. 2022. *The Role of Big Businesses in Entrepreneurship: A Cross-Country Panel Analysis Using the GEM Data.* Asian Development Bank.

Background Notes

Alano, E. and P. Quising. 2022a. *Entrepreneurship Trends in Developing Asia.* Asian Development Bank.

———. 2022b. *Information and Communication Technology and Entrepreneurship.* Asian Development Bank.

Castillejos-Petalcorin, C. 2022. *High-Valued Social Entrepreneurs: BioNTech and the Ocean Cleanup.* Asian Development Bank.

Castillejos-Petalcorin, C. and J. Kim. 2022. *Female Entrepreneurship and Gender Equality.* Asian Development Bank.

Chiyachantana, C. and P. M. Prasarnphanich. 2022. *Digital Entrepreneurship Interview Survey (DES).* Asian Development Bank.

Habaradas, R. 2022b. *Social Entrepreneurship: Conceptual Definition, Brief Literature Review and Some Examples from the Philippines.* Asian Development Bank.

Kim, J. and C. Castillejos-Petalcorin. 2022. *Entrepreneurship and Cleaner Environment.* Asian Development Bank.

Muftiandi, A. 2022b. *Business Innovation and E-commerce in Indonesia.* Asian Development Bank.

Myoda, Y. 2022. *Real-Life Entrepreneurs.* Asian Development Bank.

Myoda, Y. and C. Castillejos-Petalcorin. 2022a. *Determinants of Entrepreneurship: A Selective Literature Review.* Asian Development Bank.

———. 2022b. *A Selective Literature Review on Fiscal Incentives to Promote Entrepreneurial Activity.* Asian Development Bank.

Pham, Q. and L. P. Tan. 2022a. *Female Entrepreneurship and Gender Equity: Literature Review and Vietnamese Examples.* Asian Development Bank.

Prasarnphanich, P. M. 2022b. *Engaging Digital Entrepreneurs for Thailand's Public Health Service Delivery.* Asian Development Bank.

Quising, P. and A. Ramayandi. 2022. *Entrepreneurship and Competition Policy.* Asian Development Bank.

Vanderberg, P. and A. Hampel Milagrosa. 2022. *The Challenges of Providing Quality Advice and Mentorship through Incubators.* Asian Development Bank.

References

Ács, Z. J., E. Autio, and L. Szerb. 2014. National Systems of Entrepreneurship: Measurement Issues and Policy Implications. *Research Policy* 43(3). https://doi.org/10.1016/j.respol.2013.08.016.

Acs, Z., L. Szerb, and E. Autio. 2014. *Global Entrepreneurship and Development Index 2014.* Amazon Books.

Acs, Z., S. Desaid, and J. Hessels. 2008. Entrepreneurship, Economic Development, and Institutions. *Small Business Economics* 31.

ADB. 2020. *Asian Development Outlook 2020: What Drives Innovation in Asia?* Asian Development Bank.

———. 2021. Did Internet Access Improve during COVID-19? *Asian Development Bank blog.* 24 September. https://blogs.adb.org/blog/did-internet-access-improve-economic-resilience-during-covid-19.

Afuah, A. 2003. Redefining Firm Boundaries in the Face of the Internet: Are Firms Really Shrinking? *Academy of Management Review* 28(1).

Andries, P., K. Debackere, and B. Van Looy. 2013. Simultaneous Experimentation as a Learning Strategy: Business Model Development Under Uncertainty. *Strategic Entrepreneurship Journal* 7(4).

Armour, J. and D. Cumming. 2008. Bankruptcy Law and Entrepreneurship. *American Law and Economics Review* 10.

Arin, K. et al. 2015. Revisiting the Determinants of Entrepreneurship: A Bayesian Approach. *Journal of Management* 41(2).

Autio, E. and K. Fu. 2012. Allocation of Effort into Informal Entrepreneurship: Institutional and Individual-Level Effects. *Working Paper.* Imperial College Business School.

———. 2015. Economic and Political Institutions and Entry into Formal and Informal Entrepreneurship. *Asia Pacific Journal of Management* 32(1).

Autio, E. and Z. Acs. 2010. Intellectual Property Protection and the Formation of Entrepreneurial Growth Aspirations. *Strategic Entrepreneurship Journal* 4(3).

Autio, E. et al. 2018a. Digital Affordances, Spatial Affordances, and the Genesis of Entrepreneurial Ecosystems. *Strategic Entrepreneurship Journal* 12(1).

Autio, E. et al. 2018b. *The European Index of Digital Entrepreneurship Systems.* Publications Office of the European Union. doi:10.2760/39256, https://ec.europa.eu/jrc/sites/default/files/eides_2018.pdf.

Autio, E., K. Fu, and J. Levie. 2019. *Entrepreneurship as a Driver of Innovation in the Digital Age.* Asian Development Bank.

Autio, E. and H. Rannikko. 2017. Entrepreneurial Dynamic of the Digital Economy and Finland's International Competitiveness. In *Publications of the Government's Analysis, Assessment and Research Activities.* Finland Prime Minister's Office.

———. 2019. *EIDES 2019—The European Index of Digital Entrepreneurship Systems.* Publications Office of the European Union. doi:10.2760/107900, https://ec.europa.eu/jrc/sites/default/files/eides_2019.pdf.

———. 2020. *EIDES 2020—The European Index of Digital Entrepreneurship Systems.* Publications Office of the European Union. doi:10.2760/150797, https://ec.europa.eu/jrc/sites/default/files/eides_2020.pdf.

Bardhan, I., J. Whitaker, and S. Mithas. 2006. Information Technology, Production Process Outsourcing, and Manufacturing Plant Performance. *Journal of Management Information Systems* 23(2).

Baumol, W. J. and R. Strom. 2007. Entrepreneurship and Economic Growth. *Strategic Entrepreneurship Journal* (1).

Berdiev, A. N. and J. W. Saunoris. 2018. Corruption and Entrepreneurship: Cross-country Evidence from Formal and Informal Sectors. *Southern Economic Journal* 84(3).

Blank, S. 2013. Why the Lean Start-up Changes Everything. *Harvard Business Review* 91(5).

Bocken, N. and Y. Snihur. 2020. Lean Startup and the Business Model: Experimenting for Novelty and Impact. *Long Range Planning* 53(4).

Botero, J. et al. 2004. The Regulation of Labor. *Quarterly Journal of Economics* 119(4).

Bouwman, H., S. Nikou, and M. De Reuver. 2019. Digitalization, Business Models, and SMEs: How do Business Model Innovation Practices Improve Performance of Digitalizing SMEs? *Telecommunications Policy* 43(9).

Camuffo, A. et al. 2019. A Scientific Approach to Entrepreneurial Decision Making: Evidence from a Randomized Control Trial. *Management Science* 66(2). doi:10.1287/mnsc.

Chowdhury, F., S. Terjesen, and D. Audretsch. 2015. Varieties of Entrepreneurship: Institutional Drivers across Entrepreneurial Activity and Country. *European Journal of Law and Economics* 40(1).

Contigiani, A. and D. A. Levinthal. 2019. Situating the Construct of Lean Start-up: Adjacent Conversations and Possible Future Directions. *Industrial and Corporate Change* 28(3).

Davenport, T. H. 2005. The Coming Commoditization of Processes. *Harvard Business Review* 83(6).

Davidsson, P. and B. Honig. 2003. The Role of Social and Human Capital among Nascent Entrepreneurs. *Journal of Business Venturing* 18.

de Soto, H. 2000. *The Mystery of Capital.* Basic Books.

Di Gregorio, D., M. Musteen, and D. E. Thomas. 2008. Offshore Outsourcing as a Source of International Competitiveness for SMEs. *Journal of International Business Studies* 40(6).

Dimov, D. 2016. Toward a Design Science of Entrepreneurship. In J. A. Katz and A. C. Corbett, eds. Models of Start-Up Thinking and Action: Theoretical, Empirical and Pedagogical Approaches. *Advances in Entrepreneurship, Firm Emergence and Growth* 18.

Djankov, S. et al. 2002a. The Regulation of Entry. *Quarterly Journal of Economics* 117(1).

———. 2002b. Going Informal: Benefits and Costs. In B. Belev, ed. *The Informal Economy in the EU Accession Countries.* Center for the Study of Democracy.

———. 2003. Courts. *The Quarterly Journal of Economics* 118(2).

Dreher, A. and M. Gassebner. 2013. Greasing the Wheels? The Impact of Regulations and Corruption on Firm Entry. *Public Choice* 155(3).

Dulong De Rosnay, M. and F. Stalder. 2020. Digital Commons. *Internet Policy Review* 9(4).

Dutta, N. and R. Sobel. 2016. Does Corruption Ever Help Entrepreneurship? *Small Business Economics* 47(1).

Eckhardt, J. and S. Shane. 2003. Opportunities and Entrepreneurship. *Journal of Management* 29(3).

Ferreira, J. J. M., C. I. Fernandes, and F. A. F. Ferreira. 2019. To Be or Not to be Digital, That is the Question: Firm Innovation and Performance. *Journal of Business Research* 101.

Hartog, C., A. V. Stel, and D. J. Storey. 2010. Institutions and Entrepreneurship: The Role of the Rule of Law. *EIM Research Reports*.

Heckman, J. J. 1979. Sample Selection Bias as a Specification Error. *Econometrica* 47(1).

Hwang, H. and W. W. Powell. 2005. Institutions and Entrepreneurship. In S. A. Alvarez, R. Agarwal, and O. Sorenson, eds. *Handbook of Entrepreneurship Research: Interdisciplinary Perspectives*. Springer.

Jean, R. J., R. R. Sinkovics, and S. T. Cavusgil. 2010. *Journal of International Business Studies* 41(7).

Karmarkar, U. 2004. Will You Survive the Services Revolution? *Harvard Business Review*.

Kerr, W. R., R. Nanda, and M. Rhodes-Kropf. 2014. Entrepreneurship as Experimentation. *Journal of Economic Perspectives* 28(3).

Klapper, L., L. Laeven, and R. Rajan. 2006. Entry Regulation as a Barrier to Entrepreneurship. *Journal of Financial Economics* 82(3).

Klapper, L. and I. Love. 2010. The Impact of the Financial Crisis on New Firm Registration. In *Policy Research Working Papers*. World Bank.

Kritikos, A. 2014. *Entrepreneurs and Their Impact on Jobs and Economic Growth*. IZA World of Labor. May. https://wol.iza.org/articles/entrepreneurs-and-their-impact-on-jobs-and-economic-growth/long.

La Porta, R. et al. 1998. Law and Finance. *Journal of Political Economy* 106(6).

La Porta, R., F. Lopez-de-Silanes, A. Shleifer, and R. W. Vishny. 1999. The Quality of Government. *Journal of Law, Economics, and Organization* 15(1).

Lahiri, S. and B. L. Kedia. 2011. Co-evolution of Institutional and Organizational Factors in Explaining Offshore Outsourcing. *International Business Review* 20(3).

Levie, J. and E. Autio. 2008. A Theoretical Grounding and Test of the GEM Model. *Small Business Economics* 31(3).

———. 2011. Regulatory Burden, Rule of Law, and Entry of Strategic Entrepreneurs: An International Panel Study. *Journal of Management Studies* 48(6).

Levie, J. et al. 2014. Global Entrepreneurship and Institutions: An Introduction. *Small Business Economics* 42(3).

Lewin, A. Y. and H. W. Volberda. 2011. Co-evolution of Global Sourcing: The Need to Understand the Underlying Mechanisms of Firm-Decisions to Offshore. *International Business Review* 20(3).

Liu, A., H. Liu, and J. Gu. 2021. Linking Business Model Design and Operational Performance: The Mediating Role of Supply Chain Integration. *Industrial Marketing Management* 96.

Mani, D., A. Barua, and A. B. Whinston. 2010. An Empirical Analysis of the Impact of Information Capabilities Design on Business Process Outsourcing Performance. *Management Information Systems Quarterly* 34(1).

Massa, L. and C. L. Tucci. 2013. Business Model Innovation. In *The Oxford Handbook of Innovation Management*. Oxford University Press.

Michelle, W. L. F. 2009. Technology Leapfrogging for Developing Countries. In D. B. A. Mehdi Khosrow-Pour, ed. *Encyclopedia of Information Science and Technology, Second Edition*. IGI Global.

Mograbyan, M. and E. Autio. 2021. Internationalisation as a Business Model Design Process. Academy of International Business Conference, Florida, July.

Nambisan, S. 2017. Digital Entrepreneurship: Toward a Digital Technology Perspective of Entrepreneurship. *Entrepreneurship Theory and Practice* 41(6).

Rachinger, M. et al. 2019. Digitalization and Its Influence on Business Model Innovation. *Journal of Manufacturing Technology Management* 30(8).

Reynolds, P. D., N. Bosma, and E. Autio. 2005. Global Entrepreneurship Monitor: Data Collection Design and Implementation 1998–2003. *Small Business Economics* 24(3).

Ries, E. 2011. *The Lean Startup*. Crown Business.

Roman, A., I. Bilan, and C. Ciumas. 2018. What Drives the Creation of New Businesses? A panel-data analysis for *EU Countries, Emerging Markets Finance and Trade* 54(3). https://doi.org/10.1080/1540496X.2017.1412304.

Romme, A. G. L. and I. M. M. J. Reymen. 2018. Entrepreneurship at the Interface of Design and Science: Toward an Inclusive Framework. *Journal of Business Venturing Insights* 10.

Seung-Hyun, L., M. Peng, and J. Barney. 2007. Bankruptcy Law and Entrepreneurship Development: A Real Options Perspective. *Academy of Management Review* 32(1).

Thomas. A. S. 2000. A Case for Comparative Entrepreneurship: Assessing the Relevance of Culture. *Journal of International Business Studies* 31(2).

Thomas, L., D. Sharapov, and E. Autio. 2018. Linking Entrepreneurial and Innovation Ecosystems: the Case of AppCampus. In E. Carayannis, et al., eds. *Entrepreneurial Ecosystems and the Diffusion of Startups*. Edward Elgar.

Tilson, D., K. Lyytinen, and C. Sørensen. 2010. Research Commentary-Digital Infrastructures: The Missing IS Research Agenda. *Information Systems Research* 21(4).

Troilo, M. 2011. Legal Institutions and High-Growth Aspiration Entrepreneurship. *Economic Systems* 35.

UNCTAD. 2021a. *Data Protection and Privacy Legislation Worldwide*. United Nations Conference on Trade and Development. https://unctad.org/page/data-protection-and-privacy-legislation-worldwide (accessed 28 January 2022).

———. 2021b. *E-transactions Legislation Worldwide*. United Nations Conference on Trade and Development. https://unctad.org/page/e-transactions-legislation-worldwide (accessed 28 January 2022).

Van Alstyne, M. W., G. G. Parker, and S. P. Choudary. 2016. Pipelines, Platforms, and the New Rules of Strategy. *Harvard Business Review* 94(4).

Whitaker, J., S. Mithas, and M. S. Krishnan. 2010. Organizational Learning and Capabilities for Onshore and Offshore Business Process Outsourcing. *Journal of Management Information Systems* 27(3).

Xiong, J. et al. 2021. The Window of Opportunity Brought by the COVID-19 Pandemic: An Ill Wind Blows for Digitalisation Leapfrogging. *Technology Analysis & Strategic Management*.

Yoo, Y. R. et al. 2012. Organizing for Innovation in the Digitized World. *Organization Science* 23(5).

3

ECONOMIC TRENDS AND PROSPECTS IN DEVELOPING ASIA

THE CAUCASUS AND CENTRAL ASIA

The Russian invasion of Ukraine materially affected the outlook for the Caucasus and Central Asia. The subregional growth projection is raised because of unexpected knock-on effects from geopolitical tensions, such as large incoming money transfers from the sanctioned Russian Federation and robust hydrocarbon exports. With global commodity price hikes, inflation forecasts are raised, and larger current account surpluses are projected because of strong exports and inward transfers to some countries. However, the war's future effects remain highly uncertain and the risks may prevail.

Subregional assessment and prospects

Forecasts for aggregate economic growth in the Caucasus and Central Asia are raised from 3.6% in 2022 and 4.0% in 2023 in *Asian Development Outlook 2022 (ADO 2022)* to 3.9% in 2022 and 4.2% in 2023 in this *Update* (Figure 3.1.1). The upward revisions reflect growth in many of the subregion's eight economies due to knock-on effects from the ongoing Russian invasion of Ukraine. Growth projections are raised for Armenia, Azerbaijan in 2022, Georgia, the Kyrgyz Republic, Tajikistan, and Uzbekistan in 2023 because of large money transfers from the Russian Federation to several countries and, for petroleum exporters, larger-than-expected hydrocarbon exports. Relocation of Russian businesses and inflow of skilled workers from the Russian Federation may also favor the medium-term outlook. Meanwhile, the negative effects of the invasion have proved to be smaller than anticipated. Relaxing pandemic-related movement restrictions also helped sustain recovery. However, great uncertainty remains about how the Russian invasion of Ukraine and its economic impacts on trade and supply chain disruption will play out in the coming months and beyond, as the Russian Federation is a major trade partner for most countries in the subregion.

Figure 3.1.1 GDP growth in the Caucasus and Central Asia

Robust growth in H1 2022 prompts higher growth projections for most countries and the subregion as a whole.

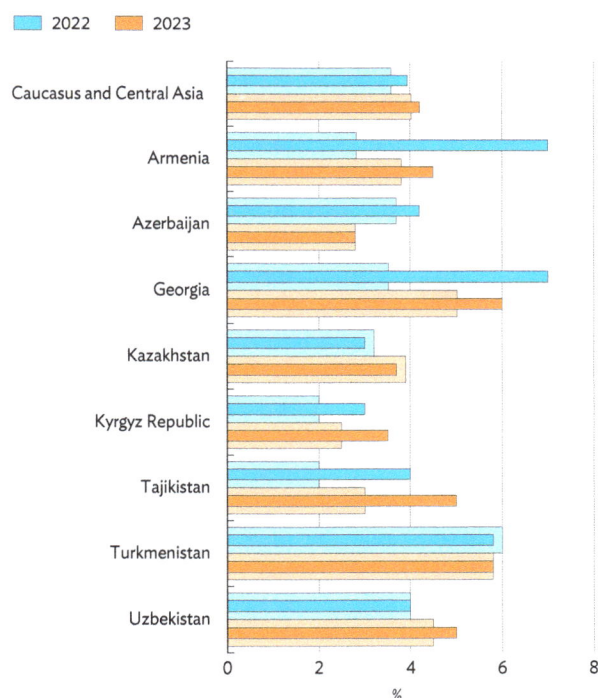

GDP = gross domestic product, H = half.
Note: Lighter colored bars are *Asian Development Outlook 2022* forecasts.
Source: *Asian Development Outlook* database.

The subregional assessment and prospects were written by Kenji Takamiya. Kazakhstan was written by Genadiy Rau, and the other economies by Muhammadi Boboev, Begzod Djalilov, Grigor Gyurjyan, Jennet Hojanazarova, George Luarsabishvili, and Nail Valiyev; and Zhamilia Bataeva, consultant. All authors are in the Central and West Asia Department of ADB.

Higher inflation observed in the subregion may also adversely affect growth by cutting consumers' real incomes. This is a reason for marginally decreasing the growth projection for Turkmenistan in 2022. By contrast, Kazakhstan's growth projections for 2022 and 2023 are slightly reduced because of waning business confidence and, outside of services, weakening activity.

Among the subregion's hydrocarbon importers, Armenia and Georgia grew especially rapidly. Armenia's economy grew by 11.0% in the first half of 2022, and Georgia's growth rate was estimated at 10.5% in the first half of 2022. Both Armenia and Georgia experienced sharp increases in money transfers from the Russian Federation as Russian firms and individuals relocated activities abroad. The Kyrgyz Republic also received inward money transfers and recorded robust growth at 7.7% in the first 7 months of 2022. Tajikistan grew by 7.4% in the first half of 2022. While remittance inflows declined because of recession in the Russian Federation, adverse effects on growth in the country were somewhat mitigated by recent appreciation of the Russian ruble against the US dollar.

Most of the subregion's hydrocarbon exporters also showed steady expansion in the first half of 2022, albeit to varying degrees. Growth in Azerbaijan accelerated to 6.2%, led by production in the non-hydrocarbon economy, along with strong hydrocarbon exports. Among gas exporters, Turkmenistan's government reported robust growth at 6.0% in the first half of 2022, whereas growth in Uzbekistan was 5.4% in the first half of the year. Kazakhstan, the subregion's largest economy, recorded growth of 3.4% during the first half of 2022, higher than in the same period in 2021, partly reflecting sharply higher exports of goods and services. Yet business confidence is beginning to fade amid geopolitical tensions, and heavy reliance on the Caspian Pipeline Consortium for oil exports through the Russian Federation poses a risk to the outlook of the country.

Accelerating global commodity prices and other factors augmented inflationary pressures throughout the Caucasus and Central Asia. Forecasts for average inflation in the subregion are thus raised from 8.8% to 11.5% in 2022 and from 7.1% to 8.5% in 2023 (Figure 3.1.2).

Figure 3.1.2 Inflation in the Caucasus and Central Asia

Higher than expected inflation in most countries during H1 2022 prompts a rise in projected inflation for the subregion in 2022 and 2023.

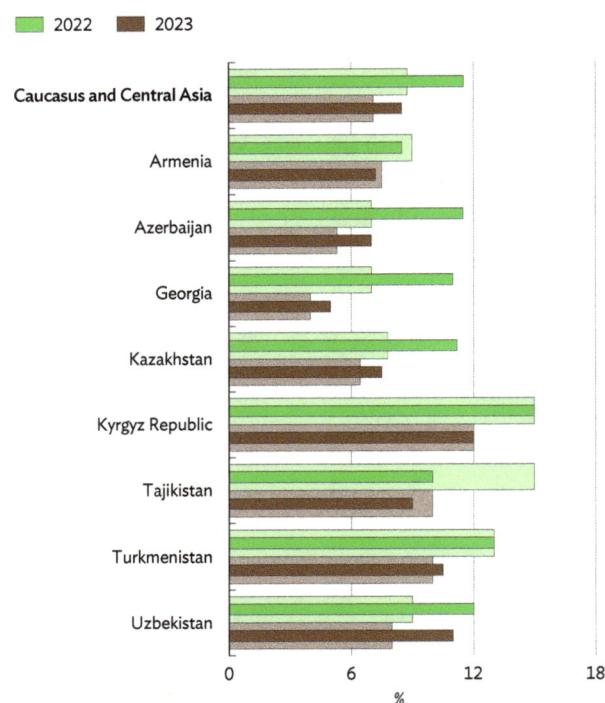

H = half.

Note: Lighter colored bars are *Asian Development Outlook 2022* forecasts.

Source: *Asian Development Outlook* database.

Most of the subregion's economies recorded double-digit inflation during the first half of 2022. This *Update* raises projections for Azerbaijan, Georgia, Kazakhstan, Turkmenistan in 2023, and Uzbekistan. Azerbaijan's inflation reached 12.9% in the first 6 months of 2022, reflecting elevated food prices and a rise in utility tariffs. In Georgia, inflation accelerated to 12.9% by July 2022, and in Kazakhstan to 12.3%, both mainly due to food prices. Inflation information is not available for recent months in Turkmenistan, but prices appear to have risen notably for food and other products with imported components. Uzbekistan's inflation was 10.6% in the first half of the year, reflecting rising wages and pensions, price deregulation for domestic wheat, and higher import costs. In the Kyrgyz Republic, sharp increases in food and energy prices lifted inflation to 13.0 % in the first 7 months of 2022. First half inflation stayed in single digits in Armenia and Tajikistan, at 8.1% and 8.3%, respectively, partly thanks to monetary tightening.

Figure 3.1.3 Current account balance in the Caucasus and Central Asia

Exceptionally high petroleum exports and inward money transfers in several countries have led to an upward revision in the average current account balance for the subregion in 2022 and 2023.

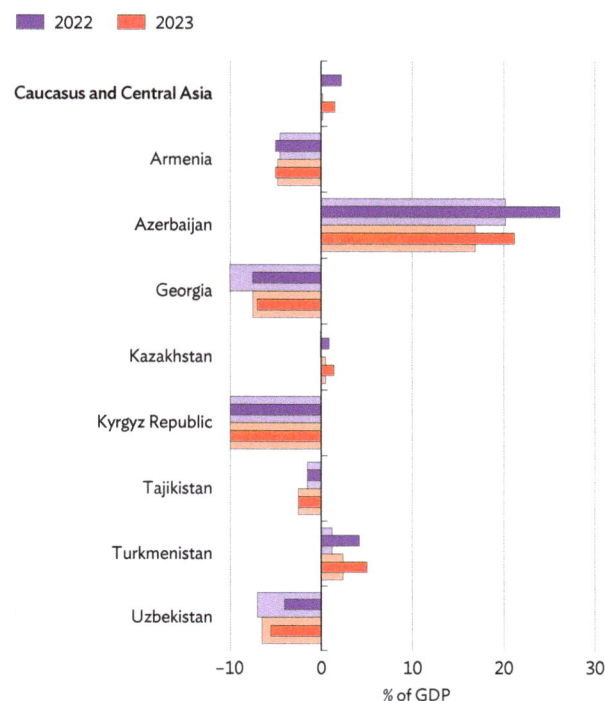

GDP = gross domestic product.
Note: Lighter colored bars are *Asian Development Outlook 2022* forecasts.
Source: *Asian Development Outlook* database.

The economies of the Caucasus and Central Asia are forecast to have a weighted average current account surplus equal to 2.2% of GDP in 2022 and 1.5% in 2023, well above earlier projections of 0.0% and 0.2% in *ADO 2022* (Figure 3.1.3). Higher surpluses or lower deficits are now projected for Azerbaijan, Georgia, Kazakhstan, Turkmenistan, and Uzbekistan. With oil prices elevated, Azerbaijan recorded a massive current account surplus equal to 22.4% of GDP in the first quarter of the year. Georgia had a current account deficit at 12.5% of GDP in the first quarter of 2022, but it is projected to narrow starting in the second quarter as an influx of Russian citizens to Georgia helped raise inward money transfers by 68.5% year on year in the first 7 months of 2022. Kazakhstan's current account is estimated to have been a surplus equal to 7.2% of GDP during the first half of 2022, with the merchandise trade surplus more than doubling thanks to higher oil and gas exports.

Gas exports from Turkmenistan to the People's Republic of China are estimated to have increased by 50% in the first half of 2022 over the same period in 2021. Uzbekistan's current account deficit narrowed sharply to 1.4% of GDP in the first half of 2022 thanks to a temporary increase in inward money transfers. In Armenia, the deficit widened to 9.3% of GDP in the first quarter of 2022 because higher imports raised the merchandise trade deficit. However, transfers from abroad and service exports including tourism may offset part of this deficit as the year progresses. While the Kyrgyz Republic recorded a deficit equal to 18.3% of GDP in the first quarter of 2022 as gold exports plunged and merchandise imports rose sharply, gold exports are expected to recover during the rest of the year. In Tajikistan, the merchandise trade deficit expanded by 70% in the first half of 2022, compared with the same period last year, as imports rose by 24.2% while exports stagnated.

Kazakhstan

With the economy adjusting only gradually to a deteriorating economic environment of supply chain disruption, exchange rate volatility, and global inflation amplified by the Russian invasion of Ukraine, this *Update* marginally reduces growth projections for 2022 and 2023. Larger-than-expected increases in global commodity prices prompt higher inflation projections for both years. Robust petroleum exports support upward revisions to projections for current account balances in both 2022 and 2023.

Updated assessment

The economy expanded at an annual rate of 3.4% in the first half of 2022, somewhat above 2.2% in the same period of 2021, as exceptionally strong export earnings financed higher government expenditure (Figure 3.1.4). Services grew by 2.1%, up from a 1.4% increase in the first half of 2021, as the removal of COVID-19 travel restrictions and quarantine measures boosted trade and transport by 6.2%, with passenger traffic up by 19.1%. Continued vaccination progress and a decline in the number of cases has allowed Kazakhstan to gradually remove COVID-19 social distancing and quarantine restrictions. In June, the authorities lifted requirements for testing and proof of vaccination status for travelers entering Kazakhstan.

Figure 3.1.4 Supply-side contributions to growth

Growth in the first half of 2022 was higher than a year earlier.

■ Agriculture
■ Construction
■ Industry
■ Services
— Gross domestic product

Percentage point

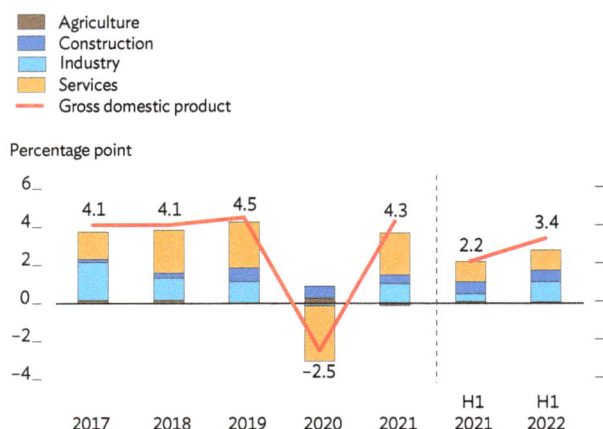

H = half.

Source: Republic of Kazakhstan. Agency for Strategic Planning and Reforms. Bureau of National Statistics (accessed 31 August 2022).

Figure 3.1.5 Average inflation

Inflation accelerated sharply in the first 7 months of 2022.

■ Food, beverages, and tobacco
■ Nonfood goods
■ Services
— All goods and services

%, period average

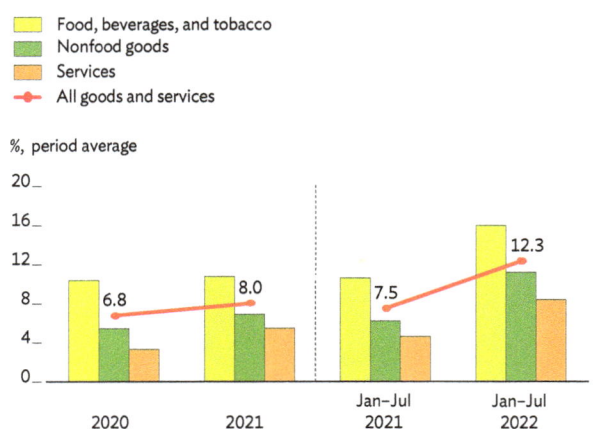

Source: Republic of Kazakhstan. Agency for Strategic Planning and Reforms. Bureau of National Statistics (accessed 31 August 2022).

Industry expanded by 3.5%, backed by a 5.8% rise in manufacturing partly due to the government's import substitution program. Mining increased by 1.9% as oil and gas production rose by 1.2% in line with production expansion quotas agreed with the Organization of the Petroleum Exporting Countries and other major oil producers (OPEC+). Growth in construction remained strong at 9.2%, benefiting from state housing and infrastructure support programs. Agriculture expanded by 1.4% on higher livestock production.

Demand-side data, available for the first quarter of 2022, show that growth came mainly from net exports, as exports of goods and services rose by 24.6% and imports by 11.8%. Consumption declined by 1.9% as private consumption fell by 0.8% and public consumption by 6.3%. Investment expanded by 1.2%, with fixed investment in housing and infrastructure projects rising by 1.6%.

Average inflation in the first 7 months of 2022 accelerated to 12.3% from 7.5% in the same period a year earlier, reflecting price increases of 16.0% for food, 11.2% for other goods, and 8.4% for services (Figure 3.1.5). Supply chain disruption from food export bans imposed by the Russian Federation led to shortages of staple foods and jumps in prices of 52.6% for sugar and 22.8% for wheat.

In the first half of 2022, the central bank actively managed adverse spillover effects from the Russian invasion of Ukraine. Following a sharp rise of 325 basis points in its key policy rate to 13.5% in February, the central bank raised it by 50 basis points in April and again in July to 14.5% (Figure 3.1.6). Broad money growth decelerated to 1.1% in the first half of 2022, following a surge by 20.8% in 2021 (Figure 3.1.7). In the first 6 months of 2022, deposits grew by 1.4% and credit by 8.4%, with lending to firms up by 4.2%, consumer credit by 7.7%, and mortgages by 17.6%. However, net international reserves fell by 2.2%, dragging down net foreign assets.

Figure 3.1.6 Policy rate

The central bank sharply raised its policy interest rate during the first half of 2022.

% end of period

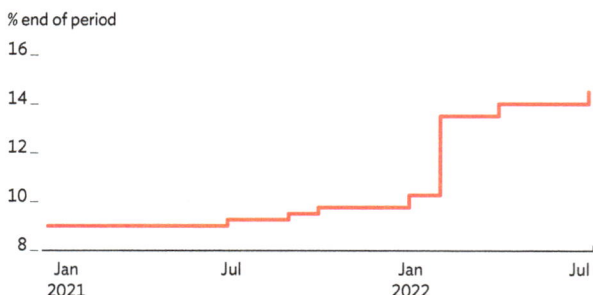

Source: Haver Analytics (accessed 31 August 2022).

Figure 3.1.7 Broad money

Growth in broad money and credit both declined during H1 of 2022.

■ Broad money growth
— Credit growth

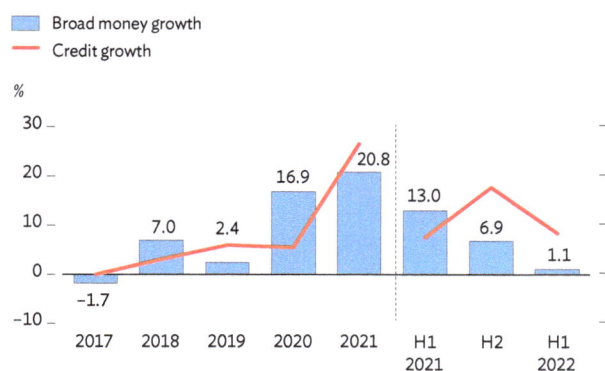

H = half.
Note: Broad money and credit growth are from December of the previous year.
Source: Republic of Kazakhstan. Agency for Strategic Planning and Reforms. Bureau of National Statistics (accessed 31 August 2022).

Figure 3.1.8 Fiscal indicators

Higher revenue and lower expenditure cut the fiscal deficit in the first half of 2022.

■ Revenue
■ Expenditure
— Fiscal balance

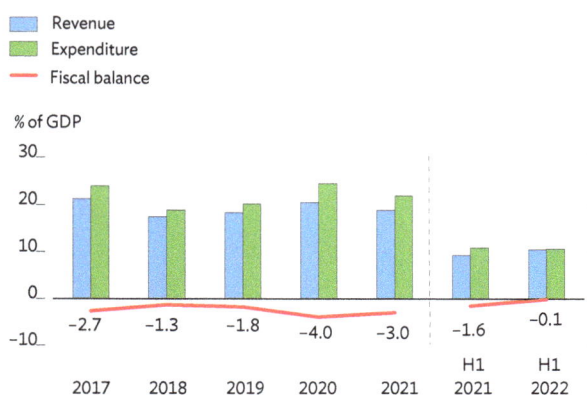

GDP = gross domestic product, H = half.
Source: Republic of Kazakhstan. Agency for Strategic Planning and Reforms. Bureau of National Statistics (accessed 31 August 2022).

Foreign currency deposits constituted 35.9% of all deposits, declining marginally over the period, while deposits in tenge, the national currency, rose by 2.6%. The share of nonperforming loans increased from 3.3% at the end of 2021 to 3.6% in June 2022.

Notably higher revenue sharply narrowed the budget deficit in the first half of 2022 (Figure 3.1.8), though state budget expenditure was 19.5% higher than in the same period of 2021 as government spending rose by 38.9% for defense, 28.7% for education, and 22.0% for security and public order. In April, planned state budget expenditure for 2022 was raised by 16.7% to support employment programs, housing and infrastructure, agriculture, and manufacturing—as well as to index salaries and pensions to inflation. Transfers from the National Fund of the Republic of Kazakhstan (NFRK), which funds almost a quarter of the planned budget, are financing the additional outlays. In the first 6 months of 2022, tax revenue grew by 46.8%, with increases of 68.8% from corporate taxes, 44.8% from value-added tax, and 38.1% from personal income tax as economic activity expanded. A doubling of oil export duty collections and the expiration of tax holidays and waivers also raised revenue substantially.

In the first half of 2022, the tenge fluctuated significantly, depreciating by 18.7% against the US dollar by mid-March despite central bank interventions exceeding $1.4 billion (Figure 3.1.9).

Figure 3.1.9 Exchange rate

The tenge–US dollar exchange rate fluctuated considerably from January to July 2022.

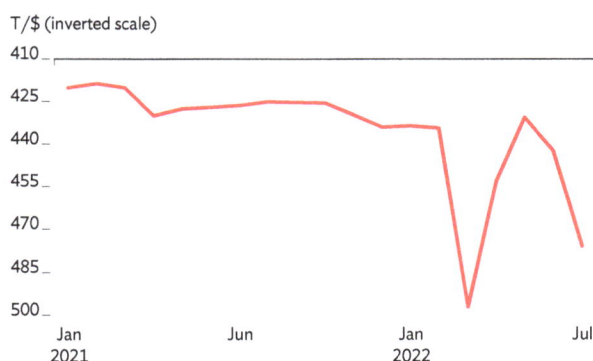

Source: National Bank of the Republic of Kazakhstan (accessed 31 August 2022).

On top of the NFRK converting $2.7 billion in foreign exchange to tenge before transferring funds to the state budget, the government asked state enterprises to sell foreign exchange earnings. These developments and rising commodity prices briefly reversed tenge depreciation in late May, though the currency subsequently depreciated by 10% to early August. During the first half of 2022, the value of the tenge against the US dollar averaged 6.1% below the average in the first half of 2021.

Figure 3.1.10 Foreign currency reserves and sovereign wealth fund assets

Gross reserves and sovereign wealth fund assets both declined from January to July 2022.

Source: National Bank of the Republic of Kazakhstan (accessed 31 August 2022).

Figure 3.1.11 External and public sector external debt

External debt declined during the first quarter of 2022, as did public sector external debt.

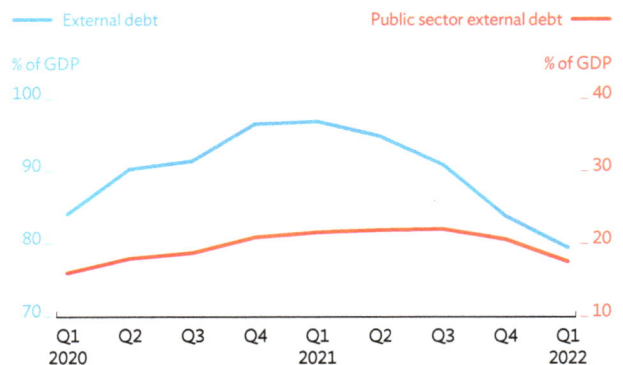

GDP = gross domestic product, Q = quarter.
Source: National Bank of the Republic of Kazakhstan (accessed 31 August 2022).

Gross foreign exchange reserves declined by 7.0% to $32.0 billion in June 2022, of which 69.9% constituted monetary gold (Figure 3.1.10). Reserves provided cover for 8.1 months of imports of goods and services. In the first half of 2022, net receipts to the NFRK were triple those in the same period of 2021 as tax payments from oil companies exceeded transfers to the state budget. However, NFRK assets declined to an estimated $51.9 billion as budget transfers and the effect of stock market decline exceeded inflow from taxes on oil export earnings. External debt declined to $160.8 billion, equal to 80.9% of GDP, at the end of March 2022 (Figure 3.1.11). Intercompany debt, primarily for oil and gas projects, declined to $94.3 billion, or 47.5% of GDP, with $15.5 billion coming due in 2022. Public sector external debt declined to $35.5 billion, or 17.9% of GDP, with $3.7 billion due in 2022.

Preliminary estimates for the first half of 2022 indicate a current account surplus of $6.6 billion, equal to 7.2% of GDP, as the trade surplus in goods more than doubled (Figure 3.1.12). Merchandise exports rose by 56.8% to $42.4 billion, reflecting an 84.7% increase in oil and gas exports. Merchandise imports expanded by 15.9%, reaching $20.7 billion, with increases of 21.5% for intermediate goods and 9.8% for consumer products. High concentration of foreign investment in mining allowed foreign investors' profit transfers to increase by 28.9% to $13.2 billion.

Figure 3.1.12 Current account balance and components

The current account moved into surplus during the first half of 2022 as higher petroleum prices sharply raised export earnings.

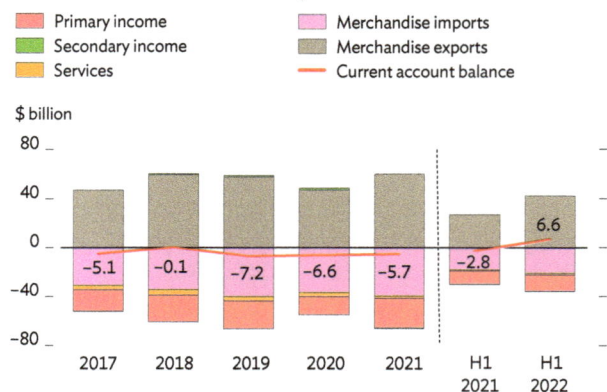

GDP = gross domestic product, H = half.
Source: National Bank of the Republic of Kazakhstan (accessed 31 August 2022).

Prospects

On the supply side, some further growth is expected in manufacturing and services. Government import substitution programs to support manufacturing are anticipated to increase local production modestly, helping address supply chain constraints. Growth in services will continue, supported by gains in hospitality, trade, and transportation from pent-up demand.

State agriculture support measures will stimulate some investment and production, though water shortages and outdated equipment constrain growth prospects. Rising global demand for commodities and higher oil production quotas agreed by OPEC+ will support mining. However, reliance on the Caspian Pipeline Consortium oil export route, which transports about 80% of Kazakhstan's oil to European markets, poses a downside risk to the outlook. The government is actively exploring ways to diversify oil export routes, which will require time and investment.

On the demand side, a projected 12.5% increase in exports should outweigh rising imports. However, consumption is projected to grow in 2022 by only 1.9%, primarily from higher private spending. Investment will stagnate, reflecting a deteriorating global economic outlook under persistent inflation, rate hikes, and declining business confidence amid the Russian invasion of Ukraine. Moreover, the latest central bank enterprise survey reported weakening activity in all sectors except services. With declining confidence and weakening activity outside of services, this *Update* marginally reduces growth projections for both 2022 and 2023 (Table 3.1.1 and Figure 3.1.13).

Inflation is accelerating, primarily from exogenous shocks. Supply chain disruption, rising energy prices, and currency depreciation have raised the cost of producing and transporting goods. Fiscal support measures help to cushion the negative effects but at the cost of adding to inflationary pressure. The central bank is expected to tighten monetary policy further by raising its key policy rate and absorbing excess liquidity, though inflation will likely remain well above the bank's target range. With record inflation during the first 7 months of 2022, this *Update* raises inflation projections for both 2022 and 2023 (Figure 3.1.14).

With the April 2022 amendment to the state budget providing additional fiscal support, expenditure is now projected to equal 22.6% of GDP this year, up from 21.7% in *ADO 2022*. The revenue forecast is also raised, from 18.7% of GDP to 19.6%, reflecting a decision to increase transfers from the NFRK by more than 55%, rather than reducing them as earlier envisioned. The 2022 budget deficit will remain at 3.0% of GDP, with the non-oil deficit rising from 8.6% of GDP to 9.8%.

Table 3.1.1 Selected economic indicators in Kazakhstan, %

Weakening activity prompts lower growth forecasts, and high commodity prices raise projections for inflation and current account surpluses.

	2021	2022		2023	
		ADO 2022	Update	ADO 2022	Update
GDP growth	4.3	3.2	3.0	3.9	3.7
Inflation	8.0	7.8	11.2	6.4	7.5
CAB/GDP	–3.0	–0.1	0.9	0.5	1.4

ADO = *Asian Development Outlook*, CAB = current account balance, GDP = gross domestic product.
Sources: Asian Development Bank estimates.

Figure 3.1.13 GDP growth

Growth projections for 2022 and 2023 are revised down.

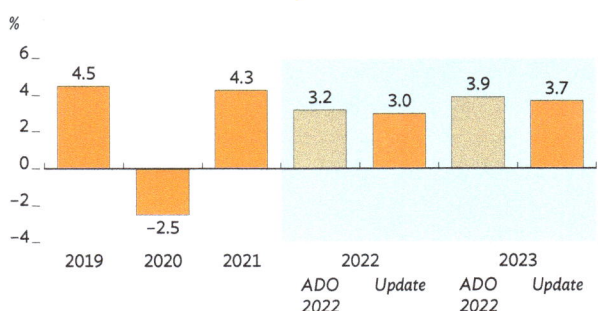

ADO = *Asian Development Outlook*, GDP = gross domestic product.
Source: *ADO* database.

Figure 3.1.14 Inflation

Inflation projections for 2022 and 2023 are increased.

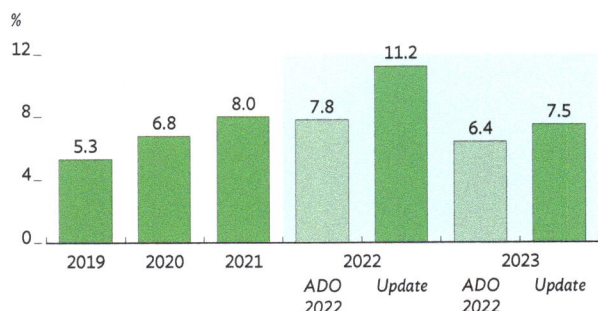

ADO = *Asian Development Outlook*.
Source: *ADO* database.

Government and government-guaranteed debt is now forecast to increase marginally in 2022 to the equivalent of 29.0% of GDP before declining to 28.5% at the end of 2023.

Higher commodity prices are projected to double the merchandise trade surplus in 2022 to a decade high of $39.8 billion, equal to 19.7% of GDP, with a further but smaller increase in 2023. Persistent deficits in services and primary income are expected to widen substantially during the rest of 2022 but by less than the rise in the merchandise trade surplus. In view of these developments, this *Update* revises up current account projections to surpluses equal to 0.9% of GDP in 2022 and 1.4% in 2023 (Figure 3.1.15).

Higher transfers to the budget are projected to trim NFRK assets to $55.5 billion at the end of 2022, below the previous forecast of $58.0 billion. Assets will then rise again to $57.0 billion at the end of 2023, less than the earlier projection of $60.0 billion. Projections for gross international reserves are unchanged at $31.5 billion at the end of 2022, cover for 7.4 months of imports of goods and services, rising to $33.8 billion at the end of 2023.

External debt including intercompany debt is now forecast to be equivalent to 82% of GDP at the end of 2022, below the earlier forecast of 87%, and to 78% at the end of 2023, revised down from 85%, as oil and mining companies use windfall profits to repay intercompany debt.

Figure 3.1.15 Current account balance

The current account is now expected to show a surplus in 2022 and a larger surplus in 2023.

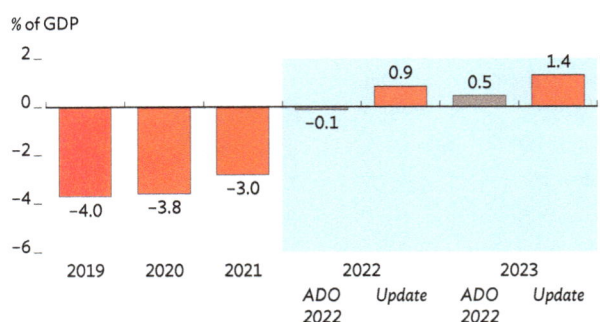

ADO = Asian Development Outlook, GDP = gross domestic product.
Source: ADO database.

Other economies

Armenia

Despite a challenging external environment, the economy grew by a strong 11.0% in the first half of 2022, more than expected and well above 3.8% growth in the first half of 2021. Growth was underpinned by buoyant private consumption and soaring investment.

On the supply side, services propelled expansion with solid growth by 14.8%, reflecting increases in all segments but led primarily by vigorous expansion of more than 25% in finance, transportation, hotels, and information and communications services. Industry expanded by 4.6% as gains in manufacturing, electricity generation, and water and waste management outweighed 11.1% decline in mining and quarrying. Construction grew by a robust 21.8%, reflecting higher investment. Less favorable weather in the first half caused agriculture to shrink by 1.8%.

On the demand side, private consumption rose by 10.6%, reflecting unusually large inward money transfers. Public consumption contracted by 2.7% as current fiscal expenditure tightened. Investment, as measured by gross fixed capital formation, grew by 17.7% on higher government and private capital spending. The deficit in net exports widened as imports grew faster than exports. With robust economic activity in the first half of the year, and despite some assumed moderation in demand in the rest of the year, this *Update* raises growth projections for 2022 and, less dramatically, 2023.

Average annual inflation jumped to 8.3% in January–July 2022 from 6.1% a year earlier, reflecting increases of 13.1% for food, 6.4% for other goods, and 3.9% for services. Buoyant domestic demand, rising global commodity prices, and the pass-through effect of higher electricity tariffs from February 2022 and natural gas price hikes from April 2022 all propelled the acceleration.

Table 3.1.2 Selected economic indicators in Armenia, %

Rapid growth during the first half of 2022 prompts an upward revision in forecast growth and current account deficits for 2022 and 2023, while inflation is now projected somewhat lower as prices rose less than expected.

	2021	2022		2023	
		ADO 2022	*Update*	*ADO 2022*	*Update*
GDP growth	5.7	2.8	7.0	3.8	4.5
Inflation	7.2	9.0	8.5	7.5	7.2
CAB/GDP	-4.0	-4.5	-5.0	-4.7	-5.0

ADO = Asian Development Outlook, CAB = current account balance, GDP = gross domestic product.
Source: Asian Development Bank estimates.

Inflation was 9.3% year on year in July, well above the Central Bank of Armenia's 2.5%–5.5% target range. To counter inflationary pressure, the central bank tightened monetary policy, raising the policy rate by 175 basis points in three steps to 9.5% in June 2022. With monetary tightening, an expected small moderation in aggregate demand, and strong appreciation of the Armenian dram against the US dollar and euro, this *Update* slightly reduces the inflation projections for 2022 and 2023.

The current account deficit widened considerably to equal 9.3% of GDP in the first quarter of 2022 from 2.8% a year earlier as a larger trade deficit more than offset surpluses in services and private transfers. The merchandise trade deficit widened to 14.1% of GDP from 9.3% a year earlier as a 44.3% increase in imports outpaced a 27.8% increase in exports. With imports expected to continue rising more quickly than exports, a further widening of the merchandise trade deficit is expected in the rest of the year. Higher transfers and increased gains from tourism, transportation, and information and communication technologies are expected to offset part of the larger trade deficit in goods. Accordingly, this *Update* revises upward current account deficit projections for 2022 and 2023.

Azerbaijan

Growth jumped to 6.2% during the first half of 2022 from 2.1% during the same period in 2021 as the economy aside from the large hydrocarbon industry expanded by 9.6%. Services grew by 9.6%, reflecting strong performance in transportation, a rebound in retail trade, and a doubling of value added in hospitality as pandemic travel bans were lifted. Manufacturing grew by 4.5% with strong gains in construction materials and metals, food processing, and textiles. Mining picked up by 2.5%, with expansion in both oil and gas production, while construction grew by 7.7%. Agriculture stalled during the period, with higher livestock production offsetting a 2.7% decline in crop output.

On the demand side, private consumption grew by 4.8% during January–May 2022 as salary increases boosted household incomes and higher consumer confidence helped raise bank lending by 5.2%. Public consumption grew by 5.1%, with civil service salary increases and higher spending on social services. While investment outside of hydrocarbons jumped by 14.6%, weaker investment in hydrocarbons, particularly for gas, cut total investment by 3.1%.

Higher oil prices encouraged the government to amend the fiscal budget in June to increase projected revenue by 8.9% and raise expenditure by 8.1%. These amendments will further stimulate the economy by raising salaries and public investment while remaining consistent with new fiscal rules limiting the non-oil deficit in the consolidated budget and the ratio of public debt to GDP. With higher oil earnings and stronger domestic demand, despite a possible decline in consumer confidence as continued inflation cuts real income, this *Update* raises the growth forecast for 2022 while maintaining a lower rate for 2023.

Inflation during January–June 2022 accelerated to 12.9% year on year from 4.3% in the same period of 2021. Prices rose by 18.4% for food, 6.7% for other goods, and 10.3% for services. High global food price inflation triggered the spike in food prices, while increased tariffs for fuel and other utilities in 2021 boosted inflation in services.

Table 3.1.3 Selected economic indicators in Azerbaijan, %

High petroleum prices prompt upward revisions to forecasts for growth in 2022 and current account surpluses in 2022 and 2023, along with higher projections for inflation in both years because of elevated global food prices.

	2021	2022		2023	
		ADO 2022	Update	ADO 2022	Update
GDP growth	5.6	3.7	4.2	2.8	2.8
Inflation	6.7	7.0	11.5	5.3	7.0
CAB/GDP	12.9	20.2	26.2	16.9	21.2

ADO = Asian Development Outlook, CAB = current account balance, GDP = gross domestic product.
Source: Asian Development Bank estimates.

A stable exchange rate kept inflation from rising even faster. The jump in inflation led the government to raise the monthly minimum wage by 20% to AZN300. In addition, the central bank raised its policy rate by 50 basis points in two steps to 7.75% in March, maintaining it through July as inflationary pressure moderated. With the jump in inflation during the first part of the year, this *Update* raises the projection for 2022 but maintains it for 2023 as administered utility prices are expected to remain unchanged.

The current account achieved a surplus equal to 22.4% of GDP in the first quarter of 2022 as oil prices rose further. Higher oil prices raised the merchandise trade surplus to $5.4 billion in the first quarter 2022 from $3.1 billion in the same period of 2021 as exports jumped by 8.1%. Imports grew by 14.5%, with high imports of food products. Elevated oil prices are expected to keep the current account surplus high for the rest of the year. Assets of the State Oil Fund of the Republic of Azerbaijan inched up by 0.5% in the first quarter of 2022 to $45.3 billion, equal to 83% of GDP. On these developments, this *Update* projects wider current account surpluses in 2022 and 2023.

Georgia

Real GDP expanded by an estimated 10.5% in the first half of 2022, driven by growth in services and manufacturing. Services increased by 15.3% on gains in accommodation, food services, trade, transport, and real estate. Industry expanded by 18.0%, led by manufacturing and utilities. Agriculture grew by 2.3%, reflecting favorable weather and a good harvest.

Growth on the demand side came from strong private consumption, higher export and tourism revenue, and a large inflow of money transfers from Georgians working abroad and Russian citizens entering Georgia. With higher inflow of money transfers and encouraging growth figures, this *Update* raises growth projections for 2022 and 2023, despite heightened geopolitical risks from the ongoing Russian invasion of Ukraine (Table 3.1.4).

Average annual inflation accelerated to 12.9% in the first 7 months of 2022 from 7.2% in the same period of 2021, led by food prices. Prices rose by 19.0% for food, 9.6% for other goods, and 7.1% for services, including increases of 19.3% for transport and 21.6% for utilities. The producer price index, which often presages increases in consumer prices, rose by 15.0% in the same period, while core inflation—excluding food, energy, and regulated tariffs, including some for transport—was 7.1%. With double-digit inflation in consumer prices, the National Bank of Georgia, the central bank, raised its policy rate by 50 basis points to 11.0% in March 2022 to help contain inflation and manage inflationary expectations. After some volatility following the Russian invasion of Ukraine, the currency appreciated significantly, helping to contain imported inflation. With higher-than-expected global commodity prices and strong domestic growth, this *Update* raises inflation forecasts for 2022 and 2023.

Solid economic growth and the gradual unwinding of pandemic response measures have effectively tightened fiscal policy. Revenue grew at an annual rate of 33.6% through June 2022 as high personal and corporate income tax receipts more than offset an increase in public pensions equal to 0.6% of GDP, a 10% hike in the public sector wage bill, and targeted support to the vulnerable.

Table 3.1.4 Selected economic indicators in Georgia, %

Growth and inflation will be higher than forecast earlier in ADO 2022, and current account deficits smaller.

	2021	2022		2023	
		ADO 2022	Update	ADO 2022	Update
GDP growth	10.4	3.5	7.0	5.0	6.0
Inflation	9.6	7.0	11.0	4.0	5.0
CAB/GDP	−10.1	−10.0	−7.5	−7.5	−7.0

ADO = *Asian Development Outlook*, CAB = current account balance, GDP = gross domestic product.
Sources: National Statistics Office of Georgia; National Bank of Georgia; Asian Development Bank estimates.

The fiscal deficit is thus projected to fall from 6.1% in 2021 to less than 4.0% in 2022, with public debt declining from the equivalent of 49.5% of GDP to 47.0%, reflecting in part reduced public borrowing.

The current account deficit widened slightly from the equivalent of 12.5% of GDP in the first quarter of 2021 to 13.0% a year later but is expected to narrow from the second quarter. In the first 7 months of 2022, merchandise exports increased by 36.3% and imports by 34.8%. Exports to Ukraine fell by 21.1%, but those to the Russian Federation remained largely unchanged. Inflow of money transfers soared by 68.5% year on year in the first 7 months of 2022 as inflow from the Russian Federation surged by nearly sixfold during April–July 2022, representing 50.3% of all such transfers, due to an influx of Russian citizens to Georgia. About 2.3 million travelers visited Georgia in the first 7 months of 2022, a 214.4% annual increase from 2021, though receipts from tourism remained about 20% below those in the same period of 2019, before the pandemic. Considering these trends, this *Update* trims forecasts for current account deficits in 2022 and 2023. Foreign direct investment more than quadrupled to $568 million in the first quarter of 2022, reflecting a high share of reinvested earnings.

Kyrgyz Republic

The economy grew by 7.7% during the first 7 months of 2022, or by 4.7% excluding output from the Kumtor gold mine, with increases nearly across the board. Industry expanded by 17.8% on gains of 45.6% in metal processing, 27.5% in wood and wood products, and 12.9% in food and tobacco. Services grew by 3.5% with an increase of 12.5% in food and accommodation as 3.8 million international visitors nearly doubled their numbers during the same period last year. Construction expanded by 3.6%, reflecting higher investment in housing and facilities for mining and manufacturing, supplying electricity, transportation, cargo storage, hotels and restaurants, education, and health care. Agriculture grew by 8.4% on gains in crop production, particularly wheat and barley.

The Russian invasion of Ukraine and resulting sanctions on the Russian Federation constrain the outlook for growth because of the Kyrgyz Republic's close economic ties through remittances, trade, investment, and tourism. The impact of the war is still evolving, and a major slowdown is expected in the second half of this year. Nevertheless, with sustained growth during the first 7 months of the year and a government anti-crisis plan estimated to equal 2.5% of GDP, this *Update* raises growth projections for 2022 and 2023 (Table 3.1.5).

During the first 7 months of 2022, average annual inflation reached 13.0%, mainly due to higher global prices for food and energy and currency depreciation against the US dollar in March and April (though later reversed). Prices rose by 12.6% for food, 5.6% for other goods, and 4.9% for services. To curb inflation and respond to depreciation, the National Bank of the Kyrgyz Republic, the central bank, raised the policy rate in March 2022 by 6.0 percentage points to 14.0%. In addition, the government cut the value-added tax on imports of key staple foods. With inflation expected to remain high in 2022 because of food and energy prices and then moderate slightly in 2023, this *Update* retains earlier inflation forecasts for 2022 and 2023.

Table 3.1.5 Selected economic indicators in the Kyrgyz Republic, %

Growth performance during the first half of 2022 prompts an upward revision to growth forecasts for 2022 and 2023.

	2021	2022		2023	
		ADO 2022	Update	ADO 2022	Update
GDP growth	3.6	2.0	3.0	2.5	3.5
Inflation	11.9	15.0	15.0	12.0	12.0
CAB/GDP	–8.7	–10.0	–10.0	–10.0	–10.0

ADO = *Asian Development Outlook,* CAB = current account balance, GDP = gross domestic product.
Sources: National Bank of the Kyrgyz Republic; Asian Development Bank estimates.

In the first quarter of 2022, the current account deficit equaled 18.3% of GDP. Data for the first half of 2022 showed merchandise exports contracting by 40.5% compared to the same period last year, mainly because of a substantial decline in gold exports. During the same period, other exports grew by a strong 52.9% over the same period in 2021, while imports jumped by 68.7%. Money transfers rose by 7.5% during the first half of the year compared to the same period of 2021, perhaps including inflows sent by firms relocating from the Russian Federation.

Meanwhile, recession in the Russian Federation, the main host country of Kyrgyz migrant workers, may reduce migrant remittances. Gold exports will likely increase in the coming months, following the recent settlement of a dispute at the Kumtor gold mine between the Kyrgyz authorities and the private investor. Exports of services will be sustained. With these developments, this *Update* sustains forecasts for a steady current account deficit in 2022 and 2023.

Tajikistan

During the first half of 2022, growth slowed to 7.4% from 8.7% a year earlier. The slowdown reflected moderating production, weak exports, and lower consumption as recession in the Russian Federation cut remittances while food prices surged and private lending diminished. Nevertheless, growth exceeded earlier projections because recovery in the value of the Russian ruble against the US dollar trimmed the decline in remittances. Expansion in industry dropped from 23.4% to 17.3%, reflecting disruption in the supply of inputs. Rising fertilizer prices and less favorable weather slowed growth in agriculture from 8.1% to 7.2%. Expansion in services moderated from 16.5% to 12.8% as a 10% fall in remittances in the first 5 months of 2022 relative to a year earlier slowed growth in retail trade from 17.1% to 9.3% and disruption to external trade cut transportation by 8.5%.

On the demand side, expansion in gross fixed investment fell from 23.7% during the first half of 2021 to 4.1% this year as cuts in nonpriority government spending and the decline in remittances and disposable household income slashed growth in construction, much of which is for private housing, from 33.5% to 2.5%. Lower remittances and surging inflation constrained growth in consumption, while rising imports opposite flat exports expanded the deficit in net exports.

The government has acted to alleviate the adverse effect of external shocks on the economy by approving in March an action plan to mitigate potential risks to the national economy, its cost estimated to equal 2.5% of GDP. The resulting higher social spending is, along with shortfalls in value-added tax collection and social insurance levies on firms, projected to widen the fiscal deficit to the equivalent of 3.5% of GDP in 2022 from 2.0% in 2021.

With growth stronger than expected during the first half of 2022, this *Update* raises growth projections for 2022 and 2023 (Table 3.1.6). However, falling remittances, continuing trade disruption, and a slowdown in the Rogun hydropower project are forecast to constrain consumption and domestic business activity later this year.

Table 3.1.6 Selected economic indicators in Tajikistan, %

Growth projections are raised for 2022 and 2023, and inflation forecasts reduced.

	2021	2022 ADO 2022	2022 Update	2023 ADO 2022	2023 Update
GDP growth	9.2	2.0	4.0	3.0	5.0
Inflation	8.0	15.0	10.0	10.0	9.0
CAB/GDP	2.6	−1.5	−1.5	−2.5	−2.5

ADO = *Asian Development Outlook*, CAB = current account balance, GDP = gross domestic product.
Source: Asian Development Bank estimates.

Reported annual inflation averaged 8.3% in the first half of 2022, down from 9.0% in the same period of 2021. Prices rose by 9.6% for food, 6.6.% for other goods, and 8.4% for services, reflecting a surge in global commodity prices. To restrain inflation, the National Bank of Tajikistan, the central bank, raised its policy rate from 13.25% to 13.50% on 22 August and expanded sales of deposit certificates to absorb liquidity. In response to pressures on the exchange rate from ruble depreciation and the drop in remittances, and to eliminate a significant gap between official and market exchange rates, on 9 March the central bank devalued the Tajik somoni by 15% against the US dollar. The somoni subsequently appreciated by 21% to the end of June as the ruble strengthened against the US dollar. In addition, a hike in electricity tariffs was postponed until 2023. With these developments, this *Update* cuts inflation forecasts for 2022 and 2023.

The merchandise trade deficit expanded by 70% in the first half of 2022 relative to the same period a year earlier as merchandise exports stagnated at $1.2 billion, while merchandise imports rose by 24.2% to $2.3 billion. Nevertheless, purchases of domestically produced gold and limited currency interventions kept international reserves stable at cover for about 7 months of imports. In view of these developments, and with remittances projected to fall by at least 25% in 2022, this *Update* maintains projections for current account deficits in both 2022 and 2023.

Turkmenistan

Growth at 6.0% for the first half of 2022, as reported by the government, was virtually unchanged from 6.1% reported for the same period in 2021.

As reported, supply side growth came from all sectors, with the large hydrocarbon economy expanding mainly from higher production and exports of natural gas, and the nonhydrocarbon economy benefiting from partial relaxation of restrictions on external trade and travel. Besides increased hydrocarbon output, growth in industry reflected higher output of electricity, chemicals, textiles, food processing, and other agro-industrial products, as well as stepped-up construction. Private firms involved in import-substitution programs received substantial government support. The gradual lifting of quarantine measures boosted services, with gains in retail trade, international and domestic transportation, catering, and hospitality relative to weak performance in the first half of 2021 under strict lockdown policies. As the government's main priority is to enhance domestic agricultural production for greater food security, support to farmers in the form of soft credit and subsidies for fertilizers, machinery, and other services is projected to boost agricultural output. Reports for the first half of 2022 indicate that strategic cotton and wheat crops have been sown toward meeting the government's annual production targets, as have a large variety of horticultural crops.

On the demand side, the government reported increased net exports and higher public investment in industrial and social infrastructure. However, notable inflation continued to limit real household incomes, as did constraints on employment from structural issues, suppressing private consumption. In view of these developments, this *Update* marginally reduces the growth projection for 2022 but maintains the projection for 2023 (Table 3.1.7).

The government has not reported data on inflation for the first half of 2022. However, observed prices for imported food and other products, medicines, and locally produced goods with imported components have continued to rise in line with earlier projections.

Table 3.1.7 Selected economic indicators in Turkmenistan, %

The projection for growth in 2022 is slightly reduced from ADO 2022, and higher gas exports prompt forecasts for substantially wider current account surpluses in 2022 and 2023.

	2021	2022		2023	
		ADO 2022	*Update*	*ADO 2022*	*Update*
GDP growth	5.0	6.0	5.8	5.8	5.8
Inflation	12.5	13.0	13.0	10.0	10.5
CAB/GDP	0.6	1.2	4.2	2.4	5.0

ADO = *Asian Development Outlook*, CAB = current account balance, GDP = gross domestic product.
Source: Asian Development Bank estimates.

Monetary policy remains focused on controlling inflation by keeping the official exchange rate unchanged, supplemented by price controls and the distribution of selected foodstuffs at subsidized prices. Access to foreign currency remains restricted, fueling a parallel market in foreign exchange with a substantial difference between official and parallel market exchange rates. In view of these developments and the lagged effects of an unusually sharp rise in global food prices earlier, this *Update* slightly raises the inflation forecast for 2023.

Gas exports to the People's Republic of China in the first half of 2022 are estimated to be 50% higher than in the same period of last year. More generally, higher demand for gas exports from Turkmenistan to the People's Republic of China and other countries in the region may raise total exports by 30% in 2022 and a further 10% in 2023. Imports are projected to rise slowly by 5%–7% annually, constrained by the government's import substitution programs and capital controls. With exports increasing faster than imports, this *Update* more than doubles the current account surpluses projected for both 2022 and 2023. Scheduled repayment of external public obligations is projected to reduce external debt by a further 35% over the forecast period to equal 5.2% of GDP in 2022 and 3.3% in 2023.

Uzbekistan

The government reported growth slowing from 7.2% in the first half of 2021 to 5.4% in the same period of 2022. Growth was nonetheless higher than expected as expansion in construction and investment remained strong despite uncertainty about investment inflows from the Russian Federation. Expansion in industry moderated from 9.2% to 5.1%, with smaller gains in manufacturing and a decline in mining and quarrying. Growth in services decreased from 9.7% to 7.3%, with slower expansion in trade, transport, and storage. Growth in construction soared from 0.3% to 6.2% on gains in housing, infrastructure, and repairs. Expansion in agriculture edged up from 2.1% to 2.7% as both crop and livestock production increased.

On the demand side, growth in gross capital formation accelerated to 9.4% from 5.9% a year earlier on higher infrastructure spending and upgrades to machinery and equipment, mainly from enterprises' own funds. Consumption grew by an estimated 4.3%, down from 7.1% a year earlier, as rapid inflation curbed real household income and demand despite rising wages and pensions. The deficit in net exports widened by 10.8%, with trade deficits expanding by 8.0% for goods and 23.6% for services.

Shocks from the Russian invasion of Ukraine on food and energy prices and sluggish future remittances will likely curb household income and consumption in the second half of 2022. With these uncertainties, this *Update* retains the growth projection for 2022 but raises it slightly for 2023 (Table 3.1.8).

Despite higher costs for imported food and capital goods, rising wages and pensions, and price deregulation for domestic wheat, inflation decelerated slightly to 10.6% in the first half of 2022 from 10.9% a year earlier. To stabilize food prices, the authorities exempted tax and customs duties on essential foodstuffs until the end of 2022, helping to slow food inflation to 14.2% from 15.5% a year earlier. Inflation for other goods accelerated from 8.6% to 9.0% but for services slowed from 8.4% to 6.6% as planned energy tariff increases were postponed.

Table 3.1.8 Selected economic indicators in Uzbekistan, %

Slower inflation and a sharp decrease in the current account deficit during the first half of 2022 prompt a decline in projected inflation and the current account deficit for 2022 and 2023.

	2021	2022		2023	
		ADO 2022	Update	ADO 2022	Update
GDP growth	7.4	4.0	4.0	4.5	5.0
Inflation	10.7	9.0	12.0	8.0	11.0
CAB/GDP	–7.0	–7.0	–4.0	–6.5	–5.5

ADO = *Asian Development Outlook*, CAB = current account balance, GDP = gross domestic product.
Source: Asian Development Bank estimates.

In response to external inflationary pressure and depreciation of the Uzbek sum against the US dollar, monetary authorities raised the policy rate from 14% to 17% in March 2022, subsequently lowering the rate to 16% in June and 15% in July to support growth as the exchange rate stabilized. With anticipated increases in energy tariffs in the second half of 2022 and continuing high prices for imported food, this *Update* raises earlier inflation projections for 2022 and 2023.

The current account deficit narrowed sharply to equal 1.4% of GDP from 10.9% a year earlier on rising inward money transfers. Exports of goods expanded by 32.3%, reflecting large increases in gold, textiles, copper, and petrochemicals. Imports rose by 21.5% on higher imports of machinery and equipment, ferrous metals, and petrochemicals. Service exports soared by 41.7% as demand for transport and tourism services increased, while imports rose by 32.4% on higher demand for tourism, cargo, business services, and information and communication services. Reported inward money transfers from the Russian Federation increased the income surplus by 138.4%, partly because small exporters and long-term migrant workers switched from informal channels to official methods of sending money to Uzbekistan in response to a recently imposed $10,000 limit on withdrawals of US dollar currency from the Russian Federation. With the current trend in the trade balance and the temporary rise in money transfers, this *Update* trims earlier projections for current account deficits in 2022 and 2023.

EAST ASIA

Subregional GDP growth slowed in the first half of 2022, subdued in particular by COVID-19 lockdowns in the People's Republic of China. The projection in this *Update* for aggregate GDP in the whole year is downgraded from *ADO 2022*, as is the forecast for 2023 but less so. Inflation has been rising, prompting projections for this year and next to be revised higher. This *Update* foresees narrowing subregional current account surpluses in 2022–2023 similar to those projected in April.

Subregional assessment and prospects

The economies of East Asia expanded in aggregate in the first half (H1) of 2022, but at a rate below what was expected in *ADO 2022*. In the People's Republic of China (PRC), economic growth slowed to 2.5% in H1 2022 from 12.7% in H1 2021, with the second quarter (Q2) particularly weak due to a pronounced growth slowdown in services in the face of COVID-19 lockdowns. Growth moderated to 2.9% in the Republic of Korea (ROK) in H1 2022, slowing from Q1 to Q2. Much of remaining growth came from exports, which rose by 6.0% in real terms, supported by robust semiconductor and petroleum product shipments. GDP in Taipei,China grew 3.4% in H1 2022 on robust domestic demand with particular impetus from investment, driven by firms' capital expenditure and green energy and 5G network infrastructure projects. The economy of Hong Kong, China saw marked deterioration in H1 2022 as GDP shrank by 2.6% following worse-than-expected contraction in Q1 and only marginal improvement in Q2 as mobility restrictions to contain a fifth wave of the COVID-19 pandemic weighed heavily on domestic demand.

Mongolia was adversely impacted by supply disruption including pandemic-induced border restrictions with the PRC.

Subregional inflation generally rose in H1 2022 by more than expected. Consumer price inflation in the PRC accelerated to 1.7% in H1 2022 from 0.5% a year earlier, with nonfood prices rising by 2.2%, driven by higher fuel prices and pass-through from increased producer prices. Inflation quickened more rapidly than expected in the ROK to average 4.9% in the first 7 months of the year, reaching 6.3% year on year in July, primarily due to higher prices for oil and food. Inflation in Taipei,China averaged 3.1% in H1 2022, driven by higher global food and oil prices and poor weather that hit fruit and vegetable harvests. Headline consumer price inflation in Hong Kong, China averaged 1.5% in H1 with elevated energy prices, rising prices for food imports from the PRC, and continuing supply chain disruption. In Mongolia, inflation continues to be much higher than elsewhere in the subregion, and it accelerated after the start of the war in Ukraine.

The section on the PRC was written by Dominik Peschel and Wenyu Liu, consultant. The part on other economies by David De Padua, Yothin Jinjarak, Matteo Lanzafame, Pilipinas Quising, Irfan Qureshi, Bold Sandagdorj, and Michael Timbang, consultant. All authors are in the East Asia and Economic Research and Regional Cooperation departments of ADB. Subregional assessment and prospects were written by Eric Clifton, consultant, Economic Research and Regional Cooperation Department of ADB.

Available information paints a mixed picture for East Asian current account balances in H1 2022. The PRC current account surplus increased from the equivalent of 1.4% of GDP in H1 2021 to 2.0% in H1 2022, driven by strengthening merchandise exports. In the ROK, the merchandise trade surplus decreased in the first 5 months of this year by more than the increase in the service trade surplus, resulting in a lower current account surplus estimated to equal 2.3% of GDP, a 41.8% drop compared to the first 5 months of 2021. The current account surplus in Hong Kong, China narrowed from 12.9% of GDP in Q4 2021 to 11.6% in Q1 2022 as falling surpluses in goods and primary income offset a growing surplus in services. In Taipei,China, trade data for H1 2022 indicate that imports grew by 8.7% while exports grew by only 6.6% due to softer global demand. Mongolia continues to experience a current account deficit.

Subregional GDP growth is forecast to slow from 7.7% in 2021 to 3.2% in 2022—significantly lower than projected in *ADO 2022*—before climbing back to 4.2% in 2023 (Figure 3.2.1). Growth in the PRC is expected to improve somewhat in H2 2022, recovering from the weak H1 performance caused by COVID-19 lockdowns. On balance, though, GDP in the PRC is expected to grow by only 3.3% in 2022, or 1.7 percentage points lower than forecast in *ADO 2022*, before expanding by 4.5% in 2023, or 0.3 points lower than forecast in April.

As global growth fades along with stimulus from economic reopening in 2021, GDP growth in the ROK in 2022 and 2023 is forecast to be lower than *ADO 2022* projections. Growth in Hong Kong, China will continue to be held back by a slowing global economy, prolonged supply chain disruption, and high global interest rates. Against this backdrop, this *Update* cuts the *ADO 2022* growth forecast sharply for 2022 but maintains it for 2023. For Taipei,China, given slowing exports stemming from weaker global demand, this *Update* revises down the forecast for growth from 3.8% to 3.4% in 2022, while the 3.0% growth forecast for 2023 is maintained. With the Mongolian economy buffeted by external shocks, its growth forecasts downgraded to 1.7% in 2022 and 4.9% in 2023.

Figure 3.2.1 GDP growth in East Asia

Growth in the subregion is now expected to be lower.

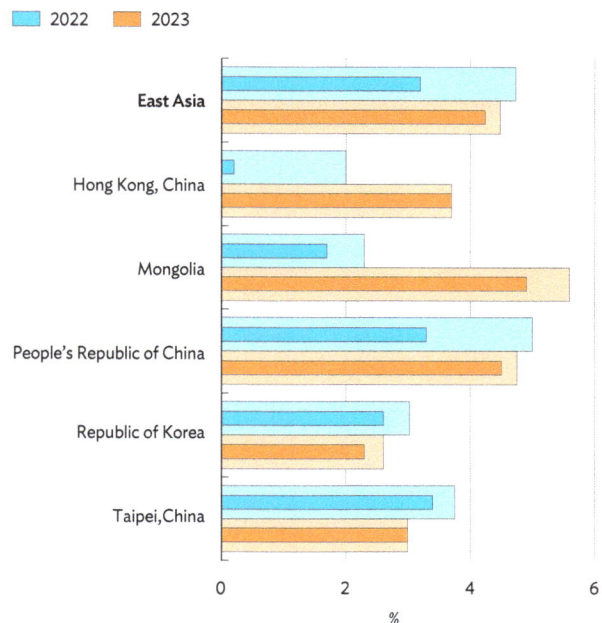

GDP = gross domestic product.
Note: Lighter colored bars are *Asian Development Outlook 2022* forecasts.
Source: *Asian Development Outlook* database.

Inflation in East Asia as a whole is forecast at 2.5% in both 2022 and 2023, close to the *ADO 2022* projection for 2022 but sharply higher for 2023 as inflation is likely to accelerate in the rest of this year (Figure 3.2.2). Consumer price inflation in the PRC is forecast to average 2.3% in 2022, unchanged from the *ADO 2022* projection, and to rise to 2.5% on average in 2023, revised up from 2.0% in *ADO 2022* given returning food price inflation and some pass-through to consumers of increased input prices. While inflation is expected to moderate in the ROK over the coming months, it is still forecast to be higher than *ADO 2022* projections in both 2022 and 2023. Price pressures in Hong Kong, China are expected to be kept in check by the slowdown in growth and higher interest rates, so the *ADO 2022* inflation forecast is lowered for 2022 but maintained for 2023. With lower oil prices and official measures in Taipei,China to dampen inflation expected to wind down, inflation there is forecast at 2.8% in 2022 and 2.0% in 2023. In Mongolia, inflation is much higher than the subregional norm and is now forecast to reach 14.7% in 2022 and 11.6% in 2023.

Figure 3.2.2 Inflation in East Asia

Inflation is now generally expected to be higher.

■ 2022   ■ 2023

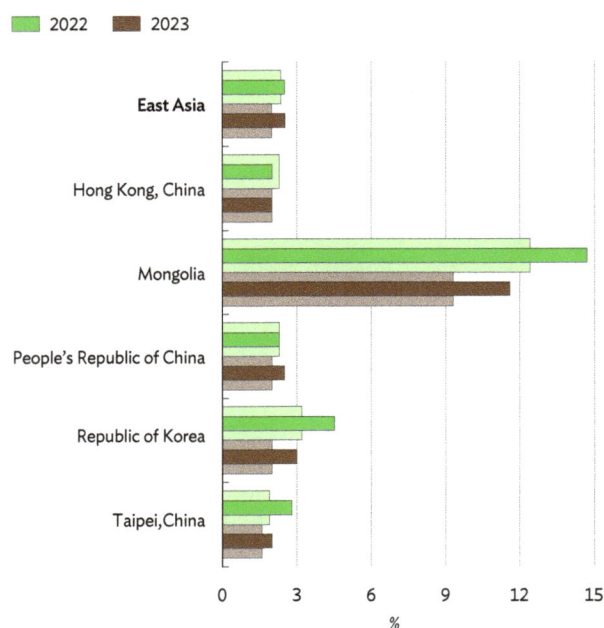

Note: Lighter colored bars are *Asian Development Outlook 2022* forecasts.
Source: *Asian Development Outlook* database.

Figure 3.2.3 Current account balance in East Asia

Projected balances are similar to those forecast in April.

■ 2022   ■ 2023

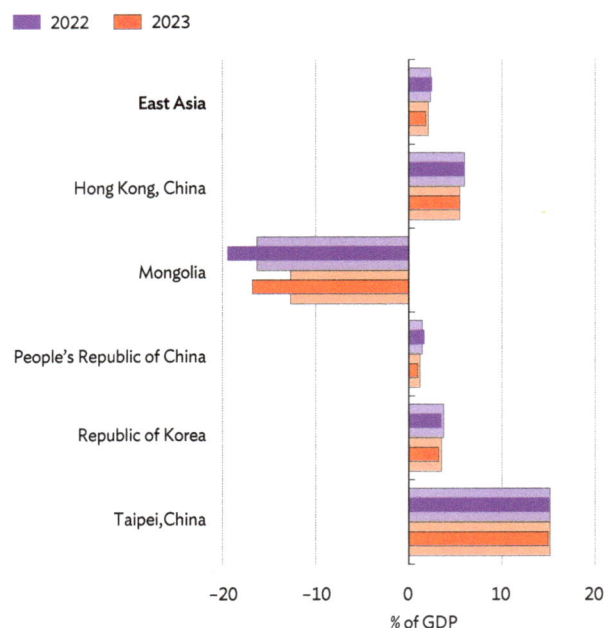

GDP = gross domestic product.
Note: Lighter colored bars are *Asian Development Outlook 2022* forecasts.
Source: *Asian Development Outlook* database.

The subregional current account surplus is forecast to narrow from the equivalent of 2.8% of aggregate GDP in 2021 to 2.5% in 2022 and 1.9% in 2023, a similar pattern to that projected in April, albeit with a larger net decline in the latter year (Figure 3.2.3). Following the same pattern, the PRC current account surplus is now forecast to decline from 1.8% of GDP in 2021 to 1.7% in 2022—a bigger surplus than forecast in April because of the strong export growth in H1. With weakening external demand during the rest of this year and next, the PRC current account surplus will narrow to 1.0% of GDP in 2023, or 0.2 percentage points lower than forecast in April. Likewise, with slowing international demand, ROK current account surpluses are expected to narrow somewhat more than forecast in April.

Earlier forecasts that current account surpluses in Hong Kong, China will fall by half from 2021 are unchanged from *ADO 2022*, as greater negative impact on exports from a decelerating global economy will likely be offset by some recovery in demand from the PRC, and slower domestic growth will dampen imports.

The current account surplus in Taipei,China is now forecast to widen only marginally to 15.1% of GDP in 2022 before narrowing again to 15.0% in 2023 as exports slow and investment stimulates imports. Mongolia will have the only current account deficits in the subregion, forecast at 19.5% of GDP in 2022 and 16.8% in 2023, increased from *ADO 2022* projections.

Downside risks weigh heavily on the outlook. The slowdown in global growth could hurt the subregion's exports by more than forecast, and aggressive monetary tightening by central banks in the advanced economies—particularly if followed by subregional central banks—could further stymie growth. Some economies could be adversely affected by any further escalation in geopolitical tensions. The war in Ukraine could induce another surge in global energy and commodity prices. Finally, risks continue from possible new breakouts of COVID-19 variants and associated lockdowns.

People's Republic of China

After economic recovery in 2021, GDP growth will moderate in 2022 even more than projected in *ADO 2022* because of COVID-19 lockdowns and tepid domestic demand. Inflation is projected to pick up in line with higher food prices. While moderating in line with softer external trade, the current account surplus is forecast to stay in surplus.

Updated assessment

Economic growth in the People's Republic of China (PRC) moderated to 2.5% in the first half (H1) of 2022 from 12.7% in H1 2021 (Figure 3.2.4). GDP growth slowed sharply from 4.8% in Q1 2022 to 0.4% in Q2 as COVID-19 lockdowns disrupted economic activity.

On the demand side, consumption contributed only 0.8 points to growth in H1 2022 because of lockdowns in Q2, a sharp fall from a contribution of 7.5 points in H1 2021 (Figure 3.2.5). Real growth in household income declined from 12.0% in H1 2021 to 3.0% a year later, while real growth in household consumption plunged from 17.4% to 0.8% (Figure 3.2.6). Retail sales are estimated to have plummeted in real terms from 21.8% growth in H1 2021 to 3.4% contraction in H1 2022.

Figure 3.2.4 Economic growth

Economic growth moderated in H1 2022, with retail sales having been hit hard.

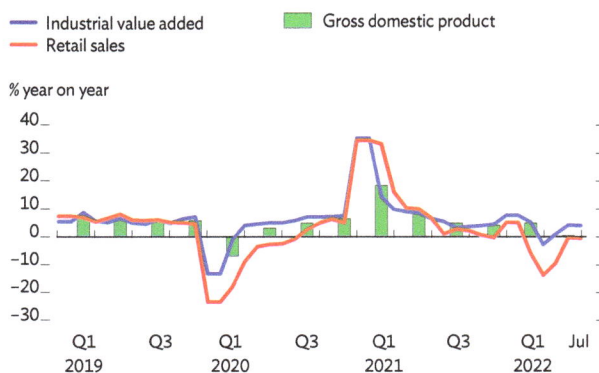

Q = quarter.
Sources: CEIC Data Company (accessed 15 August 2022);
Asian Development Bank estimates.

Figure 3.2.5 Demand-side contributions to growth

Contributions from consumption dropped sharply in H1 2022.

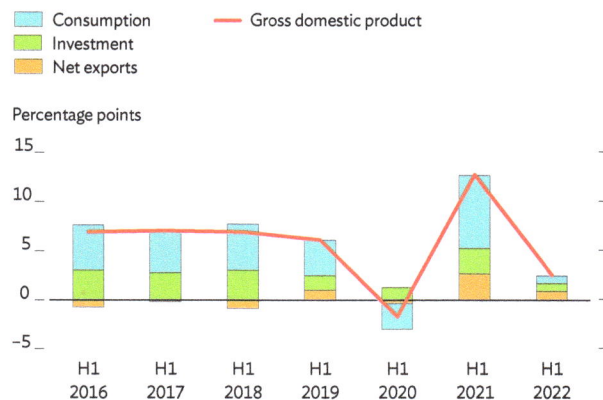

H = half.
Source: CEIC Data Company (accessed 21 July 2022).

Figure 3.2.6 Growth in income and consumption expenditure per capita

Consumption growth took a bigger hit than income growth in Q2 2022.

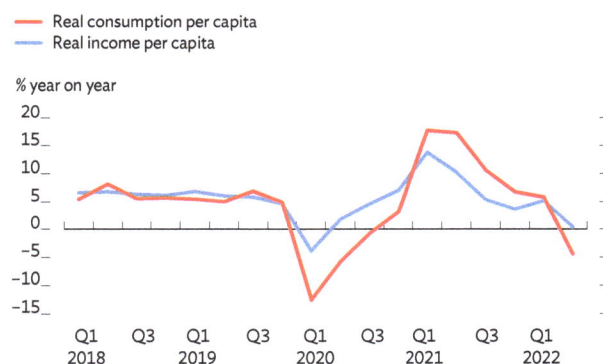

Q = quarter.
Sources: Data Company (accessed 21 July 2022); Asian Development Bank estimates.

Investment contributed 0.8 percentage points to growth in H1 2022, or 1.8 points lower than a year earlier. Nominal fixed asset investment growth slowed to 6.1% from a 12.6% increase a year earlier, dragged down by contraction in real estate investment (Figure 3.2.7). Manufacturing investment grew by 10.4% on solid high-tech manufacturing performance and ongoing export growth, while infrastructure investment increased by 7.1%. Real estate investment contracted by 5.4% in H1 due to property developers' funding shortages, declining house prices, and weak market sentiment.

Figure 3.2.7 Growth in fixed asset investment

Infrastructure investment remained broadly stable in H1 2022, while real estate investment contracted.

- All fixed assets
- Infrastructure
- Manufacturing
- Real estate

% year on year, year to date

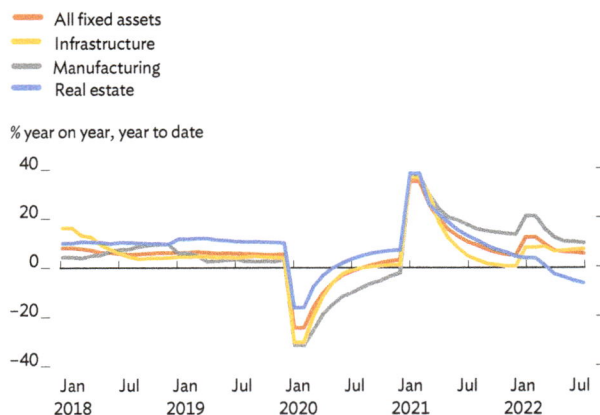

Source: CEIC Data Company (accessed 15 August 2022).

Net exports emerged as the most significant contributor to growth in H1 2022, providing 0.9 percentage points. This was down from 2.7 points in the same period of last year, though, as merchandise export growth moderated from rapid expansion in 2021.

On the supply side, the impact of lockdowns can be seen as industry outpaced services and became the main contributor to growth in H1 2022. Industry contributed 1.2 percentage points to growth, down from 5.5 points in H1 2021, while services contributed only 1.0 point, down from 6.7 points (Figure 3.2.8).

Figure 3.2.8 Supply-side contributions to growth

The contribution of services to growth declined notably in H1 2022.

- Services
- Industry
- Agriculture
- Gross domestic product

Percentage points

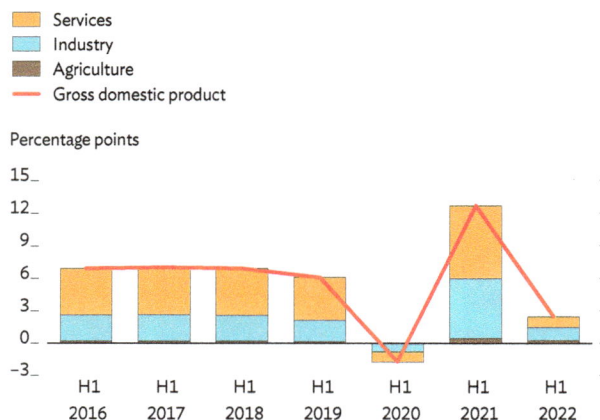

H = half.
Source: CEIC Data Company (accessed 21 July 2022).

Growth in the secondary sector fell from 14.8% in H1 2021 to 3.2% a year later. Industry growth slowed to 3.4% in H1 2022 from 15.9% a year earlier, while construction decelerated to 2.8% in H1 2022 from 8.6% a year earlier. However, in June, industry value added rebounded to 3.9%, showing signs of recovery. Meanwhile, driven by infrastructure investment, construction accelerated to 3.6% in Q2 from 1.4% in Q1.

The real estate sector contracted in H1 2022, with new housing starts and completions falling by double digits. Prices for newly constructed homes in 70 major cities were on a declining trend in H1 2022. Price growth in tier-1 cities was somewhat resilient, while tier-3 cities were hit hardest following earlier excessive construction (Figure 3.2.9).

Since June 2022, home buyers in several cities have refused to pay their mortgages on prepaid units because developers have failed to meet construction schedules. Presales are common practice in the PRC and—given that borrowing restrictions have curtailed debt-laden developers' access to fresh money—an important funding source.

Figure 3.2.9 Price increase for newly constructed homes

Housing prices showed a declining trend in H1 2022, with top-tier cities being somewhat resilient.

- Tier 1 cities
- Tier 2 cities
- Tier 3 cities
- Top 70 cities

% year on year

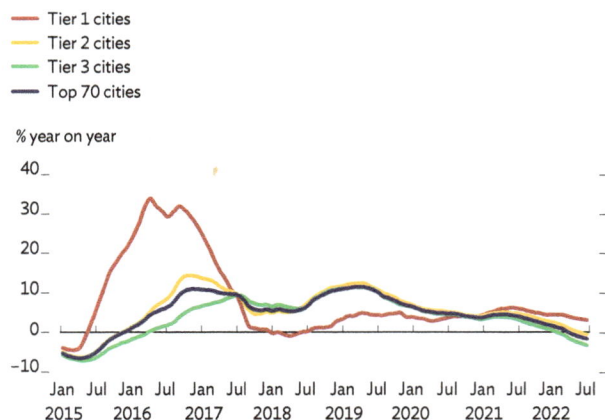

Note: Tier-1 cities are Beijing, Guangzhou, Shanghai, and Shenzhen; tier 2 has 31 provincial capitals and larger municipalities; and tier 3 has 35 other cities.
Sources: CEIC Data Company (accessed 15 August 2022); Asian Development Bank estimates.

Growth in services slowed from 11.8% in H1 2021 to 1.8% a year later. The slowdown was broad-based and most pronounced in real estate services and accommodation, while only information technology and financial intermediation expanded. Growth in agriculture moderated from an exceptionally high rate of 7.8% in H1 2021 to a still robust 5.0% a year later, thereby contributing 0.3 percentage points to growth versus 0.4 points a year earlier.

The labor market weakened in H1 2022, with the surveyed urban unemployment rate increasing from 5.3% in January to 6.1% in April, then gradually improving to 5.5% in June. In H1 2022, new urban jobs increased by 6.54 million, or 0.44 million fewer than in the same period last year, indicating a labor market under pressure. Moreover, the number of rural labor migrants working in urban areas decreased by 1.1 million from the end of June 2021 to 181.2 million at the end of June 2022, further below its 2019 value of 182.5 million in June 2019, before the COVID-19 crisis. The surveyed unemployment rate for workers aged 16–24 rose from 15.3% in January 2022 to 19.3% in June, higher than the average of 13.7% in H1 2021, indicating pressure on the youth labor market.

Consumer price inflation gradually revived to 1.7% in H1 2022 from 0.5% a year earlier (Figure 3.2.10). Though food prices picked up and rose by 2.4% in Q2, they still fell by an average of 0.3% in H1 2022 following food price deflation in Q1.

Nonfood prices rose by 2.2% in H1 2022, driven up from 0.7% a year earlier by higher fuel prices and pass-through from increased producer prices. Despite moderation for 8 consecutive months, producer price inflation still averaged 7.8% in H1 2022, half again above the average during the same period a year earlier.

Monetary policy remained supportive in H1 2022. A small cut in key policy rates in January 2022 was surprisingly followed by another one in August (Figure 3.2.11). With liquidity ample, the 7-day interbank market rate between financial institutions fell by nearly 40 basis points to average 1.72% in Q2, down from 2.10% in Q1 2022. In April 2022, the People's Bank of China, the central bank, lowered the required reserve ratio by 0.25 percentage points for all banks, thereby making additional funds available for bank loans.

Figure 3.2.10 Monthly inflation

Consumer price inflation edged up, while producer price inflation moderated in H1 2022.

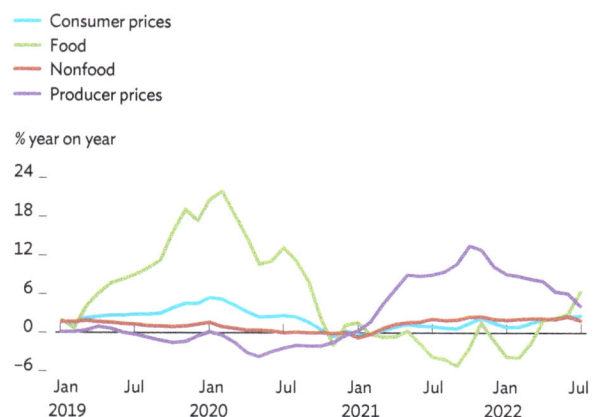

Source: CEIC Data Company (accessed 10 August 2022).

Figure 3.2.11 Banking lending and policy rates

The central bank cut key policy rates twice in the first 8 months of 2022.

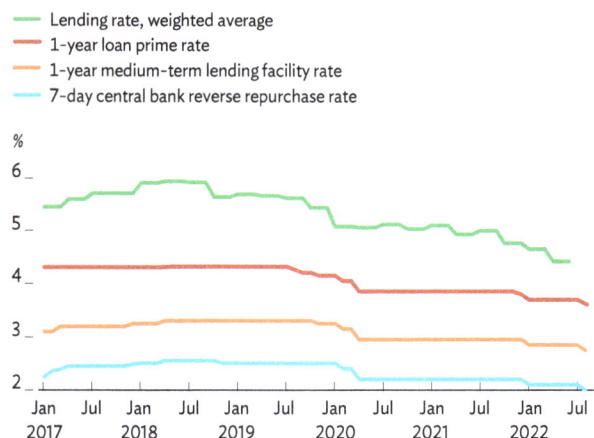

Source: CEIC Data Company (accessed 23 August 2022).

In May, to support the ailing real estate sector, the central bank reduced the 5-year loan prime rate, used for mortgage pricing, by 15 basis points to 4.45% and followed up in August with another reduction of the same magnitude to 4.3%.

Credit growth was broadly stable in H1 2022. Total social financing—a broad credit aggregate that includes bank loans, government and corporate bonds, and shadow bank and equity financing—was up by 10.8% year on year at the end of June 2022, the growth rate edging down from 11.0% a year earlier (Figure 3.2.12).

Figure 3.2.12 Growth in broad money, credit outstanding, and government bonds outstanding

Reflecting high government financing needs, government bonds outstanding rose sharply in 2022.

— Broad money (M2)
— Bank loans
— Government bonds
— Total social financing
— Shadow banking

% year on year

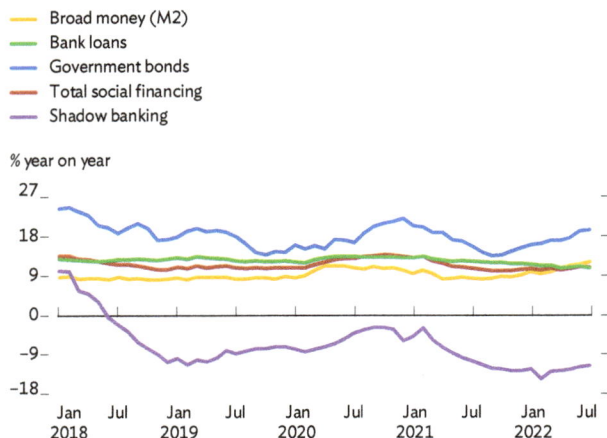

Note: Shadow banking comprises entrust loans, trust loans, and banks' acceptance bills.
Source: Asian Development Bank calculations using data from CEIC Data Company (accessed 15 August 2022).

Figure 3.2.13 General government fiscal revenue and expenditure

Value-added tax credit refunds in Q2 2022 saw fiscal revenue drop sharply, resulting in a gaping budget deficit.

— Revenue
— Expenditure
Surplus or deficit ■

% change year on year   % of GDP

GDP = gross domestic product, Q = quarter.
Note: Public finance budget only.
Source: Asian Development Bank calculations using data from CEIC Data Company (accessed 22 July 2022).

Figure 3.2.14 Local government special bond issues

New special bond issues soared in Q2 2022, with June issues alone exceeding one-third of the annual quota.

■ New issues
■ Replacement or refinancing
— New issues, year to date

CNY trillion   % of annual quota

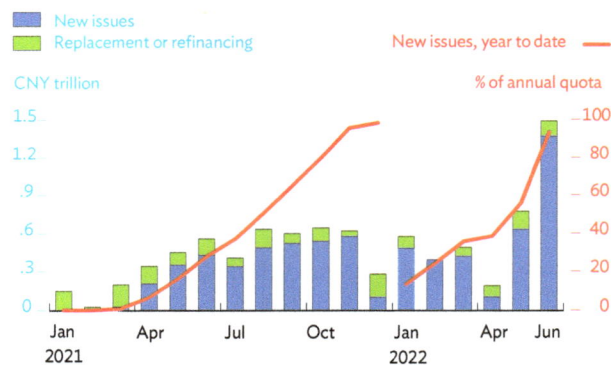

Source: Asian Development Bank calculations using data from CEIC Data Company (accessed 15 August 2022).

Government bonds outstanding rose sharply by 19.0%, reflecting high new issuance in H1 2022. Bank loans outstanding increased by 11.0% by the end of June 2022, while shadow bank financing declined by 11.9%, reflecting government efforts to rein it in. Broad money (M2) grew by 11.4% to the end of June 2022, compared with 8.6% growth a year earlier.

As fiscal revenue fell sharply, the budget deficit increased sharply to the equivalent of 4.2% of GDP in H1 2022 (Figure 3.2.13). General government fiscal revenue plummeted by 10.2% in H1 2022, which resulted from the government refunding value-added tax credit to micro and small enterprises and self-employed households in Q2 to stabilize the economy. Meanwhile, fiscal expenditure grew by 5.9% in H1 2022.

New issues of local government special bonds—not included in the general budget—amounted to CNY3.41 trillion in H1 2022, or 93.3% of the annual quota of CNY3.65 trillion (Figure 3.2.14). In June alone, new issues reached CNY1.37 trillion—more than a third of the annual quota—reflecting government efforts to boost infrastructure.

To shore up infrastructure investment, the government also increased the credit quota of policy banks by CNY800 billion in June 2022 and, in addition, allowed them to raise CNY300 billion in bonds as equity capital for key investment projects. In late August 2022, the government topped up this policy financing tool for infrastructure projects by more than CNY300 billion and allowed the issuance of additional new local government special bonds (see Economic Prospects below).

The current account surplus increased from the equivalent of 1.4% of GDP in H1 2021 to 2.0% in H1 2022. The merchandise trade surplus increased from 2.9% of GDP to 3.7% (Figure 3.2.15). Merchandise exports grew by 12.8% in H1 2022 from a high base in H1 2021. After being disrupted by widespread lockdowns in April, exports resumed in May and June. Meanwhile, import growth moderated to 8.3% in H1 2022 given its sharp slowdown in Q2 under weak domestic demand. Growth in exports was broad-based in mechanical and electrical products, high-tech products, organic chemicals, and consumer goods. However, exports of medical products declined in line with external demand for goods to contain COVID-19, such as masks and personal protective equipment. Geographically, exports to the European Union increased by 18.9% in H1 2022, to the US by 15.7%, and to Southeast Asia by 16.8%—but to Japan by only 4.4%, as exports to that destination were particularly hard hit in April. The service deficit declined from the equivalent of 0.7% of GDP in H1 2021 to 0.4% in H1 2022.

Net foreign direct investment decreased from the equivalent of 1.4% of GDP in H1 2021 to 0.9% in H1 2022 (Figure 3.2.16) as inflow growth lagged that of outflow. Reserve assets decreased to $3.25 trillion at the end of June 2022, or $99.3 billion less than a year earlier.

The renminbi depreciated by 5.3% in nominal terms against the US dollar in H1 2022 to CNY6.71 in June (Figure 3.2.17). By the end of June 2022, the currency stood unchanged from the end of 2021 in nominal effective terms, against a trade-weighted basket of currencies, but it depreciated by 4.0% in real effective terms.

Figure 3.2.16 Balance of payments

The current account surplus was solid in Q1 2022, but net capital outflow was high.

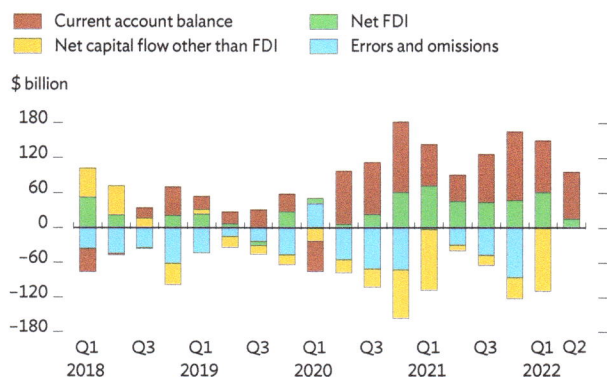

FDI = foreign direct investment, Q = quarter.
Note: For Q2 2022, published data are available only on the current account and FDI.
Sources: Asian Development Bank calculations using data from CEIC Data Company (accessed 15 August 2022).

Figure 3.2.15 Current account balance and merchandise trade

While growth in imports fell sharply, export growth has proven more resilient in H1 2022.

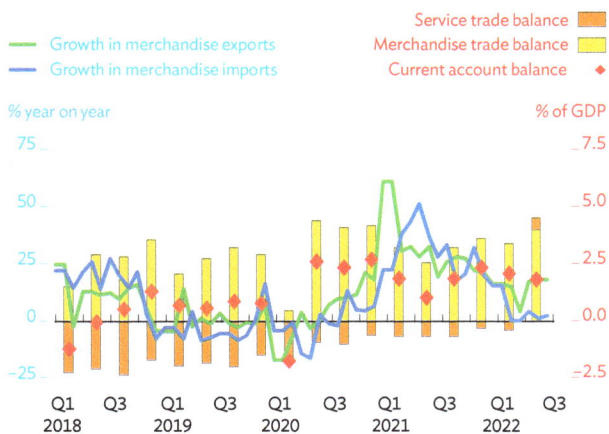

GDP = gross domestic product, Q = quarter.
Note: January and February data are combined to exclude the Lunar New Year effect.
Source: Asian Development Bank calculations using data from CEIC Data Company (accessed 15 August 2022).

Figure 3.2.17 Renminbi exchange rates

The renminbi depreciated in Q2 2022.

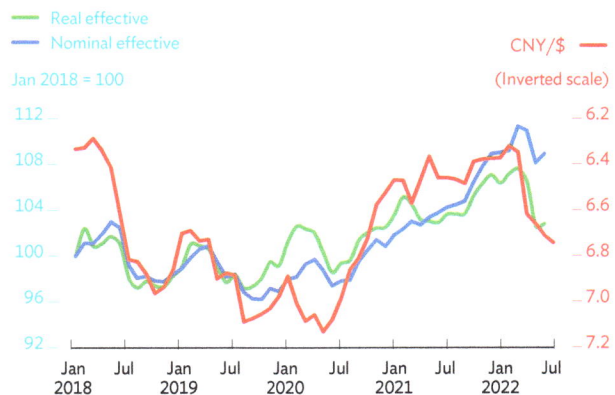

Source: Asian Development Bank calculations using data from CEIC Data Company (accessed 10 August 2022).

Prospects

Economic growth is expected to improve somewhat in H2 2022, recovering from weak H1 performance caused by COVID-19 lockdowns. At the same time, the government is unlikely to change course on its zero-COVID strategy. Merchandise exports, though moderating, are expected to support growth in industry in H2, while services should recover in line with improving household demand. Higher infrastructure investment and a pickup in fiscal outlays should support growth in H2 2022 as there is pressure on the government to address tepid household demand, support the ailing property sector, and address high youth unemployment. However, increased infrastructure spending can be only a temporary stopgap to boost growth. Government measures are needed to mitigate stress in the property market, which has linkages to many parts of the economy.

Several impediments are keeping economic growth from recovering swiftly. First, household demand got hit again and has not fully recovered. Meanwhile, household savings, especially those of migrant workers and micro businesses, suffered under income losses. Second, the housing market will likely weigh on economic recovery in H2 2022 as it has not yet stabilized and the government has been reluctant to substantially loosen housing market restrictions, particularly those on developer financing. Third, local governments lack the funds to sustain more prolonged infrastructure stimulus, which has forced the central government to allow them to accumulate additional debt. Fourth, monetary policy has only limited potential to support growth because monetary policy tightening in advanced economies inhibits scope for the People's Bank of China to lower policy rates. Finally, external trade is expected to soften in H2 2022 and moderate further in 2023 as external demand declines in line with slowing growth in advanced economies.

On balance, GDP is expected to grow by only 3.3% in 2022, 1.7 percentage points lower than forecast in *ADO 2022*, before expanding by 4.5% in 2023, or 0.3 points lower than forecast in April (Table 3.2.1).

Domestic demand is expected to improve gradually from Q2 2022. However, COVID-19 persistence continues to weigh on consumer confidence.

Table 3.2.1 Selected economic indicators in the People's Republic of China, %

Economic growth is expected to moderate more than expected in ADO 2022, while inflation rises.

	2021	2022		2023	
		ADO 2022	Update	ADO 2022	Update
GDP growth	8.1	5.0	3.3	4.8	4.5
Inflation	0.9	2.3	2.3	2.0	2.5
CAB/GDP	1.8	1.5	1.7	1.2	1.0

ADO = *Asian Development Outlook*, CAB = current account balance, GDP = gross domestic product.
Sources: CEIC Data Company; Asian Development Bank estimates.

In addition, investment will remain burdened by a property sector under stress, while moderating exports in H2 and a deteriorating outlook for external demand in 2023 should slow expansion in manufacturing investment. At the same time, infrastructure investment looks set to pick up in H2 2022, with the government possibly mobilizing additional funds later this year. As external trade moderates, the contribution of net exports to growth should ease, while those of consumption and investment are expected to recover despite the domestic economic challenges enumerated above.

On the supply side, growth in services is expected to outpace industry in H2 2022, supported by a gradual recovery in household consumption. That said, hospitality, recreation, and tourism will remain hampered by the zero-COVID policy. Given supply chain bottlenecks, rising input costs, and weakening external demand, the strong expansion of industry seen over the past 2 years will likely ebb. Industry will face headwinds from moderating exports, especially in 2023, though high-tech and innovative industries will continue to benefit from government support. The weak housing market will continue in H2 2022 to weigh on construction and related industries that suffer from rising input costs, and housing prices will likely decline on average in 2022. Agricultural production will be adversely affected this year by an extreme heat wave and severe drought that hit much of the country this summer.

The labor market outlook remains clouded. Higher infrastructure investment may suppress the unemployment rate in the short run. However, rural labor migrants in cities will continue to face difficulty finding jobs in the service sector as tepid consumer spending curtails the creation of new jobs in that labor market. Youth unemployment will likely stay elevated because construction jobs will do little to absorb the 10.76 million new college and university graduates the government expects to enter the labor market in 2022.

Consumer price inflation is forecast to average 2.3% in 2022, unchanged from the *ADO 2022* projection, as inflation picks up in H2 (Table 3.2.1). Driven by rising pork prices, food inflation should remain elevated in H2 2022 after its strong rise in July 2022. Nonfood inflation is expected to stay moderate, though some producers may pass on increased input prices. With the outlook for global energy prices providing some relief—and given expected moderation in external demand—producer price inflation should not stage a strong comeback. Consumer inflation is now expected to rise to 2.5% on average in 2023, this forecast up from 2.0% in *ADO 2022*, given returning food price inflation.

The central bank will ensure ample liquidity in the interbank market in the remainder of 2022. Still, substantial cuts to key policy rates are unlikely given that the central banks of most major economies will further tighten monetary policy. The 10-year US Treasury note yield surpassed the PRC government bond yield in May 2022 (Figure 3.2.18).

Pronounced policy rate cuts in the PRC would weaken the renminbi, which could spur hot money outflows. Also, a more negative interest rate spread would further burden the renminbi, portfolio outflows having already picked up in Q1 2022 as foreign investors unwound positions in the PRC in response to rising US interest rates. With a strong US dollar and rising rates in the US, further portfolio outflows can be expected.

While restrictions on credit to the real estate sector will remain in place, the central bank may cut the 5-year loan prime rate to help stabilize the property sector, especially if housing prices start to fall faster than expected. However, a lack of confidence in developers' ability to solve their funding challenges and deliver finished homes as promised has already manifested itself in mortgage strikes by disappointed home buyers.

Figure 3.2.18 Government bond yields

Driven by a tightening in US monetary policy, the spread over the US narrowed quickly in 2022 and even turned negative in Q2 2022.

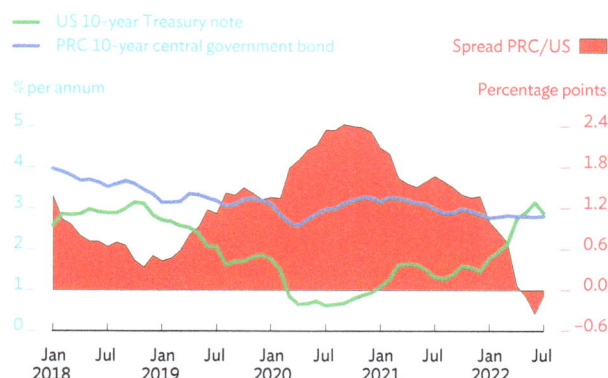

PRC = People's Republic of China, US = United States.
Note: Yields are monthly averages.
Sources: Asian Development Bank calculations using data from CEIC Data Company (accessed 10 August 2022).

Banks may be confronted with rising nonperforming loans from property developers, which could imperil smaller and local banks in particular. Local banks with weak balance sheets are often located away from economic centers, and overinvestment in property in recent years remains a challenge in many tier-3 cities.

Fiscal policy is expected to be more supportive on the spending side in H2 2022 with the rollout of infrastructure stimulus. In addition, on-budget fiscal expenditure will likely edge up in line with improving fiscal revenue in H2 2022, though lower-than-budgeted annual fiscal revenue may curtail planned 8.4% fiscal expenditure growth in the budget. More critically, infrastructure stimulus must be financed. By the end of H1 2022, 93% of the annual quota for new local government special bonds had been used. Assuming that the funds thus raised would need some months to reach construction sites, this stimulus would likely taper off in Q4 2022. To avoid this, in late August 2022 the central government approved CNY500 billion in new local government special bonds that must be issued by the end of October. As the 2022 ceiling for local government bonds outstanding is nearly CNY1.5 trillion higher than required for the original annual quota of CNY3.65 trillion in this bond category, the newly approved CNY500 billion filled only a third of the space left by previously unused quotas.

General government debt looks set to rise substantially in 2022 after a moderate increase in 2021 to equal 72.2% of GDP, according to data from the Bank for International Settlements. Strong new local government bond issuance and contracting fiscal revenue in H1 2022 are going to push general government debt higher in 2022. Another challenge is that local government revenue from land sales declined in H1 2022 as the property sector suffered stress. Furthermore, local governments in less developed regions tend to have higher public debt and lower revenue, thus lacking funds for extended infrastructure stimulus without central government support.

External trade should moderate in H2 2022 from a high base as demand softens from advanced economies. High inflation and rising energy prices in Europe will hit demand for consumer goods, many of them produced in the PRC. Import growth will reflect high commodity and energy prices as domestic demand gradually recovers. The service deficit is expected to remain broadly unchanged in 2022 before widening in 2023 with anticipated revival of international travel.

Considering strong export performance in H1 2022, the current account surplus is now forecast to edge down 0.2 percentage points less than forecast in *ADO 2022*, from the equivalent of 1.8% of GDP in 2021 to 1.7% in 2022. In tandem with weakening external trade in 2023, it will narrow more steeply to 1.0% of GDP, or 0.2 points lower than forecast in April.

Risks to the outlook are both domestic and external. Domestic risks include unpredictable COVID-19 outbreaks and virus mutations, which have prevented domestic consumer demand from fully recovering. Further deterioration in the property market is another domestic risk to the outlook. Also, mounting risks in the financial system, especially at smaller banks, could temporarily disrupt the market and trigger policy interventions. An external risk is friction in global value chains caused by temporary supply shortages or transport bottlenecks. In addition, any cooling of growth in advanced economies more pronounced than expected could similarly worsen external demand.

Other economies

Hong Kong, China

The economy suffered marked deterioration in the first half (H1) of 2022. GDP fell by 2.6% in the H1 as the economy saw a worse-than-expected contraction in the first quarter (Q1), and improved only marginally in Q2. Mobility restrictions to contain the fifth wave of COVID-19 weighed heavily on domestic demand especially in Q1. Private consumption declined by 2.8% in H1, reflecting a worsening labor market and downbeat economic sentiment. Retail sales value decreased by 2.6% in H1, and restaurant receipts by 13.6%. Fixed investment fell by 5.3% in H1 as expenditure on machinery, equipment, and intellectual property products as well as costs of ownership transfer declined.

Goods exports dropped by 6.6% in H1 as pandemic-induced labor shortages lowered production and disrupted cross-border logistics hindered trade with the People's Republic of China (PRC), adding to the impact of moderating global demand. Service exports declined by 0.6% as external demand for transportation, business, financial, and other services retreated under weak cross-border financial activity and moribund tourist arrivals. Imports of goods and services dropped by 5.7% in H1, reversing 20.1% growth in the same period last year, but net exports still subtracted 0.6 percentage points from growth.

Lackluster performance in H1 and a darkening global environment significantly worsen the growth outlook for 2022 (Table 3.2.2). Domestic demand will be the main growth driver. Private spending is expected to recover slightly in the remainder of this year, aided by abating COVID-19 infections, gradually relaxed containment measures, and the new rounds of consumption vouchers and employment support. Fiscal policy will remain supportive this year and tighten thereafter.

Surveys indicate more businesses starting to expect the economic environment to improve. Nevertheless, growth will remain stifled for the rest of 2022 by slowdowns in the PRC and the global economy and by prolonged supply chain disruption. In addition, with a currency peg forcing the Hong Kong Monetary Authority to mirror monetary tightening

Table 3.2.2 Selected economic indicators in Hong Kong, China, %

Growth will be substantially lower in 2022 than projected in April as export prospects worsen, but inflation will remain moderate.

	2021	2022		2023	
		ADO 2022	*Update*	*ADO 2022*	*Update*
GDP growth	6.3	2.0	0.2	3.7	3.7
Inflation	1.6	2.3	2.0	2.0	2.0
CAB/GDP	11.3	6.0	6.0	5.5	5.5

ADO = *Asian Development Outlook*, CAB = current account balance, GDP = gross domestic product.
Source: Asian Development Bank estimates.

in the US, interest rates are set to remain higher for longer, thus denting domestic demand. Against this backdrop, including worse-than-expected performance in H1, this *Update* projects only minimal growth in 2022. It maintains the forecast for strong growth 2023 on an expected rebound in external demand and reflecting a base effect.

Headline consumer price inflation averaged 1.5% in H1 2022, slightly lower than 1.6% underlying inflation thanks to additional electricity charge subsidies provided by the government. External price pressures have intensified from elevated energy prices, rising food prices in the PRC, and continuing supply chain disruption. Nonetheless, headline inflation should remain moderate as domestic price pressures are low, reflecting subdued domestic demand and slowing growth. The inflation forecast is lowered for 2022 but maintained at that lower rate for 2023, when domestic demand is expected to be more robust.

The current account surplus narrowed from the equivalent of 12.9% of GDP in Q4 2021 to 11.6% in Q1 2022. Falling surpluses in goods and primary income offset a growing surplus in services. The overall balance of payments deficit equaled 7.7% of GDP in Q1, and net external financial assets amounted to 5.5 times GDP. While slower domestic growth will dampen imports, worsening external demand will continue to hold down exports. On balance, the ratio of the current account surplus to GDP is projected to decline as forecast in *ADO 2022* in both 2022 and 2023.

Mongolia

In the first half (H1) of 2022, GDP expanded by 1.9% with full reopening of the economy from pandemic restrictions in February supporting recovery in services and agriculture. However, mining contracted deeply by 27.5% due to border restrictions induced by COVID-19 that curtailed exports to the People's Republic of China (PRC), subtracting 4.2 percentage points from growth. Contraction continued in manufacturing, construction, and transportation.

The prolonged restrictions at the border with the PRC disrupted trade, as did the Russian invasion of Ukraine, reducing essential imports and escalating price increases, and dampened business sentiment. But the eventual lifting of pandemic-related restrictions revived domestic demand, assisted by accommodative monetary and fiscal policies. Private consumption grew by 6.9% and contributed 4.5 points to growth as government consumption added another 0.7 points. Investment also grew rapidly, by 43.3%, and contributed 16.3 points, driven mainly by increased public capital expenditure and a 27.9% increase in net foreign direct investment. However, net exports dragged growth down by 19.6 points as exports faltered while imports rose on higher international prices, generating a threefold increase in the goods and services deficit.

Despite initial signs of recovery—recent reopening of trade portals with the PRC and gradual improvement in exports—the economy's near-term growth prospects remain uneven. Because of prolonged border restrictions compared to expectations in *ADO 2022*, sluggish growth and soaring inflation will persist this year, albeit with some improvement in 2023 (Table 3.2.3). The economy grew only slowly in H1, and recovery in industry and mining is likely to take time to materialize. However, agriculture and services will grow strongly. Contributions to growth from private investment and consumption will be moderated by higher borrowing costs and a likely decline in the availability of credit as banks lose their appetite for risk. This is in response to hikes in the central bank policy rate by 400 basis points in H1, which may continue, and to the phasing out of the regulatory forbearance regarding bank asset classification and provisioning, as well as banks' heightened liquidity concerns.

Table 3.2.3 Selected economic indicators in Mongolia, %

Low growth is forecast to persist this year before growth picks up next year, while inflation and the current account deficit outpace earlier projections.

	2021	2022		2023	
		ADO 2022	Update	ADO 2022	Update
GDP growth	1.4	2.3	1.7	5.6	4.9
Inflation	7.1	12.4	14.7	9.3	11.6
CAB/GDP	−13.0	−16.3	−19.5	−12.7	−16.8

ADO = Asian Development Outlook, CAB = current account balance, GDP = gross domestic product.
Source: Asian Development Bank estimates.

In 2023, GDP will climb slightly less than forecast in *ADO 2022*, though external risks are likely to be mitigated and border issues with the PRC resolved. Net exports will start contributing to growth in line with recovery in exports of goods and services and moderation in import growth, but the contribution of domestic demand will likely be lower than expected in April. A combination of persistently high inflation and a large current account deficit creates a pressing need for fiscal consolidation and monetary tightening to achieve better external balance, dampening consumption and investment. Further, consumption growth will fall as purchasing power deteriorates under persistently high inflation and cash transfer programs for households become better targeted or phased out.

Annual inflation escalated to 15.7% in July 2022, remaining above the central bank target of 6% for the past 15 consecutive months. The surge in inflation will continue mainly on persistent supply disruption, rising transportation costs, and higher prices for food, fuel, and imported durables. Inflation forecasts for both years are therefore revised up from *ADO 2022* projections. The current account deficit widened by 105.1% in H1 2022 and is forecast much larger in the whole of 2022 than in 2021 before narrowing somewhat in 2023. The deficit will exceed *ADO 2022* forecasts in both years, mainly because of higher imports, lower growth expected in the PRC, and continued downward corrections to coal, copper, and iron ore prices.

Downside risks to the outlook would arise from any new restrictions at major trade portals with the PRC, fall in mineral commodity prices, negative spillover from the global slowdown, aggressive monetary tightening, or rising balance sheet risks in the domestic financial sector.

Republic of Korea

Growth moderated to 2.9% in the first half of 2022, slowing from the first to the second quarter. Much of the impetus to growth came from exports, which rose by 6.0% in real terms, supported by robust exports of semiconductors and petroleum products. Government consumption spending rose by 5.4% as budget disbursements were stepped up and a substantial fiscal stimulus package was rolled out to temper the economic downturn. Private consumption rose by 4.2%, supported by a stronger labor market as the unemployment rate fell to 2.9% in June from 3.6% in January, but tempered by high household debt that weighed on consumer sentiment. Investment was hit by soaring costs for raw materials and energy and by generally weak business sentiment, which lowered construction and facility outlays in both quarters and softened investment in intellectual property products. On the supply side, manufacturing, supported by exports, maintained robust growth as the output of semiconductors, video and communication equipment, and machinery expanded. Service sector growth also continued.

Inflation quickened more rapidly than expected to average 5.0% in the first 8 months of the year and reach 6.3% year on year in July before falling to 5.7% in August, driven primarily by the higher prices for oil and food. Global supply chain disruptions contributed to higher prices, especially for durable goods. Prices for services, notably rent and dining out, also increased. Core inflation, which excludes energy and agricultural products, more than doubled in the first 8 months of the year to average 3.3%. These trends suggest an increased contribution from demand to current price pressures as the economy reopens following COVID-19 restrictions imposed earlier in the year. Rising inflation prompted the central bank to increase its policy interest rate in six steps from August 2021 and August 2022 to 2.50%. The won depreciated by 12.0% against the US dollar in the first 8 months of 2022. The government has since taken steps to support the won, including through an agreement with the US to provide foreign exchange liquidity facilities if needed.

Merchandise exports rose by 14.6% in nominal US dollar terms in the first 7 months of this year. Imports increased by 24.6%, owing to growth in domestic demand and higher global prices for oil and commodities.

Table 3.2.4 Selected economic indicators in the Republic of Korea, %

Slower global growth and higher commodity prices will lower growth and current account surpluses and raise inflation compared to ADO 2022 forecasts.

	2021	2022		2023	
		ADO 2022	Update	ADO 2022	Update
GDP growth	4.1	3.0	2.6	2.6	2.3
Inflation	2.5	3.2	4.5	2.0	3.0
CAB/GDP	4.9	3.8	3.5	3.5	3.2

ADO = Asian Development Outlook, CAB = current account balance, GDP = gross domestic product.
Source: Asian Development Bank estimates.

With imports increasing faster than exports, the merchandise trade surplus decreased by $25.1 billion, more than the increase in the service trade surplus, resulting in a lower current account surplus of $25.9 billion (or an estimated 3.0% of GDP), a 47.7% drop compared to the first 7 months of 2021.

Private consumption is expected to slow in the second half of the 2022 as stimulus from the economy's reopening fades and interest rate increases dampen consumer spending and limit business investment. Export growth is expected to weaken as well as growth in major export markets slows. Furthermore, the OECD composite leading indicator of economic activity for the Republic of Korea, which peaked in May 2021, fell to 98.2 in August, indicating slowing economic activity. Thus, GDP growth in 2022 and 2023 is now forecast to be lower than the *ADO 2022* projection.

Monetary tightening in the first half of the year and going forward, coupled with lower global oil and food prices projected for next year, should moderate price increases in the coming months, but inflation is forecast to remain higher than *ADO 2022* projections for both 2022 and 2023.

Export growth is expected to slow further in the second half of 2022 as the global economy slows, lowering external demand. This, combined with higher import prices for oil and other raw materials, will reduce the merchandise trade surplus. With net service trade remaining in deficit, the current account surplus will be lower than *ADO 2022* forecasts for both this year and next.

Taipei,China

GDP grew by 3.4% in the first half (H1) of 2022 on robust domestic demand. Investment grew by 8.8% and contributed 2.2 percentage points to growth, driven by private investment and by green energy and 5G network infrastructure projects. Government consumption grew by 2.7% and contributed 0.3 points as the government rolled out a new round of COVID-19 relief measures, consisting mostly of subsidizing costs for hard-hit industries and help for unemployed workers through retraining programs, wage subsidies, and relief loans. Private consumption picked up by 1.7% in H1 2022 and contributed 0.8 percentage points to growth following a shift from a zero-COVID policy to a disease prevention model of pursuing zero severe cases and control of all mild cases. Export growth slowed to 6.6% in H1 2022 from 22.1% in H1 2021 as exports to the People's Republic of China (PRC), a key trade partner, contracted by 4% in May and 15% in June, reflecting a slowdown in the PRC. With imports growing by 8.7%, the contribution of net exports to growth fell to 0.1 percentage points.

On the supply side, agriculture contracted by 1.5% in H1 2022 at least in part due to abnormal weather, which has hurt harvests nationwide. Manufacturing grew by 5.6%, driven by continued expansion in semiconductors, computers, electronic goods, and optical products. Services grew by 2.1%, driven largely by information and communication, which grew by 6.2%, and by wholesale and retail trade, up by 2.0%.

Departure from the zero-COVID policy and lockdowns sets the stage for a rebound in private consumption. Investment will also help drive growth as company reshoring continues and investment expands in the semiconductor industry and green energy. However, growth in industrial production slowed to 0.7% in July, in line with the slowdown in export growth in Q1, and the July manufacturing purchasing managers' index fell to a pessimistic 44.6. Export orders bounced back to double-digit growth in May and June, suggesting that exports could grow more strongly in H2 2022, albeit not as strongly as in previous years. On balance, given slowing export growth from weaker global demand, this *Update* revises down the forecast for 2022 growth but maintains the forecast for 2023 on the expectation that investment continues and consumption recovers.

Table 3.2.5 Selected economic indicators in Taipei,China %

The ADO 2022 growth forecast for 2022 is revised down slightly, the inflation forecast raised for this year and the next, and forecasts for the current account surplus lowered.

	2021	2022		2023	
		ADO 2022	Update	ADO 2022	Update
GDP growth	6.6	3.8	3.4	3.0	3.0
Inflation	2.0	1.9	2.8	1.6	2.0
CAB/GDP	14.8	15.2	15.1	15.2	15.0

ADO = *Asian Development Outlook*, CAB = current account balance, GDP = gross domestic product.

Source: Asian Development Bank estimates.

Inflation averaged 3.1% in H1 2022, driven by higher global food and oil prices and poor weather affecting fruit and vegetable harvests. In response, the central bank raised its policy rates in March and June by a total of 37.5 basis points. The government also introduced various supply-side measures such as domestic oil price controls, electricity rate freezes, and lower customs duties. With these measures, and with oil prices expected to trend downward in the rest of the year, inflation is expected to slow in H2 2022. But with the higher-than-expected outturns in H1 2022, inflation is forecast to be higher than April projections in both 2022 and 2023.

The current account is forecast to record large surpluses this year and next, as projected in *ADO 2022*. However, with exports slowing and investment driving import growth, the ratio of the current account surplus to GDP is expected to be slightly lower in both years than forecast in April.

The main risk to the outlook is escalating tensions in the region. The PRC recently restricted imports of citrus and selected fishery products from Taipei,China. While these products account for a very small part of exports to the PRC, any escalation of bans to include electronic or related products would be very disruptive to supply chains and could significantly hurt growth. Other risks include elevated price pressures from higher-than-expected global commodity prices and costlier imported goods if monetary policy tightening in the US causes currency depreciation in Taipei,China.

SOUTH ASIA

The subregional economy is forecast to grow more slowly in 2022 and 2023 than was forecast in *ADO 2022*. Higher inflation is expected and the current account deficit will be wider over the forecast horizon as domestic demand recovers. The outlooks for economies in the subregion remain largely similar to the earlier projections, but Sri Lanka is the outlier because of its deepening recession and galloping inflation.

Subregional assessment and prospects

Aggregate GDP is forecast to expand by 6.5% in 2022 and 2023 as global economic headwinds continue to reduce demand and cause supply disruptions (Figure 3.3.1). This outlook reflects the pattern of growth in India, which accounts for 80% of the subregional economy. It excludes Afghanistan because the unsettled situation there and lack of credible data preclude meaningful forecasts. Afghanistan's continued political isolation and the suspension of international development assistance will further weaken domestic demand and economic activity. Ongoing drought in some areas of the country and the breakdown of value chains are expected to reduce agricultural production, livestock health, and the livelihood of farmers. In summary, Afghanistan's economic outlook looks bleak.

India's economy grew 13.5% year on year in the first quarter of fiscal year 2022 (FY2022, ending 31 March 2023) reflecting strong growth in services. However, GDP growth is revised down from *ADO 2022*'s forecasts to 7.0% for FY2022 and 7.2% for FY2023 as price pressures are expected to adversely impact domestic consumption, and sluggish global demand and elevated oil prices will likely be a drag on net exports.

Figure 3.3.1 GDP growth in South Asia

South Asian economies except Sri Lanka will grow at a robust pace over 2022 and 2023.

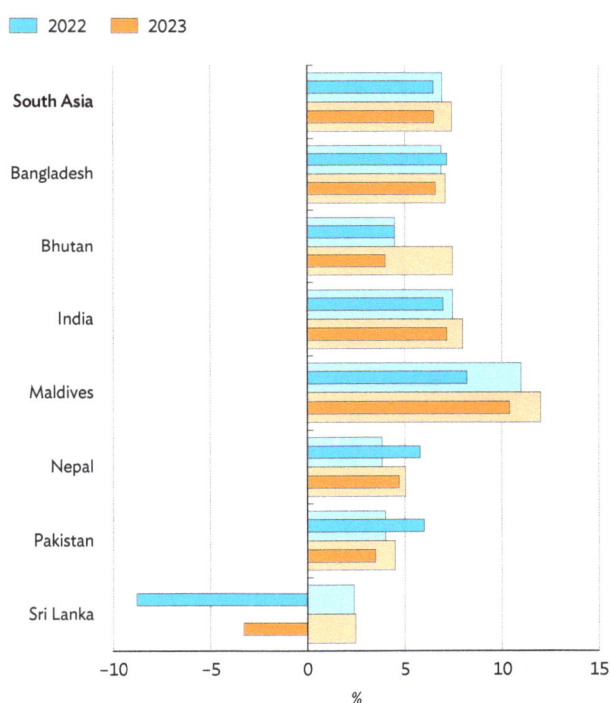

GDP = gross domestic product.
Note: Lighter colored bars are *Asian Development Outlook 2022* forecasts.
Source: *Asian Development Outlook* database.

The section on Bangladesh was written by Soon Chan Hong, Barun K. Dey, and Mahbub Rabbani; India by Shalini Mittal and Rana Hasan; Pakistan by Ali Khadija and Maleeha Rizwan. The sections on other economies were written by Abdul Hares Halimi, Nirukthi Kariyawasam, Manbar Singh Khadka, Sonam Lhendup, Ahmad K. Miraj, and Neelina Nakarmi, and consultants Abdulla Ali and Macrina Mallari. The authors are in the Central and West Asia and South Asia departments, ADB. The subregional assessment and prospects was written by Reza Vaez-Zadeh, consultant, Economic Research and Regional Cooperation Department. ADB placed on hold its assistance in Afghanistan effective 15 August 2021. ADB Statement on Afghanistan | Asian Development Bank (10 November 2021).

Growth prospects for the rest of South Asia's economies will be mixed. Sri Lanka's economy contracted in the first quarter of 2022 and will be in deep recession this year and 2023, rather than grow moderately, as was forecast in *ADO 2022*. The severe balance of payments and debt crisis that led to a default, a shortage of foreign exchange reserves, supply bottlenecks, and the need for fiscal tightening will take a heavy toll on the Sri Lankan economy this year and the next.

Growth was higher in Nepal and Pakistan in FY2022 (ended 15 July 2022 in Nepal and 30 June 2022 in Pakistan) than was forecast in April. Increased agricultural output and a robust performance in large-scale manufacturing and services lifted growth in Pakistan, while a rebound in industry and the gathering pace in tourism and related activities supported growth in Nepal. However, the FY2023 growth forecast for Nepal is revised down slightly from *ADO 2022*'s projection largely because of tight monetary policy to stem inflationary pressures. Pakistan's is also revised down, reflecting ongoing policy tightening and stabilization efforts to tackle sizable fiscal and external imbalances, and double-digit inflation. The recent severe floods heighten the risk to the country's macroeconomic outlook.

Bangladesh's growth edged up in FY2022 (ended 30 June 2022) and was above the April forecast on a broad-based recovery in industry and services, supported by rising domestic and external demand. Remittances lifted private consumption expenditure, increased subsidies and transfers raised public consumption, and investment grew on the implementation of large government infrastructure projects. The growth forecast for FY2023, however, is revised down on the likely adverse impact of the war in Ukraine on exports, domestic energy shortages, and fiscal tightening.

Bhutan's growth forecast for 2022 is unchanged from *ADO 2022*'s projections, with the removal of COVID-19 restrictions lifting growth this year. However, the forecast for 2023 is revised to well below the forecast in *ADO 2022*, mainly because of delays in completing a major hydropower plant and slower-than-expected revival in tourism. Growth in Maldives is revised down for both years as the impact on the economy from a rebound in

Figure 3.3.2 Inflation in South Asia

Inflation is on the rise in South Asia, especially in Sri Lanka.

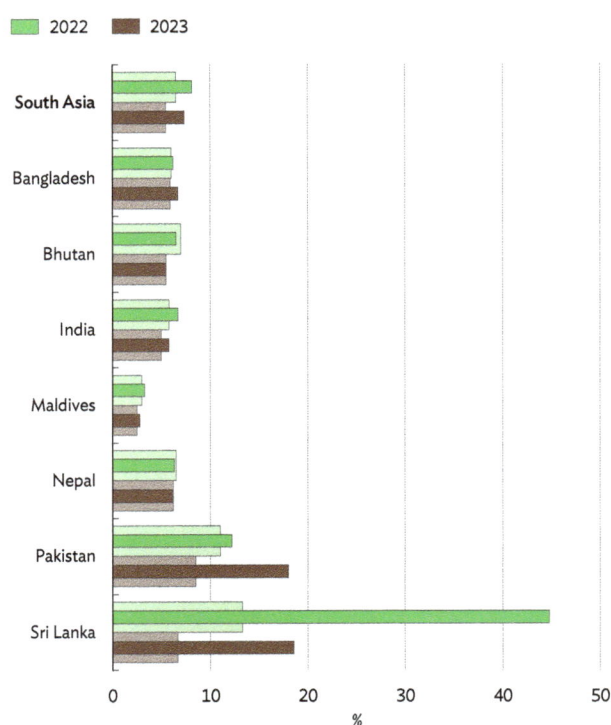

Note: Lighter colored bars are *Asian Development Outlook 2022* forecasts.
Source: *Asian Development Outlook* database.

tourism that started in the first half of this year will be tamped down by an expected slump in construction as government outlays are scaled back.

The subregional forecasts for inflation are revised up from April's projections to 8.1% for 2022 and 7.4% for 2023 (Figure 3.3.2). The revision mainly reflects the pattern of inflation in India. Headline inflation there breached the monetary policy target of 2%–6% in the first quarter of FY2022 on food price increases and pressures from rising global oil and commodity prices following the Russian invasion of Ukraine. This *Update* expects inflation in India to be higher than *ADO 2022*'s forecast, averaging 6.7% in FY2022 and moderating to 5.8% in FY2023 as demand pressures from strengthening economic activity are tamped down by easing supply bottlenecks.

Inflation soared in Sri Lanka in the first half of 2022 when food prices almost doubled and other prices rose markedly because of a fertilizer ban that stymied agricultural production, rising global oil and commodity prices, supply chain disruptions, and the depreciation of the currency. Inflation this year and next will remain substantially above *ADO 2022*'s projections, accelerated by similar factors. Pakistan's inflation forecast for FY2022 and FY2023 are revised up from April's. This reflects the steep rise in inflation in the last quarter of FY2022 (April–June) when fuel and electricity subsidies were removed, the rupee weakened against the US dollar, and international commodity prices surged. Similar factors will push inflation in Bangladesh beyond *ADO 2022*'s forecast in FY2023. The inflation forecast for Bhutan is revised down for this year from the April projection and retained for next year as rising agricultural output should moderate food price increases. Inflation in Nepal was marginally lower in FY2022 than the earlier projection and is revised slightly down for FY2023 as demand pressures moderate. Inflation in Maldives for both years are revised up on rising import prices, expected subsidy reforms, and planned increase in goods and services tax.

The combined current account deficit of all South Asian economies is now expected to equal 3.9% of subregional GDP in 2022 and 2.3% in 2023, wider in both years than April's projections, mainly due to higher oil and other commodity prices and lower export growth (Figure 3.3.3). The slowdown in global growth and high oil prices will hurt India's export prospects in FY2022. Imports are expected to grow faster on rising domestic demand, and remittances may fall as global income falters, despite a depreciating rupee. On balance, India's current account deficit in both fiscal years is expected to widen beyond the earlier forecasts, rising to 3.8% of GDP in FY2022 and narrowing to 2.1% in FY2023.

Pakistan's current account deficit widened in FY2022 more than was forecast in April due to strong domestic demand and the sharp rise in global oil and other commodity prices. The deficit will narrow in FY2023, as projected earlier. Exports and remittances will rise, supported by improved confidence, a flexible exchange rate, and the continuation of the central bank's export facilitation scheme. Import growth will slow on moderating economic growth and the rupee's depreciation. Similarly in Bangladesh, the current account deficit widened more than expected in FY2022 on a higher trade deficit and lower remittances. It will narrow in FY2023 as remittances increase, but remain higher than the earlier forecast.

Figure 3.3.3 Current account balance in South Asia

The subregion's current account deficit will rise relative to its GDP.

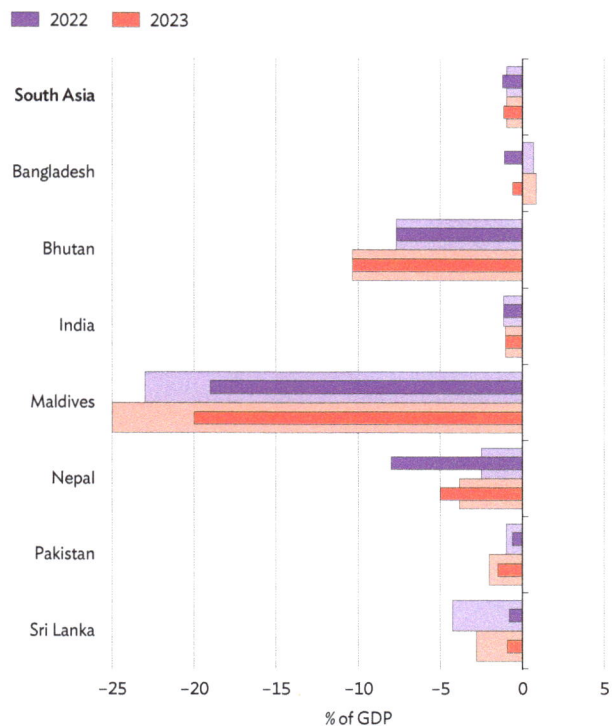

GDP = gross domestic product.
Note: Lighter colored bars are *Asian Development Outlook 2022* forecasts.
Source: *Asian Development Outlook* database.

Nepal's current account deficit was higher in FY2022 than *ADO 2022*'s forecast. It will narrow in FY2023 as import growth moderates, but remain above the earlier projection. In Bhutan, the higher-than-expected growth in investment and construction and the large increase in global import prices for food and fuel will likely lead to a substantially higher import bill, raising the current account deficit in 2022 above the earlier projection. The deficit is revised down for 2023 as energy exports are expected to rise, capital imports fall, and global food and fuel prices ease. In Maldives, rising tourism receipts will not be able to offset rising trade deficits because of higher import prices. The result will be higher current account deficits in 2022 and 2023 than the earlier projections. Sri Lanka's current account deficit is expected to be narrower in both years than was forecast in April, as imports shrink on the severe shortage of foreign exchange and net income and service receipts improve due to the suspension of external debt service and some recovery in tourism.

Bangladesh

Bangladesh maintained its growth momentum in fiscal year 2022 (FY2022, ended 30 June 2022), supported by coordinated fiscal and monetary policy measures and a sharp rise in external demand. A strong recovery in domestic demand on the receding COVID-19 pandemic and elevated global commodity prices pushed up inflation. The current account deficit widened on a sharp rebound in imports, despite strong export growth, that put pressure on the taka. Growth in FY2023 is expected to moderate on slower growth in advanced economies, inflation will accelerate, and the current account deficit narrow.

Updated assessment

GDP growth is officially estimated to have edged up to 7.2% in FY2022 from 6.9% in FY2021, driven by a broad-based recovery in economic activity on rapidly rising external and domestic demand. Both exports and imports were stronger than expected. Remittances were higher than pre-pandemic levels and contributed to strong growth in private consumption expenditure, although remittances were down from FY2021. Public consumption rose on higher recurrent expenditure for subsidies and transfers, and pay and allowances. Public investment increased as the government expedited large infrastructure projects, including the opening of the Padma Bridge, which will better connect the south-west with Dhaka. Increased private investment was reflected by solid growth in private sector credit and a sharp increase in imports of industrial raw materials and capital goods.

On the supply side, growth was lifted by industry and services. Industry grew by 10.4% in FY2022 from 10.3% in the previous fiscal year, supported by buoyant exports. Within industry, medium- and large-scale manufacturing production increased by 16.0% in the first 9 months of FY2022 from 6.5% in the same period in the previous fiscal year; small-scale manufacturing increased by 9.0% from 5.0%. Services output grew by 6.3% from 5.7% on strong performances from wholesale and retail trade, transport, accommodation, and financial services. Agriculture grew by 2.2%, down from 3.2% in FY2021 as cultivation of the summer crop area decreased due to unfavorable weather (Figure 3.3.4).

Average inflation accelerated to 6.2% in FY2022 from 5.6% in FY2021, reflecting strong domestic demand and higher global oil, gas, and commodity prices resulting from supply disruptions caused by the Russian invasion of Ukraine (Figure 3.3.5). The taka's depreciation against the US dollar also contributed to higher inflation. The government increased diesel and kerosene prices by 23.1% in November 2021 and natural gas prices by 22.8% in June 2022 due to high import costs, putting more pressure on households. Year-on-year food inflation rose moderately in the first half but accelerated rapidly in the second; nonfood inflation accelerated in the first half, but slowed in the second.

Figure 3.3.4 Supply-side contributions to growth

Growth momentum continued in 2022, but it will slow in 2023.

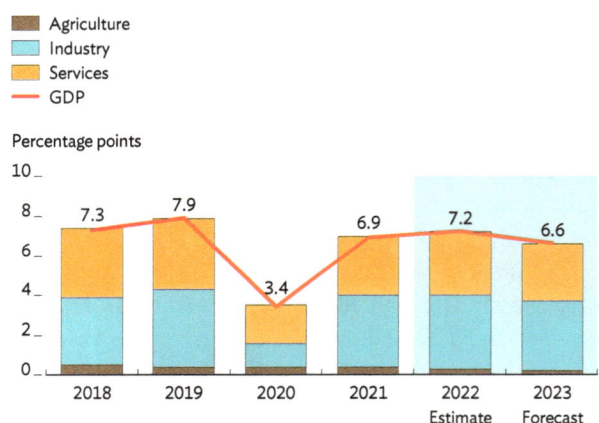

Note: Years are fiscal years ending on 30 June of that year.
Sources: Bangladesh Bureau of Statistics; Asian Development Bank estimates.

Figure 3.3.5 Monthly inflation

Inflation accelerated in 2022 on rising fuel and commodity prices.

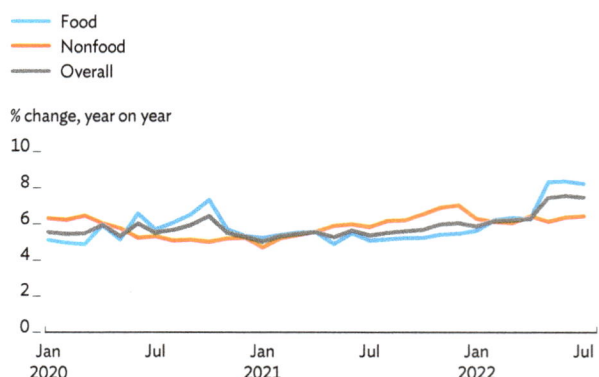

Source: Bangladesh Bank. 2022. *Monthly Economic Trends*. August.

Broad money growth decreased to 9.4% in June 2022 from 13.6% in June 2021 on a contraction in net foreign assets (Figure 3.3.6). Private sector credit in the same period grew by 13.7%, up from 8.3%, on strengthened business confidence due to COVID-19 waning. Growth in net credit to the public sector rose to 27.7% from 19.3%. Bangladesh Bank, the central bank, absorbed excess liquidity by issuing Bangladesh Bank bills during August–November 2021 and raised the repo rate by 25 basis points to 5.0% in May 2022 to contain inflationary pressure.

FY2022's revised budget targets overall revenue collection and spending growing by 18.4% (equivalent to 9.8% of GDP) and 29.0% (14.9% of GDP), respectively. Revenue collection, however, is expected to underperform the target for the fiscal year due to lower-than-targeted collection by the National Board of Revenue and lower nontax revenue. Current expenditure rose by 23.1% during the first 10 months, mainly on higher spending on subsidies and current transfers. Annual development program spending increased by 18.6% in FY2022 from the level in the previous fiscal year. Given these developments, the fiscal deficit is expected to widen to 5.1% of GDP from 3.7% in FY2021. Bangladesh is at a low risk of debt distress, with the debt-to-GDP ratio remaining at an estimated 36.3% in FY2022.

Exports grew sharply in FY2022, up 33.4% to $49.2 billion, on pent-up demand from major export destinations (Figure 3.3.7). Garment exports, accounting for about 82.0% of total exports, grew by 35.5%, bolstered by strong demand for knitwear and woven garments, the diversion of export orders from other major exporters, and competitive prices. Exports of leather and leather products, and engineering products, did well.

Imports grew by 35.9% to $82.5 billion after 19.7% growth in FY2021. About a third of the rise came from imports of intermediates for the garment industry to support sharply increased demand for exports. Intermediate goods for construction, along with pharmaceutical and fertilizer inputs, rose a robust 63.5%, contributing about 40% to the increase in total imports. Imports of capital goods rose by 26.3%, reflecting strong business confidence.

Figure 3.3.6 Monetary indicators

Credit to the private sector increased in 2022 on rising business confidence.

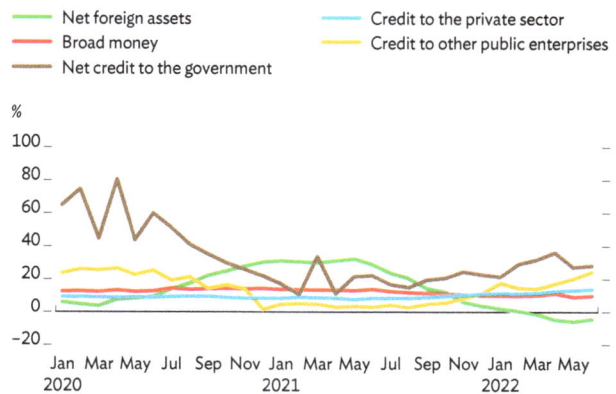

Source: Bangladesh Bank. 2022. *Major Economic Indicators: Monthly Update.* July.

Figure 3.3.7 Monthly exports and imports

Imports grew faster than exports on COVID-19 waning.

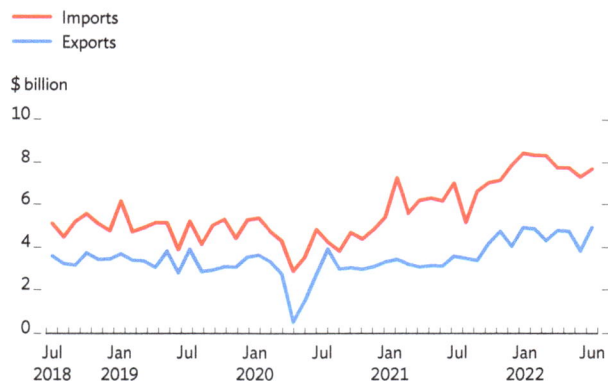

Source: Bangladesh Bank. 2022. *Major Economic Indicators: Monthly Update.* July.

A substantial rise in edible oil and wheat imports reflected higher international prices due to global supply disruptions and protective measures imposed by some key exporters.

The trade deficit widened to $33.2 billion, or 7.2% of GDP, in FY2022, as the $21.8 billion increase in imports far surpassed the $12.3 billion rise in exports. Remittances contracted by 15.1% to $21.0 billion from a high base in the previous fiscal year, reflecting the greater use of unofficial channels. Because of the higher trade deficit and lower remittances, and deficits in services and primary income, the current account deficit widened to $18.7 billion, or 4.1% of GDP (Figure 3.3.8).

Figure 3.3.8 Current account components

Current account deficit widened in 2022, reflecting robust growth in imports.

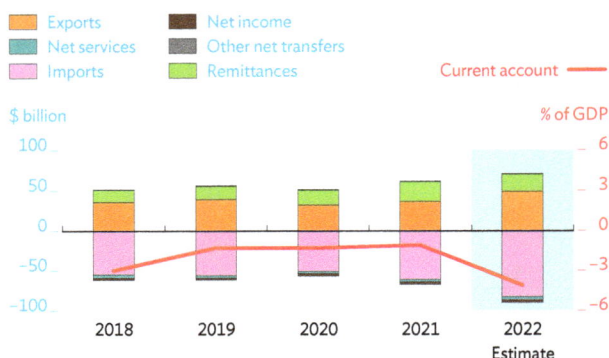

Legend:
- Exports
- Net services
- Imports
- Net income
- Other net transfers
- Remittances
- Current account

$ billion / % of GDP

X-axis: 2018, 2019, 2020, 2021, 2022 Estimate

Source: Bangladesh Bank. 2022. *Major Economic Indicators: Monthly Update*. July.

Figure 3.3.9 Gross foreign exchange reserves

Reserves declined to meet import demand.

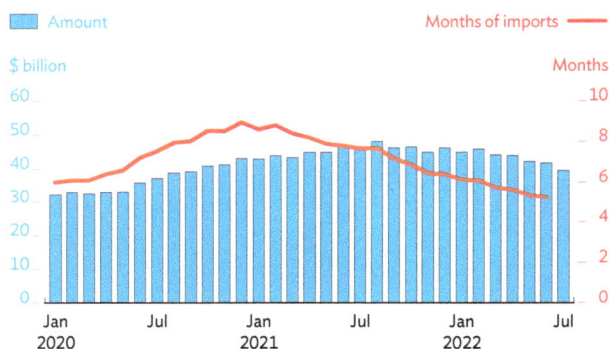

Legend:
- Amount
- Months of imports

$ billion / Months

X-axis: Jan 2020, Jul, Jan 2021, Jul, Jan 2022, Jul

Source: Bangladesh Bank. 2022. *Major Economic Indicators: Monthly Update*. August.

Figure 3.3.10 Exchange rates

Taka depreciated by 9.2% against the US dollar in 2022 on strong import demand.

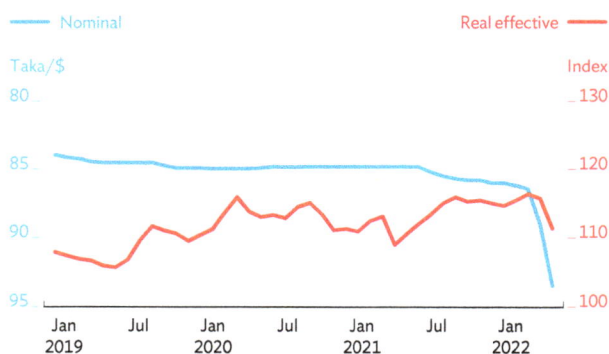

Legend:
- Nominal
- Real effective

Taka/$ / Index

X-axis: Jan 2019, Jul, Jan 2020, Jul, Jan 2021, Jul, Jan 2022

Source: Bangladesh Bank. 2022. *Monthly Economic Trends*. July.

The combined capital and financial account surplus, adjusted for errors and omissions, decreased to $13.3 billion, mainly reflecting a large decline in the use of net trade credit. With the current account deficit significantly exceeding net financial inflows, gross foreign exchange reserves fell by $4.6 billion to $41.8 billion, cover for about 5 months of imports of goods and services (Figure 3.3.9).

The taka depreciated by 9.2% against the US dollar in FY2022 in response to the strong import demand (Figure 3.3.10). Bangladesh Bank sold $7.6 billion to commercial banks to curb excessive volatility. Because of inflation differentials, the real effective exchange rate index appreciated by 0.7%—indicating further scope for the taka to depreciate.

Prospects

This *Update* revises down the forecast for GDP growth in FY2023 to 6.6% from the earlier 7.1% projection to reflect lower consumption expenditure on weaker export demand and income, an uncertain outlook, and domestic production constraints (Table 3.3.1 and Figure 3.3.11). Domestic power and energy shortages, together with rising input and transport costs, will weigh on industrial production. The economic fallout and uncertainty over the war in Ukraine will slow growth in key export destinations and substantially reduce export momentum and growth in the coming months. Public investment will slacken on government austerity measures prompted by slowing revenue growth and higher import costs. Lower private investment will also slow growth.

Table 3.3.1 Selected economic indicators in Bangladesh, %

Projections are for slowing growth, higher inflation, and persistent current account deficit.

	2021	2022		2023	
		ADO 2022	Update	ADO 2022	Update
GDP growth	6.9	6.9	7.2	7.1	6.6
Inflation	5.6	6.0	6.2	5.9	6.7
CAB/GDP	-1.1	-2.7	-4.1	-1.8	-3.6

ADO = Asian Development Outlook, CAB = current account balance, GDP = gross domestic product.

Note: Years are fiscal years ending on 30 June of that year.

Source: Asian Development Bank estimates.

Figure 3.3.11 Demand-side contributions to growth

Slower consumption will pull down growth in 2023.

- Consumption
- Investment
- Net exports
- Statistical discrepancy
- Gross domestic product

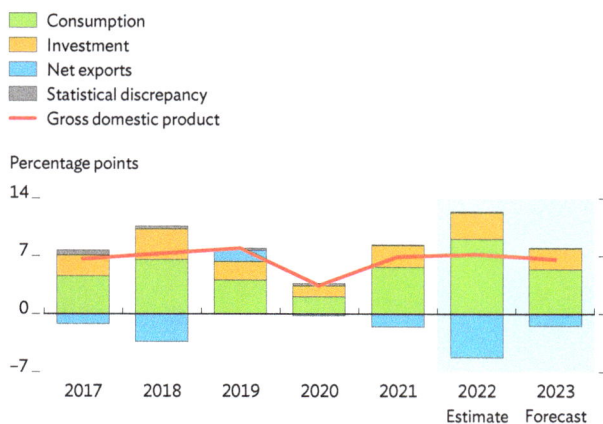

Note: Years are fiscal years ending on 30 June of that year.
Sources: Bangladesh Bureau of Statistics; Asian Development Bank estimates.

Agriculture growth is projected to decline to 2.0% in FY2023. Prolonged monsoon floods caused by an upstream onrush of water and unusually heavy rainfall inundated large parts of the north-eastern region and caused substantial damage, including to rice crops, jute, vegetables, seed beds, houses, and infrastructure. Government policy support, including increased budgetary subsidies, are expected to partly offset flood losses. Industry growth is expected to be lower at 9.5% due to lower external demand from slower growth in major export destinations and heightened economic uncertainty over the war in Ukraine. Services output is also expected to be lower, forecast at 5.8%, due to the same factors that affect agriculture and industry.

Inflation is projected to accelerate to 6.7% in the current fiscal year. Rising global commodity prices, increases in domestic-administered prices of all types of fuel, and an expected upward adjustment in domestic power tariffs are the main factors that will stoke inflation in the coming months. But increased food and agriculture subsidies, and a cut to 15.0% from 62.5% in customs duties on imported rice, should constrain food inflation.

Monetary policy will be cautious in FY2023, with a tightening bias to contain inflation and reduce pressure on the taka. Bangladesh Bank has raised its main policy repo rate by 50 basis points to 5.5% since the start of the fiscal year to tighten monetary policy.

But the impact may be limited because the 9% cap on bank lending rates still stands. In a further effort to reduce pressure on the taka, Bangladesh Bank is discouraging imports of luxury goods by significantly increasing margins on opening letters of credit, and it is promoting import substituting industries by extending new refinancing credit lines to them.

The government has implemented austerity measures to help tackle the risks from a rising fiscal deficit. FY2023's budget policy aims to underpin economic growth at a time of global economic uncertainty without adding to inflationary pressures. The budget targets revenue growth of 11.3%, or 9.7% of GDP, and spending growth of 14.2% (15.2% of GDP). Current spending is targeted at 8.4% of GDP; most of this expenditure will go on pay and allowances, subsidy and current transfers, and interest payments. Development spending is targeted at 5.8% of GDP. With the budget targeting lower revenue and higher spending, the fiscal deficit is forecast to widen to 5.5% of GDP in FY2023.

Export growth is projected to slow to 8.1% in FY2023 from the unusually large expansion in the previous fiscal year on lower growth in major trading partners. Higher prices and the limited supply of primary energy and electricity may upset timely production and the fulfillment of overseas orders for garments and other export products. Imports are expected to grow by only 10.0%—after FY2022's unusually high growth—as demand decreases for intermediates for export-oriented industries. Slower economic growth and uncertainty will depress domestic demand for consumer goods and capital equipment.

The trade deficit is forecast to widen to $37.5 billion (7.3% GDP) in the current fiscal year on faster growth in imports than exports. Remittances will rebound and are forecast to increase by 9.5%. Inflows will be buoyed by the 253% growth in Bangladeshis going abroad for employment in FY2022. Despite a wider trade deficit, the current account deficit is forecast narrowing slightly to 3.6% of GDP in FY2023 due to increased remittances.

The main downside risk to the outlook is a weakening in exports caused by global uncertainty over the prolonged war in Ukraine. Adverse weather events are perennial risk.

India

The economy grew strongly in the first quarter of fiscal year 2022 (FY2022, ending 31 March 2023), but the forecasts for GDP growth for both FY2022 and FY2023 are revised down from *ADO 2022*'s projection in April due to global economic headwinds. Inflation has turned out to be more persistent than expected, and led to a sharp tightening in monetary policy. The projections for inflation are revised up over the forecast horizon. Because of the less-than-favorable global environment, the forecasts for the current account deficit for both fiscal years are also raised.

Updated assessment

GDP grew by 13.5% year on year in the first quarter of FY2022, driven by a strong services sector that reflected pent-up demand being released for contact-intensive service sectors as the country returns to normalcy from COVID-19. Private consumption contributed 14.0 percentage points to total growth, the largest of all components of growth, followed by gross capital formation, up 6.7 points (Figure 3.3.12). Public consumption grew slowly, up 1.3% year on year in the first quarter, contributing only 0.2 points to growth. The contribution of net exports became increasingly negative over the quarter because of rising oil prices and imports.

Figure 3.3.12 Demand-side contributions to growth

Private consumption was the main contributor in Q1 2022, followed by gross capital formation.

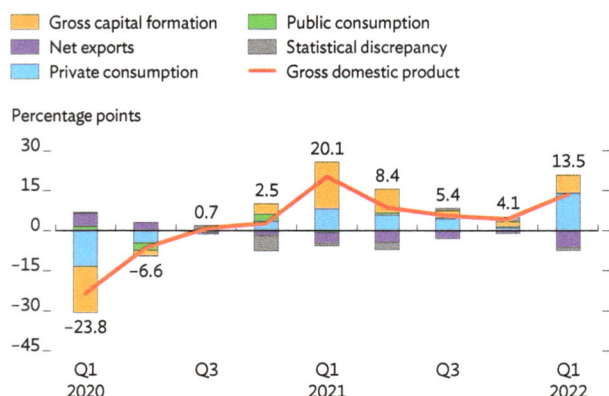

Q = quarter.

Notes: Years are fiscal years ending on 31 March of the next year. Growth rates are year on year.

Sources: Ministry of Statistics and Programme Implementation; Haver Analytics (accessed 1 September 2022).

Figure 3.3.13 Supply-side contributions to growth

Growth in Q1 2022 was driven largely by strong growth in contact-intensive service sectors.

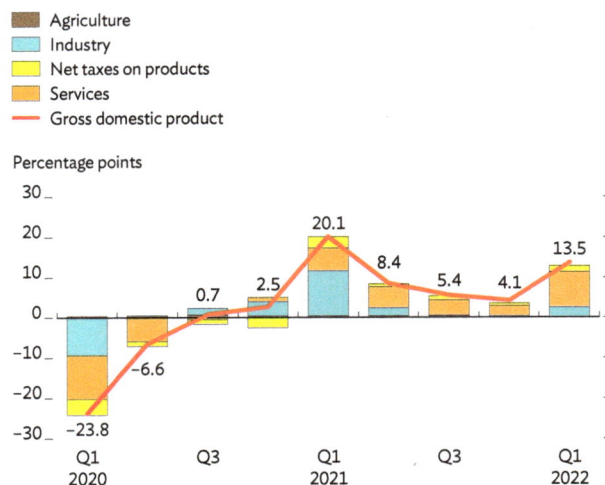

Q = quarter.

Notes: Years are fiscal years ending on 31 March of the next year. Growth rates are year on year. Net taxes on products are tax receipts minus subsidies.

Sources: Ministry of Statistics and Programme Implementation; Haver Analytics (accessed 1 September 2022).

On the supply side, double-digit growth in services was a major driver of aggregate growth (Figure 3.3.13). Trade, hotels, and transport grew by 25.7% year on year and public administration by 26.3%. Industry output contributed 2.2 percentage points to growth; construction made the largest contribution followed by manufacturing.

The headline inflation rate averaged 7.3% in the first quarter of FY2022 and continued to breach the monetary policy target of 2%–6% in July, largely on increases in food prices, which account for nearly 45% of the consumption basket (Figure 3.3.14). Food inflation was, nevertheless, below levels prevailing at the height of the pandemic. Rising prices of domestically grown vegetables accounted for 35% of food inflation, and the dependence on food imports has declined over the years to 4.3% of total merchandise imports. These developments indicate that while rising global oil and commodity prices and supply constraints following the Russian invasion of Ukraine have stoked inflation, domestic factors, such as heatwaves and heavy rainfall, are having a major impact on inflation.

Figure 3.3.14 Inflation

Inflation remains above the Reserve Bank of India's 2%–6% target.

- Headline
- Core
- Food

% year on year

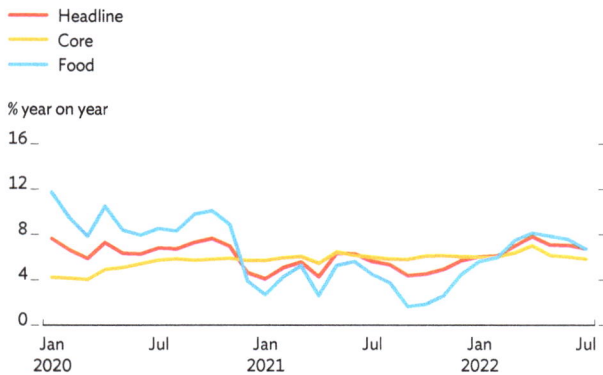

Source: CEIC Data Company (accessed 2 September 2022).

Figure 3.3.15 Interest rates

The policy rate was increased by 140 basis points during May–August 2022 to control inflation.

- Lending rate
- Policy rate

%

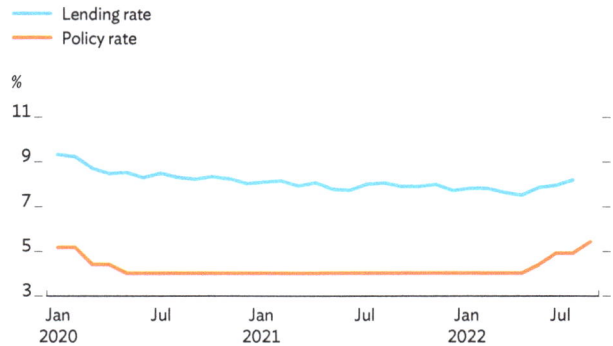

Source: CEIC Data Company (accessed 1 September 2022).

Given the elevated inflation rate, rising global financial pressures due to monetary tightening in the US, and heightened global uncertainty, the Reserve Bank of India (RBI) terminated its accommodative monetary policy stance in May. This was accompanied by an increase in the policy rate by 140 basis points over 4 months to contain inflationary expectations (Figure 3.3.15). Because economic activity remains below the pre-pandemic trend level, and inflation is largely caused by supply-side factors, the hike was primarily aimed at anchoring inflation expectations and reducing capital outflows following US monetary tightening.

The central government, too, took measures to help control inflation by cutting the excise duty on petrol and diesel, providing additional fertilizer and gas subsidies, and extending the free food distribution program. Funding these measures amounted to the equivalent of 0.9% of GDP. Their impact on the budget, however, is likely to be offset by the goods and services tax (GST) being levied in August on some essential goods, mainly packaged food. Buying cheaper Russian oil and import duty cuts also helped tame inflation.

GST revenue grew by 32.8% in the first 4 months of FY2022 (Figure 3.3.16) and the overall gross tax revenue of the central government increased by 24.9%. Nondebt capital receipts—which largely reflects disinvestment proceeds—totalled ₹301.2 billion due to the strategic sale of a major public insurance company (Figure 3.3.17).

Figure 3.3.16 Goods and services tax

GST revenue remains buoyant due to resurgent economic activity and improved compliance.

₹ million

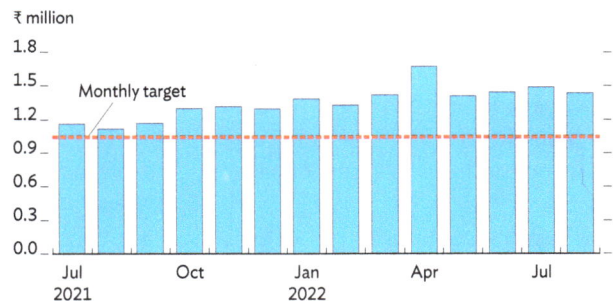

GST = goods and services tax.
Source: CEIC Data Company (accessed 2 September 2022).

Figure 3.3.17 Federal budget indicators

Revenue was lifted by a strategic divestment in May 2022.

- Revenue receipts
- Nondebt capital
- Total expenditure

₹ trillion

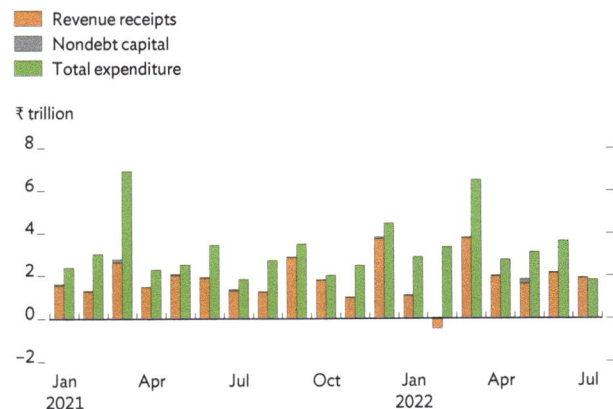

Source: CEIC Data Company (accessed 2 September 2022).

Government expenditure increased to ₹9.5 trillion in the first quarter from ₹8.2 trillion in the same period in FY2021. The budget deficit widened to ₹3.5 trillion from ₹2.7 billion.

India's states continue to grapple with fiscal issues. A June 2022 RBI report indicated that 10 states are fiscally vulnerable due to their high debt-to-GDP ratios. The liabilities of states to power distribution companies are a further source of stress on states' finances. Moreover, states receive less than 50% of total GST revenue, and their borrowing from the market has declined. Because of this, some states are tightening spending on development projects to balance their cash flows. This has the potential for adverse impacts on their future economic development.

The ratio of nonperforming loans (NPLs) to total loans is at its lowest in 6 years, at 5.9% in March 2022 down from 7.4% in the same month last year (Figure 3.3.18). While NPLs declined across all sectors, they remained high for the gems and jewelry and construction sectors. Macro-stress tests indicate that India's banks are well capitalized and capable of absorbing macroeconomic shocks even in the absence of further capital infusion. These tests indicate that the ratio of gross nonperforming assets of banks to total banking assets may decline to 5.3% by March 2023 under the baseline scenario on higher expected bank credit growth and the declining trend in the stock of these assets, among other factors. That notwithstanding, the RBI's financial stability report of June notes that banks, especially public banks, had substantial unrealized losses on their books at the beginning of the interest rate tightening cycle in May, which poses risks to their financial health. The NPLs of nonbanking financial institutions—heavy borrowers from banks and accounting for 33.5% of total bank borrowing—totaled 6.2% at the end of March 2022, a marginal dip from 6.8% in September 2021.

Credit flow improved on the fall in NPLs, although with considerable variation across sectors. Nonfood credit— which excludes public sector loans for buying crops from farmers—expanded by 2.3% from the start of April to mid-June 2022 (Figure 3.3.19). Although overall credit to agriculture expanded during the same period, priority lending to agriculture contracted by 2.3%.

Figure 3.3.18 Nonperforming loans

Declining bad loans will help spur investment.

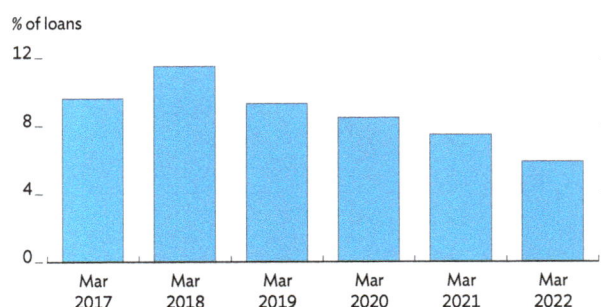

% of loans

Source: Reserve Bank of India (accessed 8 August 2022).

Figure 3.3.19 Bank credit

Rising since January 2022, especially for personal loans.

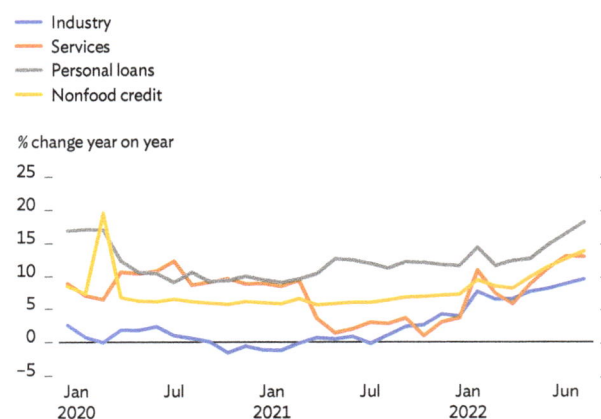

- Industry
- Services
- Personal loans
- Nonfood credit

% change year on year

Note: Nonfood credit excludes public sector loans for buying crops from farmers.
Source: Centre for Monitoring Indian Economy (accessed 23 August 2022).

Within the services sector, loans to shipping, aviation, and computer software declined sharply, and loans to large industrial firms also contracted. Loans against gold jewelry contracted, and export credit contracted 20.3%, indicating weak exports. But loans grew to the wholesale trade sector and nonbanking financial institutions. The stock market remained resilient— declining by only 2% since the start of the fiscal year— despite rising global uncertainty (Figure 3.3.20).

Imports grew by 47.9% in the first 4 months of FY2022, outpacing exports, up by 18.5%. Rising global oil prices and the depreciating rupee increased the value of imports. Slower global growth caused exports to falter.

Figure 3.3.20 Stock market

India's has performed better than peers.

— Emerging markets excluding Asia
— Bombay Stock Exchange SENSEX
— MSCI AC Asia Pacific index excluding Japan

1 January 2020 = 100

Source: Bloomberg (accessed 2 September 2022).

Figure 3.3.21 Gross international reserves

Using reserves to prevent the rupee from depreciating further caused a sharp drop in import cover.

■ Foreign exchange reserves
■ Gold reserves and special drawing rights
— Import cover

$ billion   Months of imports

Note: Years are fiscal years ending on 31 March of the next year.
Source: CEIC Data Company (accessed 1 September 2022).

Figure 3.3.22 Exchange rate

The exchange rate breached the psychologically important level of ₹80 = $1 in July 2022.

₹/$ (inverted scale)

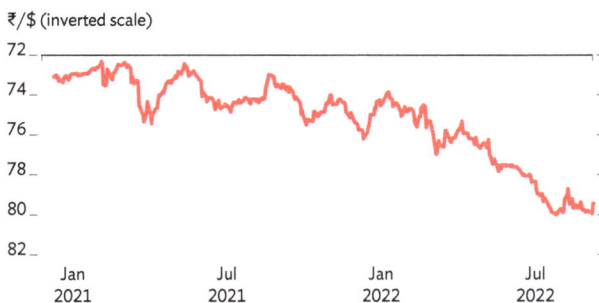

Source: Bloomberg (accessed 2 September 2022).

Despite a growing surplus in services, the overall goods and services deficit, at a record $100.8 billion in the first 4 months, points to a widening current account deficit.

Foreign direct investment (FDI) inflows declined to $16.1 billion in the first quarter of FY2022 from $17.2 billion in the same period in FY2021. Nevertheless, they have been sufficiently strong to cover foreign portfolio outflows of $6.4 billion by the end of August. Foreign exchange reserves declined by $65.9 billion since January 2022 to $564.1 billion in August, covering 8.2 months of imports compared to 13 months in January 2022 (Figure 3.3.21).

The rupee depreciated from ₹74.3 to the US dollar in January 2022 to ₹80.0 in July 2022 (Figure 3.3.22). The RBI has been active in preventing the rupee from depreciating further, resulting in the biggest drawdown of foreign exchange reserves since the 2008–2009 global financial crisis. To minimize the loss of reserves, future interventions should be aimed at reducing wide short-term exchange rate swings rather than stabilizing the rate, thereby allowing it to reflect underlying market conditions and remain an automatic stabilizer.

Prospects

Elevated oil and commodity prices and high inflation will likely require the continued tightening of monetary policy to ensure that inflation expectations do not get entrenched, which would likely hinder economic growth in the short run. Weaker than expected global demand over the next 2 years will also adversely affect exports and growth, despite the structural reforms being undertaken by the government. Nevertheless, the economy is expected to grow strongly over the forecast horizon, with investment playing a catalytic role. On the assumption that global demand will remain sluggish and oil prices elevated, this *Update* revises down the forecasts for growth to 7.0% for FY2022 from *ADO 2022*'s 7.5% projection and to 7.2% from 8.0% for FY2023 (Table 3.3.2).

Private consumption will be affected by higher inflation eroding consumer purchasing power even though consumer confidence continues to improve (Figure 3.3.23). Sticky core inflation will adversely impact spending over the next 2 years if wages fail to adjust.

Table 3.3.2 Selected economic indicators in India, %

Growth will be lower and inflation and the current account deficit higher in 2022 and 2023 than was forecast in ADO 2022.

	2021	2022		2023	
		ADO 2022	Update	ADO 2022	Update
GDP growth	8.7	7.5	7.0	8.0	7.2
Inflation	5.5	5.8	6.7	5.0	5.8
CAB/GDP	–1.2	–2.8	–3.8	–1.9	–2.1

ADO = *Asian Development Outlook*, CAB = current account balance, GDP = gross domestic product.
Note: Years are fiscal years ending on 31 March of the next year.
Source: Asian Development Bank estimates.

Figure 3.3.23 Consumer confidence

Consumer confidence continues to improve despite higher inflation.

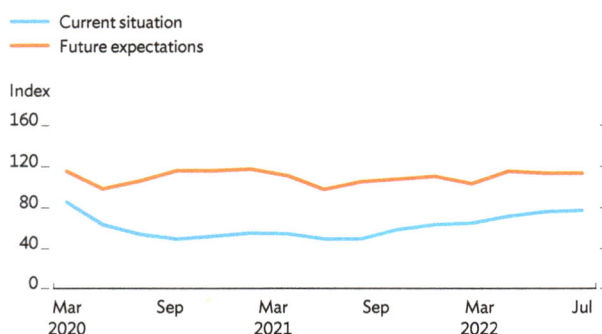

Source: Reserve Bank of India (accessed 2 September 2022)

Figure 3.3.24 Business sentiment

Business expectations dipped marginally in Q1 2022, but remain elevated in Q2.

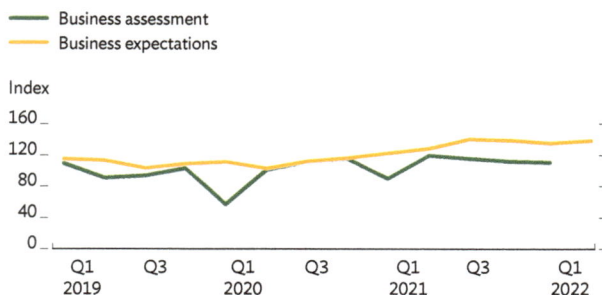

Q = quarter.
Note: Years are fiscal years ending on 31 March of the next year.
Source: Reserve Bank of India (accessed 2 September 2022).

Subsidized fertilizer and gas, the free food distribution program, and the excise duty cuts will help offset some of the effects of high inflation on consumers, but the tax on packaged food products will likely be a burden on consumers already dealing with rising inflation.

Higher government revenue from rising oil prices will help boost public consumption. Current government expenditure is expected to rise due to subsidy programs. But the overall impact on the ratio of the fiscal deficit to GDP may turn out to be minimal because of higher-than-expected nominal GDP.

Investment growth is likely to be lower than projected in April as the RBI raises policy rates, increasing the cost of borrowing for investors amid rising global uncertainty. Banks have been quick to pass on the policy rate increases to lenders, and lending rates have already risen by 43 basis points since the last hike in June. The business expectations index for the first quarter of FY2022 declined marginally, but remained elevated in the second quarter (Figure 3.3.24). Investment will nevertheless grow strongly during the forecast horizon, led by public rather than private investment (Figure 3.3.25). Government capital expenditure in the current fiscal year is budgeted at a record high of 2.9% of GDP, and the ratio of completed projects to the new projects announced remains higher for the public than the private sector.

Figure 3.3.25 Investment projects

The ratio of project completions over announced new projects was higher for the public sector in Q3 2021.

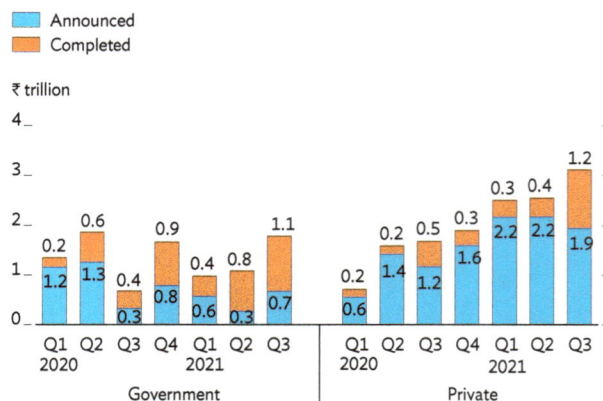

Q = quarter.
Note: Years are fiscal years ending on 31 March of the next year.
Source: Centre for Monitoring Indian Economy (accessed 23 August 2022).

Agriculture value-added is likely to be marginally lower this fiscal year as the sown area declined and the monsoon remains uneven. Agriculture incomes will, however, be largely protected, as the government is expected to increase minimum support prices to defray rising input costs.

The index of industrial production over April–May grew a strong 12.9% and the purchasing managers' index (PMI) remained above 50 in the first 4 months of FY2022, indicating robust manufacturing growth. The PMI in July—at 56.4 after 53.9 in June— was the highest in 8 months (Figure 3.3.26). The manufacturing sector, however, is expected to grow slower than previously anticipated because of rising input-cost inflation, which rose for the 22nd successive month in May before stabilizing in June and easing in July. For manufacturing to take off in FY2023 and growth to remain buoyant, it is imperative that the government's plan to reform the logistics ecosystem proceeds well. Mining output will do well because of rising commodity prices.

Services are expected to remain buoyant as this is the first year that COVID-19 restrictions have been significantly eased. Contact-intensive activities will get a big boost from this. Tourism is expected to increase, although foreign tourist arrivals remain below their pre-pandemic level, indicating room for further improvement (Figure 3.3.27). A depreciating rupee will increase net exports of services and net income. The global slowdown may, however, tamp the recovery in services.

Inflation will remain elevated in this and the next fiscal year. This *Update* forecasts the inflation rate averaging 6.7% in FY2022 before moderating to 5.8% in FY2023, just below the central bank target range of 2%–6%. Both forecasts are higher than *ADO 2022*'s projections. Even though supply pressures are expected to ease in FY2023, upward pressure on inflation could continue because of demand-side pressures caused by increasing economic activity.

Figure 3.3.26 Purchasing managers' index

PMI continues to be in the expansionary territory.

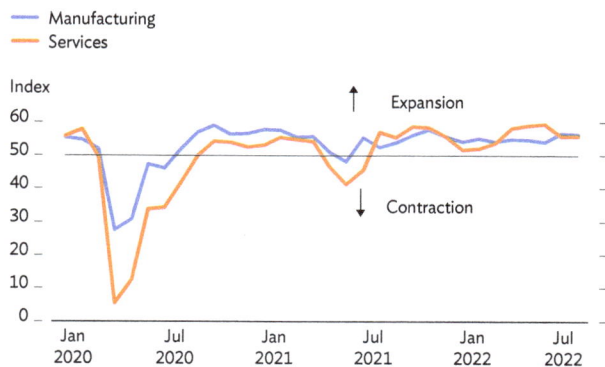

Source: Bloomberg (accessed 1 September 2022).

Figure 3.3.27 Foreign tourist arrivals

Arrivals continue to improve, but remain below pre-pandemic levels.

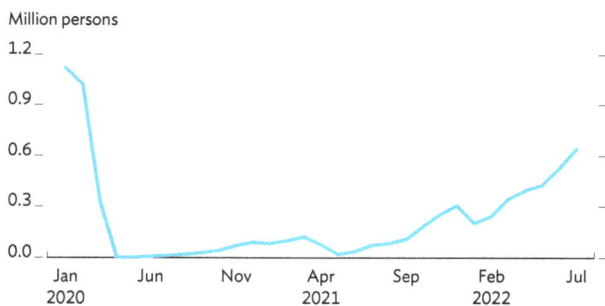

Source: CEIC Data Company (accessed 1 September 2022).

Fiscal pressure could also remain as a rising policy rate increases the cost of borrowing for the government, which largely borrows from the domestic market. Further fiscal pressures may be felt as the subsidy burden rises due to multiple overlapping schemes, such as minimum-support prices for farmers, the free food distribution program, fertilizer and gas subsidies, and excise duty cuts on petrol and diesel. The government needs to rationalize the subsidy program and mobilize domestic revenue to move onto a path of fiscal sustainability.

The RBI is expected to increase policy rates even though economic activity is still below the pre-pandemic trend and inflation continues to be driven more by domestic supply conditions than international factors. The RBI may, however, consider slowing the pace of policy rate hikes until next year because economic activity, although increasing, remains below the pre-pandemic trend. At the same time, allowing the exchange rate to serve as an automatic stabilizer will help improve the balance of payments position.

The slowdown in global growth will hurt India's export prospects in FY2022. Imports are expected to accelerate, despite purchases of cheaper Russian oil, as the country is a net oil importer. A depreciating rupee may raise the local currency value of remittances even as global income falters. On balance, the current account deficit is forecast to widen to 3.8% of GDP in FY2022 and narrow to 2.1% of GDP in FY2023, as oil and other import prices moderate. The revised forecasts are higher than ADO 2022's projections (Figure 3.3.28). Higher US interest rates and an increase in bond purchases may trigger capital outflows as foreign investors search for higher returns (Figure 3.3.29). This together with the RBI using foreign exchange reserves to manage the exchange rate and a rising import bill may put further pressure on reserves.

Risks to the outlook tilt to the downside and depend on how the war in Ukraine unfolds. Notwithstanding external pressures, structural reforms, including a concerted effort to improve the regulatory climate for businesses and physical infrastructure, should spur private investment and create more jobs over the medium-term.

Figure 3.3.28 Current account balance

The deficit is expected to widen in 2022 on rising oil prices before narrowing in 2023.

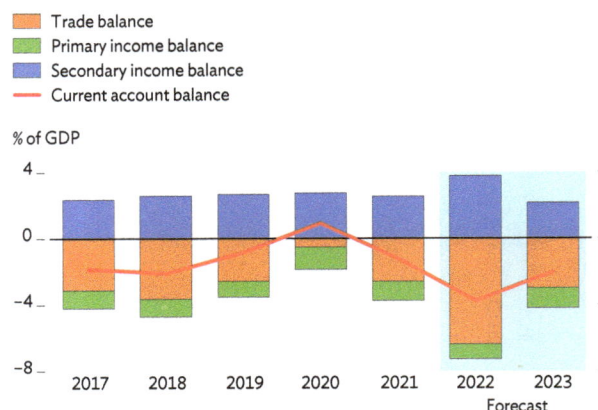

GDP = gross domestic product.
Note: Years are fiscal years ending on 31 March of the next year.
Sources: CEIC Data Company (accessed 2 September 2022); Asian Development Bank estimates.

Figure 3.3.29 Portfolio capital flows

Net capital outflows were negative since October 2021 before turning positive in July 2022.

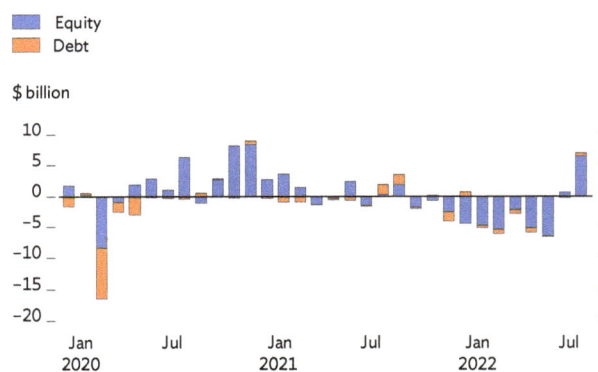

Source: Security and Exchange Board of India (accessed 2 September 2022).

Pakistan

The economy grew strongly in fiscal year 2022 (FY2022, ended 30 June 2022), supported by agriculture, services, and industry, especially large-scale manufacturing. Growth is expected to slow in FY2023 amid ongoing policy tightening and stabilization efforts to tackle sizable fiscal and external imbalances and double-digit inflation. The medium-term economic outlook will be largely shaped by the restoration of political stability and the continued implementation of reforms under the revived International Monetary Fund (IMF) program to stabilize the economy and restore fiscal and external buffers. The recent floods have severely damaged farmland, property, and livelihoods, adding a serious risk to the outlook, including for the already elevated inflation rate.

Updated assessment

The economy grew by a robust 6.0% in FY2022, propelled by higher private consumption. This followed a strong recovery in FY2021 on 5.7% growth after a 0.9% contraction in FY2020 caused by the COVID-19 pandemic. Private consumption expanded by 10.0% in FY2022, contributing 9.3 percentage points to growth (Figure 3.3.30).

The increase reflects improved employment conditions and higher household incomes—the latter against a backdrop of resilient remittances. Private consumption was also lifted by fuel and electricity subsidies in response to the sharp rise in global oil prices. These subsidies, however, were unsustainable. Investment growth slowed during FY2022, despite a noticeable rise in public investment from government efforts to expand infrastructure and affordable housing. Despite strong GDP growth, macroeconomic vulnerabilities quickly arose as a sharp expansion in domestic demand and a steep rise in global oil and commodity prices caused imports to grow much faster than exports. Net exports reduced growth by 2.7 percentage points. A notable widening of the trade deficit, along with fiscal slippages, lackluster progress on structural reforms, and limited capital inflows, also contributed to Pakistan's balance of payments difficulties.

On the supply side, agriculture output increased by 4.4% in FY2022, up from 3.5% in the previous fiscal year, supported by a strong performance in crops and livestock (Figure 3.3.31). Crop value-added grew by 6.6% as favorable weather boosted cotton output and a rise in the area under cultivation sharply increased rice, sugarcane, and maize production.

Figure 3.3.30 Demand-side contributions to growth

Growth in 2022 was supported by higher private consumption.

- Net exports
- Changes in stocks & valuables
- Fixed investment
- Government consumption
- Private consumption
- Gross domestic product at market prices

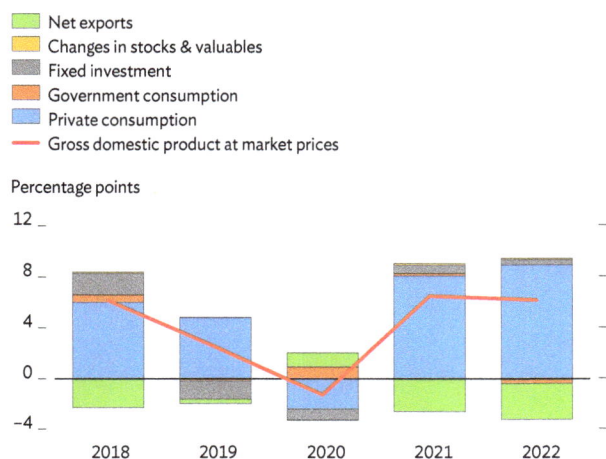

Note: Years are fiscal years ending on 30 June of that year.
Source: Pakistan Bureau of Statistics. *National Accounts: Table 9: Expenditure on Gross Domestic Product at constant prices of 2015–16* (accessed 29 July 2022).

Figure 3.3.31 Supply-side contributions to growth

Growth remained robust in 2022, led by services and industry.

- Agriculture
- Industry
- Services
- Gross domestic product at factor cost

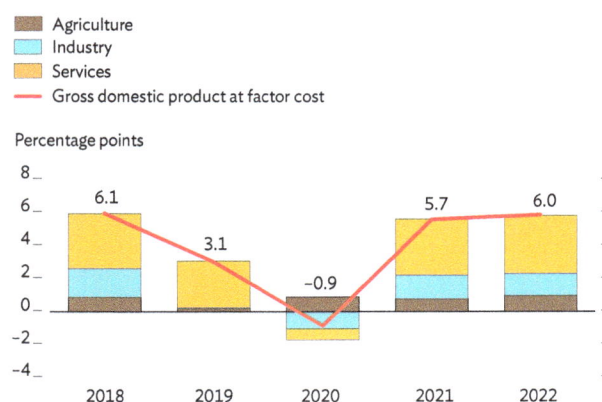

Notes: Years are fiscal years ending on 30 June of that year. Gross domestic product at basic prices excludes indirect taxes less subsidies.
Source: Pakistan Bureau of Statistics. *National Accounts: Table 5: Gross Domestic Product of Pakistan (at constant basic prices of 2015–16)* (accessed 29 July 2022).

The expansion of livestock, which accounts for over 60% of value-added in agriculture, increased by 3.3% from 2.4% in FY2021, boosting the overall growth in agriculture. The sector's contribution to growth increased to 1.0 percentage point from 0.8 points in FY2021.

Industry growth continued strong, led by a robust and broad-based expansion in large-scale manufacturing. Here, output increased by 11.7% in the first 11 months of FY2022, up from 10.2% in the same period in the previous fiscal year. The main contributions to the increase in large-scale manufacturing were textiles (4.7 percentage points), food (1.7 points), automobiles (1.5 points), furniture (1.2 points), chemicals (0.7 points), and iron and steel products (0.7 points).

Services output remained strong in FY2022, growing by 6.2% from 6.0% in FY2021. Growth was led by wholesale and retail trade and transport and storage. Faster growth raised the sector's contribution to GDP to 3.6 percentage points from 3.5 points.

Inflation accelerated sharply in the fourth quarter (April–June) of FY2022, although pressure on prices had been accumulating since the second quarter. Inflation in the fourth quarter was spurred by the pass-through effects of removing fuel and electricity subsidies, a significant depreciation in the rupee, and the surge in international commodity prices from geopolitical tensions. Inflation spiked to 21.3% year on year in June, its highest since 2008, lifting average headline inflation to 12.2% in FY2022 from 8.9% in the previous fiscal year (Figure 3.3.32). The inflation surge was broad-based, with double-digit increases for the food and nonfood price indices. The State Bank of Pakistan, the central bank, has raised its policy rate by a cumulative 800 basis points (bps) since September 2021 to help counter rising inflation and tackle mounting external imbalances and unrelenting pressure on the rupee (Figure 3.3.33). The tightening reversed an accommodative policy stance adopted at the start of the COVID-19 pandemic in March 2020. Higher interest rates notwithstanding, credit to the private sector surged by 20.5% in the year to May 2022 in response to robust domestic demand. Credit to the private sector was led by higher lending for manufacturing, consumer financing, telecommunication, wholesale and retail trade, electricity generation, and construction.

Figure 3.3.32 Monthly inflation

Food and energy prices kept inflation elevated in 2022.

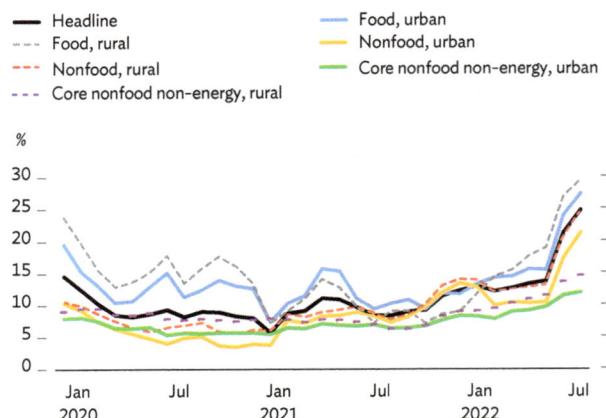

Source: State Bank of Pakistan. *Economic Data: Inflation Snapshot (2015–16 = 100)* (accessed 1 August 2022).

Figure 3.3.33 Interest rates and inflation

The central bank raised its policy rate to 15% in July 2022 to combat inflation.

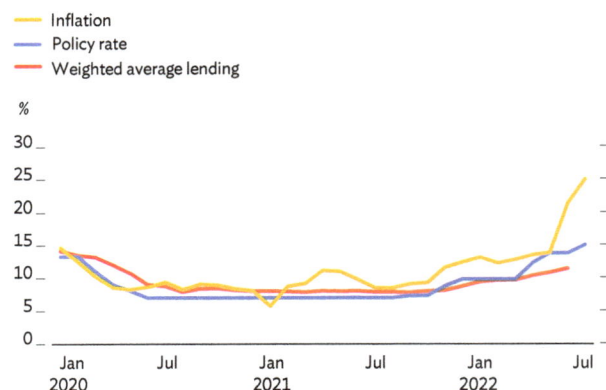

Source: State Bank of Pakistan. *Economic Data* (accessed 22 August 2022).

The consolidated fiscal deficit of the federal government and provincial governments was at 7.9% of GDP in FY2022, 1.8 percentage points higher than in FY2021. The increase reflects lower levies on petroleum products and, until May 2022, increased petroleum subsidies in the wake of the global oil price shock. The primary balance posted a deficit equivalent to 3.1% of GDP in FY2022, up from FY2021's 1.2% deficit. Revenue collection in the period slipped by 0.4 percentage points to 12.0% of GDP, as a large decline in nontax revenue outweighed strong tax collection (Figure 3.3.34).

Figure 3.3.34 Government budget indicators

The fiscal deficit widened to 7.9% of GDP in 2022 on lower petroleum stock levies and higher petroleum subsidies.

- Bank
- Current
- Development
- External
- Net lending
- Nonbank
- Nontax
- Tax

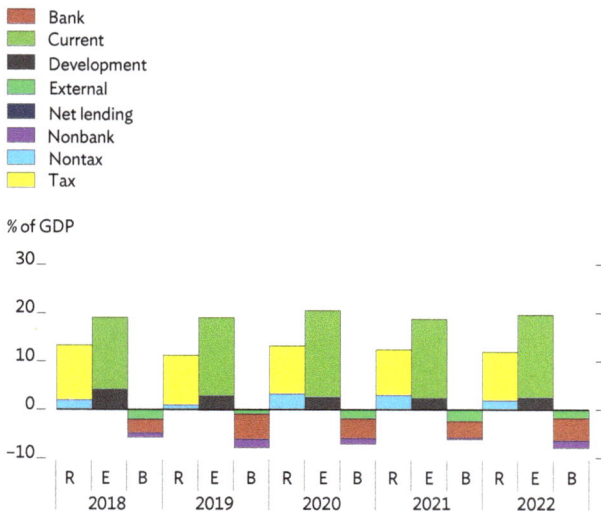

B = budget financing, E = expenditure, GDP = gross domestic product, R = revenue.

Note: Years are fiscal years ending on 30 June of that year.

Source: Ministry of Finance. *Pakistan Summary of Consolidated Federal and Provincial Fiscal Operations, 2021–22* (accessed 19 August 2022).

Figure 3.3.35 Current account components

The current account deficit widened in 2022 on surging imports.

- Current transfers including remittances
- Exports
- Services
- Income
- Imports
- Current account balance

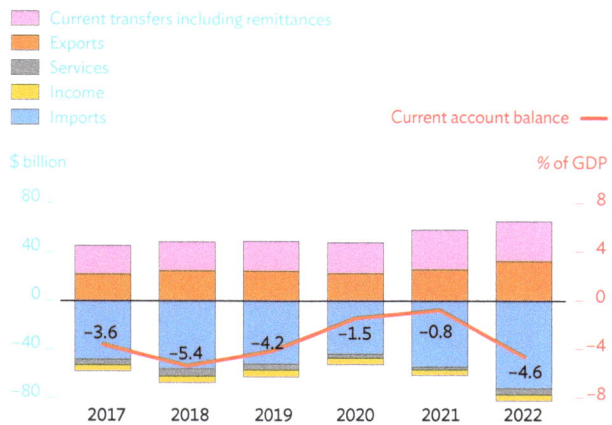

GDP = gross domestic product.

Note: Years are fiscal years ending on 30 June of that year.

Source: State Bank of Pakistan. *Economic Data: External Sector. Summary Balance of Payments as per BPM6 July 2022* (accessed 1 August 2022).

Figure 3.3.36 Trade balance

The trade deficit widened in 2022 as imports grew faster than exports.

- Merchandise imports
- Merchandise exports
- Trade balance

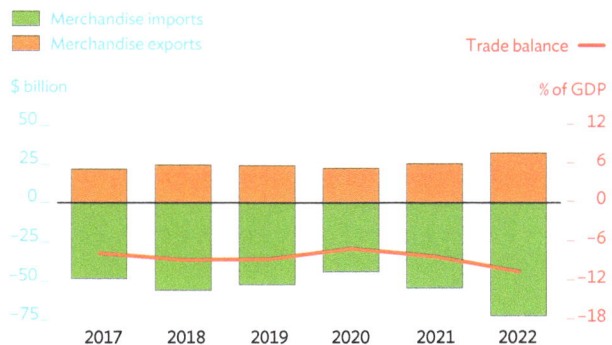

GDP = gross domestic product.

Note: Years are fiscal years ending on 30 June of that year.

Source: State Bank of Pakistan. *Economic Data: External Sector. Summary Balance of Payments as per BPM6 July 2022* (accessed 1 August 2022).

Tax revenue rose to 10.1% of GDP from 9.5% in FY2021, helped by the strong domestic recovery and higher import values. Nontax revenue declined to 1.9% of GDP from 2.9% in the previous fiscal year, reflecting smaller transfers of central bank profits and the government's decision to suspend the petroleum levy to stabilize domestic fuel prices. Total expenditure increased to 19.9% of GDP in FY2022—up from 18.5% in FY2021—due to increases in fuel and electricity subsidies and development spending. Domestic borrowing financed 77.6% of FY2022's fiscal deficit: 76.0% from banks and the rest from nonbank sources. External borrowing financed the remaining 22.4% of the deficit.

The current account deficit rose some sixfold to $17.4 billion (4.6% of GDP) in FY2022 from $2.8 billion (0.8%) in FY2021 (Figure 3.3.35). About 75% of the increase came from the merchandise trade deficit widening to 10.5% of GDP from 8.2% (Figure 3.3.36). The higher deficit came mainly from a surge in imports from strong domestic demand and the sharp rise in global oil and other commodity prices. The deficit in petroleum accounts for 51% of the overall increase in FY2022's current account deficit.

The easing of global travel restrictions and higher import-related freight and financial services expanded the deficit in services to 1.4% of GDP from 0.7% in FY2021. Consequently, the deficit in goods and services widened to 11.9% of GDP from 9.0% in FY2021. Continued strong remittance inflows, at a record $31.4 billion (8.4% of GDP) in FY2022, partly offset the impact of the larger deficit in goods and services on the overall current account deficit (Figure 3.3.37).

Figure 3.3.37 Remittances

Remittances remained strong in 2022 but grew more slowly than in 2021.

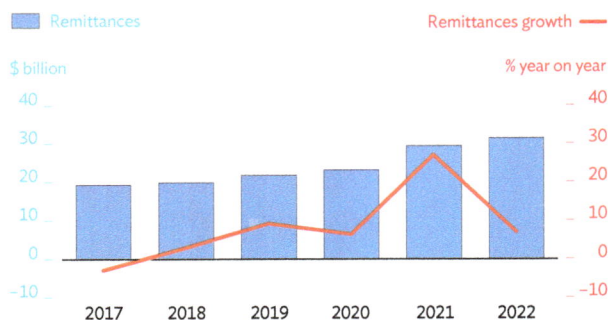

Note: Years are fiscal years ending on 30 June of that year.
Source: State Bank of Pakistan. *Economic Data: External Sector. Workers' Remittances (Credit) Seasonally Adjusted* (accessed 1 August 2022).

Challenges in getting enough financing to cover the significantly higher current account deficit and mounting debt repayments amid limited multilateral inflows persisted throughout FY2022. Despite substantial bilateral financing from the People's Republic of China and Saudi Arabia, much of the current account deficit was financed by drawing down official reserves, thereby reducing critical buffers for absorbing exogenous shocks. The central bank's gross foreign reserves plunged by 43.4% to $9.8 billion at the end of FY2022, cover for only 1.4 months of imports (Figure 3.3.38). Because of these growing external imbalances, the rupee depreciated by 26.4% against the US dollar over the fiscal year.

Figure 3.3.38 Gross official reserves and exchange rate

The central bank's gross foreign reserves declined significantly by the end of 2022.

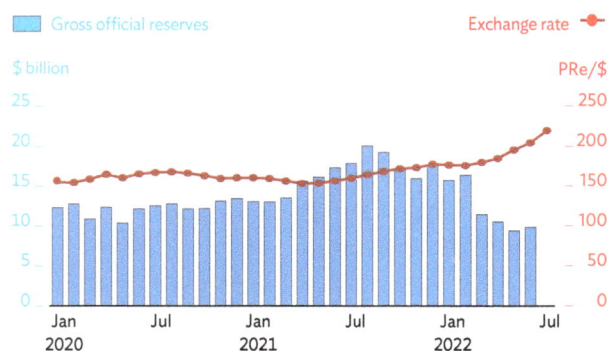

Source: State Bank of Pakistan. *Economic Data* (accessed 1 August 2022).

Prospects

On 29 August 2022, the IMF revived and augmented the Extended Fund Facility (EFF) program aimed at restoring macroeconomic stability. This allowed an immediate disbursement of 894 million in special drawing rights (about $1.1 billion), bringing total purchases for budget support under the arrangement to about $3.9 billion. In addition, the IMF extended the arrangement to the end of 2023 and augmented access by 720 million in special drawing rights, bringing total potential purchases under the EFF to about $6.5 billion. It is hoped that economic reforms in the program will catalyze significant international financial support and promote sustainable and balanced growth. The government has implemented key measures to sharply reduce fiscal and quasi-fiscal deficits. These include an ambitious revenue mobilization effort to generate 1% of GDP in additional taxes, while also ensuring cost recovery in the energy sector. To anchor inflationary expectations to the medium-term inflation target, the central bank raised its policy rate by a cumulative 675 bps to 13.75% at the end of FY2022 and by another 125 bps to 15.00% in July. The central bank also introduced measures to curtail imports and ease pressure on the rupee. These include requiring prior approval from the central bank for importing disassembled automobiles for reassembly and for all types of machinery under chapters 84 and 85 of the Harmonized System classification codes, introducing a 100% cash margin requirement on imports of several items, and prohibiting consumer financing for imported automobiles. Continued exchange rate flexibility will help absorb external shocks and support the rebuilding of foreign exchange reserves.

This *Update* revises down the growth forecast for FY2023 to 3.5% from the 4.5% projection made in *ADO 2022* in April, as economic activity will be curtailed by ongoing stabilization efforts to tackle sizable fiscal and external imbalances (Table 3.3.3 and Figure 3.3.39). Fiscal consolidation, apart from relief for flood damage, and monetary tightening are expected to suppress domestic demand. A contraction in demand, together with capacity and input constraints created by higher import prices from the rupee's large depreciation, will reduce industry output. Agriculture growth is expected to moderate on high input costs, including electricity, fertilizers, and pesticides.

Table 3.3.3 Selected economic indicators in Pakistan, %

Growth will moderate in 2023 with stabilization efforts, accompanied by a lower current account deficit and higher inflation.

	2021	2022		2023	
		ADO 2022	*Update*	*ADO 2022*	*Update*
GDP growth	5.7	4.0	6.0	4.5	3.5
Inflation	8.9	11.0	12.2	8.5	18.0
CAB/GDP	−0.8	−3.5	−4.6	−3.0	−3.0

ADO = Asian Development Outlook, CAB = current account balance, GDP = gross domestic product.
Note: Years are fiscal years ending on 30 June of that year.
Sources: Pakistan Bureau of Statistics. *National Accounts Tables*; State Bank of Pakistan. *Economic Data: Inflation Snapshot (2015–16 = 100)*, and *External Sector Summary Balance of Payments as per BPM6 July 2022*; Asian Development Bank estimates.

Figure 3.3.39 GDP growth

Growth is projected to slow to 3.5% in 2023 as stabilization efforts curtail economic activity.

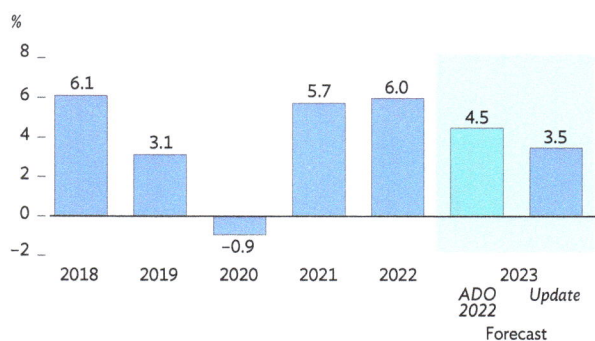

ADO = Asian Development Outlook, GDP = gross domestic product.
Note: Years are fiscal years ending on 30 June of that year.
Sources: Pakistan Bureau of Statistics. *National Accounts: Table 5: Gross Domestic Product of Pakistan (at constant basic prices of 2015–16)* (accessed 29 July 2022); Asian Development Bank estimates.

Slower growth in agriculture and industry will in turn diminish services growth, particularly wholesale and retail trade.

Inflation is expected to accelerate in FY2023 as new tax measures announced in the budget, together with an increase in the wheat support price and planned upward adjustments to electricity tariffs, are expected to keep inflationary pressures high. The year-on-year consumer price index inflation rate was at 24.9% in July 2022. This *Update* substantially revises up the forecast for headline inflation for FY2023 to 18.0% from the earlier 8.5% projection due to a potentially strong second-round impact from the rupee's depreciation and fuel and energy price adjustments (Figure 3.3.40).

On 29 June, parliament approved an FY2023 budget consistent with EFF program targets that aims for a primary surplus equivalent to 0.4% of GDP for the fiscal year. The fiscal deficit is expected to decline to 4.9% of GDP through a mix of ambitious revenue-mobilization efforts and subsidy cuts. Revenue growth is expected to increase, underpinned by the new tax measures in the Finance Act of 2022, the resumed collection of the petroleum levy, a renewed focus on curtailing tax expenditure, and additional policy and administrative measures to broaden the tax base. Expenditure is projected to decline in FY2023 as a percentage of GDP, led by a 1.4 percentage point of GDP cut in budgeted subsidies.

Figure 3.3.40 Inflation

Inflation will continue to remain elevated in 2023.

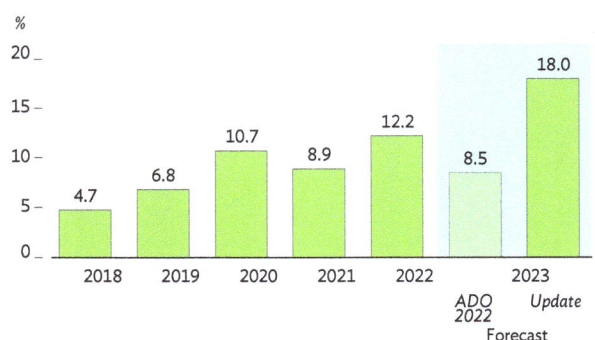

ADO = Asian Development Outlook.
Note: Years are fiscal years ending on 30 June of that year.
Sources: State Bank of Pakistan. *Economic Data: Inflation Snapshot (2015–16 = 100)* (accessed 29 July 2022); Asian Development Bank estimates.

The government aims to preserve social and development spending to protect the vulnerable and limit the slowdown in growth amid efforts to stabilize the economy. The government has already raised domestic fuel prices to bring them in line with international oil prices and is undertaking a phased withdrawal of electricity and gas subsidies, which will contribute to higher inflation in FY2023.

The current account deficit is forecast to narrow to 3.0% of GDP in FY2023, unchanged from *ADO 2022*'s projection, on a sharp slowdown in economic growth, measures to curtail nonessential imports, and the pass-through effect of the rupee's large depreciation against the US dollar (Figure 3.3.41). Exports and remittances are expected to remain resilient in FY2023, supported by improved confidence, a flexible exchange rate, the continuation of the central bank's export facilitation scheme, and government initiatives to reduce the cost of doing business. While foreign capital inflows are expected to increase, financing challenges will remain given the large sums needed to cover the current account deficit and service debt repayments. Maturing external public debt will be at about $21 billion in FY2023. Foreign direct investment should revive as investor confidence is restored by the implementation of the IMF stabilization and reform program. This should also help bring additional finance from multilateral institutions and other international partners, thus supporting the buildup of foreign exchange reserves.

Pakistan's medium-term prospects hinge critically on the restoration of political stability and the continued implementation and deepening of reforms under the revived IMF EFF program to stabilize the economy and rebuild fiscal and external buffers.

Figure 3.3.41 Current account balance

The current account deficit will shrink in 2022 as economic growth slows.

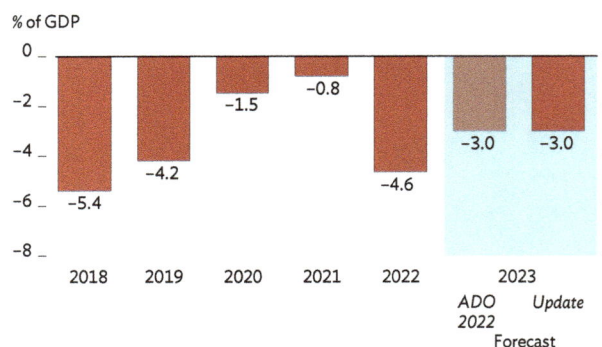

ADO = Asian Development Outlook, GDP = gross domestic product.
Note: Years are fiscal years ending on 30 June of that year.
Sources: State Bank of Pakistan. *Economic Data* (accessed 29 July 2022); Asian Development Bank estimates.

The economic outlook will also depend on the continued availability of adequate external financing under challenging domestic and global economic and political conditions. The potential economic consequences of the recent severe floods heighten the already significant risks to the outlook, including the elevated inflation rate, possible fiscal slippage as general elections approach, and a higher-than-projected increase in global food and energy prices.

Other economies

Afghanistan

Afghanistan continues to experience major turmoil, with the economic and political situation remaining highly uncertain. Humanitarian assistance from the international community in response to the ongoing socioeconomic crisis has had limited stabilizing effects on the economy in expanding the supply of basic household goods, increasing the supply of US dollars in the economy, helping stabilize the exchange rate, and facilitating transactions and payments. At the same time, the continued suspension of broader international development assistance poses serious challenges to normalizing economic activity in Afghanistan.

Continued political uncertainties and the limited international development assistance will further weaken domestic demand and economic activity in the second half of 2022. Weak domestic demand, limited access to international markets, and the disruption in the financial market will likely keep activity in services and industry subdued. An ongoing drought is expected to significantly reduce agricultural production and affect livestock health and the livelihoods of subsistence farmers. The drought reflects below average precipitation and snowfall from December 2021 to April 2022, which diminished the formation of snowpacks during the winter months and reduced the availability of water and irrigation during spring and summer. Unemployment has increased significantly. More than 900,000 people are estimated to have become unemployed since August 2021, reflecting jobs lost because of the economic crisis, the change in the political administration, and restrictions on employing women.

Supply-side shocks and currency depreciation in the fourth quarter of 2021 propelled average annual inflation to 15.5% in the first half of 2022 from 2.5% in the same period of 2021. The sharply higher inflation rate reflects price increases of 22.7% for food and 8.0% for other items. Annual inflation was at 17.5% in June 2022. Inflationary pressures will remain until borders open and aid flows broadly resume to help finance the current account.

These pressures will compound uncertainties on trade, investment, and macroeconomic stability. The ongoing drought combined with heightened food and energy prices in the international market and supply chain disruptions will increase inflationary pressures, adding to industry costs and reducing consumers' real incomes. Monetary policy is likely to be ineffective in curbing inflation in an economy with extensive dollarization.

Domestic capacity has been further constrained with the exit of part of the educated population from the country. This has hampered economic activities. In the first half of 2022, public revenue totaled AF75.6 billion, 56% of which came from customs duties. Non-tax sources were the biggest contributors to domestic revenue. However, public revenue is insufficient to cover basic services and expenditure, including salaries for public sector employees. Fiscal challenges, the afghani's depreciation, and the inability to access foreign exchange have also severely hampered the ability of the Taliban regime to provide basic public goods and services, such as electricity (77% imported), further compounding the economic crisis and its humanitarian impacts.

Imports have sharply contracted in line with subdued domestic demand and limitations on international payments. In the first quarter of 2022, imports from Pakistan, Afghanistan's biggest trading partner, were 54% below the same period in 2021. But a surge in exports of coal and fruit propelled exports of goods to Pakistan to $408 million in the first quarter of 2022 from $200 million in the same period last year. Services inflows have diminished sharply since the departure of international security forces and diplomats. Because of these developments, the combined deficit in goods and services is expected to narrow in 2022.

Bhutan

The economy grew by 4.1% in 2021 after a record 10.0% contraction in 2020 due to disruptions caused by the COVID-19 pandemic. Strong domestic demand supported by the government's countercyclical programs and monetary relief measures and eased COVID-19 restrictions enabled all sectors of the economy to expand last year. Services grew by 6.3%, mainly reflecting a marked increase in wholesale and retail trade from the release of pent-up demand and revived economic activity triggering a sharp rise in transportation and communications services output. Despite an 8.8% increase in construction, industry output grew by only 2.0%, held back by a 4.9% decline in hydroelectricity production owing to low rainfall and weak water flows. Below-average rainfall constrained agricultural production, up only 2.1%. On the demand side, aggregate consumption expenditure revived, rising by 5.1% after contracting 4.3% in 2020. The growth mainly reflects private spending and fixed investment, mostly by government, which was up by a robust 12.6%.

This *Update* maintains the forecast for 2022 growth in *ADO 2022* made in April, as supportive macroeconomic policies have been continued (Table 3.3.4). Government investment will continue to be the key driver of growth as the government ramps up efforts to complete ongoing projects in the 12th Five-Year Plan, 2018–2023. Aggregate consumption expenditure is expected to ease since current government expenditure can be funded only through available tax revenue. Construction growth, forecast at 17.5%, will underpin moderate 6.3% industry growth because electricity output is expected to increase by only 1%–2% due to the temporary shutting down of the Tala plant, the country's largest hydropower plant, for maintenance. Manufacturing output is forecast to double to 4.1%; mining and quarrying production will decline slightly. Services growth is expected to slip to 3.9% on slower consumption expenditure. Agriculture production is forecast at 2.3% due to better weather.

GDP growth in 2023 is revised down to 4.0%, well below *ADO 2022*'s 7.5% forecast, mainly due to delays in completing the 1,020 megawatt Punatsangchhu II hydropower plant and a slower-than-expected revival in tourism. Public investment is expected to decline due to the transition from the 12th to the 13th Five-Year Plan and private investment is expected to slacken in tandem with the decline in public investment.

Table 3.3.4 Selected economic indicators in Bhutan, %

GDP growth and current account deficits in 2023 are lowered from ADO 2022's forecasts.

	2021	2022		2023	
		ADO 2022	Update	ADO 2022	Update
GDP growth	4.1	4.5	4.5	7.5	4.0
Inflation	7.4	7.0	6.5	5.5	5.5
CAB/GDP	–22.0	–10.6	–15.0	–10.5	–7.5

ADO = *Asian Development Outlook*, CAB = current account balance, GDP = gross domestic product.
Sources: Royal Government of Bhutan publications; Asian Development Bank estimates.

Bhutan's near-term outlook will depend on global, regional, and domestic circumstances. The global economic uncertainties due to geopolitical tensions are affecting Bhutan through higher oil and commodity prices. The risk of more potent COVID-19 variants poses health and economic risks. Other risks include further delays to hydropower projects, a lower-than-expected services' performance, and erratic rainfall patterns affecting energy and agriculture output.

Headline inflation in the first half of 2022 averaged 6%, mainly due to rising fuel prices. The increase in nonfood prices was relatively higher than food prices. Since fuel prices have eased since mid-July and the outlook for agriculture is positive, the forecast for inflation is revised down in 2022 from the earlier projection; the forecast for 2023 is retained.

The current account deficit for 2022 is projected to be well above *ADO 2022*'s forecast because of a widening trade deficit. This mainly reflects somewhat higher-than-expected growth in investment and construction, and the large increase in global import prices for food and fuel. The current account deficit for 2023 is revised down; the forecast takes into consideration the improvement in the balance of trade on higher power exports, a substantial fall in capital imports as investment slackens, and easing global fuel and food prices. Higher remittances are expected because of the growing numbers of Bhutanese travelling overseas for work.

Maldives

Tourism performed strongly in the first half of 2022, with tourist arrivals growing by 59.3% year on year. This was still 5.7% lower compared to the same period of 2019. The impact of the Russian invasion of Ukraine caused a decline in tourists from both countries. Even so, Maldives managed to attract tourists from its traditional and new markets that compensated for this loss. Europe was the biggest market, accounting for 63.1% of total arrivals and growing by 52.5%. India was the largest single-source market, with arrivals up by 14.8%, followed by the United Kingdom. Arrivals from the People's Republic of China, which had a 16.7% market share in 2019, were nominal, reflecting the country's stringent travel policies to mitigate the spread of COVID-19.

Construction activity increased in the first half of 2022, as was evident from the 70.4% year on year rise in imports of construction materials. Total government tax collection rose by 49.4% in the first half from the same period in 2021, reflecting the robust recovery of businesses. Based on official estimates, the economy grew by 19.3% in the first quarter year on year.

Prospects are favorable for the peak tourist season in the fourth quarter. Maldives had 813,211 tourist arrivals in the first half of 2022; this exceeded the projection in *ADO 2022* in April for arrivals in this period. Construction activity is expected to slow in the second half as the government reprioritizes spending and delays part of its public investment program to cover higher financing and interest costs and increased subsidies due to soaring global oil and food prices. At the end of June, subsidy spending was 191% higher than in the same period in 2021 and 21% above the approved allocation in the 2022 budget. Because of limited fiscal space and increased spending requirements, the government might surpass its earlier fiscal deficit projection for 2022 of 11.2% of GDP. Given all these developments and the base effect from the revised higher 2021 GDP growth rate, this *Update* revises down the forecast for growth for 2022 and 2023 from the earlier projections (Table 3.3.5).

The main downside risks to the outlook are the emergence of new viruses dampening the recovery in tourism and a sharp increase in global interest rates raising the cost of borrowing.

Table 3.3.5 Selected economic indicators in Maldives, %

The forecasts for growth are revised down; the projections for inflation and the current account deficit to GDP ratios are revised up.

	2021	2022		2023	
		ADO 2022	Update	ADO 2022	Update
GDP growth	37.1	11.0	8.2	12.0	10.4
Inflation	0.5	3.0	3.3	2.5	2.8
CAB/GDP	−9.2	−19.5	−20.0	−17.5	−19.0

ADO = *Asian Development Outlook,* CAB = current account balance, GDP = gross domestic product.
Sources: Maldives Monetary Authority. *Monthly Statistics.* July 2022; Asian Development Bank estimates.

Both would put pressure on debt sustainability in the face of the country's very high public debt-to-GDP ratio and limited foreign exchange reserves. The government's proposed increase in the goods and services tax and subsidy rationalization reforms, which are planned to take place next year, are corrective measures to tackle the fiscal imbalance and the high level of debt.

The government's subsidies on food staples, fuel, and electricity largely kept inflation in check in the first half of 2022, at an average 1.8%, despite a big increase in energy prices and non-energy imports. However, inflationary pressure from high-priced imports appears to have intensified—June's inflation rate was 5.2%—and inflation is now expected to be higher than *ADO 2022*'s projection. Inflation will ease in 2023 due to an expected moderation in global oil and food prices, but the level will remain elevated as the government increases the goods and services tax and streamlines subsidies. On balance, the inflation forecasts are revised up for 2022 and 2023.

The trade deficit in the first half of 2022 increased by 47.3% from the same period in 2021; all import items rose, especially petroleum products, due to geopolitical tensions. Robust tourism, however, boosted the services balance, with travel receipts up by 39.1% in the first 5 months of 2022 year on year. Because supply constraints will continue to exert inflationary pressure on import prices, the trade gap is expected to be wider than earlier estimates. Accordingly, the current account deficit forecasts are revised up from *ADO 2022*'s projections.

Nepal

The economy continued to recover in fiscal year 2022 (FY2022, ended 15 July 2022) after rebounding in FY2021 from a contraction in FY2020. This *Update* revises up the growth forecast for FY2022 from the projection made in *ADO 2022* in April (Table 3.3.6) with official preliminary estimates showing GDP growth at 5.8%. The official preliminary estimates reflect the authorities' expansionary fiscal and monetary policies in FY2022. Industry rebounded by 10.2%, up from 4.5% in FY2021, on increased electricity and manufacturing output and construction activity. Services grew by 5.9%, up from 4.2%, as tourism and related activities gathered pace on rising international tourist arrivals. Even so, arrivals and tourist revenue are still well below pre-pandemic 2019. Wholesale and retail trade, transport, and financial services picked up due to a significant containment of COVID-19 infections and the removal of mobility restrictions. Agriculture output slowed to 2.3% from 2.8% because of unexpected rains and floods in mid-October that damaged ready-to-harvest crops. On the demand side, strong 5.4% growth in private consumption expenditure helped underpin GDP growth. Fixed investment growth declined to 4.6% from 9.8% on a 6.0% slump in public investment because of budget implementation delays. Private investment, however, rose by 8.8%.

The forecast for growth in FY2023 is revised down from the earlier projection because of the effect of needed policy tightening to stem a rapid rise in imports, a marked decline in foreign exchange reserves, and the increasing inflationary pressure in FY2022. These developments if they had continued would have jeopardized macroeconomic stability. To tackle rising inflation and pressure on foreign exchange reserves, Nepal Rastra Bank, the central bank, announced an increase in its policy rate in July to 7.0% from 5.5%, which took effect in August. The fiscal policy for FY2023 is somewhat expansionary, focusing on strengthening agriculture, industry, infrastructure, and social protection. But some expenditure trimming may be needed to strengthen macroeconomic stability.

The inflation rate was at 8.1% at the end of FY2022. The elevated level mainly reflects higher global oil and commodity prices caused by the Russian invasion of Ukraine. This somewhat dampened domestic agriculture production and the recovery in domestic demand.

Table 3.3.6 Selected economic indicators in Nepal, %

The current account deficit will moderate in 2023 due to tight monetary policy.

	2021	2022		2023	
		ADO 2022	Update	ADO 2022	Update
GDP growth	4.2	3.9	5.8	5.0	4.7
Inflation	3.6	6.5	6.3	6.2	6.1
CAB/GDP	-7.8	-9.7	-12.9	-6.1	-8.1

ADO = *Asian Development Outlook*, CAB = current account balance, GDP = gross domestic product.
Note: Years are fiscal years ending 15 July of that year.
Source: Asian Development Bank estimates.

The marked rise in prices, however, occurred mostly in the final months of FY2022, as inflation was quite low early in the fiscal year. Annual inflation in FY2022 averaged 6.3%, a tad lower than *ADO 2022*'s projection. The inflation forecast for FY2023 is revised down as international crude oil prices have begun receding and on anticipation of a further rise in interest rates. The 22 July increase in Nepal Rastra Bank's policy rate is expected to keep inflationary pressures in check.

The current account deficit increased by 81.9% in FY2022 to $5.2 billion, the equivalent of 12.9% of GDP, well above *ADO 2022*'s projection. Imports grew rapidly, especially in the first half of FY2022, as economic activity surged with the lifting of COVID-19 restrictions. The trade deficit widened by 19.5%, but workers' remittances, the major offset of the traditional trade deficit, grew by only 2.2% from 8.2%. Financial inflows slackened and were not enough to offset the current account deficit. Foreign exchange reserves fell to $9.5 billion in FY2022—cover for only 6.9 months of imports of goods and services—from $11.8 billion the previous fiscal year (10.2 months). The current account deficit is forecast narrowing in FY2023 from FY2022 due to moderating merchandise imports amid stable remittance inflows, but the deficit will be wider than *ADO 2022*'s projection.

Downside risks to the outlook could arise from further stringent measures by the authorities that may be necessary to curb imports and tame inflationary pressure, which would depress domestic production and consumption, adversely affecting growth. A resurgence in COVID-19 leading to lockdown measures, intensified geopolitical turmoil, or a disaster triggered by a natural hazard are also risks to the outlook.

Sri Lanka

Economic conditions deteriorated significantly since *ADO 2022* in April on a deepening debt crisis, severe shortage of foreign exchange, and major supply shocks. These are the results of persistent and large fiscal deficits, the impact of the COVID-19 pandemic, an ill-timed move to switch from chemical to organic fertilizers, and the Russian invasion of Ukraine. On 18 May, Sri Lanka defaulted on its external sovereign debt for the first time after suspending service payments on certain categories of its commercial and official bilateral debt. This resulted in its sovereign credit rating being downgraded to the restrictive/selective default category. Limited external financing avenues and dwindling foreign reserves have led to an acute energy crisis and shortages of essential goods and services that have threatened food security and hit consumer and business confidence.

GDP contracted by 1.6% year on year in the first quarter of 2022. Agriculture felt the impact of a temporary ban on chemical fertilizers, with output contracting by 6.8% in the quarter. The slight pick-up in overall services output was due to growth in information technology services and a brief revival in tourism in early 2022 as the pandemic subsided. Sri Lanka's multifaceted crisis caused private consumption to fall in the first quarter, but government consumption rose. Gross capital formation declined on a sharp fall in inventories. But the deficit in net exports narrowed substantially because of the squeeze on imports and resilient export growth.

The Central Bank of Sri Lanka and the government have taken several measures to stabilize the economy. The central bank raised policy rates by a cumulative 950 basis points over the first 8 months of 2022 that included a record rate hike of 700 basis points in April. Energy prices have been raised on numerous occasions since mid-2021. As of August 2022, fuel prices tripled on a year-on-year basis. And electricity prices were raised on 18 August, the first increase since 2013.

A reform-oriented interim budget for 2022 was presented to Parliament on 30 August, necessitated by the drastic change in Sri Lanka's economic situation since the original budget was approved in December 2021. Proposed reforms include rationalizing the size of the public sector;

Table 3.3.7 Selected economic indicators in Sri Lanka, %

A multidimensional crisis will lead to sizeable contractions in growth and galloping inflation in 2022 and 2023.

	2021	2022		2023	
		ADO 2022	Update	ADO 2022	Update
GDP growth	3.3	2.4	–8.8	2.5	–3.3
Inflation	6.0	13.3	44.8	6.7	18.6
CAB/GDP	–3.8	–4.3	–0.8	–2.8	–0.9

ADO = *Asian Development Outlook*, CAB = current account balance, GDP = gross domestic product.
Sources: Central Bank of Sri Lanka; Asian Development Bank estimates.

setting up dedicated units for managing public debt and public–private partnerships and restructuring state-owned enterprises; a new central bank law to strengthen the monetary authority's independence; reducing dependence on monetization of the budget deficit; strengthening fiscal oversight; liberalizing trade by phasing out para-tariffs; and improved bankruptcy laws. Proposed expenditure measures aim to increase outlays on social protection through higher allocations and repurposing project spending. Capital expenditure is likely to be limited to essential projects. The budget's revenue proposals complement measures that were introduced on 31 May; these include increasing value-added tax (VAT) in two steps from 8% to 15%, thereby fully reversing December 2019's VAT reduction. Revenue is forecast rising to the equivalent of 8.8% of GDP this year from 8.3% in 2021 and expenditure declining to 18.6% of GDP from 19.9%. The government projects the overall fiscal deficit at 9.8% of GDP in 2022, up from 11.6% in 2021, and the primary deficit declining to 4.0% from 5.7%.

Sri Lanka reached a staff-level agreement with the International Monetary Fund (IMF) on 1 September for a 4-year $2.9 billion extended fund facility program. Prior actions need to be implemented and progress on debt treatment is required before the IMF's management and the executive board approve the program. Proposals in the interim budget are in line with the key elements of the IMF program.

The severe macroeconomic challenges, including the impact of the ongoing crisis, which worsened in mid-2022 are likely to have resulted in sharp contractions in the second and third quarters.

Contractionary monetary policy and tight fiscal policy will further weigh on growth. This *Update* revises down the growth forecasts for Sri Lanka for 2022 and 2023 from the projections made in *ADO 2022*. Contractions, not growth, are now projected for both years.

Inflation soared to 64.3% in August from 14.2% in January, averaging 37.1% in the first 8 months. This was largely driven by food inflation, at 93.7% in August. The core inflation rate also rose sharply, from 8.3% at the end of 2021 to 46.6% in August, signaling underlying inflationary pressures. Import restrictions, supply chain disruptions, poor agriculture output following the chemical fertilizer ban, rising global oil and commodity prices, energy price revisions, and exchange rate depreciation are stoking inflation. The inflation forecasts are therefore revised sharply up for both years, with inflationary pressures abating over time.

Merchandise exports grew a robust 12.9% year on year in the first 7 months of 2022, spurred by 20.0% growth in garment exports, Sri Lanka's largest export item. But tea and several other key agriculture exports contracted as output declined. Merchandise imports contracted by 3.5% on the shortage of foreign exchange and higher commodity prices. Although fuel imports increased in value amid rising oil prices, volumes fell. Because of this, the merchandise trade deficit narrowed by 26.1% in the first 7 months over the same period in 2021. The recovery in tourism was brief, as arrivals fell again in the second quarter on the effects of the Russian invasion of Ukraine—both countries have been key source markets since the pandemic—and the domestic crisis. Remittance inflows fell by 47.6% year on year in the first 8 months, despite measures introduced to promote inflows through formal channels.

Foreign exchange reserves remain perilously low at $1.72 billion at the end of August—cover for about 1 month of imports—compared to $3.10 billion at the end of 2021. Usable reserves, which exclude $1.50 billion in bilateral currency swaps, are far lower. The rupee depreciated by 44.1% against the US dollar from March to August, as the central bank abandoned the de facto peg it had maintained since April 2021 before allowing greater exchange rate flexibility in March 2022. Since 12 May 2022, to limit currency volatility, the central bank introduced an indicative mid-point based on the preceding day's spot market rate with a margin on both sides.

Imports will be constrained by the contraction in domestic demand and the scarcity of foreign exchange, which together with the recovery in exports should help narrow the goods-trade deficit. Remittances are likely to be lower this year, but net income and service receipts may improve for the full year due to a decline in interest payments following the suspension of external debt service payments and some recovery in tourism in the last quarter as travel advisories are relaxed. Overall, smaller ratios of the current account deficit to GDP are expected this year and the next than were projected earlier.

The downside risks to the outlook include global economic headwinds, geopolitical factors, spillovers from sovereign exposure to the financial sector, external financing constraints, delays in securing the IMF program, and political uncertainty.

SOUTHEAST ASIA

Two factors—stronger domestic demand from the reopening of markets and borders, and reduced external demand from increased global risks—are shaping Southeast Asia's growth. Because of stronger consumption, this *Update* revises slightly up the forecast for the subregion's growth in 2022 from *ADO 2022*'s projection in April. The forecast for 2023 is lower, reflecting the cloudier global outlook. Continuing supply disruptions because of the war in Ukraine, higher commodity and food prices, and higher global interest rates will accelerate inflation. The current account surplus will likely narrow this year.

Subregional assessment and prospects

Since April, the performance of Southeast Asia's economies has been mixed. The reopening of markets on easing COVID-19 restrictions, coupled with pent-up consumer demand, lifted private consumption and investment growth for most economies. The reopening of borders facilitated a quick rebound in domestic and intra-regional tourism that increased output in travel, accommodation, and hospitality services. For the first half of 2022, aggregate GDP growth for Southeast Asian economies with quarterly data was 5.3%.

The stringency index for the subregion fell on aggregate to 34% in August from almost 60% in December 2021—despite a recent spike in COVID-19 cases. Lower COVID-19 deaths helped people gain confidence that they can live with COVID-19. Consumer spending on services, consumer durables, and discretionary items buoyed domestic demand, particularly for the bigger economies. Growth was also supported by higher employment and income, and government cash transfers to vulnerable groups.

A nascent resurgence of private investment is coming mainly from manufacturing even though public investment remains constrained.

Export growth continues to bounce back. Solid demand for digital products is supporting stronger electronics exports in Malaysia, the Philippines, Thailand, and Viet Nam. Higher garments and textiles sales in Cambodia and Myanmar are supporting exports of these goods. Thailand's agricultural product and Singapore's processed food exports are significantly benefiting from heightened global demand to secure food supplies. And higher commodity prices, particularly for palm oil and energy exports, provided windfall gains to Brunei Darussalam, Indonesia, and Malaysia.

However, higher imports of oil and food products widened trade deficits, particularly for the smaller economies but also for the Philippines and Thailand. Imports increased on rising consumption and investment demand, and higher commodity prices.

The subregional assessment and prospects were written by James Villafuerte and Dulce Zara. The section on Indonesia was written by Henry Ma and Priasto Aji; Malaysia by James Villafuerte and Maria Theresa Bugayong; the Philippines by Cristina Lozano and Teresa Mendoza; Thailand by Chitchanok Annonjarn; Viet Nam by Cuong Minh Nguyen, Nguyen Luu Thuc Phuong, and Chu Hong Minh. The other economies, by Emma Allen, Poullang Doung, Kavita Iyengar, Yothin Jinjarak, Soulinthone Leuangkhamsing, Eve Cherry Lynn, Nedelyn Magtibay-Ramos, Joel Mangahas, Duong Nguyen, Shiu Tian, Marcel Shroeder, and Mai Lin Villaruel. The authors are in the Southeast Asia and Economic Research and Regional Cooperation departments, ADB.

Services exports expanded in the first half of 2022 after countries eased travel restrictions for foreign visitors. International tourist arrivals in Thailand totaled 2.1 million, up from 40,000 in the first half of 2021; 1 million in Malaysia, which has achieved half of its full-year target; and 500,000 in Cambodia, up from 100,000 in the first half of 2021. Indonesia's services exports surged by 60% in the second quarter, as more international flights were allowed.

Fiscal policy continued to support domestic demand, which is still affected by the lingering effects of COVID-19 and being dampened by rising energy and food prices. In addition to pandemic-assistance measures, governments across Southeast Asia have rolled out measures to protect vulnerable groups from elevated fuel and food prices. Fuel subsidies were implemented in Cambodia, Indonesia, Malaysia, the Philippines, Thailand, and Timor-Leste. Excise taxes on fuel products were suspended in the Lao People's Democratic Republic (Lao PDR), and Viet Nam reduced its environment protection tax to cool inflationary pressures. Fiscal policies will likely become tighter as fiscal consolidation measures are introduced to contain rising fiscal deficits and debt.

Growth in the Southeast Asia subregion for 2022 is revised up to 5.1% from the earlier 4.9% projection due to stronger growth forecasts for Indonesia, Myanmar, and the Philippines (Figure 3.4.1). Consumer spending in these economies accelerated after their borders reopened. Growth in Indonesia is benefiting from windfall export gains. Investment in the Philippines is also rising. The projections for growth this year for the Lao PDR, Singapore, Thailand, and Timor-Leste are revised down because of weaker external demand from major economies, which will dampen growth in these four economies. The forecasts for Brunei Darussalam, Cambodia, Malaysia, and Viet Nam are unchanged. The growth forecast for the Southeast Asia subregion for 2023 is revised down to 5.0% from the earlier 5.2% projection because of weaker global growth, supply chain disruptions, continuing lockdowns in the People's Republic of China, and higher inflation. Growth forecasts for seven of the subregion's 11 economies are revised down and the rest unchanged.

Figure 3.4.1 GDP growth in Southeast Asia

Growth lifted by eased COVID-19 mobility restrictions and reopened borders.

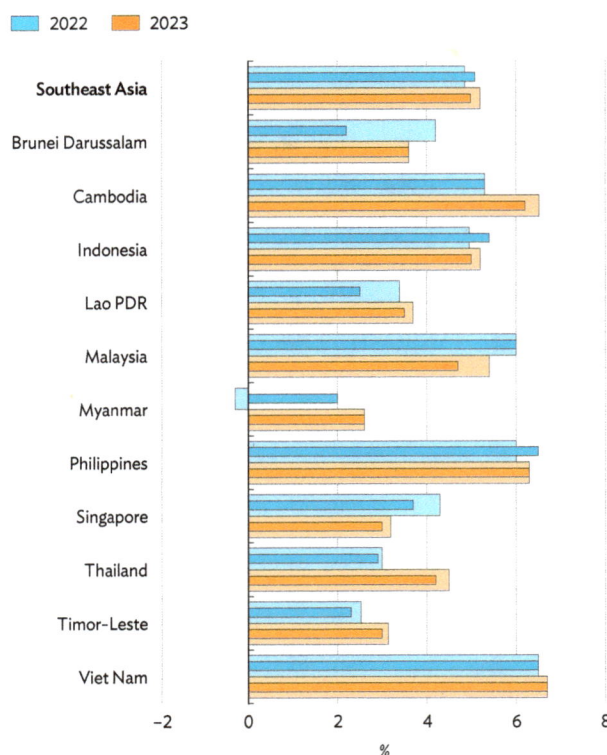

GDP = gross domestic product, Lao PDR = Lao People's Democratic Republic.
Note: Lighter colored bars are *Asian Development Outlook 2022* forecasts.
Source: *Asian Development Outlook* database.

Inflation remains elevated at a weighted average of 4% in the first half of 2022. Inflation rose in nine economies, reflecting higher fuel and food prices. Inflation was contained in Viet Nam and decelerated in Malaysia due to government subsidies and price controls. The subregion's smaller import-dependent economies are grappling with higher food prices. Noticeably higher prices apply to maize in the Philippines, meat in Thailand, eggs in Singapore, and oils and fats in Brunei Darussalam. Among the varied reasons for rising prices are supply disruptions caused by the war in Ukraine, higher energy prices and the cost of credit, and lower agricultural production from bad weather. Most local currencies have depreciated against the US dollar, led by the Lao PDR's kip, Myanmar's kyat, and the Philippine peso as of end August, contributing to inflationary pressures in these economies.

Figure 3.4.2 Inflation in Southeast Asia

Supply disruptions, elevated energy prices, and bad weather are stoking inflation.

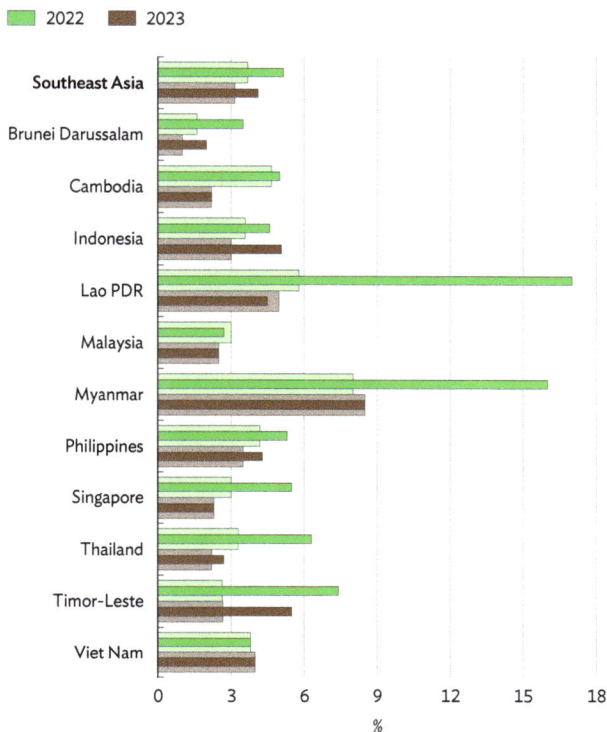

■ 2022   ■ 2023

Southeast Asia
Brunei Darussalam
Cambodia
Indonesia
Lao PDR
Malaysia
Myanmar
Philippines
Singapore
Thailand
Timor-Leste
Viet Nam

0   3   6   9   12   15   18
%

Lao PDR = Lao People's Democratic Republic.
Note: Lighter colored bars are *Asian Development Outlook 2022* forecasts.
Source: *Asian Development Outlook* database.

Figure 3.4.3 Current account balance in Southeast Asia

Imports surging in many economies on higher oil prices and weaker local currencies.

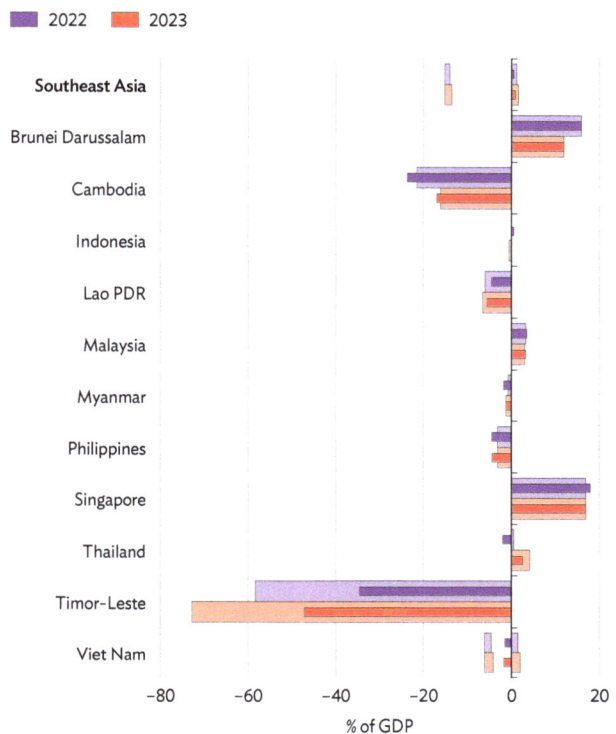

■ 2022   ■ 2023

Southeast Asia
Brunei Darussalam
Cambodia
Indonesia
Lao PDR
Malaysia
Myanmar
Philippines
Singapore
Thailand
Timor-Leste
Viet Nam

−80   −60   −40   −20   0   20
% of GDP

GDP = gross domestic product, Lao PDR = Lao People's Democratic Republic.
Note: Lighter colored bars are *Asian Development Outlook 2022* forecasts.
Source: *Asian Development Outlook* database.

Because of these developments, the forecasts for inflation in 2022 for the Southeast Asia subregion are revised up to 5.2% from the earlier 3.7% projection and to 4.1% from 3.1% for 2023 (Figure 3.4.2).

Monetary policy is still largely accommodative, although several authorities have started tightening to manage rising inflation, led by the Philippines, which has raised its policy rate by 175 basis points (bps), Malaysia by 50 bps, and Thailand and Indonesia by 25 bps each. Some central banks have also imposed foreign exchange controls to shore up much-needed US dollars, notably in the Lao PDR and Myanmar.

The subregion's current account balance will remain positive, but narrow to a forecast 0.5% in 2022 from the earlier projection of a 1.2% surplus (Figure 3.4.3).

Imports are rising mainly on higher prices of fuel and food imports. Consumer demand is lifting imports of consumer items. Imports of machinery and equipment are up on robust manufacturing output and ongoing infrastructure projects. Hefty gains by oil exporting countries and rising financial and international tourist receipts are helping the subregion to maintain a current account surplus. The current account balance will improve next year on lower fuel and food prices. Larger tourism receipts will increase the services balance, because Southeast Asia is a popular destination for international tourists.

Indonesia

Growth in 2022 is expected to be higher than the forecast in *ADO 2022*. Consumption and exports are holding up to global shocks. The current account surplus will increase this year, but inflation will also be significantly higher. With the recovery strengthening, fiscal and monetary support is being unwound. In 2023, a slower global economy will reduce growth and the current account, and inflation will remain elevated.

Updated assessment

The economy is coping well with threats to growth. An outbreak of the COVID-19 Omicron variant in the first quarter of 2022 had a minimal impact on economic activity. The commodity price shock following the Russian invasion of Ukraine produced an export and revenue windfall for Indonesia. And growth in the first half was stronger than expected. Real GDP grew by 5.2%, the fastest pace since the second half of 2013 (Figure 3.4.4). Quarter-on-quarter growth of seasonally adjusted GDP rose to 1.8% in the second quarter from 1.6% in the first.

Private consumption drove growth in the first half of 2022, contributing 4.8 percentage points to growth and more than offsetting lower government consumption (Figure 3.4.5). Eased COVID-19 mobility restrictions stimulated greater spending in transportation, restaurants, and hotels. Private consumption was also lifted by lower unemployment and measures to protect households from higher prices.

The export boom continued on strong demand for primary commodities (Figure 3.4.6). Net exports contributed 1.5 percentage points to growth in the first half, their largest contribution since late 2020. Buoyant consumer spending stimulated imports, but exports grew much faster. Services exports jumped by 60% in the second quarter, as more international flights were allowed.

Government consumption contracted by 6.3% in the first half, as less stimulus was needed and in line with reducing the fiscal deficit to 3.0% of GDP by 2023. Fixed investment rose by 3.6%, somewhat lower than in the second half of 2021. Construction, which accounts for 74% of fixed investment, grew slowly, probably because of rising construction material prices.

Figure 3.4.4 Quarterly GDP growth

Domestic demand is driving growth.

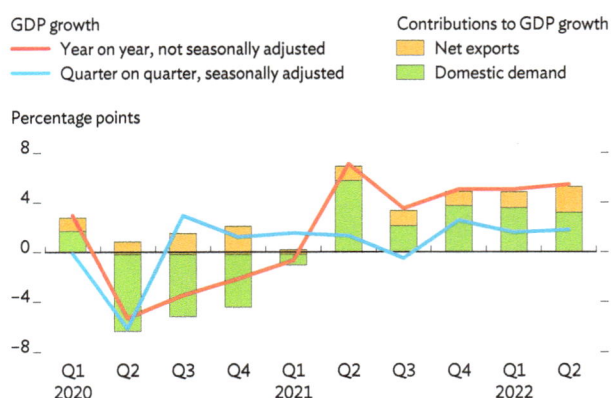

GDP = gross domestic product, Q = quarter.
Note: The statistical discrepancy is distributed proportionately to domestic demand and net exports.
Source: Statistics Indonesia (accessed 19 August 2022).

Figure 3.4.5 Contributions to consumption growth

Contact-intensive spending recovered on eased COVID-19 mobility restrictions.

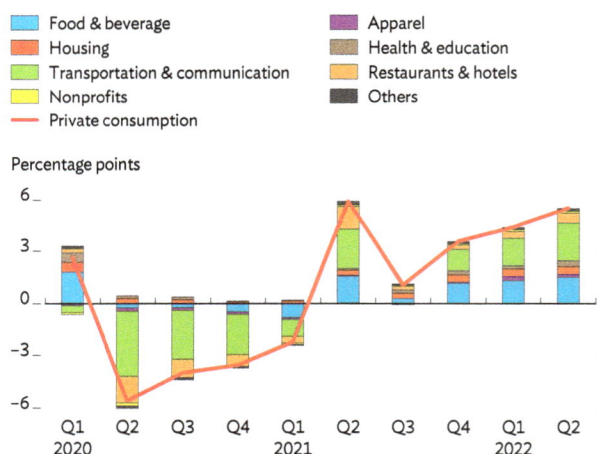

COVID-19 = coronavirus disease, Q = quarter.
Source: Statistics Indonesia (accessed 19 August 2022).

Inventory buildup was also modest due to consumer spending outpacing restocking.

High commodity prices spurred inflation, which rose to 4.7% in August—above Bank Indonesia's 4.0% inflation ceiling—after averaging 3.1% in the first half (Figure 3.4.7). The fastest price increases were for food and transportation, as supply shocks hit petroleum, coal, wheat, cooking oil, and soybeans.

Figure 3.4.6 Commodity exports have boomed

A. Commodity prices

Prices of key commodity exports have risen faster than those of key imports ...

- Prospera commodity price index
- Coal export price
- Petroleum
- Food

Jan 2022 = 100

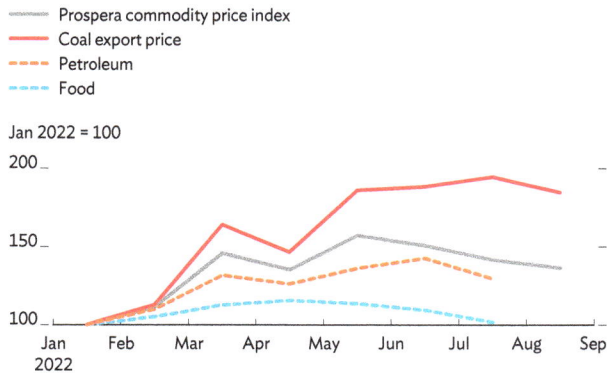

B. Export decomposition

... and export volume growth has been strong, ...

- Price contribution
- Volume contribution
- Export growth

Percentage points

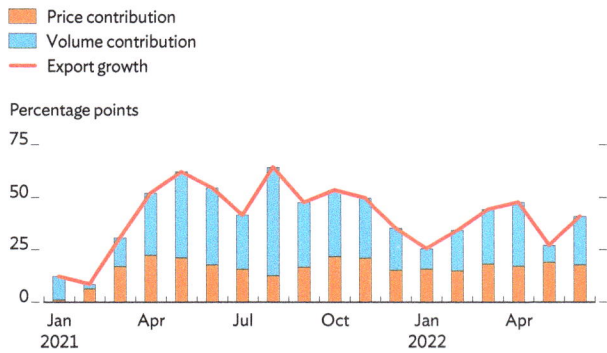

C. Merchandise trade

... as a result, trade surpluses have been registered since mid-2020.

- Export growth
- Import growth
- Trade balance

% year on year $ billion

GDP = gross domestic product.

Note: The Prospera commodity price index comprises crude palm oil, coal, nickel, rubber, and copper, weighted by export shares of these commodities in 2019.

Sources: A. International Monetary Fund. Primary Commodity Price System; Prospera (both accessed 23 August 2022); B and C. Statistics Indonesia (accessed 23 August 2022).

Figure 3.4.7 Inflation

Inflation jumped, but core inflation remains moderate.

- Headline
- Core
- WPI
- PPI
- GDP deflator

% year on year

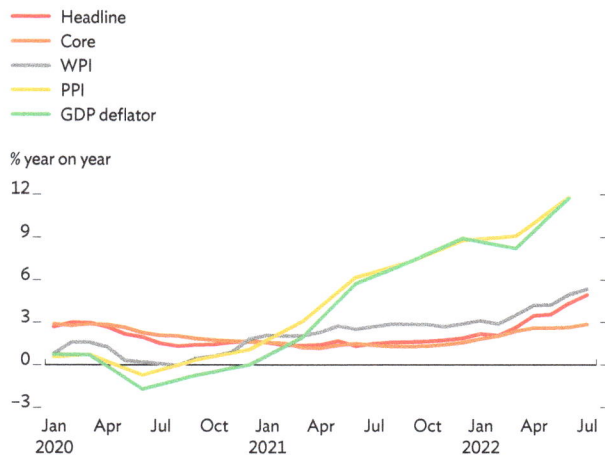

GDP = gross domestic product, PPI = producer price index, WPI = wholesale price index.

Source: Statistics Indonesia (accessed 23 August 2022).

Broader measures—the GDP deflator and producer prices—also rose fast. To prop up purchasing power, the government used subsidies and price controls for fuel and electricity, temporary export bans for coal and palm oil, and temporary cash assistance totaling Rp15.7 trillion over April–June for low-income households and low-paid workers. Still, the prices of some fuels and airline tickets have increased, as have electricity rates for better-off households. On 3 September, the government raised key fuel prices by about 30%.

Inflationary pressures so far do not appear to be becoming entrenched (Figure 3.4.8). The increase in headline inflation was mainly due to imported inflation from commodity supply shocks rather than the economy overheating or inflationary expectations rising. Core inflation averaged 2.5% over the first half and was 3.0% in August, lower than headline inflation. Survey measures of inflation expectations have been steady. Inflation rates for the components of the consumer price index have dispersed, indicating that inflationary shocks are not generalized. And the economy is still about 5.0% below its full potential.

The current account has been in surplus since 2021, on record trade surpluses. Exports of goods in the first half grew by 37% in US dollar terms and imports by 30%.

Figure 3.4.8 Inflation pressures

Inflation expectations and dispersion indicate that inflation has not yet become entrenched.

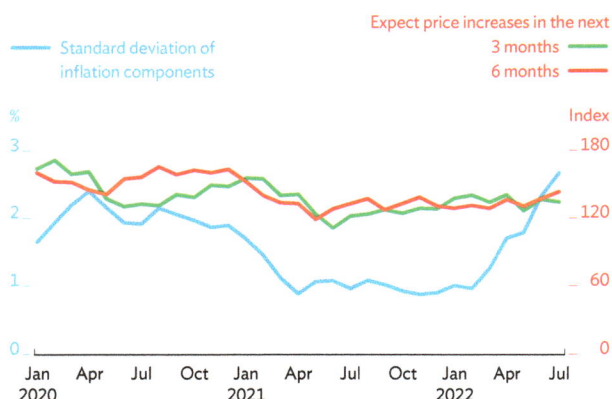

Note: The expectations index shows the weighted net balance of respondents who expect prices to increase in the next 3 or 6 months.
Sources: Bank Indonesia. Retail Sales Survey June 2022 (accessed 13 September 2022); Asian Development Bank estimates.

Figure 3.4.9 Portfolio flows

Debt financing is shrinking, but equity flows are steady.

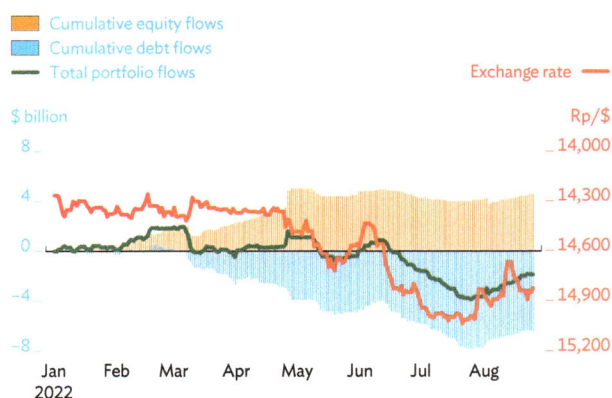

Sources: Bank Indonesia; Institute of International Finance online database (both accessed 1 September 2022).

Although prices of imported fuel and food rose, prices of exports rose faster and export volumes were also strong. An example of this is coal: although Indonesia is a net oil importer, it is a net energy exporter due to its coal reserves and has benefited from the disruptions to Russian energy supplies that drove up the demand for and price of coal. Indonesia's large trade surpluses have offset persistent deficits in services and incomes—and this produced a current account surplus of $4.2 billion in the first half, up from $3.5 billion for the whole of 2021.

Financial outflows increased in the first half, reducing external debt but also international reserves. Although equity capital inflows and foreign direct investment were healthy, the financial account had a deficit, largely due to portfolio debt finance chasing rising yields in advanced economies (Figure 3.4.9). The government and corporations repaid some external debt due to their improved financial situation. External debt fell to $403 billion—equivalent to 32% of GDP—at the end of June from $417 billion at the end of 2021. International reserves fell to $132 billion at the end of August—cover for 6.1 months of imports and debt payments—from $145 billion at the end of last year (Figure 3.4.10). International reserves in August were about twice the amount of external debt due in 1 year. Sovereign credit ratings are stable.

Figure 3.4.10 Balance of payments

Financial outflows reduced international reserves.

Q = quarter.
Notes: The change in international reserves may not equal the overall balance due to the revaluation of reserve holdings and foreign exchange intervention. Net errors and omissions are included in the financial and capital accounts.
Source: Bank Indonesia (accessed 23 August 2022).

Financial volatility increased in June–July, as it did in many emerging markets, but soon abated. Following the Federal Reserve's higher-than-expected policy rate hikes in June and July and higher-than-expected US inflation, the interest rate on Indonesia's 10-year government bonds and its credit default swap spread temporarily spiked, and the rupiah depreciated by 4% against the US dollar, but later recovered (Figure 3.4.11).

Figure 3.4.11 Financial volatility indicators

Financial volatility increased in June–July on negative financial shocks in the United States.

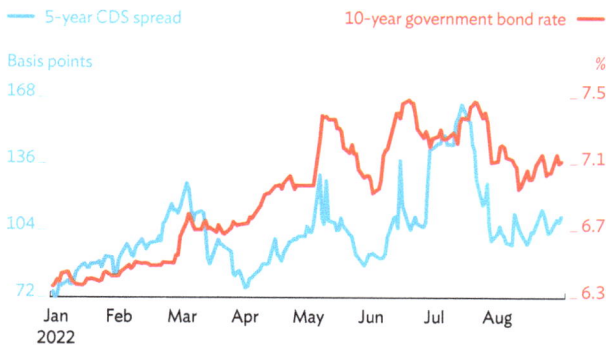

CDS = credit default swap.
Source: Bloomberg (accessed 1 September 2022).

Figure 3.4.12 Fiscal indicators

Returning to the 3% fiscal deficit ceiling is on track.

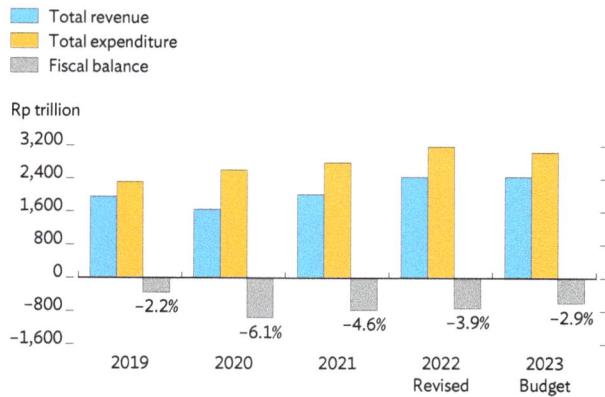

Note: Numbers in percentages are fiscal balances as percent of gross domestic product.
Source: Ministry of Finance.

With the economy recovering, fiscal stimulus is being withdrawn. A fiscal surplus was achieved in the first half, and the government is aiming for a lower deficit this year of Rp732 trillion (3.92% of GDP) from the original target of Rp868 trillion (4.85%) (Figure 3.4.12). Outlays were cut for COVID-19 measures and the national economic recovery plan. Revenue grew by 52% on the recovery, high commodity prices, and new tax measures, including an increase in the value-added tax rate to 11% in April. However, the implementation of the carbon tax has been postponed, pending technical regulations. Revenue from natural resources grew by 92%. Buoyant revenue enabled outlays for fuel and electricity subsidies to increase to Rp502 trillion from Rp139 trillion, while still reducing the deficit. To cap these untargeted subsidies, fuel prices were increased. Instead of increasing subsidies, the government will provide Rp24.2 trillion cash assistance for low-income households, low-paid workers, motorcycle taxi drivers, and fishers.

With financial conditions normalizing and inflation picking up, monetary policy support is also being withdrawn. On 23 August, Bank Indonesia raised the policy rate—the 7-day reverse repo rate—by 25 basis points from 3.5%, which had been its level since February 2021. The central bank is taking other steps to tighten monetary policy. In May, it announced that banks will have to meet by September a 9.0% reserve requirement ratio, higher than the previous 6.5%.

The central bank has reduced its claims on the central government by Rp112 trillion since the end of 2021, and its direct purchases of government bonds (Rp831 trillion in 2020–2021; Rp56 trillion so far in 2022) will end in December. Credit grew by 10.7% in June, and business lending by almost 10.0% (Figure 3.4.13). The nonperforming loan ratio was at 2.9% in the same month, and the capital adequacy ratio, at 24.7%, was above the regulatory minimum.

Figure 3.4.13 Loans and deposits

Lending has picked up on improved activity and confidence.

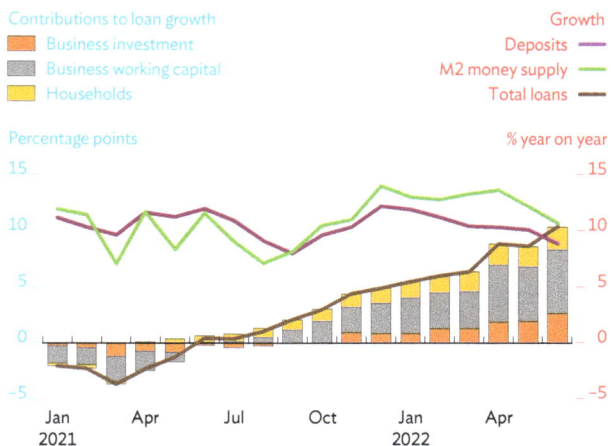

Source: Bank Indonesia (accessed 23 August 2022).

Social indicators continue to improve. People living below the poverty line fell to 26.2 million (9.5% of the population) in February 2022 from 26.5 million (9.7%) in August 2021 (Figure 3.4.14). The unemployment rate fell to 5.8% from 6.5% in the same period. Some 81% of the targeted population was fully vaccinated at the end of June and 23% had received a booster.

Prospects

This *Update* revises up the forecast for growth for 2022 to 5.4% from the 5.0% projection made in *ADO 2022* in April and revises down the projection for 2023 to 5.0% from 5.2% (Table 3.4.1). Domestic demand should remain strong through the rest of this year, despite higher inflation, and so should external demand. But financial market volatility is still present, a small wave of COVID-19 infections started in July, and global growth was worsening at the time of writing. Headwinds from these sources will continue through 2023, when macroeconomic policy will tighten.

Leading indicators point to strong demand through the fourth quarter (Figures 3.4.15 and 3.4.16). The manufacturing purchasing managers' index and the consumer confidence index have been above their expansion thresholds since late 2021. The CEIC leading indicator index in June was 25% above its level at the start of the pandemic. Retail sales volume in July was up by about the same.

Figure 3.4.14 COVID-19 indicators

Infections have been contained; vaccination is approaching 100%.

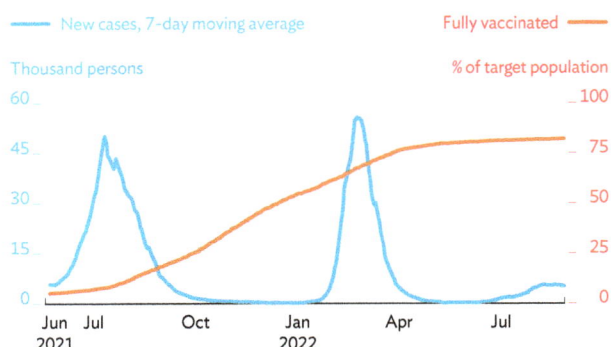

COVID-19 = coronavirus disease.
Source: Our World in Data (accessed 1 September 2022).

Table 3.4.1 Selected economic indicators in Indonesia, %

The forecasts for growth, inflation, and the current account in 2022 are revised up.

	2021	2022		2023	
		ADO 2022	Update	ADO 2022	Update
GDP growth	3.7	5.0	5.4	5.2	5.0
Inflation	1.6	3.6	4.6	3.0	5.1
CAB/GDP	0.3	0.0	0.5	−0.5	0.0

ADO = Asian Development Outlook, CAB = current account balance, GDP = gross domestic product.
Sources: Statistics Indonesia; Asian Development Bank estimates.

Figure 3.4.15 Consumer activity

Leading indicators are now above their pre-pandemic levels.

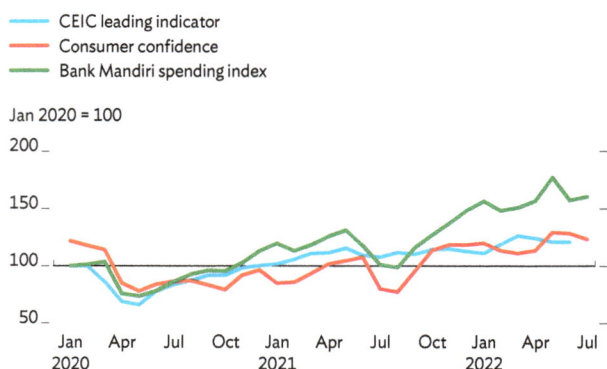

Notes: For the CEIC and the Bank Mandiri indices, January 2020 = 100. For consumer confidence, values above 100 indicate optimism.
Sources: Bank Mandiri; CEIC Data Company; Statistics Indonesia (all accessed 23 August 2022).

Figure 3.4.16 Manufacturing activity

Manufacturing has regained its pre-pandemic pace.

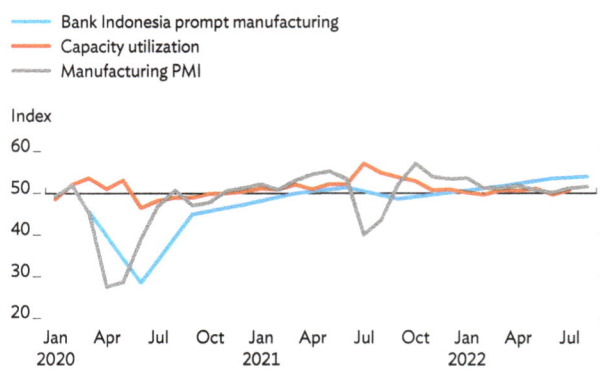

PMI = purchasing managers' index.
Note: PMI values above 50 indicate expansion.
Sources: Bank Indonesia; CEIC Data Company (accessed 1 September 2022).

The Bank Mandiri spending index was 60% above its level at the start of the pandemic. International tourist arrivals rose by 173% in June, although arrivals are still only 25% of their pre-pandemic level.

"Revenge spending" will drive consumption in 2022; normalization, in 2023. Consumption is projected to grow by 6% in 2022, but return in 2023 to its pre-pandemic trend growth of 5%. Consumer confidence and purchasing power this year will be supported by increasing jobs and incomes, food and fuel subsidies, and the minimal impact on the economy of the mild COVID-19 wave. The projection for 5% consumption growth in 2023 is in line with 2013 and 2014, when fuel prices were also increased by about 30%.

In the revised projections, export growth will slow somewhat this year, but the external balance is forecast to have a surplus of 0.5% of GDP, up from the earlier projection of zero. The growth of goods exports will ease to about 13% in the second half due to slower global growth, but tourism earnings will continue to grow fast. Demand for imports will be healthy. For the full year, the contribution of net exports should be about 1 percentage point, the same as in 2021. Slower global growth in 2023 will result in net exports contributing less to growth. Exports of goods will likely grow at half 2022's pace; import growth will keep step with normalized domestic demand. Tourism should grow robustly as international arrivals normalize.

Government consumption and investment will not significantly contribute to growth this year and next. Government consumption in national income account terms is forecast to contract by 5%–10% in both years, consistent with fiscal consolidation. Investment is projected to grow by only about 5.0%–5.5% in both years, amid rising interest rates, moderating demand, and increasing financial volatility.

The inflation rate will jump in September and remain high through December because of the increase in fuel prices. This *Update* revises up the inflation forecast for 2022 to 4.6% from 3.6% in the earlier projection. Because of the base-year effect of subdued inflation in the first half of 2022, inflation is forecast at 5.5%–6.0% through June 2023 and easing to 3.8% in December. Inflation is forecast averaging 5.1% in 2023, up from the earlier 3.0% projection.

Tighter fiscal and monetary policy will hold down growth. The budget deficit is targeted at 3.92% of GDP in 2022 and 2.85% in 2023, but the deficits could come in lower due to higher revenue on buoyant domestic demand and subsidies being scaled down. The central bank will likely further raise the policy rate in 2022 and in early 2023 to forestall inflationary expectations and in response to higher rates abroad and possible downward pressure on the rupiah.

Risks to 2022's outlook are approximately balanced. Consumption and investment could turn out to be more robust than expected, offsetting weaker exports. For 2023, the risks are on the downside. Growth in advanced economies could fall more than expected. If inflation turns out to be much higher than expected, consumer demand will be weaker. And higher inflation, together with a smaller export windfall, will reduce the scope for subsidies to support purchasing power.

Lao People's Democratic Republic

Supply disruptions and rising commodity prices have increased inflationary pressures and delayed economic recovery in the Lao People's Democratic Republic (Lao PDR). This *Update* revises down the GDP growth forecasts for 2022 and 2023 from the projections made in *ADO 2022* in April. Inflation is forecast to be significantly higher this year before moderating in 2023. Lower domestic demand should contribute to a larger narrowing in the current account deficit over the forecast horizon than was expected in *ADO 2022*.

Updated assessment

The impact of COVID-19 restrictions on the labor market has decreased. Most businesses returned to operating at normal levels in the first half of 2022 (Figure 3.4.17). In May, the country reopened its borders, and had 175,369 international arrivals by June.

Volatile prices linked to the Russian invasion of Ukraine, particularly for oil, saw households trim daily consumption spending, which dampened output growth. Sharp increases in the prices of fertilizers, animal feed, food, and fuel discouraged farm and plantation activity. Foreign direct investment inflows halved to $280 million in the first half amid slower growth in the Lao PDR's trading partners, constraining the contribution of fixed investment to growth.

Fuel shortages in June hit consumers and businesses hard through supply disruptions and cost increases. The headline inflation rate in August was at a 22-year high of 30.0%. The rate averaged 15.5% in the first 8 months (Figure 3.4.18). Administered prices for fuel were increased 13 times from January to September, resulting in a 90.3% rise in diesel prices and a 62.3% increase in gasoline prices. The kip fell by 37.4% against the US dollar and 32.9% against the baht in the official market from January to August (Figure 3.4.19). The gap between the official and parallel foreign exchange markets was 38.6% by mid-June, but it narrowed to an average of 15.9% in August.

In response to these developments, the government, in June, increased the availability of foreign exchange for fuel importers and issued letters of credit to shore up fuel supplies. The central bank also announced

Figure 3.4.17 Mobility changes

Signs of a gradual recovery from COVID-19 from January to April, but the economy plateaued after Pi Mai on fuel supply disruptions.

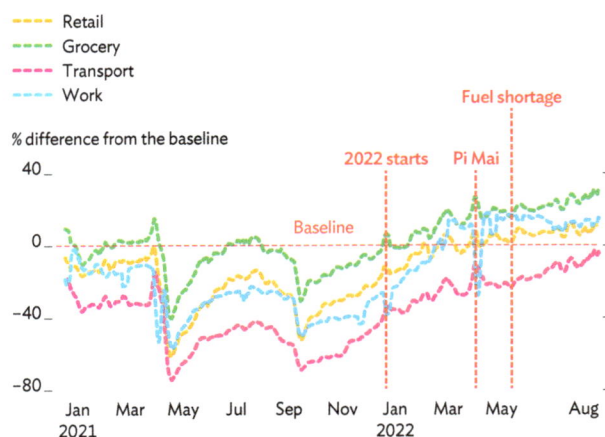

COVID-19 = coronavirus disease.
Note: Pi Mai is the Lao New Year.
Source: *COVID-19 Community Mobility Reports* (accessed 7 September 2022).

Figure 3.4.18 Monthly inflation

Rising food and transport prices from fuel shortages and the weaker kip pushed inflation to double digits in May–August 2022.

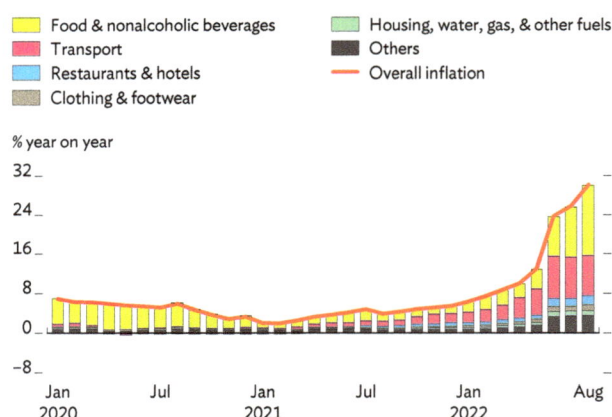

Source: Lao Statistics Bureau (accessed 7 September 2022).

a savings bond issuance of KN5 trillion, the equivalent of 3% of money supply, to reduce excessive liquidity in the economy and shore up demand for the kip.

Rising inflation and the country's high public debt reinforced off-risk sentiment among analysts and market investors. In June, Moody's Investors Service downgraded the Lao PDR's rating to Caa3 from Caa2 on external liquidity risks. Fitch Ratings downgraded in August.

Public and publicly guaranteed debt—a large portion of which is external—climbed to 88% of GDP in 2021, up from 72% in 2020, as the government raised domestic borrowing. The US dollar value of this debt increased because of the weaker kip. Foreign currency public debt service over 2022–2026 averaged $1.3 billion annually, equivalent to over half of projected government revenue. Debt relief from several creditors, totaling to $984 million over 2019–2021, helped to mitigate near-term pressures. International reserves continue to be below adequacy standards and were reported at $1.3 billion at the end of March 2022, cover for 2 months of imports.

Demand for the Lao PDR's exports remained robust in the first half, at $4.1 billion after $3.9 billion in the same period in 2021, despite slowing growth in major trading partners. Sufficient rainfall helped many hydropower plants reach capacity, and first-half electricity exports rose 1% to $1 billion. Continuing weak domestic demand weighed on imports, which totaled only $3.1 billion in the first half 2022. The relatively light import bill enabled the balance of trade to turn a higher surplus of $1.1 billion in the first half, up from $841 million in the same period in 2021.

Prospects

This *Update* lowers the forecasts for GDP growth for 2022 to 2.5% from *ADO 2022*'s 3.4% projection and to 3.5% from 3.7% for 2023 (Table 3.4.2). The rising cost of living has decreased consumer purchasing power, and input supply constraints have reduced the growth prospects for agriculture and industry. These trends, coupled with the economic slowdown in the People's Republic of China, delayed the Lao PDR's recovery.

Next year will see a gradual recovery, supported by new investment and higher renewable energy and mining output. A consortium of lenders is preparing finance for the 600 megawatt Monsoon Wind project that, once completed, will export all the power it generates and be Southeast Asia's biggest wind energy project.

The forecast for inflation is sharply revised up to 17.0% for 2022 on higher-than-expected oil prices and the weaker kip. Inflation next year is expected to moderate to 4.5% on lower global oil prices. Low interest loans for local food producers to buy agriculture inputs should help boost domestic food production and relieve pressure on food prices.

Figure 3.4.19 Exchange rate

The kip fell sharply in June 2022 on fuel supply disruptions and speculation on foreign exchange shortages.

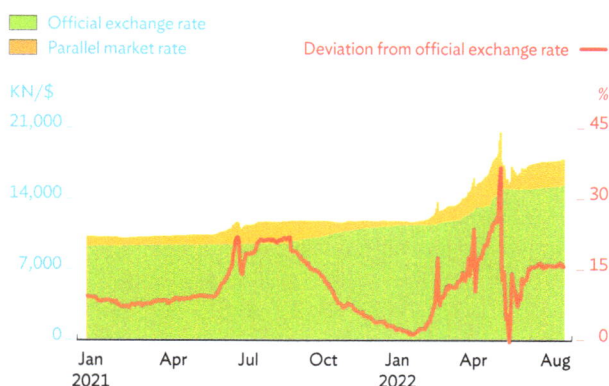

Source: Bank of the Lao PDR.

Table 3.4.2 Selected economic indicators in the Lao People's Democratic Republic, %

Growth in 2022 and 2023 will be lower than projected in ADO 2022; inflation will be much higher in 2022.

	2021	2022		2023	
		ADO 2022	Update	ADO 2022	Update
GDP growth	2.3	3.4	2.5	3.7	3.5
Inflation	3.7	5.8	17.0	5.0	4.5
CAB/GDP	−5.0	−6.0	−4.5	−6.5	−5.5

ADO = Asian Development Outlook, CAB = current account balance, GDP = gross domestic product.
Source: Asian Development Bank estimates.

Energy exports will remain robust with seven hydropower projects scheduled to come online in 2022, adding 4.1 billion kilowatt hours to the country's export earnings. The current account deficit is expected to narrow to the equivalent of 4.5% of GDP from 5.0% in 2021 on buoyant export growth outpacing imports. A recovery in domestic demand is expected to stimulate imports of capital and consumer goods in 2023, widening the current account deficit to 5.5%.

Downside risks to the outlook include liquidity risks due to low foreign exchange reserve adequacy and a high public debt burden. The continuing weak external demand is a key risk. A coordinated effort across all creditors that is focused on shifting to sustainable and transparent public financing practices will be important for reducing the country's high risk of debt distress.

Malaysia

Growth accelerated in the first half of 2022 as economic activity continues to improve on eased COVID-19 mobility restrictions and the reopening of Malaysia's borders on 1 April. Growth, at 6.9%, was a tad lower than 7.0% in the first half of 2021. The 6.0% growth forecast for 2022 made in *ADO 2022* in April is maintained on expectations that consumption growth will stay robust. Growth will slow in 2023 on an expected slowdown in export opportunities and interest rate hikes in advanced economies, particularly the United States.

Updated assessment

GDP growth in the second quarter of 2022 rose sharply to 8.9% from the first quarter's 5.0%. Private consumption growth rose by 11.5% in the first half; spending was fastest on restaurants, hotels, and recreation services—and this growth was supported by higher household income due to government assistance under the Bantuan Keluarga Malaysia program. This increased wage subsidies from May and improved labor market conditions. Public consumption also increased, but at the slower pace of 4.7%, down from 6.9%.

Investment growth declined to 2.9% in the first half of 2022 from 5.5% in the same period last year (Figure 3.4.20). Last year's strong investment growth failed to gain traction, partly because of weaker global growth and unresolved domestic political uncertainties. Although digitalization pushed up investment in machinery and equipment, investment in structures and other assets declined. Growth in private investment declined to 3.3% from 8.7%. Public investment was up a meager 1.0%—an improvement, nevertheless, on the 6.9% contraction in the first half of 2021—mainly on investments in oil and gas and telecommunications.

Export growth fell to 9.2% from 23.3% due to weaker growth in the People's Republic of China, Singapore, and the US, which are among Malaysia's largest trading partners (Figure 3.4.21). Demand for electronics and electrical products, which comprise more than a third of total exports, rose by 30%. Higher international oil, fats, and base metals prices benefited Malaysia's commodity exports. Imports of goods and services rose by 12.6%. The economic recovery stimulated large imports of intermediate and investment goods for manufacturing and consumption.

Figure 3.4.20 Demand-side contributions to growth

Growth accelerates on strong private consumption.

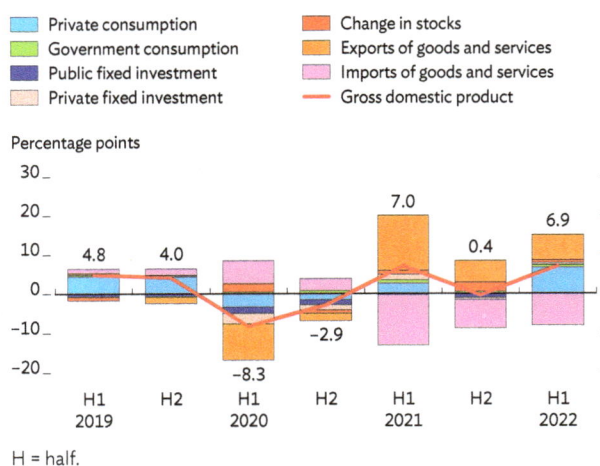

H = half.
Sources: Department of Statistics Malaysia; Haver Analytics (both accessed 29 August 2022).

Figure 3.4.21 Merchandise exports

Exports moderated on weaker global demand.

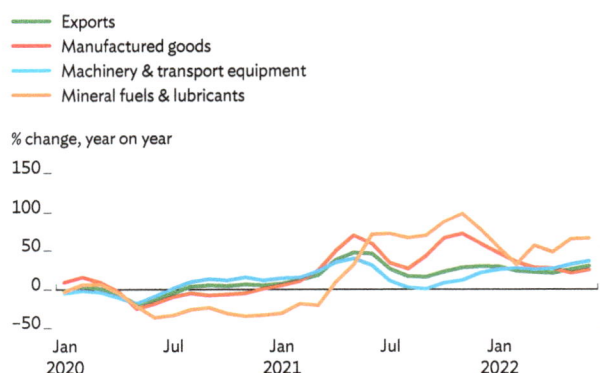

Source: Haver Analytics (accessed 29 August 2022).

Services and industry continue to be the main growth drivers (Figure 3.4.22). The economy's reopening invigorated businesses catering to consumer durables and leisure activities that, in turn, benefited the services sector. Services growth in the first half, at 9.2% after 4.9% in the same period last year, was strongest in accommodation, transport, and storage. Industry output grew by 5.0%—albeit slower than 11.9% growth in the first half last year—on continued strong demand for electrical, electronic, and optical products. The pull-forward effect from lifting the exemption on the sales and services tax on 30 June increased demand for transport equipment and machinery in the first half.

Figure 3.4.22 Supply-side contributions to growth

Services output rose after Malaysia's borders reopened on 1 April 2022.

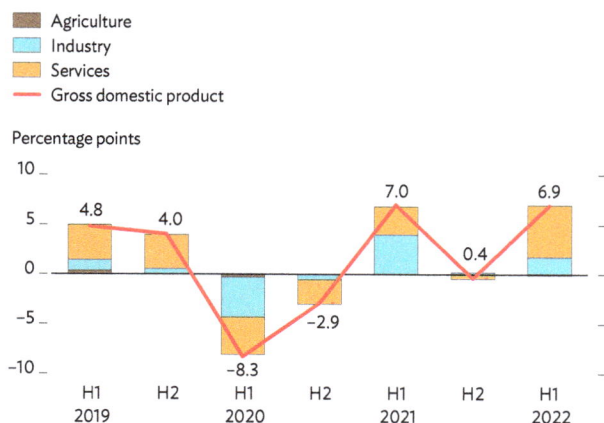

- Agriculture
- Industry
- Services
- —— Gross domestic product

Percentage points

[Figure: Bar chart with values labeled 4.8, 4.0, −8.3, −2.9, 7.0, 0.4, 6.9 across periods H1/H2 2019, H1/H2 2020, H1/H2 2021, H1 2022]

H = half.

Sources: Department of Statistics Malaysia; Haver Analytics (both accessed 29 August 2022).

Figure 3.4.23 Labor market indicators

The unemployment rate eased and wages increased, particularly services.

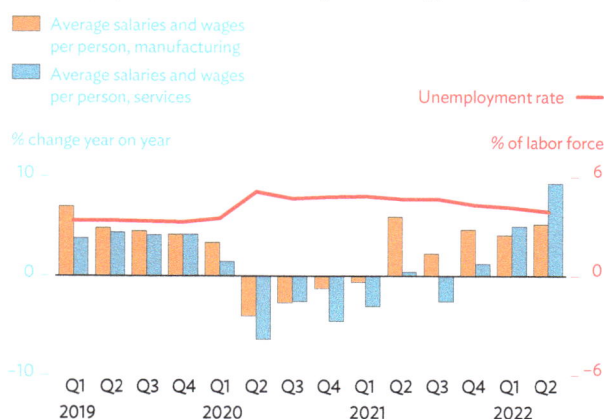

- Average salaries and wages per person, manufacturing
- Average salaries and wages per person, services
- —— Unemployment rate

% change year on year   % of labor force

[Figure: Bar and line chart from Q1 2019 to Q2 2022]

Q = quarter.

Note: Salaries and wages refers to cash payments, including bonuses, commissions, overtime pay, cost of living allowances, and other allowances made to employees during the quarter.

Source: Haver Analytics (accessed 30 August 2022).

Manufacturing output slowed to 7.9% in the first half from 15.8% in the first half of 2021, reflecting weaker external demand from advanced economies. Construction contracted by 2.4% in the first half of 2022 because of fewer large nonresidential projects and small-scale projects compared to an 8.3% expansion in the same period in 2021. Mining output contracted by 0.8% after growing 2.4% in the period, because of closures for maintenance at some oil and gas facilities.

Agriculture output contracted by 1.2% in the first half, deepening the contraction that started last year. Rising input costs, including feeds and fertilizers, affected livestock and other agricultural production, and labor shortages affected palm oil harvests. Heavy rains early this year hit harvests, prompting farmers and agro-entrepreneurs to tap funds for food production administered by Bank Negara Malaysia, the central bank.

The unemployment rate eased to 3.9% in the second quarter from 4.1% in the first as more businesses resumed operations or increased capacity after COVID-19 restrictions were lifted (Figure 3.4.23). The further improvement in labor conditions is evidenced by an increase in the labor force participation rate and a decline in the underemployment rate. Wages rose, notably in manufacturing and services, on an increase in minimum wages from May. Under the government's wage subsidy as part of its social amelioration package implemented in 2020

in response to COVID-19, financial assistance paid to employers to continue their operations and retain employees benefitted close to 3 million employees as of July 2022.

The inflation rate in the first half of 2022 averaged 2.5%, down from 2.3% in the same period last year (Figure 3.4.24). Inflation accelerated to 2.8% in May and to 3.4% in June on brisker economic activity following the reopening of Malaysia's borders, the effects of more expensive inputs and logistics bottlenecks caused by the Russian invasion of Ukraine, and labor shortages in agricultural areas.

Figure 3.4.24 Monthly inflation

Inflation accelerated mainly from spikes in food prices.

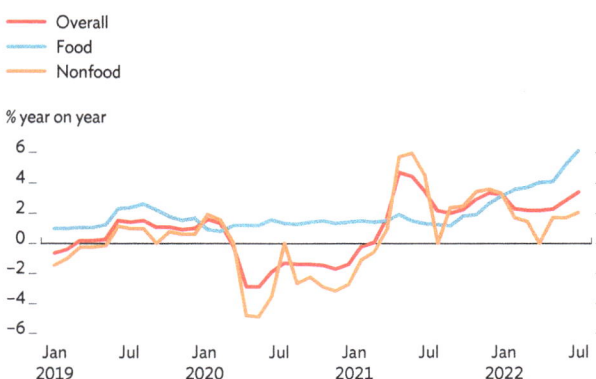

- —— Overall
- —— Food
- —— Nonfood

% year on year

[Figure: Line chart from Jan 2019 to Jul 2022]

Source: Haver Analytics (accessed 29 August 2022).

To contain food price rises from higher fuel costs, the government has allocated a RM30 billion fuel subsidy for this year. In February, subsidies to poultry farmers were provided up to June, and import permits for certain goods abolished. The first half saw significant price increases for transport (4.1%), restaurants and hotels (3.2%), and furnishings, household equipment, and maintenance (3.0%). Core inflation accelerated to 2.2% from 0.7% in the first half of 2021.

The government granted subsidies to ease the surging cost of living, particularly in the second quarter. This was done because 2022's allocation to the COVID-19 fund—a RM110 billion fund set up to tackle the effects of the pandemic on incomes through direct cash transfers, wage subsidies for employment retention, and social amelioration packages—had a lower allocation than in 2020 and 2021.

The current account surplus narrowed to an estimated equivalent of 0.9% of GDP in the first half of 2022 from 3.4% in the same period last year due to lower trade and primary income balances (Figure 3.4.25). Imports grew more than exports on the recovering domestic demand. The deficit in services trade narrowed due to gains in finance, travel, and tourism receipts—the latter since borders reopened in April. Increased capital and financial account inflows resulted in a surplus in the balance of payments in the first half, estimated at RM17.7 billion. International reserves totaled $107 billion on 15 July, cover for 5.7 months of imports of goods and services, and 1.1 times total short-term foreign debt.

Bank Negara Malaysia raised the overnight policy rate on 11 May and 6 July by a cumulative 50 basis points to 2.25%. The rate hikes were in response to tightening global financial conditions, inflationary pressures from higher commodity prices, and strong domestic demand.

Malaysia's external debt totaled RM1.13 trillion, equal to 67.7% of GDP, at the end of June. About 33% was ringgit-denominated and therefore not affected by fluctuations in the ringgit–US dollar exchange rate. The rest is denominated in other foreign currencies, which are mostly medium- to long-term in tenures. In the foreign exchange market, the ringgit depreciated by 4.4% in the first half, averaging $1 = RM4.289, down from $1 = RM4.110 in the same period last year. Higher commodity prices continued to cushion downward pressure on the ringgit from external factors.

Prospects

This *Update* maintains the forecast for GDP growth in 2022 at 6.0% made in *ADO 2022* in April. The forecast for 2023 is revised down to 4.7% from 5.4% due to increasing global headwinds (Table 3.4.3 and Figure 3.4.26). Two factors are driving Malaysia's near-term prospects: consumer demand is recovering strongly, supported by the reopening of markets and borders, and improving employment and income for households; and the continuance of a strong COVID-19 vaccination effort. As of 22 August, 84% of the population was fully vaccinated and almost 50% had received their first booster. All these factors are significantly lifting consumer confidence and retail trade, allowing for a solid recovery in consumer demand (Figure 3.4.27).

Figure 3.4.25 Current account balance and components

Surplus in the current account dipped as imports outpaced exports.

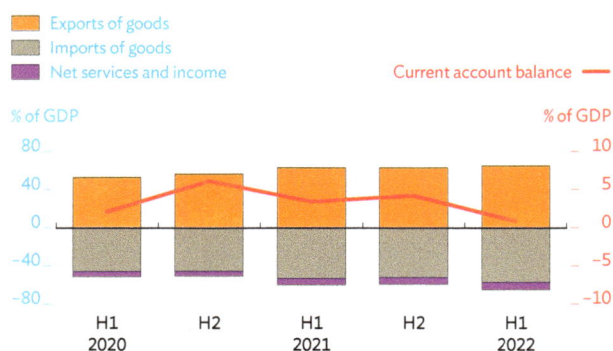

GDP = gross domestic product, H = half.
Source: Haver Analytics (accessed 29 August 2022).

Table 3.4.3 Selected economic indicators in Malaysia, %

Growth will be subdued in 2023, inflation tamed, and the current account in surplus.

	2021	2022		2023	
		ADO 2022	Update	ADO 2022	Update
GDP growth	3.1	6.0	6.0	5.4	4.7
Inflation	2.5	3.0	2.7	2.5	2.5
CAB/GDP	3.8	3.3	3.5	3.0	3.2

ADO = *Asian Development Outlook*, CAB = current account balance, GDP = gross domestic product.
Source: Asian Development Bank estimates.

Figure 3.4.26 GDP growth

Growth strengthens in 2022, but will weaken in 2023.

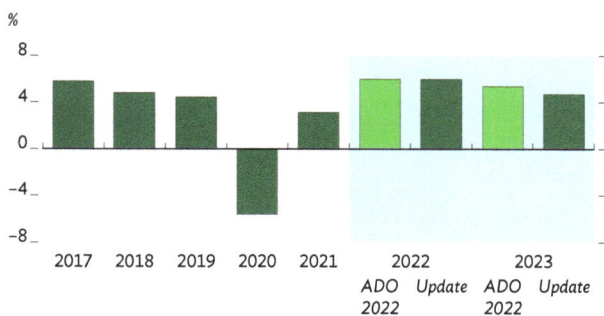

ADO = Asian Development Outlook, GDP = gross domestic product.
Source: ADO database.

Figure 3.4.27 Consumer sentiment and retail trade

Consumption appears to be anchored on solid economic recovery.

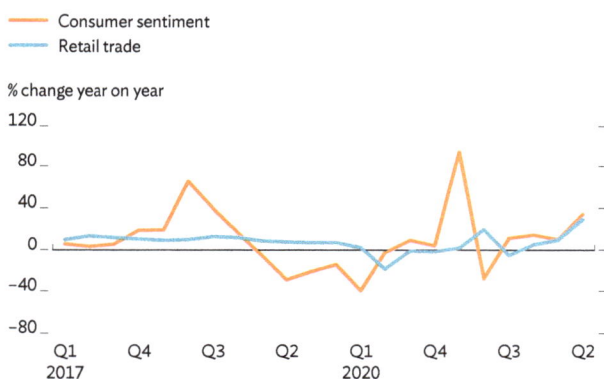

Q = quarter.
Source: Haver Analytics (accessed 29 August 2022).

Private consumption will lead growth in the near term. The consumer sentiment index rose an average 22% in the first half and retail trade was up 12%. The bright consumption picture is expected to stay given the stable macroeconomic environment and stronger output in key sectors, including hospitality, retail and digital shopping, and tourism. Spending on services and discretionary items is also expected to gain further momentum in the second half as domestic tourism gains traction while the country learns to live with COVID-19.

Growth in domestic investment will likely remain weak this year and next because of tighter global and domestic financial conditions, domestic political uncertainty, and a sluggish business climate, which will

encourage a wait-and-see attitude among international and local investors. The purchasing managers' index was at 50.6 in July, implying a slight expansion in market activity from June, particularly for manufacturing. The business tendency survey confidence indicator, a short-term indicator that shows a net balance view of the business climate in various sectors remained positive at 3.5% in the second quarter, but lower than 7.6% in the first, suggesting that the share of firms that were optimistic about business conditions declined in the second quarter.

Public investment will not grow this year because of domestic political uncertainty and a low revenue base continuing to reduce the space for public investment. This will likely recover somewhat next year on infrastructure investments in transport, industrial parks, rural areas, digital connectivity, and education. Major upcoming infrastructure investments include RM15 billion on transport projects, including the Pan Borneo Highway and the rapid transit system link connecting Singapore and Malaysia; RM2.7 billion on rural infrastructure projects to help narrow the rural–urban divide; and the RM825 million to upgrade school buildings and improve internet connectivity in the education system.

Services and industry will lead the economy's recovery over the forecast horizon on pent-up spending on services and leisure, consumer durables, and electronic products, which will support wholesale and retail trade and other services. Industry output will also expand, underpinned by rising demand for electrical and electronic products and transport equipment and machinery. The output of resource-based products will also benefit from rising oil and commodity prices. If weather conditions are normal over the rest of the year, agriculture output is expected to grow modestly in 2022, which, if this happens, will reverse two consecutive years of contractions.

Bank Negara Malaysia's tighter monetary policy is expected to continue given elevated commodity prices and continuing increases in US interest rates.

Although inflation accelerated to 2.8% in the second quarter from 2.2% in the first quarter as more expensive inputs were absorbed in production, inflation will remain stable in the near-term due to generous government subsidies and the tightening cycle of monetary policy.

The headline inflation rate is forecast at 2.7% in 2022, down from the earlier 3.0% projection. The inflation forecast for 2023 is maintained at 2.5% (Figure 3.4.28).

Although export volume could fall on weaker external demand, the US dollar value of exports should hold up well in the next 2 years, reflecting higher international commodity prices. The volume and value of imports will also expand at a faster rate, underpinned by buoyant consumer demand for imported goods. A smaller deficit for trade in services is expected. Since borders reopened, about 1 million international tourists arrived—about half this year's target. This *Update* projects a current account surplus equal to 3.5% of GDP in 2022 and 3.3% in 2023, slightly higher than the forecasts in April (Figure 3.4.29).

Fiscal policy will continue to support growth in 2022 with the fiscal deficit expected at about 6% of GDP. For this year, the government will increase development expenditure to mobilize infrastructure investment to promote stronger digital connectivity, improve health care facilities, and for projects to upskill and reskill the workforce. The fiscal policy challenges are the fiscal space being constrained by large and increasing priority spending, a weaker revenue base, and rising debt. To tackle these challenges, changes to the fiscal framework have been introduced, including raising the statutory debt ceiling to 65% of GDP, up from 60% in 2020. For next year, the government will gradually consolidate its budget commitments to support the Twelfth Malaysia Plan, 2021–2025.

Several downside risks could undermine the near-term outlook. Externally, weaker growth in advanced economies, continuing economic disruptions from the Russian invasion of Ukraine, and tightening global financial conditions could affect Malaysia's growth momentum. The war in Ukraine has elevated trade and logistics costs and disrupted supply chains, creating upward pressure on prices. Continuing monetary tightening in the US and European Union has raised the country's borrowing costs, as local bond yields move in parallel with US yields. Domestically, weakened vaccine efficacy to new COVID-19 variants could still see a return of some degree of mobility restrictions if the pressures on the country's health system mount.

Figure 3.4.28 Annual inflation

Inflation picks up in 2022, but tapers in 2023.

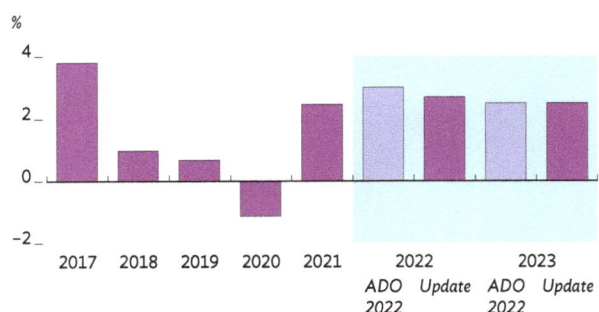

ADO = Asian Development Outlook.
Source: ADO database.

Figure 3.4.29 Current account balance

The surplus in the current account is expected to narrow in 2022 and 2023.

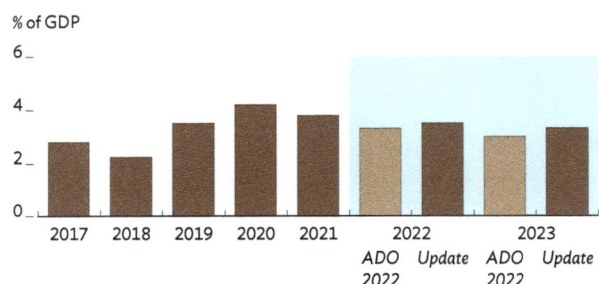

ADO = Asian Development Outlook, GDP = gross domestic product.
Source: ADO database.

Malaysia's credit ratings have remained stable. In February, Fitch Ratings affirmed its BBB+ rating for the country's long-term currency issuer default rating with a stable outlook. This was based on Malaysia's strong and broad-based medium-term growth, varied export base, high public debt, and the domestic political uncertainty. In June, S&P Global Ratings reaffirmed its A– sovereign rating and revised the outlook from negative to stable on expectations that Malaysia's solid growth momentum and strong external position will remain over the next 2 years.

Philippines

Economic growth this year is projected to be higher than forecast in *ADO 2022* in April, buoyed by a strong rebound in domestic demand. The inflation forecasts are revised up on price pressures, largely from global commodity prices, and some domestic supply limitations. Growth in 2023 will ease on the impact of monetary policy tightening and broader price pressures. Weaker-than-expected export demand is contributing to a wider current account deficit.

Updated assessment

The economy's recovery accelerated in the first half of 2022, with GDP rising by 7.8% from 3.9% the same period in 2021. Strong domestic demand underpinned growth that was marked by rebounds in household consumption and investment as COVID-19 mobility restrictions were eased further. Wider vaccination coverage allowed the economy to remain open.

Household consumption was the most significant contributor to GDP growth, rising by 9.3% from 0.9% in the first half of 2021 (Figure 3.4.30). Spending on recreation, travel, and restaurants bounced back. The labor market continued to recover. The labor force participation rate rose to 65.2% in July from 62.1% in pre-pandemic July 2019, and the unemployment rate slid to 5.2% from 5.4% over the same period.

An additional 5.7 million jobs were generated from July 2021 to July 2022, two-thirds in services, largely in wholesale and retail trade. Jobs in accommodation and food services recorded significant gains. Employment in agriculture rose and increased construction activity lifted employment in industry. Remittances from Filipinos working overseas, up by 2.8% year on year in the first half, continued to support household spending. Government consumption growth picked up to 7.8% on social services and economic recovery programs.

Investment rose on higher fixed capital and inventory buildups. Fixed investment growth quickened to 12.6% from 6.9% in the first half of 2021; here, construction was the biggest driver (Figure 3.4.31). Private construction grew by 15.7%, reversing a 12.5% contraction in the first half of 2021. Public construction, up 14.9% from 37.6%, continued to grow at a double-digit pace, lifted by large ongoing infrastructure projects. Investment in machinery and transportation equipment rose by 10.7%.

Because the 14.5% growth in imports of goods and services outpaced the 7.3% export growth, net exports weighed on GDP growth in the first half. Weak external demand was behind a 2.1% decline in merchandise exports in the second quarter in real terms to 1.8% growth in the first half. Exports of electronic products, about half of total exports, decreased.

Figure 3.4.30 Demand-side contributions to growth

Household consumption bounced back in H1 2022.

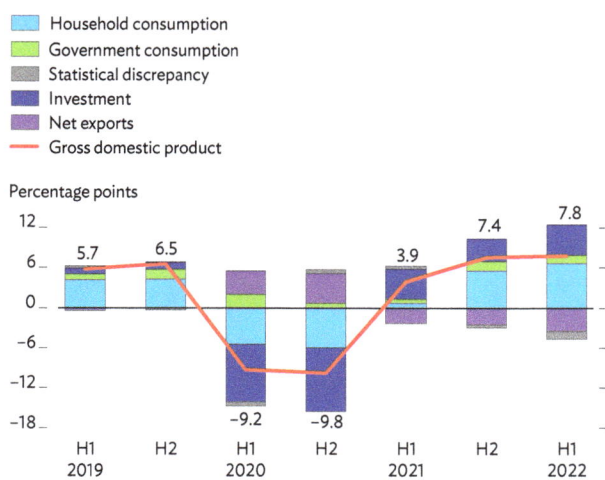

- Household consumption
- Government consumption
- Statistical discrepancy
- Investment
- Net exports
- Gross domestic product

H = half.
Sources: Philippine Statistics Authority; CEIC Data Company (accessed 2 September 2022).

Figure 3.4.31 Contributions to fixed investment growth

Private construction growth in H1 2022 reversed a sharp contraction in H1 2021.

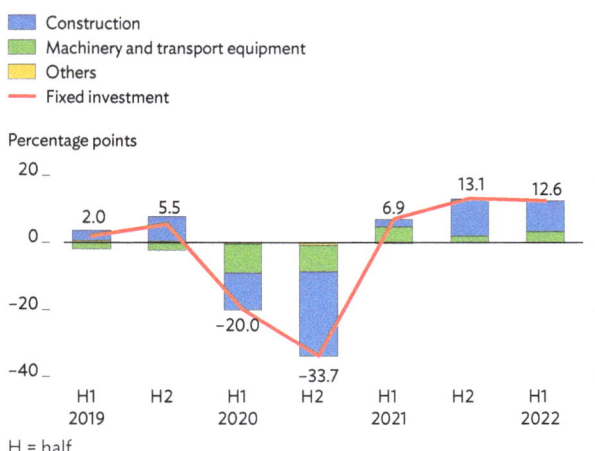

- Construction
- Machinery and transport equipment
- Others
- Fixed investment

H = half.
Sources: Philippine Statistics Authority; CEIC Data Company (accessed 2 September 2022).

Services exports, up 14.5%, recovered strongly, reversing the 3.2% contraction in the first half of 2021. Tourism bounced back after borders reopened in February, and growth continued strong for business and information services. The rapid rise in first-half imports was in line with higher demand for capital and consumer goods.

On the supply side, services output grew by 8.7% from 2.8% in the first half of 2021, contributing two-thirds of GDP growth (Figure 3.4.32). The expansion was broad-based across services activities. Retail trade rose by 8.9% and was the biggest contributor to growth in services. Transport rose by 26.6%, accommodation by 38.8%, and food and beverage services by 20.1%. Finance, information and communication, and business services continued to expand.

Industry grew by 8.3% in the first half of 2022 from 7.8% in the same period in 2021, driven mainly by manufacturing and construction (Figure 3.4.33). Manufacturing grew by 5.9%, down from 10.5%. Although strong domestic demand lifted manufacturing output, the slowdown in exports tamped growth. Manufactures of food and beverage, chemical products, and construction material gained strongly, but computers and electronic products slowed. Construction growth quickened to 17.3%, up from 1.7% in the first half of 2021.

Crop damage caused by several typhoons depressed agriculture growth, at just 0.2% in the first half. Rice production fell by 0.7%, and output was lower for sugar and some other crops. Fisheries output declined; poultry and livestock production rose.

Elevated fuel and food prices lifted the inflation rate to 6.3% year on year in August from 6.4% in July. The rate averaged 4.9% in the first 8 months, exceeding the government's 2%–4% target for the year. Food inflation, weighted at 34.8% of the consumer price index, rose to 6.5% in August, although rice inflation was lower at 2.2% (Figure 3.4.34). High global oil prices kept transport inflation elevated at 14.6%, but down from July's 18.1%. Public utility jeepney fares and minimum wages were increased in June. Core inflation accelerated to 4.6% in August, averaging 2.9% in the first 8 months, and was lower than headline inflation. The central bank raised its policy rate by a cumulative 175 basis points from May to August, bringing the overnight reverse repurchase rate to 3.75%.

Figure 3.4.32 Supply-side contributions to growth

Services bounced back on a further easing in COVID-19 mobility restrictions.

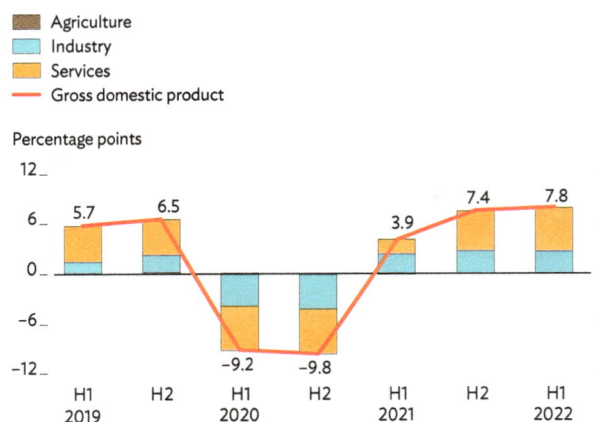

COVID-19 = coronavirus disease, H = half.
Sources: Philippine Statistics Authority; CEIC Data Company (accessed 2 September 2022).

Figure 3.4.33 Contributions to industry growth

Manufacturing and construction led industry growth in 2022.

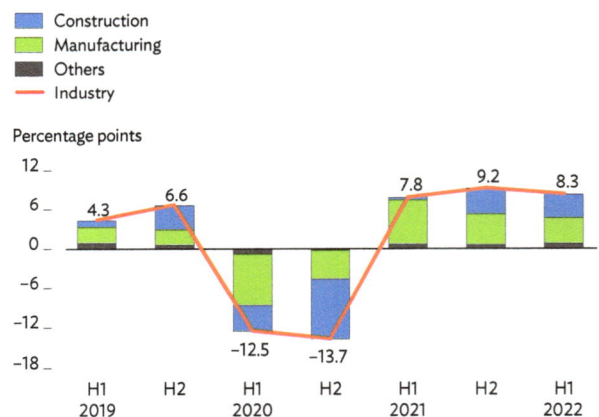

H = half.
Sources: Philippine Statistics Authority; CEIC Data Company (accessed 2 September 2022).

Domestic liquidity (M3) growth has eased since January, and was at 7% year on year in July.

The average inflation rate for the bottom 30% income households was 4.3% in the first 8 months of 2022, lower than the 4.9% national average inflation rate. This is the reverse to the surge in food price inflation in 2018, when the bottom 30% income households was more adversely affected.

Figure 3.4.34 Monthly inflation

Elevated commodity prices fueled inflation.

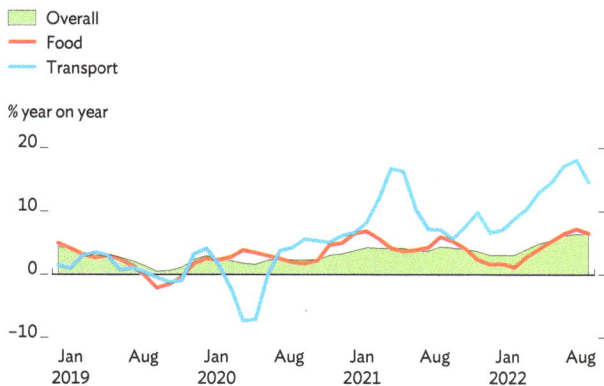

Sources: Philippine Statistics Authority; CEIC Data Company (accessed 7 September 2022).

Figure 3.4.35 Fiscal indicators

Rising revenue kept the fiscal deficit in check.

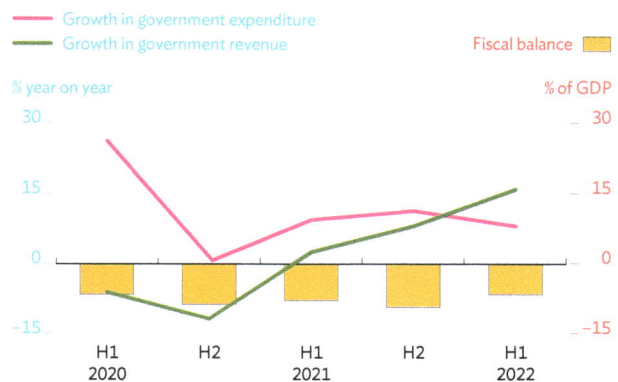

GDP = gross domestic product, H = half.
Source: CEIC Data Company (accessed 2 September 2022).

The main reasons for this were the lower usage of fuel and higher consumption of rice in the consumption basket. The rice sector reforms in 2019 provide a clear example of how trade policy reforms stabilized food prices and promoted food security. The rice tariffication law of 2019 replaced quantitative import restrictions with a 35% import tariff. The result has been stable rice prices throughout the pandemic and during 2022, resulting in lower food price inflation for the bottom 30% income households.

As a social protection measure, the government is giving fuel subsidies and discount vouchers to public transport drivers, farmers, and fishers to help them cope with rising fuel and production costs. Targeted cash transfers are being given to poor households in addition to other social protection programs, such as the Pantawid Pamilyang Pilipino Program.

The fiscal deficit narrowed to the equivalent of 6.5% of GDP in the first half of 2022 from 7.8% in the first half of last year. Revenue, up 15.9% year on year, picked up on revived business activity, surpassing 8.9% expenditure (Figure 3.4.35). Expenditure covered increases in funding for infrastructure, health and education programs, and social assistance.

The current account deficit widened to 5.03% of GDP in the first quarter of 2022 from a 0.04% deficit in the same period in 2021. Merchandise imports rose by 28.6%, outpacing 11.3% export growth. The merchandise trade deficit widened to 17.1% of GDP from 12.1%. Rising remittances and services exports partly cushioned the merchandise trade deficit. In the financial account, net inflows of foreign direct investment rose slightly in the first quarter; net portfolio investment outflows were lower. The overall balance of payments was in surplus, equal to 0.5% GDP, after a 3.1% deficit in the first quarter of 2021. Preliminary data show the balance of payments turned a deficit over April–July largely on the merchandise trade deficit widening further. This brought the balance of payments in the first 7 months to a $4.9 billion deficit, up from a $1.3 billion deficit in the same period of last year.

Gross international reserves declined to $99 billion at the end of August—cover for 8.3 months of imports and service and income payments—from $108.8 billion at end of 2021. The peso slid to a record low against the US dollar in early September, depreciating by 11% from the end of 2021. The higher balance-of-payment deficit contributed to the pressure on the peso, as did the Federal Reserve's aggressive monetary policy tightening. The ratio of external debt to GDP was 27.5% at the end of March, up from 27.0% at the end of 2021.

Prospects

Growth this year should be higher than was projected in April, and higher inflation and a wider current account deficit are expected through 2023. This *Update* raises the forecast for growth for 2022 to 6.5% from the earlier 6.0% projection on the basis of the stronger-than-expected first half (Table 3.4.4). Broad-based domestic demand will continue to underpin growth through 2023. The growth forecast for 2023 is maintained at 6.3%, as financial tightening and a broader pass-through of price pressures will likely weigh on consumption and investment.

Domestic economic activity is expected to remain firm on eased COVID-19 mobility restrictions, higher vaccination and booster shot coverage, and improving consumer confidence. A central bank survey in July showed increasingly upbeat consumer sentiment for the next 12 months on an improved employment outlook. Mobility data across several activities, including work and recreation, are back to or even surpassing pre-pandemic levels (Figure 3.4.36). The resumption of classroom learning and a rebound in tourism will boost services, the economy's biggest sector, comprising 60% of GDP. The share of tourism to GDP was at 12.9% in pre-pandemic 2019, but fell to about 5.0% in 2020 and 2021 due to lockdowns and border closures.

More businesses have reopened and increased capacity, boding well for jobs and investment. Industry output will continue to be supported by robust domestic demand. The manufacturing capacity utilization rate rose to 71.3% in July, the highest since the start of the pandemic. The manufacturing purchasing managers' index has remained above the 50 threshold that indicates expansion since February 2022. It rose to 51.2 in August from 50.8 in July on strong gains in employment on expectations of higher production (Figure 3.4.37). Nevertheless, firms surveyed cited headwinds from subdued external demand and inflationary pressures. Bank lending to businesses expanded by 11.6% year on year in July (Figure 3.4.38). Lending growth was brisk to information and communication (29.3%), manufacturing (16.2%), and wholesale and retail trade (9.3%). Imports of capital goods continued to rise at a double-digit pace, to 11.2% year on year in the first 7 months on higher purchases of transport equipment and industrial machinery.

Table 3.4.4 Selected economic indicators in the Philippines, %

Growth this year should be higher than projected in April. Higher inflation and a wider current account deficit are expected through 2023.

	2021	2022		2023	
		ADO 2022	Update	ADO 2022	Update
GDP growth	5.7	6.0	6.5	6.3	6.3
Inflation	3.9	4.2	5.3	3.5	4.3
CAB/GDP	−1.8	−3.2	−4.5	−3.1	−4.4

ADO = *Asian Development Outlook*, CAB = current account balance, GDP = gross domestic product.

Source: Asian Development Bank estimates.

Figure 3.4.36 Mobility

Mobility has steadily improved on eased COVID-19 restrictions.

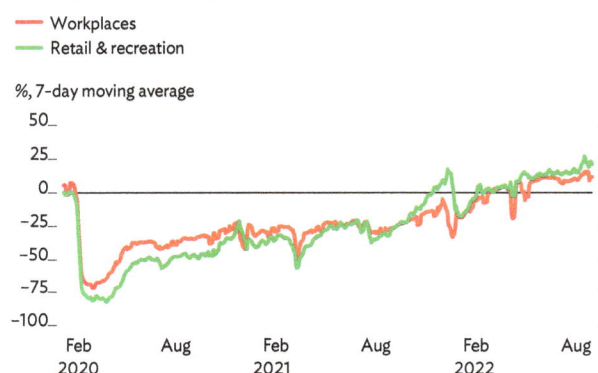

COVID-19 = coronavirus disease.

Note: Mobility refers to the average change in visitors or time spent in workplaces and retail and recreation, relative to the baseline period from January to February 2020.

Sources: Google COVID-19 Community Mobility Trends; CEIC Data Company (both accessed 7 September 2022).

Figure 3.4.37 Manufacturing purchasing managers' index

The manufacturing PMI in expansionary territory since February 2022.

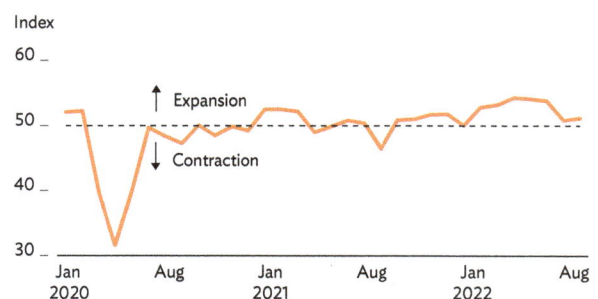

PMI = purchasing managers' index.

Note: A purchasing managers' index reading >50 signals improvement, <50 deterioration.

Sources: S&P Global; Bangko Sentral ng Pilipinas (both accessed 9 September 2022).

Figure 3.4.38 Bank lending

Credit picked up since Q3 2021 as economic activity rebounded.

% year on year

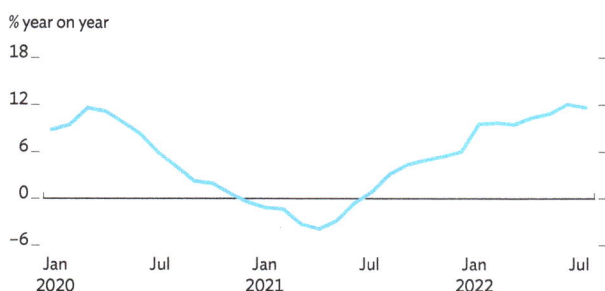

Q = quarter.
Sources: Bangko Sentral ng Pilipinas; CEIC Data Company (both accessed 9 September 2022).

Large public infrastructure projects are ongoing, including bridges, expressways, ports, and railways. Sustained public investments will continue to boost construction and manufacturing.

The government is proposing a ₱5.3 trillion budget for 2023, 4.9% higher than 2022's. Under the fiscal program, revenue is planned to rise by 10.0% next year, with the fiscal deficit narrowing to 6.1% of GDP from this year's 7.6% of GDP deficit ceiling. Larger outlays for infrastructure and social programs are planned. Infrastructure spending this year and next is planned at 5.0%–6.0% of GDP after 5.8% in 2021. Social spending includes programs on universal health care, conditional cash transfers for poor families, livelihood assistance, and education programs.

The new administration, which took office in June, has set out an eight-point socioeconomic agenda comprising food security; improved transportation; affordable and clean energy; improved health care, social services, and education; bureaucratic efficiency; and sound fiscal management. The agenda has strategies to reinvigorate the creation of quality jobs and reduce poverty. The pandemic has reversed gains in poverty alleviation. Poverty incidence declined from 23.5% of the population in 2015 to 16.7% in 2018. But it rose to 18.1% in 2021, equivalent to 20 million poor people, an increase of 2.3 million from 2018.

The government is implementing targeted social assistance, reforms to enhance the investment climate, digitalization programs, climate mitigation and adaptation, and sustained infrastructure

development through, among other things, public–private partnerships. The Corporate Recovery and Tax Incentives for Enterprises Law, approved in March 2021, included a reduction in the corporate tax rate from 30% to 25% (20% for micro, small, and medium-sized enterprises) and enhanced fiscal incentives for investors by making incentives time-bound and performance-based.

Restrictions on the participation of foreign investors in key sectors have been eased. Amendments to the Foreign Investment Act and the Public Service Act allow full foreign ownership in telecommunications, airlines, shipping, railways, and expressways. The Retail Trade Liberalization Act was amended to ease capitalization requirements for foreign investors in retail trade. The government has reduced regulatory compliance costs for businesses by launching the Central Business Portal, an online site for business information and transactions, including getting business permits, licenses, and clearances. The rollout of the Philippine Identification System for a national identification is a major digitalization program to improve the targeting and delivery of public services.

Under the government's medium-term fiscal framework, fiscal consolidation will be pursued by unwinding support provided during the pandemic. Rising revenue as economic growth gains traction will also advance fiscal consolidation. The budget deficit is programmed to narrow by about 1.0% of GDP yearly from 6.1% in 2023 to 3.0% by 2028. The deficit was at 3.4% of GDP in pre-pandemic 2019. The government has set priorities to make spending and revenue mobilization more efficient— and measures have already been taken to broaden the value-added-tax base and increase excise taxes on petroleum products, cigarettes, and alcohol. Measures to clamp down on smuggling, including fuel marking, are lifting tax collection. The government is ramping up digitalization programs to further improve tax administration. The Bureau of Internal Revenue reports that in 2021, 93% of tax returns were filed electronically. Customs procedures are also being digitalized, and 155 out of 170 customs processes are already automated. Other digitalization measures are underway to streamline customs processes. Additional tax reforms are pending in Congress, including to real-property taxes to promote an efficient valuation system and to broaden the tax base for property taxes of the national government and local governments. The government is considering imposing value-added tax on digital goods and services, and an excise tax on single-use plastics, among other measures.

In line with the narrowing fiscal deficit, the ratio of debt to GDP is programmed to start declining in 2023. At the end of June, national government debt totaled 62.1% of GDP, up from 60.4% at the end of 2021. Debt is largely domestic at two-thirds of the total (Figure 3.4.39). The country's investment grade sovereign credit ratings have been affirmed.

This *Update* revises up the forecast for inflation for 2022 to 5.3% from the earlier 4.2% projection. Inflation is expected to remain elevated over the rest of the year due primarily to supply-side factors, including elevated global commodity prices. Bad weather has constrained the domestic supply of some agriculture commodities, and petitions for additional transport fare increases have been submitted by transport groups to the government. Inflation is forecast decelerating to 4.3% in 2023 as global oil and non-oil prices start to ease. The cumulative policy rate adjustment will also contribute to slowing inflation.

Export demand is expected to weaken as growth in major export markets slows. Growth in exports to the United States, comprising 15.6% of total exports, slowed in the second quarter through July, while shipments to the European Union (11.4% share in total exports) have contracted since June. Exports to the People's Republic of China, another key market that has a 14.3% share of total exports, fell sharply by 23.9% year on year in July and contracted by 3.4% in the first 7 months. Exports of electronic products contracted by 7.9% in July. The merchandise trade deficit on a customs basis rose by 66.6% year on year in the first 7 months on import growth (25.9%) outpacing export growth (5.4%).

Figure 3.4.39 National government debt

Debt is largely domestic.

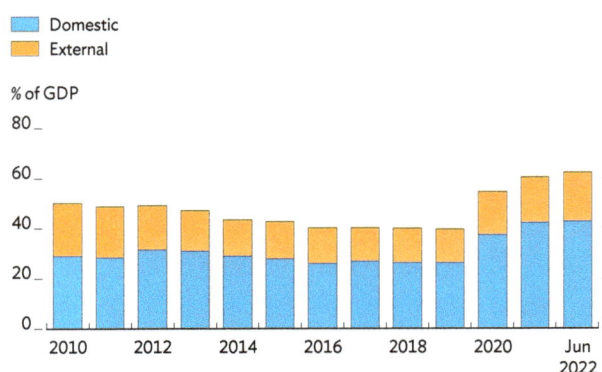

GDP = gross domestic product.
Sources: Bureau of the Treasury; CEIC Data Company (both accessed 2 September 2022).

As prospects for merchandise exports soften, growing domestic investment and consumption will continue to attract imports, keeping merchandise trade and the current account in deficit. Rising remittances and services exports on growing business processing outsourcing receipts and the recovery in tourism will partly cushion the deficit. On balance, the current account deficit is forecast to widen to 4.5% of GDP in 2022 from the earlier 3.2% projection and to 4.4% from 3.1% in 2023.

Downside risks to the outlook include a sharper slowdown in major advanced economies, heightened geopolitical tensions, and the possibility of elevated commodity prices being sustained because of the war in Ukraine.

Thailand

Growth forecasts for 2022 and 2023 are trimmed from *ADO 2022*'s projections in April. Inflation is expected to accelerate on rising energy and fresh food prices. Although economic activity recovered in the first half of 2022, the impact of the Russian invasion of Ukraine on prices and global activity will soften merchandise exports, domestic investment, and consumer spending over the rest of the year. Prolonged supply chain disruptions will affect manufacturing. Rising inflation, the global slowdown, and high household debt are significant downside risks.

Updated assessment

GDP in the first half of 2022 grew by 2.4% from 2.0% in the first half of 2021 on stronger domestic demand and surging international tourist arrivals (Figure 3.4.40). Exports of goods and services rose by 10.2% from 6.0%. The US dollar value of merchandise exports increased by 7.3%, down from 15.6%. Agriculture exports picked up on increased fruit shipments to the People's Republic of China (PRC), facilitated by improved logistics. Increased rice exports were buoyed by demand from Africa, Asia, and the United States—and especially Iraq, which started importing Thai rice in late 2021 for the first time in 7 years. Exports of computer parts and accessories, electrical appliance parts, metal, machinery, and chemical and petrochemical products also increased in the first half, lifted in part by eased COVID-19 restrictions. But exports of automotive parts declined due to shortages of intermediate products. Services exports grew by 43.2% due to the continued increase in international tourist arrivals, particularly from Southeast Asia and India. Relaxed COVID-19 travel restrictions in Thailand and abroad made this possible. International tourist arrivals totaled 2.1 million, up from 40,447 in the first half of 2021 (Figure 3.4.41).

Imports of goods and services increased by 7.6% in the first half of 2022; merchandise imports rose by 5.7%. Imports of consumer goods increased in line with stronger household consumption. Imports of capital goods rose on higher demand for machinery and equipment in all categories. Imports of raw material goods increased, especially electronic parts and electrical appliances, on better global demand.

Figure 3.4.40 Demand-side contributions to growth

The economy continues to recover, led by merchandise exports.

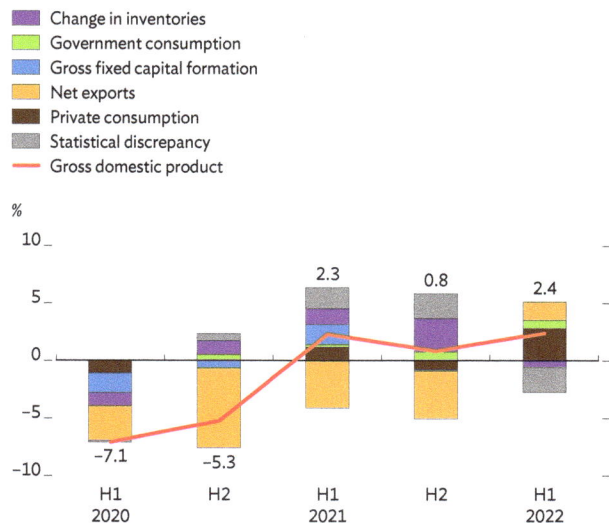

H = half.
Source: Office of the National Economic and Social Development Council (accessed 24 August 2022).

Figure 3.4.41 International tourist arrivals

Started to pick up in Q2 2022 on relaxed COVID-19 travel restrictions in Thailand and abroad.

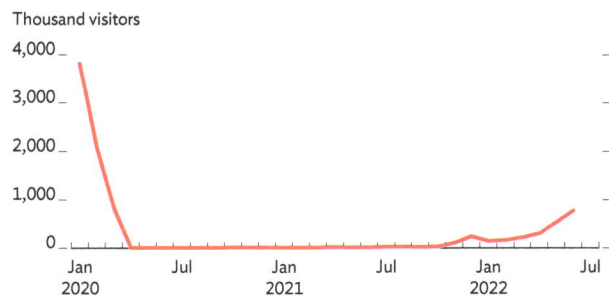

COVID-19 = coronavirus disease, Q = quarter.
Source: CEIC Data Company (accessed 24 August 2022).

And services imports rose by 15.2%, supported in part by higher freight costs due to the growth in international trade. The trade balance turned a surplus in the first half.

Private consumption expanded by 5.2%, aided by the government's economic stimulus measures that helped to create additional jobs. Private consumption also benefited from relaxed COVID-19 restrictions.

Farm income improved, mainly due to higher prices of agricultural products. But higher inflation, especially from rising prices of energy and fresh and instant food, affected private consumption. In May, the government extended the We Travel Together program, a domestic tourism subsidy scheme, to the end of September. It also extended cash handout and subsidy measures from July to September to support people on lower incomes. Additional measures include cash back for fuel bought by motorcycle taxi drivers, a cap on natural gas vehicle prices for taxi drivers, and a cooking gas price subsidy for state welfare cardholders and street vendors. Spending on durable and semi-durable goods, and services, particularly tourism, rebounded. The unemployment rate fell to 1.4% in the second quarter, its lowest since the start of the COVID-19 pandemic. Consumer confidence, however, continued to decline on concerns over the rising cost of living. While household debt as percentage of GDP edged down to 89.2% in the first quarter from 90.0% at the end of 2021, the level remains high.

Private investment rose by 2.6% in the first half on higher imports of capital goods and registrations of commercial vehicles. Both increases are in line with improving domestic demand. Still, investment in construction declined because major infrastructure projects, including the Metropolitan Rapid Transit Yellow and Pink lines, were completed and new projects are not in the construction phase.

Public consumption rose by 4.7% in the first half, mainly from higher social transfers for health care but also because of outlays by the National Health Security Fund and the Social Security Fund to tackle a resurgence of COVID-19 in the first quarter. Public investment fell by 6.8% in the first half due to construction delays in transportation projects and lower disbursements for road and bridge projects. The fiscal deficit remained large. In the first 9 months of fiscal year 2022 (FY2022, ending 30 September 2022), the deficit as a share of GDP narrowed to 4.3% from 10.4% in the same period in the previous fiscal year. Public debt in June 2022 was at 61.1% of GDP, up from 58.4% at the end of FY2021 but below the 70% debt ceiling (Figure 3.4.42).

Agriculture output rose by 4.6% year on year in the first half of 2022, driven by higher crop yields. Livestock production increased on demand from the PRC, Malaysia, India, the US, and Africa.

Some exports of agricultural products increased on concerns over food security due to the Russian invasion of Ukraine. Industry output declined by 1.0% on lower production of capital goods and technology products, especially computers and peripheral equipment, electrical equipment, and machinery. Services grew by 4.2%, largely on increased demand for accommodation and food services due to the jump in international tourist arrivals (Figure 3.4.43).

External stability remains sound even though the current account balance as a share of GDP turned into a 1.7% deficit in the first quarter of 2022.

Figure 3.4.42 Public debt

Public debt is below the 70% GDP ceiling.

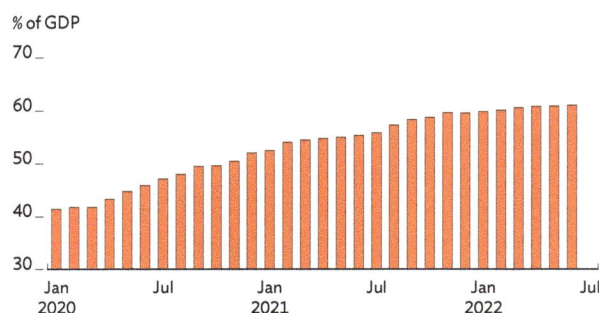

% of GDP

GDP = gross domestic product.
Source: Public Debt Management Office (accessed 24 August 2022).

Figure 3.4.43 Supply-side contributions to growth

Services rebounded on relaxed COVID-19 restrictions.

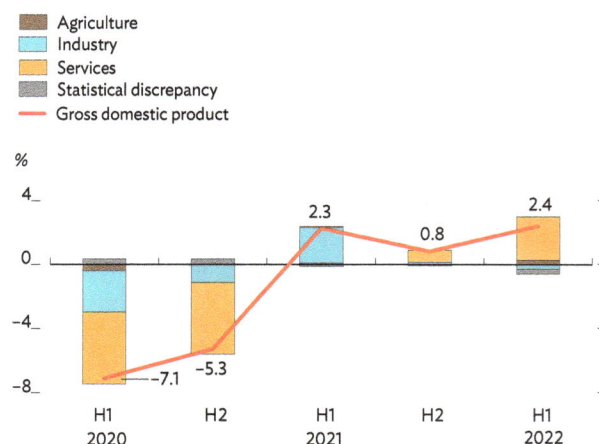

- Agriculture
- Industry
- Services
- Statistical discrepancy
- Gross domestic product

H = half.
Source: Office of the National Economic and Social Development Council (accessed 24 August 2022).

Figure 3.4.44 Balance of payments

Turned a surplus on robust Q1 2022 merchandise exports and foreign direct investment.

- Financial account: other depository corporations
- Financial account: government
- Financial account: central bank
- Current account balance
- Balance of payments

$ billion

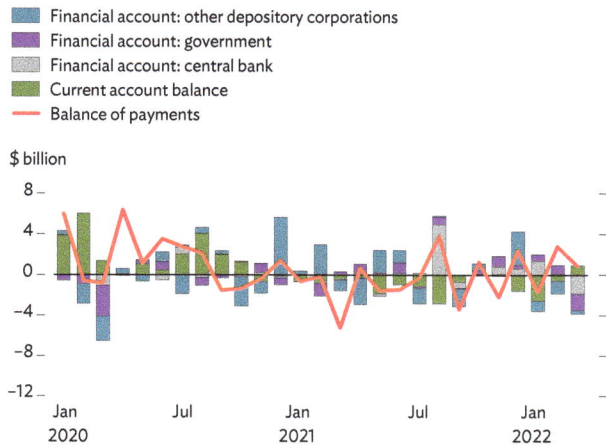

Q = quarter.
Source: CEIC Data Company (accessed 24 August 2022).

Figure 3.4.45 Inflation and policy interest rate

Inflation is accelerating on higher energy and food prices; the policy interest rate was hiked for the first time since May 2020.

- Headline inflation
- Core inflation
- Policy rate

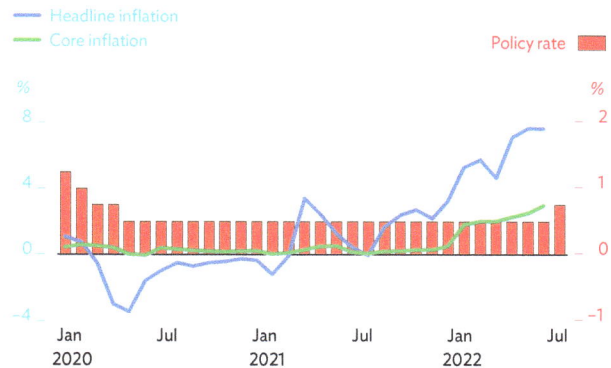

Source: CEIC Data Company (accessed 24 August 2022).

The deficit was propelled by a higher deficit from net services, income, and the transfers balance following large remittances of profits and dividends by foreign businesses. The trade balance was in surplus in the first quarter of 2022 in tandem with the recovery in merchandise exports. The capital and financial accounts posted net inflows due mainly to higher foreign direct investment in the energy sector, wholesale and retail trade, and financial and insurance services (Figure 3.4.44). The external payments position remained sustainable, with the level of international reserves providing cover for 9.6 months of imports, equal to 37.7 times short-term external debt.

Bank of Thailand, the central bank, raised its policy rate by 0.25 percentage points to 0.75% from 0.50% in August in response to two factors: the extraordinarily accommodative monetary policy because of the COVID-19 pandemic has become less needed and the economic recovery is expected to continue gaining momentum. The headline inflation rate averaged 5.6% in the first half, up from 0.9% in the same period of 2021, on higher energy and food prices (Figure 3.4.45). Price control measures for energy and public transport should help contain the cost of living. But these measures nevertheless seem inadequate since the cost pass-through is expected to broaden into a wider range of products.

Prospects

Although the economy improved in the first half of 2022, this *Update* revises down the outlook for growth in 2022 to 2.9% from *ADO 2022*'s 3.0% projection and to 4.2% from 4.5% for 2023 (Table 3.4.5 and Figure 3.4.46). The softer expected growth is largely due to higher global commodity prices following the Russian invasion of Ukraine, weaker growth in the economies of Thailand's trading partners, lower domestic investment, and higher inflation undermining consumer purchasing power.

Table 3.4.5 Selected economic indicators in Thailand, %

Despite the economy strengthening in H1 2022, growth is revised down a tad for 2022 and 2023.

	2021	2022		2023	
		ADO 2022	Update	ADO 2022	Update
GDP growth	1.5	3.0	2.9	4.5	4.2
Inflation	1.2	3.3	6.3	2.2	2.7
CAB/GDP	-2.2	0.5	-2.0	4.2	2.6

ADO = *Asian Development Outlook*, CAB = current account balance, GDP = gross domestic product, H = half.
Sources: Office of the National Economic and Social Development Council; Asian Development Bank estimates.

Figure 3.4.46 GDP growth

Growth is revised down for 2022 and 2023 mainly on heightened external risks.

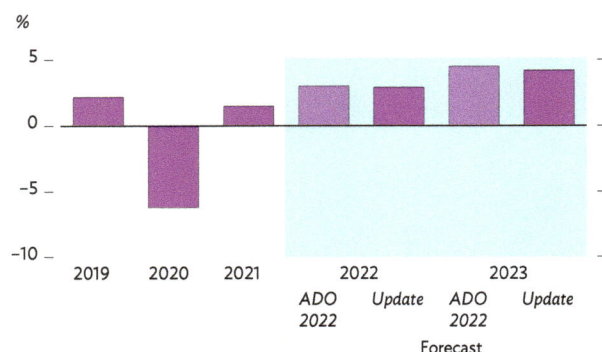

ADO = Asian Development Outlook, GDP = gross domestic product.
Source: ADO database.

External demand is expected to continue expanding, but at a slower pace. The forecast growth for 2022's exports of goods and services is revised down a tad, to 5.9% from 6.1%—and to 8.4% from 9.4% in 2023, due mainly to an expected slowdown in merchandise exports in line with slowing global demand. Supply disruptions, particularly for semiconductors, are expected to persist over the rest of 2022. Exports of automobile parts and some electronic products are likely to decline this year. Thailand's food and beverage exports could be a 2022 bright spot, as many Asian countries have curbed shipments of agricultural products to protect their consumers from surging prices.

Services exports are expected to continue rising. The forecast for international tourist arrivals this year is revised up to 6 million from *ADO 2022*'s projection of 5 million and to 17 million from 12 million in 2023. The higher forecasts are prompted by almost all travel restrictions having now been lifted by the government. The government has abolished the $10,000 health insurance requirement for foreign tourists. At points of entry into Thailand, visitors now only need to show either a COVID-19 vaccination certificate, a negative reverse transcription polymerase chain reaction test, or a professional antigen test kit result within 72 hours of travel. Thailand's color-coded system to signify the severity of the COVID-19 situation—which placed limits on dining, gatherings, and travel—was removed at the start of July, allowing for the resumption of normal business and other activities nationwide.

The growth forecast for private consumption this year is revised down from 3.3% to 3.0% on expectations that household purchasing power will deteriorate due to a significant rise in food and energy prices. Government support is expected to have only a limited impact on boosting private consumption. An example of government support for this is the extended domestic tourism subsidy that covers 40% of the cost of a hotel room not exceeding B3,000 a night. The burden of household debt could restrain consumer spending when financial assistance measures, including debt restructuring and mortgage and retail loan debt consolidation, are stopped at the end of next year. The forecast for private consumption growth in 2023 is unchanged at 3.0%—a level that is in line with the strength of economic recovery. Private investment is now forecast to grow by 4.7% in 2022, down from the earlier projection of 5.0%, due mainly to higher production costs from the sharp rise in oil prices and the baht's depreciation, which has made raw material imports more expensive. The baht fell to a lower range of B35 to B37 against the US dollar over the first half of 2022 from an average of B32 in 2021 due to the monetary policy tightening in advanced economies. The weaker trend is likely to continue in the near term. The global economic slowdown and supply disruptions are expected to reduce investment in Thailand's export-oriented sectors.

Public consumption in 2022 is forecast to contract by 1.9%, much sharper than *ADO 2022*'s projected 0.4% contraction. Public consumption is forecast to contract by 0.6% in 2023. The projection for growth in public investment this year is revised down on more expected delays and increasing costs of raw material imports due to the baht's continued depreciation and rising energy prices. Public investment in 2023 is expected to pick up as projects delayed in 2022 begin construction next year. The forecast for growth in imports of goods and services in 2022 is revised up to 4.6% from 1.1% on expectations that the prices of capital and raw material imports will rise. Earnings from international tourist arrivals should strengthen further now that the government has downgraded COVID-19 to an endemic disease, which will enable a return to normal life.

Agriculture output is expected to rise by 4.5% in 2022, higher than the earlier 3.0% projection. Paddy, sugarcane, soybean, maize, and fruit production will be supported by favorable weather, particularly sufficient water for cultivation. Agriculture output in 2023 is revised down to 2.4% from a higher base. The forecast for industrial production is revised down to 2.7% for 2022 from 3.2% due to rising energy prices and supply disruptions. Services output in 2022 is revised up to 4.6% from 4.5%. The tourism industry will continue strengthening next year in line with expectations of a global economic recovery and the further lifting of COVID-19 restrictions in Thailand. Services output next year is projected to expand by 10.3%, higher than *ADO 2022*'s 8.6% forecast.

Inflation will accelerate fast this year. The forecast for the inflation rate in 2022 is revised up to 6.3% from the earlier projection of 3.3% on a significant rise in global energy and commodity prices. Inflation will moderate in 2023, to a forecast 2.7% from the earlier 2.2% projection—a forecast that still reflects rising food and persistently high energy prices (Figure 3.4.47). Although the government has rolled out several measures to counter rising prices, including targeted subsidies on cooking gas and reducing social security contributions, the cost pass-through is expected to broaden into a wider range of products.

The current account balance as a share of GDP is now projected to register a deficit of 2% this year—reversing the surplus forecast in *ADO 2022*—due mainly to rising prices of merchandise imports (Figure 3.4.48). Net earnings from services exports are likely to increase over the rest of this year on higher remittances of profits and dividends by foreign businesses. Even though tourism receipts are expected to continue rising, this will not be enough to offset the transfer of remittance payments abroad. The current account is expected to return to a surplus next year. The capital and financial accounts are likely to turn net outflows because of tightening US monetary policy and worsening investor confidence because of the Russian invasion of Ukraine.

Risks to the outlook remain tilted to the downside. A major risk is that domestic consumer demand could weaken on higher global inflation caused by a protracted war in Ukraine. The impact of higher prices of imported of capital and raw material costs could constrain production. And slowing global demand could hurt exports. The elevated level of household debt poses a major domestic risk.

Figure 3.4.47 Inflation

Inflation in 2022 will accelerate faster than projected earlier on sharp rises in global energy and commodity prices.

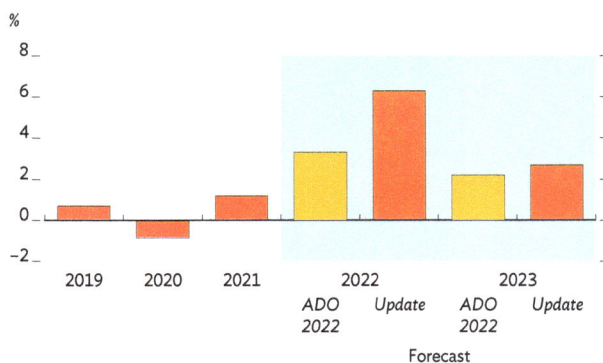

ADO = Asian Development Outlook.
Source: ADO database.

Figure 3.4.48 Current account balance

The current account will turn a deficit in 2022 on rising prices of merchandise imports.

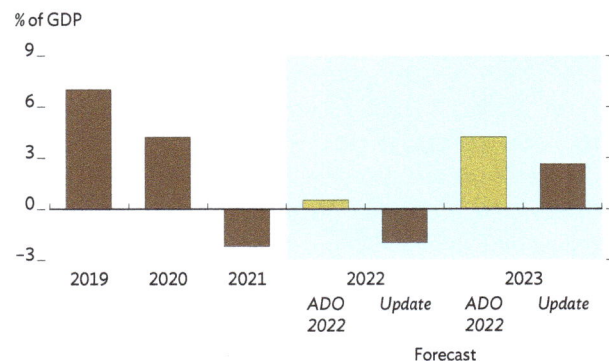

ADO = Asian Development Outlook, GDP = gross domestic product.
Source: ADO database.

Viet Nam

Strong economic fundamentals are driving an economic rebound. Risks from global inflation have been mitigated by easing global cost pressures, a stable exchange rate, effective price controls, and a steady domestic supply of food. This *Update* maintains the forecasts for growth and inflation made in *ADO 2022* in April. Still, risks to these forecasts are high—and a global economic slowdown in particular could weigh on Viet Nam's economic recovery and worsen the current account balance in the near term.

Updated assessment

The economy bounced back much faster than expected in the first half of 2022. Growth accelerated by 7.7% in the second quarter and averaged 6.4% over the first half—higher than in the same period in 2021 and 2020, but still lower than 6.8% in pre-pandemic 2019 (Figure 3.4.49). Higher input prices constrained industry growth, down to 7.7% from 8.5% in the first half of 2021. Manufacturing output moderated to 9.7% due to lower-than-expected demand from advanced economies. The sector contributed 2.3 percentage points to the overall GDP growth rate in the first half. Systemic delays in public investment disbursements depressed construction growth, which fell to 3.7% from 6.5% in the first half of 2021.

Services growth rebounded by 6.6% in the first half from 3.9% in the same period in 2021 on a sharp rise in local tourists to 60.8 million. There were 1.9 times more local tourists than in the first half of 2021 and 1.3 times more than the level before COVID-19. The rebound in local tourism lifted tourism-related services by 7% in the first half after they contracted by 1% in the same period of last year. The economic rebound boosted banking and financial services growth, up 9.5% from 9.1%, and much higher than before the pandemic.

High global input prices slowed agriculture output in the first half to 2.8% from 3.8% in the same period last year. Farm production grew by 2.3%, down from 3.6%. But forestry rose by 5.0% from 3.9% on higher exports of timber products.

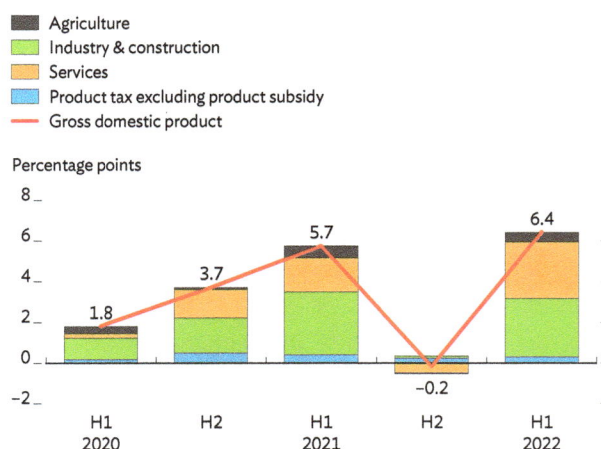

Figure 3.4.49 Supply-side contributions to growth

GDP growth bounced back strongly in H1 2022.

Legend:
- Agriculture
- Industry & construction
- Services
- Product tax excluding product subsidy
- Gross domestic product

H = half.
Source: General Statistics Office (accessed 5 August 2022).

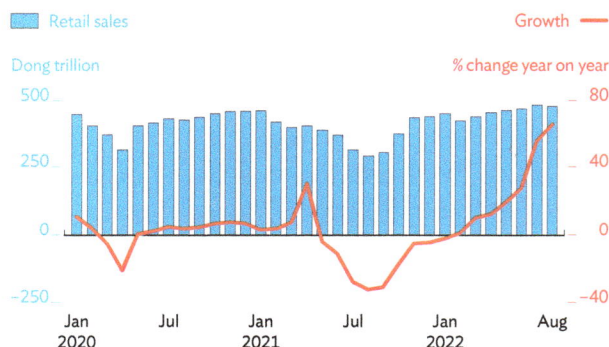

Figure 3.4.50 Retail sales

Improving retail sales supported the economic recovery.

Legend: Retail sales (Dong trillion); Growth (% change year on year)

Sources: General Statistics Office; Haver Analytics (both accessed 29 August 2022).

The final consumption of goods and services rose by 6.1% from 3.6%, lifted by 6.5% growth in consumer expenditure. The economic rebound boosted retail sales, up 65.9% year on year in August; retail sales in the first 8 months rose by 20.6% (Figure 3.4.50).

The slow disbursement of public investment in the first half—estimated at $6.5 billion or only 27% of the government's annual plan—depressed total domestic investment, which rose by 3.9% from 5.7% in the first half of last year. Only $2 billion of the $15 billion Economic Recovery Development Program has been disbursed.

The disbursement of foreign direct investment (FDI) in the first 8 months rose to an estimated $12.8 billion—10.5% higher than in the same period in 2021—on an improved business environment and revived economic activity. New FDI, however, dropped by 12.3% due to global geopolitical tensions and tighter global financial conditions (Figure 3.4.51).

The improved business environment and revived economic activity boosted business start-ups: some 101,300 firms were registered in the first 8 months, a 24.2% increase in the number of firms and a 16.2% rise in the number of total employees from the same period in 2021. In addition, 48,100 firms resumed operations, up 43.8%, bringing the total number of new and reopened firms to 149,500, up 31.1%. Although the supply of labor has normalized, labor-intensive sectors, such as textiles and garments, still face labor shortages due largely to less competitive wages that in part reflect Viet Nam's labor market moving into higher value-added sectors.

Self-sufficiency in food supply, a recovered domestic supply chain, and the effective control of the prices of key commodities and services (e.g., petroleum, electricity, health care, and education) contained headline inflation at an average of 2.6% in the first 8 months amid spiraling global price pressures (Figure 3.4.52). Core inflation averaged 1.6%.

The State Bank of Vietnam (SBV), the central bank, has successfully maintained an accommodative but flexible monetary policy to facilitate low-cost financing to help support the economic recovery while containing inflation. It has kept policy interest rates unchanged since the last rate cuts in October 2020; expanded credit, which grew by an estimated 15.9% year on year in June; and prudently monitored credit to high-risk sectors (e.g., real estate and equity). To ease inflationary pressures and support the dong, the SBV absorbed excess liquidity, estimated at D100 trillion in the first half of 2022, by selling SBV bills through open market operations, which contributed to slowing the total liquidity growth rate to 9.2% from 14.2% in the first half of 2021 (Figure 3.4.53). The SBV tightened the reins on a rising US dollar by selling about $7 billion in the first 7 months of 2022 to stabilize the exchange rate, keeping the dong's depreciation against the US dollar at 2% and leaving the dong more stable than some other currencies in Southeast Asia.

Figure 3.4.51 Foreign direct investment

Revived economic activity and an improved business climate lifted FDI disbursement, although new FDI declined.

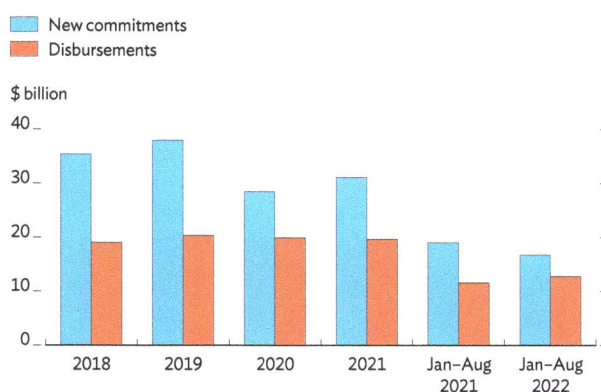

FDI = foreign direct investment.
Source: Haver Analytics (accessed 29 August 2022).

Figure 3.4.52 Monthly inflation

Recovered domestic supply chains and effective price controls helped contain headline inflation.

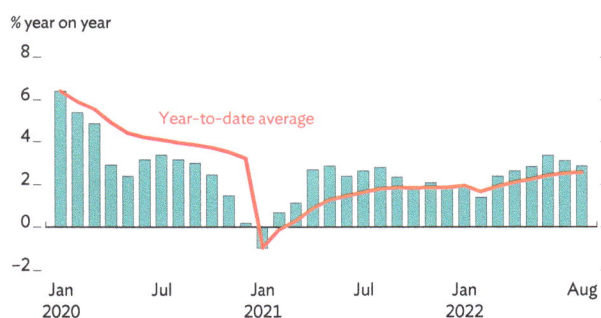

Source: General Statistics Office (accessed 29 August 2022).

Figure 3.4.53 Credit and money supply growth

Credit growth continued to support the recovery.

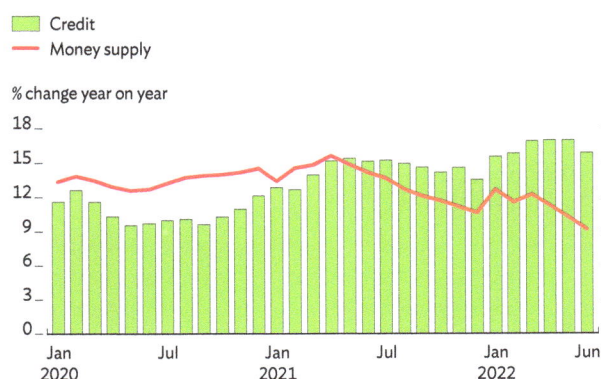

Sources: State Bank of Vietnam; Asian Development Bank estimates.

The merchandise trade surplus narrowed to an estimated 0.4% of GDP in the first half of 2022 from 2.7% in 2021 because of weakening global demand. But revived economic activity and the stable exchange rate increased exports, up 17.1% to $250.8 billion year on year in the first 8 months. The recovery in domestic production lifted imports by 13.6% to $246.8 billion, resulting in a $4.0 billion trade surplus.

Rising global inflation and tightening financial conditions lowered remittances in the first half by an estimated 20% from the level in the same period in 2021. Weakening global demand and reduced remittances turned the current account balance into a deficit of an estimated 1.5% of GDP in the first half after a deficit of 3.7% in the same period last year.

Low disbursements of foreign borrowing narrowed the financial account surplus to 3.8% of GDP in the first half from 8.8% in the same period of last year. The current account deficit and a declining surplus of the financial account turned the balance of payments to an estimated deficit of 1.5% of GDP (Figure 3.4.54). By June, foreign reserves were estimated to cover 3.7 months of imports, down from 3.9 months at the end of 2021, because of the narrowing trade surplus and the SBV selling US dollars to stabilize the exchange rate.

Profits from crude oil and earnings from imports and exports lifted government revenue by 19.4% in the first 8 months from the same period in 2021. The ratio of domestic to total revenue declined to 79% from 81.4%. Revenue from the transfer of land use rights rose sharply to around 13% from 8% of total revenue. Spending on health care, social security, and income support modestly increased, by 4.2%. The preliminary on-budget fiscal balance turned an estimated surplus of 5% of GDP in the first half, up from 2% in 2021.

Prospects

The economic rebound is expected to continue over the second half of 2022, supported by strong economic fundamentals, flexible monetary policy, and a faster-than-expected recovery in manufacturing, services, and domestic consumption from July to December. This *Update* maintains the growth forecasts made in *ADO 2022*: 6.5% for 2022 and 6.7% for 2023 (Table 3.4.6 and Figure 3.4.55).

Figure 3.4.54 Balance of payments indicators

The current account balance was under pressure from a narrowing trade surplus and reduced remittances.

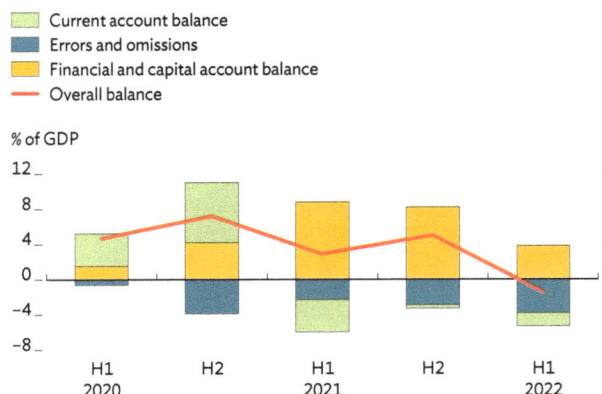

GDP = gross domestic product, H = half.
Sources: Haver Analytics (accessed 19 August 2022); State Bank of Vietnam; Asian Development Bank estimates.

Table 3.4.6 Selected economic indicators in Viet Nam, %

Economic fundamentals remain strong, supporting growth.

	2021	2022		2023	
		ADO 2022	Update	ADO 2022	Update
GDP growth	2.6	6.5	6.5	6.7	6.7
Inflation	1.8	3.8	3.8	4.0	4.0
CAB/GDP	–2.0	1.5	–1.5	2.0	–1.7

ADO = Asian Development Outlook, CAB = current account balance, GDP = gross domestic product.
Sources: General Statistics Office; Asian Development Bank estimates.

Figure 3.4.55 GDP growth

Forecasts for strong growth in 2022 and 2023 unchanged.

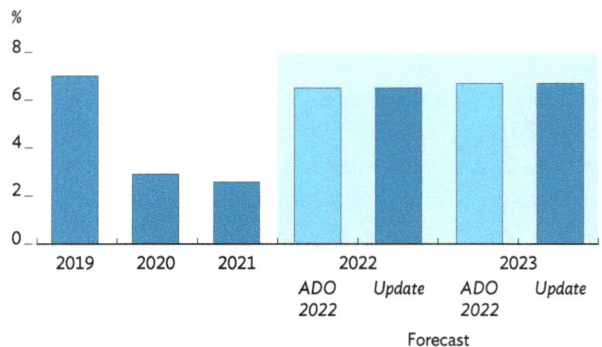

ADO = Asian Development Outlook, GDP = gross domestic product.
Source: ADO database.

Global food shortages and restored global food supply chains will boost agriculture production this year. But the forecast for agriculture growth is revised down to 3.0% from the earlier 3.5% projection because high input costs may still constrain the sector's growth. Softening global demand has already slowed manufacturing. The manufacturing purchasing managers' index in August reduced to 52.7 from 54.0 in June (Figure 3.4.56). Because of this, the forecast for industry growth is lowered to 8.5% from 9.5%, but the outlook for industry remains bullish given strong FDI disbursement in the sector. Fully normalized domestic mobility and the lifting of COVID-19 travel restrictions for foreign visitors will support a rebound in tourism in the second half that will be stronger than was expected in April. This will drive services growth, revised up to 6.6% for 2022 from the earlier 5.5% projection. The raised forecast is nevertheless below services growth of 7.3% in pre-pandemic 2019.

Figure 3.4.56 Purchasing managers' index

Manufacturing PMI moderated in August 2022, but it was still in expansionary territory.

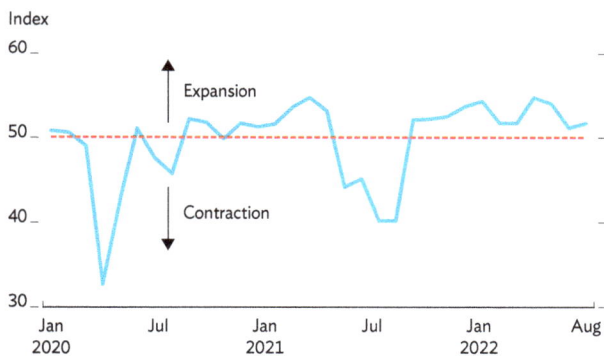

PMI = purchasing managers' index.
Source: CEIC Data Company (accessed 5 September 2022).

Weaker global demand should slow exports. The dong's depreciation is making the value of imports more expensive than exports, which is expected to result in a trade deficit in 2022. High global inflation, though gradually decelerating, and tightened financial conditions will continue to depress remittances. Because of all this, the current account is forecast to turn a deficit of 1.5% of GDP this year; *ADO 2022* forecast a surplus. A current account deficit, at 1.7% of GDP, is projected for 2023 on expectations of softer global growth.

Total investment is expected to rise this year. Although global geopolitical tensions and tightening financial conditions will continue to limit FDI inflows in 2022, FDI disbursement will be strong on the continued confidence of foreign investors and doing business in Viet Nam becoming easier. A determined effort by the government to disburse public investment, including the implementation of the Economic Recovery Development Program, would offset the effect of softer exports caused by weaker global demand. The SBV will continue to pursue a flexible and prudent monetary policy by continuing to keep its policy rates unchanged. It will also roll out the interest rate subsidy program to provide low-cost financing for the economy. However, monetary accommodation, such as the interest rate subsidy, loan restructuring, and regulatory forbearance, could delay classification of nonperforming loans, forecast at 5% of outstanding loans in 2022. Efforts to keep the exchange rate stable to support exports and imports could also stress foreign reserves.

The fiscal deficit is forecast to widen to 4% of GDP this year on continued price controls, tax cuts, targeted fiscal support, and spending on social security, health care, and COVID-19 vaccinations. Sufficient fiscal space, however, is provided by well-controlled public debt. At an estimated 43.1% of GDP in 2021, this is comfortably below the 60% statutory level. National external debt is forecast at 38.4% of GDP, which is within the statutory 45.0% limit. A strong fiscal position and low public debt have considerably aided Viet Nam's robust economic recovery, despite rising global inflation and interest rates.

Viet Nam's prudent monetary policy and effective price controls of gasoline, electricity, food, health care, and education should keep inflation in check at 3.8% in 2022 and 4.0% in 2023, the same as projected in *ADO 2022* (Figure 3.4.57). Increasing investment, controlled inflation, and accommodative monetary and fiscal conditions are expected to drive domestic consumption, boosting 2022's ongoing economic recovery. Rising consumption over the rest of the second half and possible increases in some government-administered prices may increase inflationary pressure.

Figure 3.4.57 Inflation

Flexible and prudent monetary policy and price controls keeping inflation in check; forecasts unchanged.

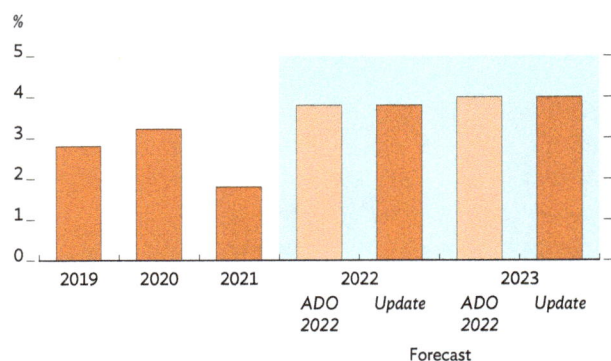

ADO = Asian Development Outlook.
Source: ADO database.

Figure 3.4.58 Business entry

Although the business environment improved in H1 2022, challenges to the business recovery remain.

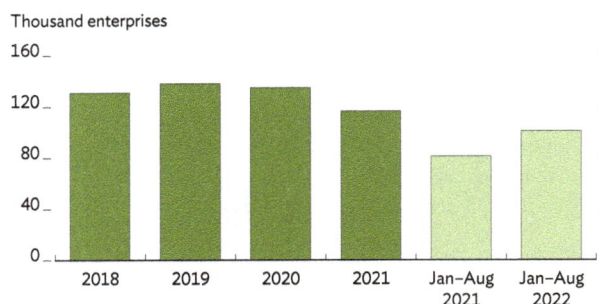

H = half.
Source: General Statistics Office (accessed 30 August 2022).

Although the overall business environment improved in the first 8 months, business momentum has started to slow and the registration of new firms declined slightly in August even though the accumulated number of new firms increased. The decline nevertheless reflects challenges in the business recovery; for example, labor shortages and lower new orders (Figure 3.4.58).

Risks to Viet Nam's economic outlook remain elevated. The global economic slowdown could weigh more heavily on exports than forecast, which would worsen the current account balance.

Although aggressive interest hikes by the central banks of major economies have helped dampen global price pressures, an intensification of global geopolitical uncertainties could push up commodity prices, worsening inflation in Viet Nam. A resurgence of COVID-19 infections is possible amid lower readiness in the health care system due to the recent resignations of many health care workers and shortages of medical equipment and drugs. A labor shortage would impede the fast recovery of services and the labor-intensive export sector in 2022. A failure to deliver public investment and social spending as planned could slow growth this year and next.

Other economies

Brunei Darussalam

The economy contracted by 4.2% in the first quarter (Q1) of 2022, the sixth consecutive quarter of negative growth. The slowdown reflects a 9.0% decline in oil and gas output because of maintenance work. Economic activity normalized in other sectors in the absence of tight COVID-19 restrictions, despite a surge in cases earlier this year. As a result, sectors other than the oil and gas expanded by 1.0% in Q1, although the performance across sectors was mixed. Agriculture, forestry, and fisheries grew by 1.0%; services increased by just 0.4%. Services were marked by a rebound in transportation and accommodation, but finance, communication, and restaurants dragged sector growth. By expenditure, Q1 household consumption rose by 5.5% year on year and government consumption by 3.8%. Gross fixed capital formation declined by 4.2%. Net exports fell by 28% in real terms, consistent with the decline in oil and gas output.

Because of the unexpected contraction in Q1 growth, this *Update* revises down the forecast for 2022 growth in *ADO 2022* made in April (Table 3.4.7). The further easing of COVID-19 restrictions in June and the reopening of borders for nonessential travel in August will help economic activity this year. The forecast for 2023 is unchanged from the earlier projection on the assumption that crude oil prices will remain elevated in the medium term. Growth in 2023 will also be supported by the construction of the second phase of Hengyi Industries' oil refinery and petrochemical project.

The global economic impact of the Russian invasion of Ukraine and ongoing global supply chain disruptions pushed the headline inflation rate to 3.9% in April, its highest since 1995. In May, the rate eased to 3.8%. Price increases were especially pronounced for food, up by 6.0% year on year in May, clothing and footwear (2.6%), and transport (4.9%). Subsidies on electricity and petrol, and the exchange rate parity with the Singapore dollar, cushioned even higher prices. Although inflation should moderate in the second half of this year on normalizing food prices, average inflation in 2022 is forecast to be higher than the projection in April.

Table 3.4.7 Selected economic indicators in Brunei Darussalam, %

An unexpected contraction in oil and gas output slowed GDP growth in 2022; global headwinds pushed up inflation.

	2021	2022		2023	
		ADO 2022	Update	ADO 2022	Update
GDP growth	–1.6	4.2	2.2	3.6	3.6
Inflation	1.7	1.6	3.5	1.0	2.0
CAB/GDP	12.5	16.0	16.0	12.0	12.0

ADO = *Asian Development Outlook*, CAB = current account balance, GDP = gross domestic product.
Sources: CEIC Data Company; Asian Development Bank estimates.

Buoyant commodity prices increased the US dollar value of exports of goods and services by 59.2% in Q1. Exports of mineral fuels and liquefied natural gas were both up by some 35% from the level in Q1 2021. Brunei Fertilizer Industries began commercial production of ammonia and urea in January and exported its first shipments to the Republic of Korea and Thailand in February. Q1 imports increased by 29.8% on higher mineral fuel and chemical imports. The current account surplus is estimated at $1.1 billion in Q1, generally in line with *ADO 2022*'s projection.

Risks to the outlook are fairly evenly balanced. An unanticipated disruption to oil and gas output is the main downside risk that could delay Brunei Darussalam's recovery. Persistently high inflation expectations could dampen domestic demand and a rebound in economic activity other than the oil and gas sector. An upside risk is another surge in oil and gas prices caused by the war in Ukraine intensifying.

Cambodia

This *Update* maintains the growth forecast for 2022 made in *ADO 2022* in April, but revises down the forecast for 2023 (Table 3.4.8.). While Cambodia's merchandise exports grew strongly in the first half of 2022, the economy faces challenges from weaker global growth. Inflation accelerated faster than anticipated in the first half due to the strong pass-through effects of fuel price increases caused by the Russian invasion of Ukraine. Because of this, the inflation forecast for 2022 is revised up from the earlier projection. The surge in fuel prices has moderated the projected narrowing of the current account deficit for this year and next.

Growth in Cambodia's garments, travel goods, and footwear output was robust in the first half, with this segment's exports rising by 39.8% year on year despite the economic slowdown in the United States and Europe. Nongarment manufacturing continued its strong growth. Construction gradually recovered, with imports of construction materials growing by 22.8% year on year in the first half. Industry output is projected to grow 9.1% this year before moderating to 8.6% in 2023 due to weaker external demand.

Surging fuel and fertilizer prices following the war in Ukraine and heavy rains lowered crop production. Milled rice exports rose marginally, increasing 0.6% year on year in the first half. Export growth for rubber fell to 15.3% from 123.2% and bananas to 24.7% from 75.7%. The forecast for agricultural growth is cut to 0.8% for 2022 and 1.1% for 2023.

The implementation of the Strategic Framework and Program for Economic Recovery in the Context of Living with COVID-19 in the New Normal, 2021–2023 is supporting the recovery in services. With the economy's reopening and an over 90% COVID-19 vaccination rate, demand for food, accommodation, transportation, and communication, as well as other in-person services has increased, although unevenly. A fifth COVID-19 vaccine dose is being rolled out to ensure the economy can safely stay open. International visitor arrivals rebounded by 394.1% year on year to 506,762 in the first half of 2022 from a low base of 102,560 in the first half of 2021. Bank credit to wholesale and retail trade rose by 9.0%, transportation by 7.9%, and hotels and restaurants by 7.6%.

Table 3.4.8 Selected economic indicators in Cambodia, %

The recovery will continue in 2022 and through 2023.

	2021	2022		2023	
		ADO 2022	Update	ADO 2022	Update
GDP growth	3.0	5.3	5.3	6.5	6.2
Inflation	2.9	4.7	5.0	2.2	2.2
CAB/GDP	–45.7	–21.5	–23.8	–16.1	–17.0

ADO = *Asian Development Outlook*, CAB = current account balance, GDP = gross domestic product.
Source: Asian Development Bank estimates.

Real estate lending increased by 19.5%. Services output is projected to grow 4.0% in 2022 and accelerate to 6.5% in 2023 as the sector strengthens further.

Foreign direct investment and other capital inflows decreased by 1.2% year on year in the first quarter of 2022, contributing to a small decline in gross international reserves to $19.5 billion by the end of June, covering about 7 months of imports. The current account deficit is expected to narrow from the previous year, although the surge in oil and commodity prices over the first half slowed the pace of narrowing. The forecast is contingent on the unbalanced gold trade ceasing and a gradual improvement in tourism.

The government is continuing with its socioeconomic interventions to support the recovery. The Cash Transfer Program for Poor and Vulnerable Households—which is mitigating the impact of the COVID-19 pandemic and surges in food and fuel prices for about 2.7 million people—disbursed $744.6 million by July 2022. Some regulatory forbearances continue to support the banking sector's recovery, but the National Bank of Cambodia's loan restructuring program, started in March 2020, was phased out at the end of June 2022.

Risks to the outlook include the emergence of a new deadly COVID-19 variant and the monkeypox outbreak, a rapid increase in nonperforming loans, the weakened growth of major trading partners, global supply chain disruptions, and a worse-than-expected surge in energy and commodities prices.

Myanmar

Economic activity improved moderately since March 2022, despite domestic political turmoil continuing to impede investment and consumption, as well as the overall economy. But because of the pick-up in activity, growth is now expected in fiscal year 2022 (FY2022, ending 30 September 2022) after a contraction was forecast in *ADO 2022* in April. The economy, however, remains vulnerable to macroeconomic instability from the political uncertainties.

A gradual improvement in garment and light manufacturing export earnings is buoying industrial output, forecast to grow by 5.0% in FY2022 from the earlier 2.7% projection. The S&P global purchasing managers' index for Myanmar's manufacturing sector trended higher in the first 10 months of FY2022, suggesting more firms expect increased output in the near term. Exports of manufactured products rose by 27.7% in the first 10 months. Construction is expected to benefit from the resumption of infrastructure and other public work projects. Private investment seems to have picked up, albeit slowly. New registered companies rose by 27.0% in the first 10 months after a 38.4% decline in the whole of the previous fiscal year.

Leading indicators on mobility trends, bank liquidity, and internet penetration indicate a mild acceleration in services' growth. Tourism services—hotels, restaurants, transportation, and communication—outperformed earlier forecasts due mainly to domestic travel. But international tourism remains subdued because of security concerns. The services sector is estimated to grow by 2.6% in FY2022, up from the 1.2% contraction forecast in April. Agriculture production, however, has been constrained by supply chain disruptions, higher input and energy prices, limited access to finance, and the security situation in rural areas. Agriculture production is expected to contract by 3.5%, far more than was forecast in April. Because of these constraints, agriculture exports fell by 13% in the first 10 months of FY2022.

The gradual relaxation of COVID-19 restrictions helped increase the volume of merchandise exports, up 7.4% in the first 10 months. Merchandise imports rose by 10.5%, reflecting strong growth in cut-make-pack and intermediate imports. Because of the strong import growth, Myanmar's trade and current account deficits are seen widening further than projected in April.

Table 3.4.9 Selected economic indicators in Myanmar, %

Growth remains low in the near term; inflation to remain elevated.

	2021	2022		2023	
		ADO 2022	Update	ADO 2022	Update
GDP growth	−5.9	−0.3	2.0	2.6	2.6
Inflation	3.6	8.0	16.0	8.5	8.5
CAB/GDP	−1.3	−0.8	−1.8	−1.3	−1.3

ADO = *Asian Development Outlook*, CAB = current account balance, GDP = gross domestic product.
Sources: https://www.mopf.gov.mm; https://www.cbm.gov.mm; Asian Development Bank estimates.

Foreign investment commitments, at $669 million in the first 9 months of FY2022, were down 82.2% compared to commitments in the whole of the previous fiscal year, mainly due to political tension.

The fiscal deficit is expected to widen further in FY2022 on a resumption in public infrastructure spending and tax and other revenue remaining low. It widened to the equivalent of 8.1% of GDP after revenue collection sharply declined in FY2021. This *Update* therefore revises up the fiscal deficit forecast for FY2022 to 7.5% of GDP from 6.5% projected earlier.

In the first 6 months of FY2022, the year-on-year inflation rate climbed to 17.3% on sharp increases in food and nonfood prices, largely caused by domestic trade disruptions, a depreciating kyat, and soaring international commodity and oil prices. Inflationary pressures are expected to rise in the near term on higher international oil prices and the kyat's continued depreciation. Despite measures by the Central Bank of Myanmar to limit the depreciation, the kyat fell by 27.2% against the US dollar in the first 10 months, and the gap between the reference rate and the parallel market rate rose by 45.9%. The average annual inflation rate is now expected to be double April's forecast.

The outlook for the economy is clouded by protracted domestic political tensions, a volatile security situation, and restrictions on trade and foreign exchange markets. The main external risks are rising global headwinds and slowdowns in Myanmar's major trading and investment partners.

Singapore

GDP grew by 4.1% year on year in the first half (H1) of 2022, buoyed by strong services and manufacturing output. Services rose by 4.8% on robust growth in information technology and real estate, and gains in tourism and domestic-oriented services in the second quarter as COVID-19 domestic and border restrictions eased from April. Tourist arrivals in H1, at 1.5 million, were almost five times higher than for the whole of 2021; first quarter tourism receipts totaled S$1.3 billion, up by 212.9% from the same quarter last year. Manufacturing grew by 5.6% year on year in H1, sustained by output growth in transport engineering and electronics. Construction rose by 2.8% on a pick-up in public and private sector construction. Domestic demand improved on higher private consumption and investment offsetting slower growth in government spending. Growth in exports slowed by 4.5% in real terms due to declining domestic oil exports, while imports expanded by 6.5% on higher oil imports.

The robust H1 growth is unlikely to continue in H2 due to the deteriorating external environment. Slower-than-expected growth in most major trading partners, continued inflationary pressures from global supply disruptions, and rising commodity prices due to the COVID-19 pandemic and the Russian invasion of Ukraine still pose downside risks. Higher financing costs amid tightening financial conditions could depress investment. Private consumption will rise as pandemic-related restrictions are lifted, but elevated inflation will curb growth. On balance, the GDP growth forecasts for 2022 and 2023 are revised down (Table 3.4.10). Growth will continue to be driven by robust information technology and financial services, sustained manufacturing growth, and the recovery in tourism and domestic-oriented services.

The inflation rate, as measured by changes in the consumer price index (CPI), rose to 7.0% year on year in July 2022 as all CPI components increased except for communication, which declined by 1.3% on competition lowering the cost of telecommunication services. Monetary Authority of Singapore (MAS) core inflation—which excludes private transport and accommodation—accelerated to 4.8% year on year in July from 4.4% in June on higher prices for food and electricity and gas. CPI inflation averaged 5.5% and MAS core inflation 3.3% in the first 7 months.

Table 3.4.10 Selected economic indicators in Singapore, %

Slower growth in trading partners, supply disruptions, and higher commodity prices will lower growth and raise inflation.

	2021	2022		2023	
		ADO 2022	Update	ADO 2022	Update
GDP growth	7.6	4.3	3.7	3.2	3.0
Inflation	2.3	3.0	5.5	2.3	2.3
CAB/GDP	18.1	17.0	18.0	17.0	17.0

ADO = Asian Development Outlook, CAB = current account balance, GDP = gross domestic product.
Sources: Ministry of Trade and Industry. *Economic Survey of Singapore Second Quarter 2022*; Asian Development Bank estimates.

Crude oil prices will remain elevated in the near term, and commodity prices are expected to stay high. MAS adjusted the rate of the Singapore dollar nominal effective exchange rate policy band in January, April, and July to ease inflationary pressures. In July, MAS revised up its 2022 forecast for CPI-All-Items average inflation to 5.0%–6.0% and average core inflation to 3.0%–4.0%. Based on these developments and trends, the inflation forecast for 2022 is revised up from *ADO 2022*'s projection, but the forecast for 2023 is unchanged—assuming global and domestic cost pressures easing next year.

Singapore's merchandise exports, mainly driven by higher prices, rose by 19.9% in US dollar terms in H1 2022, while imports grew by 23.5%, raising the trade surplus marginally to the equivalent of 28.9% of GDP. Supported also by strong net financial services receipts and lower net income deficit, the current account surplus widened to 19.5% of GDP. Given these recent developments, this *Update* revises up the forecast of the ratio of the current account surplus to GDP for 2022, but maintains the ratio's forecast for 2023 based on expected improvements in net services and income balances.

Timor-Leste

This *Update* revises down the growth forecasts for 2022 and 2023 made in April in *ADO 2022*, due to weaker private sector consumption and investment (Table 3.4.11). The original government budget for 2022 set public expenditure at $1.9 billion and included funding for social protection schemes, such as the Cesta Básica basic food basket program. In April, the government approved fuel subsidies for public transport operators, and agricultural and fishing activities. In May, the government promulgated measures, increasing the total budget to $3.1 billion, the largest in the country's history. However, the impact of the additional spending on growth is expected to be limited as 89% of the increase is for setting up a veterans' fund. Moreover, the budget execution rate is low, at 24% in January–July compared to 32% in the same period last year. The increased annual withdrawal from the Petroleum Fund, the sovereign wealth fund, will affect its sustainability. The fund had a net decline of $910 million in the first quarter of 2022 due to falling investment income—the fund's largest quarterly loss.

Timor-Leste has been exposed to rising global commodity prices, including surging food and energy costs, since the Russian invasion of Ukraine. After a decade of steady prices, inflation accelerated to 3.8% in 2021 from 0.5% in 2020. The headline inflation rate rose to 8.0% year on year in June 2022. Food and nonalcoholic drinks, comprising 54% of the consumer price index (CPI) basket, is the main inflation driver. The rise in fuel prices is affecting road and ocean transport costs, which in turn are putting upward pressure on domestic commodity prices. The rising cost of construction material globally is already apparent in the CPI through the maintenance and repair of dwellings housing subcategory, up 8.1% year on year in June.

The current account deficit as a share of GDP is revised down because inflation is expected to dampen imports. Still, coffee exports rose in value by 213% in the first half of 2022 from the same period last year. Higher hydrocarbon prices are expected to increase petroleum export revenue.

Table 3.4.11 Selected economic indicators in Timor-Leste, %

Growth will slow in 2022 and 2023, inflation accelerate sharply, and the current account deficit shrink with lower imports.

	2021	2022		2023	
		ADO 2022	Update	ADO 2022	Update
GDP growth	1.5	2.5	2.3	3.1	3.0
Inflation	3.8	2.6	7.4	2.7	5.5
CAB/GDP	–22.9	–58.4	–34.6	–72.8	–47.2

ADO = Asian Development Outlook, CAB = current account balance, GDP = gross domestic product.
Source: Asian Development Bank estimates.

So far in 2022, Timor-Leste's oil production has remained steady, although the current oil fields are expected to be depleted by the end of 2023. Remittances—which rose from $100.4 million in 2019 to $155.5 million in 2020—are the economy's largest non-oil contributor. The government is developing a national diaspora engagement policy for 2023–2027 and a remittance mobilization strategy to attract more financial flows into the country and support efforts to mobilize domestic revenue.

Growth in 2023 will be driven by another large government budget in line with the Economic Recovery Plan. Next year's budget is forecast to rise to $3.2 billion: $2.2 billion across 16 strategic areas in central government, the special administrative region, and social security, and $1.0 billion for the veterans' fund.

As Timor-Leste depends heavily on crude petroleum exports and food imports, it is exposed to volatilities in the global economy. Price swings caused by supply disruptions could further aggravate food insecurity in the country. Climate-related disaster risks are an increasing threat to livelihoods, economic performance, and infrastructure. The political context of next year's elections could delay public management reforms for long-term fiscal sustainability.

THE PACIFIC

The subregional growth projection is increased on the strength of rapid recovery in tourism for Fiji and the Cook Islands, and in mineral exports for Papua New Guinea. However, community transmission of COVID-19 continues to pose a significant downside risk to the outlook for many of the smaller economies. Higher inflation is also now expected because the impact of the Russian invasion of Ukraine on global prices has been greater than expected. The projected current account surpluses have also been raised.

Subregional assessment and prospects

This *Update* expects the Pacific subregional economy to grow by 4.7% in 2022, faster than 3.9% projected in *Asian Development Outlook 2022 (ADO 2022)*. The revised forecast largely reflects stronger-than-expected rebound in tourism in Fiji, the subregion's second-largest economy. This *Update* also adopts a more favorable growth outlook for Nauru and Vanuatu because of higher government spending on COVID-19 response and economic stimulus measures in these economies. Further, Vanuatu reopened its borders to international visitors on 1 July 2022, paving the way for recovery in tourism and related businesses. A slight upward adjustment is also made to the 2022 growth forecast for Papua New Guinea (PNG) following a small contraction in 2021. Recovery in mining and in petroleum and gas production helps drive growth this year, as does stimulus from election spending. In the absence of renewed virus outbreaks, other segments of the PNG economy are expected to normalize in 2022 (Figure 3.5.1).

Figure 3.5.1 GDP growth in the Pacific

Subregional growth projections are revised up, driven largely by recovery in larger economies.

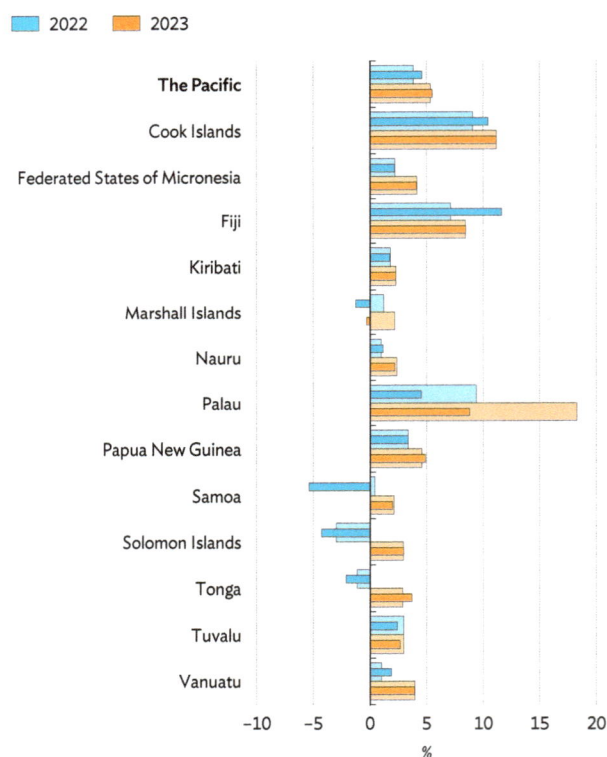

GDP = gross domestic product.
Note: Lighter colored bars are *Asian Development Outlook 2022* forecasts.
Source: *Asian Development Outlook* database.

The write-up on the Pacific economies was prepared by Jacqueline Connell, Lily-Anne Homasi, Magdelyn Kuari, Remrick Patagan, Rommel Rabanal, Cara Tinio, Isoa Wainiqolo, and James Webb of the Pacific Department of ADB, Marcel Schroder of the Economic Research and Regional Cooperation Department of ADB, and Prince Cruz and Noel Del Castillo, consultants to the Pacific Department.

The higher subregional forecast for 2022 masks downward revisions to the outlook for several economies: Tonga, due to the larger-than-expected impact from a volcanic eruption and tsunami in January 2022; Palau, where tourism is recovering more slowly than anticipated; Solomon Islands, where the economy is significantly stymied by COVID-19 mobility restrictions; and Tuvalu, where high fuel prices and continued border closures are significant drags on growth. This *Update* now sees contractions in the Marshall Islands and Samoa, both of which have suffered extended border closures and experienced local COVID-19 outbreaks in fiscal year (FY) 2022.

The 2023 growth forecast for the Pacific is adjusted slightly upward from *ADO 2022*. Faster expansion is anticipated in PNG, driven largely by the expected reopening of the Porgera gold mine, and in Tonga, as post-disaster reconstruction projects are implemented and borders are gradually reopened. On the other hand, slower growth is projected for Palau, where slow tourism recovery is seen to continue, and in small island economies facing community transmission of COVID-19. These include the Federated States of Micronesia and the Marshall Islands, where higher international commodity prices are also seen to hamper business and construction activity; and Nauru, where downscaling at the Regional Processing Centre is expected to slow economic expansion.

The 2022 forecast for subregional inflation is increased from *ADO 2022* as international prices remain elevated from the ongoing Russian invasion of Ukraine and as its impact on Pacific economies becomes more apparent (Figure 3.5.2). Faster inflation is projected in seven economies including PNG and Fiji. The biggest upward adjustments are observed in the forecasts for smaller island economies, which, with their narrow economic bases and high import dependence, are particularly sensitive to international price movements. However, slower inflation is now seen this year in Solomon Islands due to weaker economic activity as well as lower costs for betel nut. In Kiribati and Nauru, government subsidies and tax and duty reductions or suspensions have similarly helped temper fuel and utility costs to keep inflation stable.

Figure 3.5.2 Inflation in the Pacific

The impacts of high international prices are seen to linger in 2023.

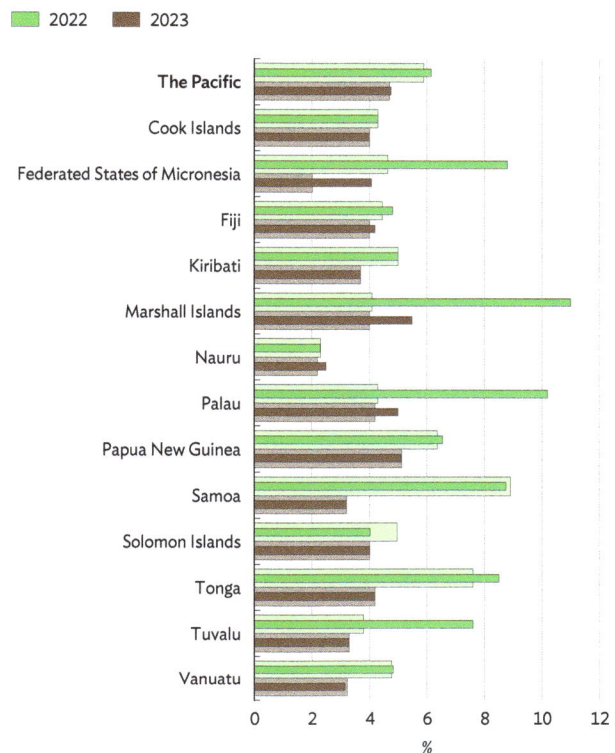

Note: Lighter colored bars are *Asian Development Outlook 2022* forecasts.
Source: *Asian Development Outlook* database.

This *Update* slightly increases the 2023 inflation projection from *ADO 2022*. Forecasts for Fiji and the North Pacific economies are adjusted upward because of lingering impacts from high international prices.

The consolidated current account surplus in 2022 is now seen to be larger than projected in *ADO 2022*, driven largely by expectations that rising commodity prices and a stronger rebound in petroleum and gas output will spur exports from PNG (Figure 3.5.3). Higher tourism receipts in Fiji and stronger-than-expected remittances and government transfers in Vanuatu should mean smaller current account deficits in these economies. However, logging exports from Solomon Islands are now expected to decline by more than initially anticipated, driving a larger current account deficit. Current account surpluses are seen to be smaller and deficits bigger in several of the smaller economies due to significantly more expensive imports.

Figure 3.5.3 Current account balance in the Pacific

Higher exports of goods and services are expected to widen the subregional current account surplus.

■ 2022   ■ 2023

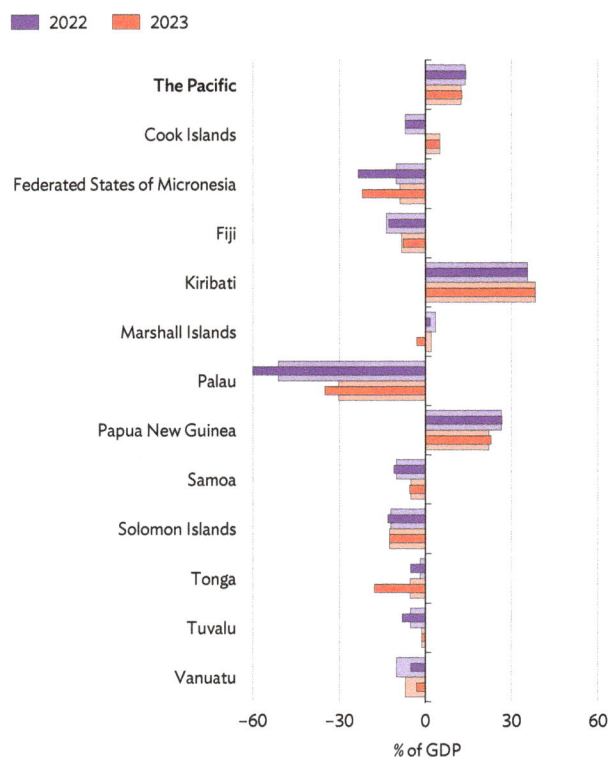

GDP = gross domestic product.

Note: Lighter colored bars are *Asian Development Outlook 2022* forecasts.

Source: *Asian Development Outlook* database.

A bigger current account surplus is expected in 2023 compared with the *ADO 2022* forecast, as PNG exports pick up after the reopening of the Porgera gold mine and higher expected prices for key agricultural and mineral products. Fiji's tourism receipts and Vanuatu's exports are also seen to continue to grow. Larger current account deficits are projected for Tonga, driven largely by substantial increases in imports for post-disaster reconstruction and rehabilitation; Palau, because of a slow recovery in tourism receipts and rising import bill; and the Federated States of Micronesia and the Marshall Islands, where imports are seen to pick up with border reopening.

Fiji

The rate of economic recovery projected for 2022 in *ADO 2022* is upgraded (Table 3.5.1). Stronger-than-expected tourism recovery has been driven by visitor arrivals from traditional source markets in Australia, New Zealand, and North America and aided by streamlined entry requirements into Fiji. Visitor arrivals in July 2022 were almost 82% of those before the COVID-19 pandemic, with the number of tourists from Australia at 101% of the July 2019 count, Canada 76%, New Zealand 90%, and United States 94%. Arrivals in the first 7 months of the year were 56% of the comparable period in 2019.

Table 3.5.1 Selected economic indicators in Fiji, %

Strong economic recovery is expected despite the threat of higher inflation.

	2021	2022		2023	
		ADO 2022	*Update*	ADO 2022	*Update*
GDP growth	−4.1	7.1	11.7	8.5	8.5
Inflation	0.2	4.5	4.8	4.0	4.2
CAB/GDP	−13.2	−13.6	−12.7	−8.3	−7.7

ADO = *Asian Development Outlook,* CAB = current account balance, GDP = gross domestic product.

Source: Asian Development Bank estimates.

ADO 2022 assumed a gradual increase in visitor arrivals as uncertainty surrounding newer variants of COVID-19 and potentially intense competition from competing destinations were expected to moderate pent-up demand. This *Update* now projects that the strong tourism rebound will be sustained throughout the year in the absence of more severe variants of COVID-19. With the benefit of being the first mover, Fiji is likely to attract more business meetings, travel promotions and incentives, international conferences, and exhibitions in the coming months.

Other sectors of the economy likewise posted higher-than-expected output in the first half of 2022. Mahogany, sawn timber, and cement production reported double-digit expansion, though from low bases. Construction increased in the first quarter of 2022 but remained below pre-pandemic levels. The projection for strong growth in 2023 is maintained.

The tourism rebound has translated into increased government revenue. In fiscal year 2022 (FY2022, ended 31 July 2022), tax revenue increased as value-added tax collection jumped by 48% over FY2021 and income tax collection rose by 7%, reflecting gradual job restoration. Government expenditure was less than budgeted for FY2022, leaving the fiscal deficit equal to 13.8% of GDP, lower than forecast earlier but still significantly above the target. The government is expected to ramp up spending with an election-year budget in FY2023 to sustain the pace of economic recovery with higher expenditure on social protection, increased pension contributions, and the hiring of additional staff. This is forecast to translate into a fiscal deficit equal to 7.4% of GDP in FY2023, which is higher than expected in *ADO 2022* in April.

The impact of the Russian invasion of Ukraine on commodity prices has been more intense than expected in *ADO 2022*. Inflation averaged 4.0% in the first half of 2022 with fuel-dependent sectors posting the most significant price jumps. Compared to the same period in 2021, transport prices soared by 13.2%, while prices for food commodities and utilities each increased by 5.0%. This *Update* therefore increases inflation forecasts for 2022 and 2023 to take into account second-round effects of the commodity shock, including higher wages, bus fares, and taxi fares.

The forecast for the current account deficit in 2022 is lower than previously projected. Higher-than-expected earnings from tourism are likely to be only partly offset by a surge in the cost of commodity imports. Further, personal remittances have been higher than expected, jumping by 16.7% year on year in the first 5 months of 2022 to equal 3.5% of GDP. Similarly, the current account deficit in 2023 is now projected to be lower than earlier forecast as payments for merchandise imports are likely to moderate and tourism inflows continue to rise.

Papua New Guinea

The forecast for growth in 2022 is revised up (Table 3.5.2). This mostly reflects base effects stemming from a downward revision to 2021 GDP and recovery in mining and in petroleum and gas production. Production at the Ok Tedi gold and copper mine and the Lihir gold mine is expected to normalize after disruptions from two COVID-19 waves last year. A higher-than-expected uptick in liquefied natural gas production in the first half of 2022 also contributed to growth.

Table 3.5.2 Selected economic indicators in Papua New Guinea, %

Rebounding natural resource output will accelerate growth this year and next, while inflation remains elevated amid global supply chain disruption.

	2021	2022		2023	
		ADO 2022	Update	ADO 2022	Update
GDP growth	−0.2	3.4	3.5	4.6	4.9
Inflation	4.5	6.4	6.5	5.1	5.1
CAB/GDP	18.9	26.5	26.7	22.1	22.9

ADO = Asian Development Outlook, CAB = current account balance, GDP = gross domestic product.
Source: Asian Development Bank estimates.

Operations in other sectors have normalized this year in the absence of renewed virus outbreaks and with borders reopened for fully vaccinated travelers in February. Spending on the national general election during the 3 months of campaigning from May to July 2022 provided additional stimulus to the economy. In addition to individual candidates' expenses for accommodation, transport, and food and beverages, the government committed for security arrangements and logistics K600 million, equal to 0.6% of GDP.

On the downside, the scheduled reopening of the Porgera mine in the second half of 2022 has now been delayed until next year. Palm oil output will be lower than expected in April. Global supply chain issues continue to affect business operations, delaying deliveries, raising costs, and deferring investment. In 2023, the resumption of mining at Porgera will play a major role in boosting growth, faster than anticipated in *ADO 2022*.

The forecast for inflation in 2022 is revised up as the national election fueled domestic spending and inflationary pressures from global supply chain disruption persisted. In the first quarter of 2022, inflation reached 6.9%, up from 4.6% a year earlier. Prices for alcoholic beverages, tobacco, and betelnut increased by 13.2%; transportation 11.7%; household equipment 9.9%; food and nonalcoholic beverages 6.2%; and housing 2.9%. Inflation is still projected to moderate in 2023 with easing price pressure on crude oil and less supply chain disruption.

The current account surplus is projected to widen slightly in 2022 and 2023 above *ADO 2022* forecasts. Even with Porgera's contribution removed from the 2022 forecast, rising commodity prices and a better-than-expected rebound in petroleum and gas output will spur exports this year. The upward revision to the surplus in 2023 is justified by higher expected exports of some agricultural products, copper, liquefied natural gas, and nickel.

Revenue windfalls from higher commodity prices probably boosted government revenue in the first half of the year, but expenditure risks related to the salary bill and the election may have eroded these gains, potentially pushing the deficit above the equivalent of 5.9% of GDP, as planned in the national budget. The newly formed government has announced a supplementary budget, and it is likely that expenditure will be reprioritized to accommodate any overruns and new commitments. The government has yet to release the 2022 Mid-Year Economic and Fiscal Outlook Report. Multilateral and bilateral support will continue to supplement the government's budget.

Risks to the outlook are balanced. A surge in commodity prices triggered by an intensifying war in Ukraine and additional sanctions on the Russian Federation could strengthen exports. Meanwhile, unanticipated disruption to natural resource output, such as a further delay to Porgera's reopening, could derail the economic rebound. And with only 3% of individuals fully vaccinated as of 9 August, a resurgence of COVID-19 remains a constant threat.

Solomon Islands

This *Update* projects worsening GDP contraction in 2022, deeper than forecast in *ADO 2022*, but no change to the forecast for positive growth in 2023 (Table 3.5.3). Economic fallout from measures to contain COVID-19 community transmission in the first quarter has been severe, consistent with earlier expectations. However, as production continued to suffer through the second quarter, recovery is now possible only in the second half of the year, buoyed by the lifting of restrictions.

Table 3.5.3 Selected economic indicators in Solomon Islands, %

Measures to contain COVID-19 depressed production more than expected, especially from logging, so the revised forecast is for sharper economic contraction in 2022.

	2021	2022		2023	
		ADO 2022	Update	ADO 2022	Update
GDP growth	–0.5	–3.0	–4.2	3.0	3.0
Inflation	–0.2	5.0	4.0	4.0	4.0
CAB/GDP	–4.9	–12.0	–13.0	–12.5	–12.5

ADO = Asian Development Outlook, CAB = current account balance, GDP = gross domestic product.
Source: Asian Development Bank estimates.

Log output fell by 37% to 679,000 cubic meters in the first half of 2022. Logging production has an outsized impact on the economy because logs and timber accounted for 70% of exports from 2015 to 2020, export duties on them accounted for 18% of domestic revenue, and logging employs about 20% of workers. Other areas in agriculture also contracted, with cocoa output down by 83%, copra by 38%, and the fish catch by 2%, while palm oil fared better with output rising by 20%.

The government lifted most restrictions on domestic shipping by the end of May, easing trade and supply-chain constraints. Restrictions on international travel were lifted in July, though incoming passengers to Solomon Islands must still be fully vaccinated and provide a negative COVID-19 test. After community transmission of COVID-19 was detected in January 2022, the cumulative case count reached 21,544 on 8 August, including 153 deaths.

The official number of active cases peaked in March 2022 at about 8,000, but the true number was likely higher because of limited capacity to test and trace across the archipelago. Vaccination remained low as of 22 August compared to other Pacific countries, with only 37% of those 12 years and older vaccinated with two doses (57% with just one dose), according to the Pacific Data Hub.

As envisaged in *ADO 2022*, the government's target for the budget deficit in 2022 increased to the equivalent of 7.4% of GDP from 4.7%. Planned expenditure—equal to 34.4% of GDP and 10.1% higher than expected in October 2021—includes measures aimed at economic recovery and stimulus (6.8% of GDP), COVID-19 response (1.4%), and reconstruction and rehabilitation following civil unrest in 2020 (1.0%). Projected tax revenue is 7.1% lower, largely because of weaker demand and production under COVID-19 restrictions.

A large part of the fiscal deficit will be financed through external and domestic borrowing. Overall debt remained low at the equivalent of 14.0% of GDP as of June 2022, with most of the 60% that is external also concessional. Debt is expected to increase sharply as project implementation accelerates, especially development for the 2023 Pacific Games.

The forecast for inflation in 2022 is revised down due to lower-than-projected first quarter inflation and the weaker economy. Muted inflation at 0.6% in the first quarter of 2022 accelerated to 3.8% in the second quarter, driven mainly by imported items, prices for which rose by 10.6%. Higher inflation in the second quarter was severe for transport, food, and household utilities including water, electricity, and gas. The index for alcoholic beverages and tobacco fell over the same period mainly because of a lower price for betel nut.

The government reduced in June the import duty on fuel by 50% and exempted fuel from the sales tax, which lowered retail prices by about 2.4%. In September, the import duty on fuel was fully eliminated. Savings from tax exemptions, which will continue until December 2022, are expected to be passed on to customers of Solomon Power through lower electricity tariffs.

Inflation is expected to accelerate in the rest of the year, with diesel prices up by more than 75% in August from a year earlier, petroleum by 50%, and liquefied petroleum gas by 15%. The price of rice rose by more than 15% over the same period. Despite higher inflation, the Central Bank of Solomon Islands maintained its expansionary monetary policy.

In the first quarter of 2022, the current account deficit reached the equivalent of 9.5% of GDP. While remittances and government transfers rose significantly, they were overwhelmed by export decline and increased imports of goods and services. Goods exports fell by 19.1%, mainly because of lower exports of logs and timber by 33.2%. The decline occurred despite increases by 150.1% in mineral exports, 22.7% in copra and coconut oil, and 5.5% in fish. Imports rose by 11.1%, led by food at 38.7% and fuel at 29.7%, while imports of machinery and transport equipment fell by 24.1%. Higher remittances pushed up primary income by 78.5% and secondary income by 152.3%.

The forecast for the current account deficit in 2022 is adjusted upward mainly because of the sharper-than-expected decline in exports in the first half of the year. The central bank reported gross foreign reserves falling by 3.5% to $677 million in the second quarter of 2022 from the previous quarter. Reserves were sufficient to cover 13.8 months of imports of goods and services, more than twice the central bank target of 6 months. The current account forecast for 2023 is unchanged.

Vanuatu

The forecast for growth in 2022 is revised up from *ADO 2022* (Table 3.5.4). International borders reopened on 1 July, paving the way for recovery in tourism and related enterprises. Demand is expected to be further boosted by remittances from Ni-Vanuatu hired as seasonal workers in Australia and New Zealand. Stronger-than-expected revenue from honorary citizenship programs in the first half of this year and higher grants from development partners allowed the government to increase planned spending for COVID-19 response and economic stimulus.

Domestic transmission of COVID-19 was first recorded in March 2022. By 4 August, 11,724 cases and 4 deaths had been reported. As of 17 July 2022, 76.1% of adults had received two or more vaccine doses and another 7.5% just one dose, according to the Ministry of Health.

Table 3.5.4 Selected economic indicators in Vanuatu, %

Higher-than-expected remittances and revenues from honorary citizenship programs led to revisions to GDP growth and current account balance.

	2021	2022		2023	
		ADO 2022	Update	ADO 2022	Update
GDP growth	1.0	1.0	2.0	4.0	4.0
Inflation	2.3	4.8	4.8	3.2	3.2
CAB/GDP	–3.8	–10.0	–5.0	–7.0	–3.0

ADO = Asian Development Outlook, CAB = current account balance, GDP = gross domestic product.
Source: Asian Development Bank estimates.

Most containment measures and restrictions imposed following the onset of domestic transmission were lifted by 16 June, easing constraints on supply chains and demand. Following border reopening, visitors to Vanuatu require a negative COVID-19 test (or proof of recovery from recent infection) for entry; vaccination is encouraged but not required. Air Vanuatu has resumed regular commercial flights from the main tourist source markets in Australia, New Caledonia, and New Zealand, as well as from Fiji and Tuvalu.

In April, the government announced a third package of COVID-19 stimulus, which included small business grants and wage subsidies effective from March to August. In May, the passage of a supplementary budget increased the allocation for recurrent expenditure by 6.3% and for capital expenditure by 15.5%. Budgeted expenditure is now 7.6% higher than foreseen in *ADO 2022*. With revenue forecast to rise by only 4.1%, the government now projects the 2022 fiscal deficit to equal 6.1% of GDP, compared with 4.4% estimated in April.

The *Half Year Economic and Fiscal Update of 2022* listed issues that adversely affect the honorary citizenship program, which is a major source of revenue. These include: correspondent banking relationship discontinued in 2021, suspension of a European Union visa waiver program in March 2022, and discontinuity in the change of name policy under the Civil Registry Act. It noted further that the Real Estate Option Program, introduced in December 2021, has very low revenue potential. Nontax revenue in the first half of 2022 was down by 17.7% from a year earlier, but this decline was less than projected in *ADO 2022*.

Growth in agriculture in the remainder of 2022 is expected to benefit from government approval in May that allows the harvest and export of sandalwood, setting the quota for the rest of 2022 at 90 tons. Sawn timber had already jumped to become in 2021 the third-biggest export after kava and copra, accounting for 8.8% of export value.

Inflation forecasts are retained, with aggregate price increases in the first quarter of 2022 at 2.8%, in line with estimates in *ADO 2022*. Price rises for food at 4.4%, alcoholic drinks and tobacco at 3.9%, and education at 2.5% drove the inflation, while indexes for household supplies, health care, communication, and recreation fell from a year earlier. Inflation is expected to accelerate in the rest of the year, with fuel prices reported to have doubled in August 2022 from a year earlier.

Inflation in 2022 is expected to be above the 1%–4% target of the Reserve Bank of Vanuatu, the central bank, which nevertheless has kept its key policy rate at 2.25% since March 2020. Broad money supply rose by 9.6% in the year to June 2022. Private sector credit grew by only 1.6% in the same period but is expected to accelerate in the second half of this year as economic recovery gains momentum. Inflation is still expected to ease to 3.2% in 2023, in line with global commodity prices.

The 2021 current account deficit equaled 3.8% of GDP, much less than the *ADO 2022* estimate of 7.0%, mainly because inflows were higher than expected from remittances and government secondary-income transfers including honorary citizenship program revenue. The ratification in May of the Pacific Agreement on Closer Economic Relations Plus is expected to boost exports of goods and services. The forecasts for 2022 and 2023 current account deficits are therefore substantially lowered.

Central Pacific economies

Growth forecasts are mixed. For Kiribati, they remain unchanged from *ADO 2022*, with economic activity seen picking up with support from border reopening in mid-2022. In Nauru, higher government spending is expected to mitigate a forecast growth slowdown in 2022, but with lower growth in 2023 and a slightly higher inflation.

Growth forecasts for Tuvalu are downgraded for both years as higher inflation in 2022 threatens growth. Forecasts for other economic indicators are retained, except that Tuvalu is now expected to have a higher current account deficit in 2022.

Kiribati

Forecasts are unchanged for steadily accelerating growth in 2022 and 2023 (Table 3.5.5). Economic activity will pick up with the incremental implementation of high-value infrastructure projects, as Kiribati reopened its borders in mid-2022. With support from development partners, the government managed to control COVID-19 transmission. Since the number of new cases peaked at 222 in February 2022, there has been a downward trend in new cases, with 82 active cases as of 22 July 2022. A high vaccination rate, with about 90% of the eligible population having had two vaccine doses, has helped to control transmission. However, any future outbreak of COVID-19 could become unmanageable, and another natural emergency such as the drought declared on 11 June 2022 could arise. Either risk could divert government attention and resources and delay the rollout of projects, thus posing risks to forecasts. Relief support provided by development partners is expected to moderate the impact of the drought on the economy.

Fishing revenue, which accounts for almost three-fourths of total revenue, is projected to recover with growth at 20.8% in 2022 and 2.1% in 2023. Meanwhile, tax revenue is expected to increase by 8.7% in 2022, supported by the reopening of borders and gradual resumption of economic activity.

These developments are expected to push total revenue in 2022 up by 27.4% over 2021 and leave fiscal surpluses in both 2022 and 2023, as projected in the *ADO 2022*.

Forecasts for inflation and current account balances in 2022 and 2023 remain unchanged. While the Russian invasion of Ukraine has resulted in soaring fuel prices in many economies in the Pacific, inflation in Kiribati is mitigated by the government's policy to subsidize fuel, which is implemented by the state-owned Kiribati Oil Company. Other subsidies provided by the government to other state-owned enterprises, including the Public Utilities Board, moderate the costs to households of their energy consumption.

Nauru

Economic growth in fiscal year 2022 (FY2022, ended 30 June 2022) is estimated to have exceeded the forecast in *ADO 2022*, the anticipated slowdown from FY2021 turning out less than initially projected (Table 3.5.6). The passage of supplementary budgets—partly funded by additional revenue from the Regional Processing Centre (RPC)—pushed government expenditure higher than expected, providing economic stimulus. Recipients of additional allocations were notably health care and the COVID-19 taskforce, Nauru Community Housing, RPC operations, public administration and infrastructure, and subsidies to state-owned enterprises. With expenditure rising by 11.6% and revenue by only 1.2%, the estimated fiscal surplus declined to the equivalent of 29.4% of GDP in FY2022 from 43.8% in FY2021.

Table 3.5.5 Selected economic indicators in Kiribati, %

Forecasts are unchanged as border reopening accelerates growth in both years.

	2021	2022 ADO 2022	2022 Update	2023 ADO 2022	2023 Update
GDP growth	1.5	1.8	1.8	2.3	2.3
Inflation	1.0	5.0	5.0	3.7	3.7
CAB/GDP	32.3	35.7	35.7	38.2	38.2

ADO = Asian Development Outlook, CAB = current account balance, GDP = gross domestic product.
Source: Asian Development Bank estimates.

Table 3.5.6 Selected economic indicators in Nauru, %

Supplementary budgets financed higher government spending, and moderated the forecast slowdown of GDP growth in 2022.

	2021	2022 ADO 2022	2022 Update	2023 ADO 2022	2023 Update
GDP growth	1.6	1.0	1.2	2.4	2.2
Inflation	1.2	2.3	2.3	2.2	2.5
CAB/GDP	4.1	...	...	...	...

... = unavailable, ADO = Asian Development Outlook, CAB = current account balance, GDP = gross domestic product.
Note: Years are fiscal years ending on 30 June of that year.
Source: Asian Development Bank estimates.

After being held at bay for more than 2 years, domestic transmission of COVID-19 was recorded in June 2022. By 2 August, more than 4,600 cases had been detected, giving Nauru the highest case load per capita in the Pacific. Nauru's vaccination rate is high, with 100% of people aged 12 and over having received at least two doses, according to the Pacific Data Hub. Further, 71% of children aged 5–11 were fully vaccinated as of 20 August. On 8 August, the government eased COVID-19 restrictions, allowing offices, churches, and recreational places to reopen, but not primary schools. Lingering disruption and health impacts from domestic transmission and containment measures are expected to continue to affect business and construction activity in FY2023.

The FY2023 budget, passed in May 2022, projects revenue 21.5% lower than in FY2022 and expenditure 17.1% lower, but these estimates are subject to considerable uncertainty. The FY2023 budget indicates the RPC will likely transition to an "enduring capability" arrangement in 2023: Nauru will receive a hosting fee from the Government of Australia in return for maintaining the facility and keeping it capable of being scaled up. Other RPC revenue streams may decline, and this downscaling of the RPC is expected to curb economic expansion. The domestic transmission of COVID-19 is also holding back growth. The GDP growth outlook for FY2023 is therefore downgraded from the ADO 2022 forecast.

The projection for inflation in FY2022 is unchanged, but it is raised for FY2023. While Nauru relies on fuel imports, government measures are expected to cushion the impact of imported inflation on households and businesses. The government reduced import duties on diesel and gasoline in June 2022, and the FY2023 budget maintained subsidies to the state-owned electricity utility to prevent consumer prices from rising too much. Subsidies to the state-owned airline and shipping company were also maintained to contain import costs. In June, the price control act was revised to raise the maximum retail price of petrol by 2% above the October 2021 price, diesel by 12%, and jet fuel by 26%.

Tuvalu

Growth forecasts for Tuvalu in 2022 and 2023 are somewhat downgraded from ADO 2022 (Table 3.5.7). While the number of COVID-19 cases in the country has remained manageable, higher-than-expected import prices brought about by the Russian invasion of Ukraine are likely to create additional spending pressures and delay expenditure on lesser priorities in 2022. Growth is expected to accelerate slightly in 2023, but lower planned expenditure is likely to keep it below the ADO 2022 forecast.

Table 3.5.7 Selected economic indicators in Tuvalu, %

Much higher inflation this year is expected to drag down growth prospects.

	2021	2022		2023	
		ADO 2022	Update	ADO 2022	Update
GDP growth	1.5	3.0	2.5	3.0	2.7
Inflation	6.7	3.8	7.6	3.3	3.3
CAB/GDP	-1.8	-5.1	-8.0	-1.2	-1.2

ADO = Asian Development Outlook, CAB = current account balance, GDP = gross domestic product.
Source: Asian Development Bank estimates.

The government's 2022 national budget projects a fiscal deficit in 2022 equal to 9.7% of GDP, reflecting lower recurrent revenue and budget support from development partners along with higher recurrent spending. The current high-cost environment compared with assumptions in ADO 2022 may demand budget reallocation. The government projected in April a small budget surplus for 2023 as expenditure moderated, but the fiscal balance is likely to deteriorate due to cost overruns caused by recent high prices.

The inflation projection for 2022 is significantly upgraded from ADO 2022, reflecting surges in meat and petroleum prices in the first half of the year. Meat prices have soared by 27% since the beginning of the year because of supply constraints and high import prices. Fuel and electricity prices have increased by at least 8% in the same period because of market disruption since the Russian invasion of Ukraine. The projection for inflation in 2023 is maintained as supplies normalize.

Reflecting high import prices and slightly lower allocation commitments from development partners to support the budget, the 2022 current account deficit is now projected to increase more than forecast in *ADO 2022*. Meanwhile, the projection for a much lower deficit in 2023 is retained because fishing license revenue is expected to recover as borders reopen.

North Pacific economies

The Federated States of Micronesia (FSM) reopened its borders in August 2022, and the Marshall Islands in September 2022, but the near-term outlook for these economies is skewed toward the downside by concerns about high international commodity prices and the ongoing COVID-19 pandemic. The growth outlook for Palau is similarly muted as high fuel prices and concerns about COVID-19 variants dampen prospects for tourism. Higher inflation and lower current account balances are forecast because of elevated international commodity prices and pass-through of price trends in the United States, the main trade partner of all three North Pacific economies.

Federated States of Micronesia

This *Update* retains the GDP growth forecast for the FSM in fiscal year 2022 (FY2022, ends 30 September 2022, as in the Marshall Islands and Palau) as economic activity picks up following the gradual unwinding of mobility restrictions (Table 3.5.8).

Table 3.5.8 Selected economic indicators in the Federated States of Micronesia, %

Elevated commodity prices are expected to drive higher inflation and current account deficits.

	2021	2022 ADO 2022	2022 Update	2023 ADO 2022	2023 Update
GDP growth	–1.2	2.2	2.2	4.2	4.1
Inflation	2.0	4.6	8.8	2.0	4.1
CAB/GDP	0.5	–10.2	–23.4	–8.8	–22.0

ADO = *Asian Development Outlook*, CAB = current account balance, GDP = gross domestic product.

Source: Asian Development Bank estimates.

This trend is expected to sustain recovery in hotels and restaurants, transport, and construction despite rising prices for key international commodities. Government support and price stabilization measures are expected to delay any second-round effects of higher inflation to FY2023. Consequently, economic growth in FY2023 is now projected marginally lower than forecast in *ADO 2022* because of slower growth in import-dependent and labor-intensive construction.

Downside risks to the growth outlook are primarily (i) recent community transmission of COVID-19 and its impact on general mobility despite the reopening of international borders this August, and (ii) possible worsening of supply shocks and price volatility affecting international commodities.

The impact of the Russian invasion of Ukraine on prices both globally and in the FSM has been greater than expected earlier this year. Inflation forecasts are therefore revised up for both FY2022 and FY2023. Preliminary estimates indicate that inflation has accelerated in FY2022 and it is expected to remain elevated in FY2023 given the country's dependence on imports of food and fuel. This is partly mitigated, however, by a pricing policy framework that stabilizes domestic retail prices in the short term. Retail fuel prices in the FSM have steadily increased since March but at a lesser pace than in other Pacific developing member countries. Uncertainty about the outlook is considerable, however, as international commodity prices remain volatile due to low global inventories.

Increased commodity costs are expected to deepen the current account deficit in FY2022 because demand for imported fuel and food is largely inelastic, with the deep deficit persisting in FY2023 as economic recovery gathers pace and demand consequently increases. The fiscal surplus is estimated to have narrowed further in FY2022 as development partners taper their budgetary support and pandemic-response grants. It will widen again in FY2023 as output returns to its pre-pandemic level.

Marshall Islands

This *Update* anticipates continued economic contraction in FY2022, not a return to growth as projected in *ADO 2022* (Table 3.5.9). Quarantine restrictions have persisted, keeping economic activity subdued, and on 8 August the government announced the first locally transmitted cases of COVID-19 in Majuro, the capital. Travel to neighboring islands was suspended but no other mobility restrictions have been imposed. As of 1 September, 15,042 cases had been reported, 28 of them in the previous 24 hours, as well as 17 deaths.

Table 3.5.9 Selected economic indicators in the Marshall Islands, %

High prices and community transmission of COVID-19 are expected to dampen growth.

	2021	2022		2023	
		ADO 2022	Update	ADO 2022	Update
GDP growth	–3.3	1.2	–1.2	2.2	–0.3
Inflation	1.0	4.1	11.0	4.0	5.5
CAB/GDP	23.5	3.5	1.7	2.0	–3.0

ADO = Asian Development Outlook, CAB = current account balance, GDP = gross domestic product.

Source: Asian Development Bank estimates.

The government declared on 12 August 2022 a state of health disaster for COVID-19, but after a quick decline in daily confirmed cases reopened borders on 8 September 2022 to all vaccinated travelers. Meanwhile, prices are likely to remain elevated, particularly for fuel. Together with community transmission of COVID-19, this is seen dampening any uptick in business activity after border reopening. This *Update* therefore forecasts continued but smaller contraction in FY2023.

Inflation forecasts are revised up. The impact of the Russian invasion of Ukraine on commodity prices has been larger than initially expected. Prices are seen to remain high in FY2023, tracking price trends in the United States.

Higher-than-expected international prices have raised import costs by more than previously forecast, necessitating downward adjustment to the current account surplus forecast for FY2022. A deficit is now projected for FY2023 as borders reopen and business activity and the implementation of public investment projects resume in earnest, and as related imports become more expensive.

Palau

Community transmission of the Omicron variant started in January 2022, peaked in February, and dissipated to low levels by early April. With solid vaccination progress that saw 100% of Palau's eligible population fully vaccinated by April 2022, COVID-19 deaths at the end of August had been contained at six.

The nascent tourism recovery remained relatively resilient under the outbreak, with 1,536 arrivals in January–March pushing the total in the first half of FY2022 to just above the low FY2021 full-year figure of 3,407. A major international conference on oceans in April further boosted tourism, contributing an additional 2,976 arrivals in the third quarter of FY2022. However, achieving the earlier projection of about 25,000 arrivals in FY2022 is now unlikely.

Tourism has recovered less in the North Pacific than in the South, where destinations enjoy strong rebounds driven by resurgence in outbound travel from Australia and New Zealand. By contrast, tourists visiting Palau are largely from East Asia, which has seen more gradual recovery in outbound tourism. This also subjects Palau to more direct competition from major tourist destinations in Southeast Asia. Thus, monthly arrivals in Palau have remained at about 10% of pre-pandemic levels since reopening in the second half of 2021, with only a slight pickup to 13% during April–July 2022 after the Omicron outbreak faded.

With full-year arrivals expected to reach about 12,000 at most, the GDP growth forecast for FY2022 is revised down (Table 3.5.10). With lingering uncertainty regarding the strength and sustainability of recovery in international tourism amid concerns about COVID-19 variants and high fuel prices, the GDP growth forecast for FY2023 is likewise cut.

Rising international commodity prices following the Russian invasion of Ukraine have further fueled inflation, which reached double digit rates year on year in the second and third quarters of FY2022.

Table 3.5.10 Selected economic indicators in Palau, %

Muted tourism recovery is denting growth, while high prices fuel inflation and an expanding current account deficit.

	2021	2022		2023	
		ADO 2022	*Update*	*ADO 2022*	*Update*
GDP growth	−17.1	9.4	4.6	18.3	8.8
Inflation	0.5	4.3	10.2	4.2	5.0
CAB/GDP	−55.9	−51.3	−60.0	−30.3	−35.0

ADO = *Asian Development Outlook*, CAB = current account balance, GDP = gross domestic product.

Source: Asian Development Bank estimates.

With average inflation over the first 3 quarters of the fiscal year at 10.2%—led by 20.0% inflation for transportation and 13.8% for food and nonalcoholic beverages—the FY2022 inflation forecast is revised significantly upward. The FY2023 inflation forecast is likewise raised in line with expectations of a potentially prolonged period of elevated international crude oil prices.

Weaker-than-expected recovery in tourism receipts and an expanding merchandise import bill with high international commodity prices will likely mean wider current account deficits in both FY2022 and FY2023 than forecast in April. Instead of narrowing steadily as envisaged in *ADO 2022*, the deficit is now seen to expand further in FY2022 before narrowing in FY2023.

South Pacific economies

In line with *ADO 2022* estimates, the reopening of the Cook Islands to tourism in January 2022 supported a significant rebound in fiscal year 2022 (FY2022, ended 30 June 2022 for all South Pacific economies). Conversely, delayed reopening in Niue, Tonga, and especially Samoa degraded their results. The economic impact of a volcanic eruption in Tonga has been even more severe than initially expected, but significant capital commitments are now expected to support more rapid recovery in FY2023 than previously forecast. Notwithstanding strong recovery in tourism in the Cook Islands, all South Pacific economies face continued risks to their fiscal positions, current account balances, and, because of elevated inflation, household purchasing power.

Cook Islands

Growth in FY2022 was higher than projected in *ADO 2022* (Table 3.5.11). This was driven by quicker-than-expected recovery in tourism, with tourist arrivals exceeding the government's projection by 37.5%. Arrivals in June 2022 were 13,939, or 87.5% of the pre-pandemic level for that month. Spurring recovery is an effective vaccination program supported by development partners that has administered two doses of COVID-19 vaccine to 99% of the population aged 12 years and above and a booster shot to 76% of the population aged 16 years and above. Other measures implemented by the Cook Islands Tourism Corporation have helped to restore tourists' confidence. The growth forecast for FY2023 is unchanged, assuming smooth recovery in tourist arrivals.

Table 3.5.11 Selected economic indicators in the Cook Islands, %

Higher tourist arrivals pushed growth in FY2022 above the April forecast.

	2021	2022		2023	
		ADO 2022	*Update*	*ADO 2022*	*Update*
GDP growth	−29.1	9.1	10.5	11.2	11.2
Inflation	2.2	4.3	4.3	4.0	4.0
CAB/GDP	−12.5	−7.0	−7.0	5.1	5.1

ADO = *Asian Development Outlook*, CAB = current account balance, GDP = gross domestic product.

Note: Years are fiscal years ending on 30 June of that year.

Source: Asian Development Bank estimates.

The government posted a fiscal deficit in FY2022 equal to 7.8% of GDP, less than projected in *ADO 2022*. This was driven by lower-than-expected recurrent spending and by tax revenue 24.4% higher than in FY2021. The fiscal deficit projection for FY2023 is unchanged as tax revenue continues to improve and spending normalizes to pre-pandemic levels. The ratio of debt to GDP in FY2022 was, at 44.6%, slightly higher than projected in *ADO 2022*. The forecast for FY2023 remains unchanged.

In its FY2023 budget document, the government estimated inflation at the end of FY2022 at 4.3%, consistent with *ADO 2022*. With supply disruption in New Zealand, the main trade partner of the Cook Islands, and effects on commodity markets from the Russian invasion of Ukraine, costs have risen for transportation, dairy products, and other imported food items. The forecast for FY2023 is unchanged, with inflation easing slightly.

Forecasts for the current account remain as in *ADO 2022* for lack of data to substantiate any revision. Rising commodity prices driven by supply chain constraints and associated higher inflation in trade partners are expected to widen the trade deficit before it is balanced by higher tourist receipts. Gradual recovery in tourist arrivals is expected to restore a current account surplus in FY2023.

Niue

The government posted a fiscal deficit in FY2022 equal to 13.3% of FY2019 GDP, higher than 10.0% as forecast in *ADO 2022* as recurrent expenditure outweighed moderate growth in recurrent revenue. Official grants declined by 19%. In FY2023, the recent border reopening will boost government revenue, but the government still forecasts a larger fiscal deficit, equal to 21.4% of GDP, due to much larger increases in both capital and recurrent spending.

The trade deficit in calendar year 2021 widened to equal 39.6% of 2019 GDP, higher than the *ADO 2022* forecast and rising from 36.8% in 2020. Imports increased by 8.4% to NZ$19.6 million, overshadowing a notable increase in exports to NZ$1.6 million. Imports were mainly food and petroleum products and machinery. The Russian invasion of Ukraine is likely to cause the trade balance to deteriorate further and accelerate inflation.

Samoa

Revised GDP data released since *ADO 2022* deepened the contraction in FY2020 to 3.1% but reduced the contraction in FY2021 to 7.1% (Table 3.5.12). Border reopening delayed until August 2022 meant a second full fiscal year without tourism. GDP data for the second and third quarters of FY2022 show much deeper impact on the Samoan economy than previously suspected. The GDP growth estimate for FY2022 is thus revised down from weak recovery forecast in *ADO 2022* to significant contraction despite countercyclical government programs.

The forecast for modest recovery in FY2023 is little changed from *ADO 2022*. The profile of tourism recovery in Fiji and the Cook Islands suggests a gradual return of tourist arrivals over a period of 6–9 months, but with Samoa reopening later than other major Pacific destinations, recovery may be slower than in competing markets. There are some upside risks to the forecasts, however, particularly the potential for a faster recovery in visitor arrivals as Samoans living overseas become able to visit friends and family more easily. Returning Samoans typically account for 30%–40% of all arrivals.

Actual inflation in FY2022 was close to the *ADO 2022* projection. It featured significant increases in food and transportation prices, which stemmed from high global oil prices and imported food costs, partly related to the ongoing Russian invasion of Ukraine. As in *ADO 2022*, inflation is expected to moderate in FY2023 as these effects dissipate but still remain somewhat elevated.

A fiscal deficit equal to 2.5% of GDP is estimated for FY2022, broadly in line with expectations in *ADO 2022*. Current expenditure remained elevated under COVID-19 support measures, and tax revenue continued to decline, but an increase in budget support from development partners prevented more serious fiscal deterioration. The persistent need for elevated public spending, and a decline in development partner grants from their recent record, is expected to outweigh partial recovery in tax revenue going into FY2023, with the fiscal deficit projected to equal 3.6% of GDP.

The current account deficit in FY2022 is estimated to have been slightly larger than forecast in *ADO 2022* but still a significant improvement on FY2021.

Table 3.5.12 Selected economic indicators in Samoa, %

A local COVID-19 outbreak and continued lack of tourism degraded the economy significantly more than expected in FY2022.

	2021	2022		2023	
		ADO 2022	Update	ADO 2022	Update
GDP growth	–7.1	0.4	–5.3	2.2	2.0
Inflation	–3.0	8.9	8.8	3.2	3.2
CAB/GDP	–15.9	–10.0	–10.8	–5.0	–5.5

ADO = *Asian Development Outlook*, CAB = current account balance, GDP = gross domestic product.
Note: Years are fiscal years ending on 30 June of that year.
Source: Asian Development Bank estimates.

Remittances continued to grow strongly, increasing by 20.8% in FY2022 and partly compensating for an expected decline in household income. The deficit in FY2023 is still projected to be lower, driven by higher tourism arrivals and despite a slight fall in remittances, but larger than earlier forecast.

Tonga

The Hunga Tonga–Hunga Ha'apai volcanic eruption and subsequent tsunami in January 2022 affected agricultural production and exports more than initially anticipated. A consequence is that GDP decline in FY2022 was greater than predicted in *ADO 2022* (Table 3.5.13). The eruption and tsunami caused damage estimated to equal 18.5% of GDP. The delayed reopening of borders, competition for returning tourists, and losses from repeated disasters are likely to hobble the long-term recovery of tourism. However, with border reopening in August 2022 now allowing Tongans to visit relatives at home, and increased capital spending supporting reconstruction, stronger GDP recovery is projected for FY2023.

Table 3.5.13 Selected economic indicators in Tonga, %

A volcanic eruption and tsunami hit FY2022 GDP and the CAB, while global inflationary pressures were slightly higher than expected.

	2021	2022		2023	
		ADO 2022	Update	ADO 2022	Update
GDP growth	–2.7	–1.2	–2.0	2.9	3.7
Inflation	1.4	7.6	8.5	4.2	4.2
CAB/GDP	6.5	–1.8	–5.2	–5.2	–17.7

ADO = *Asian Development Outlook*, CAB = current account balance, GDP = gross domestic product.
Note: Years are fiscal years ending on 30 June of that year.
Source: Asian Development Bank estimates.

Inflation outpaced the *ADO 2022* forecast due to higher-than-expected import prices and domestic food prices, with food contributing 3.5 percentage points to annual inflation, transportation 2.7 points, and housing and utilities 2.1 points. The forecast for FY2023 is retained, with domestic price pressures becoming more important and imported inflation less so.

The fiscal deficit likely expanded to equal 1.2% of GDP in FY2022, lower than the 2.8% deficit forecast in *ADO 2022*. Emergency response to the eruption was facilitated by rapid financial and material assistance from development partners, which contained immediate damage to government finances. Reconstruction will require an estimated $240 million, but this will likely be spread across several years.

The current account surplus equaled 6.5% of GDP in FY2021, considerably higher than the previously estimated 0.1%. Estimate revision reflected mostly higher remittances, which increased by 38.9% in FY2021. A deeper current account deficit than previously forecast is now estimated for FY2022, caused by urgent import needs following the volcanic eruption and tsunami. With more information on disaster impacts than was available for *ADO 2022*, the deficit is now expected to widen further in FY2023 with higher imports of reconstruction materials, a decline in remittances from current exceptional levels, and disruption to local agricultural production, which both diminishes exports and heightens the need for food imports. Notwithstanding the post-disaster increase in development partner aid and private transfers, the deterioration in the current account balance will generate a sizable external financing gap.

4

STATISTICAL APPENDIX

STATISTICAL NOTES AND TABLES

This statistical appendix presents economic indicators for the 46 developing member economies in the Asian Development Bank (ADB) in three tables: gross domestic product (GDP) growth, inflation, and current account balance as a percentage of GDP. The economies are grouped into five subregions: the Caucasus and Central Asia, East Asia, South Asia, Southeast Asia, and the Pacific. The tables contain historical data for 2019–2021 and forecasts for 2022 and 2023. Lack of updated data precludes forecasts for Niue.

The data are standardized to the degree possible to allow comparability over time and across economies, but differences in statistical methodology, definitions, coverage, and practice make full comparability impossible. National income accounts are based on the United Nations System of National Accounts, while data on the balance of payments use International Monetary Fund (IMF) accounting standards. Historical data are ADB estimates variously based on official sources, statistical publications and databases, and documents from ADB, the IMF, and the World Bank. Projections for 2022 and 2023 are generally ADB estimates based on available quarterly or monthly data, though some projections are from governments.

Most economies report by calendar year. The following report all variables by fiscal year: Afghanistan, Bangladesh, Bhutan, India, Nepal, and Pakistan in South Asia; Myanmar in Southeast Asia; and the Cook Islands, the Federated States of Micronesia, the Marshall Islands, Nauru, Palau, Samoa, and Tonga in the Pacific.

Regional and subregional averages are provided in the three tables. Averages are weighted by purchasing power parity (PPP) GDP in current international dollars. PPP GDP data for 2019–2020 were obtained from the IMF World Economic Outlook Database, October 2021 edition. Weights for 2020 are carried over to 2023.

The following paragraphs discuss the three tables in greater detail.

Table A1: Growth rate of GDP (% per year).
The table shows annual growth rates of GDP valued at constant market prices, factor costs, or basic prices. GDP at market prices is the aggregate value added by all resident producers at producers' prices including taxes less subsidies on imports plus all nondeductible value-added or similar taxes. Most economies use constant market price valuation. Pakistan uses constant factor costs, and Fiji basic prices. Some historical data for Turkmenistan are not presented for lack of uniformity. A fluid situation permits no data and forecasts for 2021–2023 for Afghanistan.

Table A2: Inflation (% per year). Data on inflation rates are period averages. Inflation rates are based on consumer price indexes. The consumer price indexes of the following economies are for a given city only: Cambodia is for Phnom Penh, the Marshall Islands for Majuro, and Sri Lanka for Colombo. 2021 data on Afghanistan was collected from international sources. A fluid situation permits no forecasts for 2022–2023 for Afghanistan.

Table A3: Current account balance (% of GDP).
The current account balance is the sum of the balance of trade in merchandise, net trade in services and factor income, and net transfers. The values reported are divided by GDP at current prices in US dollars. Some historical data for Turkmenistan are not presented for lack of uniformity. A fluid situation permits no data and forecasts for 2021–2023 for Afghanistan.

Table A1 GDP growth rate, % per year

	2019	2020	2021	ADO 2022	2022 Update	ADO 2022	2023 Update
Developing Asia	**5.0**	**−0.7**	**7.0**	**5.2**	**4.3**	**5.3**	**4.9**
Developing Asia excluding the PRC	**3.9**	**−3.5**	**5.9**	**5.5**	**5.3**	**5.8**	**5.3**
Caucasus and Central Asia	**4.7**	**−2.0**	**5.7**	**3.6**	**3.9**	**4.0**	**4.2**
Armenia	7.6	−7.2	5.7	2.8	7.0	3.8	4.5
Azerbaijan	2.5	−4.3	5.6	3.7	4.2	2.8	2.8
Georgia	5.0	−6.8	10.4	3.5	7.0	5.0	6.0
Kazakhstan	4.5	−2.5	4.3	3.2	3.0	3.9	3.7
Kyrgyz Republic	4.6	−8.4	3.6	2.0	3.0	2.5	3.5
Tajikistan	7.5	4.5	9.2	2.0	4.0	3.0	5.0
Turkmenistan	...	...	5.0	6.0	5.8	5.8	5.8
Uzbekistan	5.7	1.9	7.4	4.0	4.0	4.5	5.0
East Asia	**5.5**	**1.8**	**7.7**	**4.7**	**3.2**	**4.5**	**4.2**
Hong Kong, China	−1.7	−6.5	6.3	2.0	0.2	3.7	3.7
Mongolia	5.6	−4.6	1.4	2.3	1.7	5.6	4.9
People's Republic of China	6.1	2.2	8.1	5.0	3.3	4.8	4.5
Republic of Korea	2.2	−0.7	4.1	3.0	2.6	2.6	2.3
Taipei,China	3.1	3.4	6.6	3.8	3.4	3.0	3.0
South Asia	**4.0**	**−5.2**	**8.1**	**7.0**	**6.5**	**7.4**	**6.5**
Afghanistan	3.9	−2.4	...	...	...	...	...
Bangladesh	7.9	3.4	6.9	6.9	7.2	7.1	6.6
Bhutan	5.8	−10.0	4.1	4.5	4.5	7.5	4.0
India	3.7	−6.6	8.7	7.5	7.0	8.0	7.2
Maldives	6.9	−33.5	37.1	11.0	8.2	12.0	10.4
Nepal	6.7	−2.4	4.2	3.9	5.8	5.0	4.7
Pakistan	3.1	−0.9	5.7	4.0	6.0	4.5	3.5
Sri Lanka	2.3	−3.6	3.3	2.4	−8.8	2.5	−3.3
Southeast Asia	**4.7**	**−3.2**	**3.3**	**4.9**	**5.1**	**5.2**	**5.0**
Brunei Darussalam	3.9	1.1	−1.6	4.2	2.2	3.6	3.6
Cambodia	7.1	−3.1	3.0	5.3	5.3	6.5	6.2
Indonesia	5.0	−2.1	3.7	5.0	5.4	5.2	5.0
Lao People's Democratic Republic	4.7	−0.5	2.3	3.4	2.5	3.7	3.5
Malaysia	4.4	−5.5	3.1	6.0	6.0	5.4	4.7
Myanmar	6.8	3.2	−5.9	−0.3	2.0	2.6	2.6
Philippines	6.1	−9.5	5.7	6.0	6.5	6.3	6.3
Singapore	1.1	−4.1	7.6	4.3	3.7	3.2	3.0
Thailand	2.2	−6.2	1.5	3.0	2.9	4.5	4.2
Timor-Leste	2.1	−8.6	1.5	2.5	2.3	3.1	3.0
Viet Nam	7.0	2.9	2.6	6.5	6.5	6.7	6.7
The Pacific	**3.1**	**−6.4**	**−1.5**	**3.9**	**4.7**	**5.4**	**5.5**
Cook Islands	5.3	−5.2	−29.1	9.1	10.5	11.2	11.2
Federated States of Micronesia	2.7	−3.8	−1.2	2.2	2.2	4.2	4.1
Fiji	−0.6	−17.2	−4.1	7.1	11.7	8.5	8.5
Kiribati	−0.5	−0.5	1.5	1.8	1.8	2.3	2.3
Marshall Islands	6.6	−2.2	−3.3	1.2	−1.2	2.2	−0.3
Nauru	1.0	0.7	1.6	1.0	1.2	2.4	2.2
Niue	4.9	...	...	...	...	...	...
Palau	−1.9	−9.7	−17.1	9.4	4.6	18.3	8.8
Papua New Guinea	4.5	−3.5	−0.2	3.4	3.5	4.6	4.9
Samoa	4.5	−3.1	−7.1	0.4	−5.3	2.2	2.0
Solomon Islands	1.7	−3.4	−0.5	−3.0	−4.2	3.0	3.0
Tonga	0.7	0.5	−2.7	−1.2	−2.0	2.9	3.7
Tuvalu	13.9	1.0	1.5	3.0	2.5	3.0	2.7
Vanuatu	3.2	−5.0	1.0	1.0	2.0	4.0	4.0

... = unavailable, ADO = *Asian Development Outlook*, GDP = gross domestic product, PRC = People's Republic of China.

Notes: Because of the uncertain situation, no data and forecasts are provided for 2021–2023 in Afghanistan. Some historical data for Turkmenistan are not presented for lack of uniformity.

Table A2 Inflation, % per year

	2019	2020	2021	2022 ADO 2022	2022 Update	2023 ADO 2022	2023 Update
Developing Asia	3.3	3.2	2.5	3.7	4.5	3.1	4.0
Developing Asia excluding the PRC	3.6	3.8	4.1	5.1	6.6	4.2	5.5
Caucasus and Central Asia	7.3	7.7	8.9	8.8	11.5	7.1	8.5
Armenia	1.4	1.2	7.2	9.0	8.5	7.5	7.2
Azerbaijan	2.6	2.8	6.7	7.0	11.5	5.3	7.0
Georgia	4.9	5.2	9.6	7.0	11.0	4.0	5.0
Kazakhstan	5.3	6.8	8.0	7.8	11.2	6.4	7.5
Kyrgyz Republic	1.1	6.3	11.9	15.0	15.0	12.0	12.0
Tajikistan	8.0	9.4	8.0	15.0	10.0	10.0	9.0
Turkmenistan	13.0	10.0	12.5	13.0	13.0	10.0	10.5
Uzbekistan	14.6	12.9	10.7	9.0	12.0	8.0	11.0
East Asia	2.6	2.2	1.1	2.4	2.5	2.0	2.5
Hong Kong, China	2.9	0.3	1.6	2.3	2.0	2.0	2.0
Mongolia	7.3	3.7	7.1	12.4	14.7	9.3	11.6
People's Republic of China	2.9	2.5	0.9	2.3	2.3	2.0	2.5
Republic of Korea	0.4	0.5	2.5	3.2	4.5	2.0	3.0
Taipei,China	0.6	−0.2	2.0	1.9	2.8	1.6	2.0
South Asia	5.0	6.5	5.8	6.5	8.1	5.5	7.4
Afghanistan	2.3	5.6	5.2	...	...	...	...
Bangladesh	5.5	5.7	5.6	6.0	6.2	5.9	6.7
Bhutan	2.8	5.6	7.4	7.0	6.5	5.5	5.5
India	4.8	6.2	5.5	5.8	6.7	5.0	5.8
Maldives	0.2	−1.4	0.5	3.0	3.3	2.5	2.8
Nepal	4.6	6.2	3.6	6.5	6.3	6.2	6.1
Pakistan	6.8	10.7	8.9	11.0	12.2	8.5	18.0
Sri Lanka	4.3	4.6	6.0	13.3	44.8	6.7	18.6
Southeast Asia	2.6	1.5	2.0	3.7	5.2	3.1	4.1
Brunei Darussalam	−0.4	1.9	1.7	1.6	3.5	1.0	2.0
Cambodia	1.9	2.9	2.9	4.7	5.0	2.2	2.2
Indonesia	3.8	2.0	1.6	3.6	4.6	3.0	5.1
Lao People's Democratic Republic	3.3	5.1	3.7	5.8	17.0	5.0	4.5
Malaysia	0.7	−1.1	2.5	3.0	2.7	2.5	2.5
Myanmar	8.6	5.7	3.6	8.0	16.0	8.5	8.5
Philippines	2.4	2.4	3.9	4.2	5.3	3.5	4.3
Singapore	0.6	−0.2	2.3	3.0	5.5	2.3	2.3
Thailand	0.7	−0.8	1.2	3.3	6.3	2.2	2.7
Timor-Leste	1.0	0.5	3.8	2.6	7.4	2.7	5.5
Viet Nam	2.8	3.2	1.8	3.8	3.8	4.0	4.0
The Pacific	2.9	2.9	3.1	5.9	6.2	4.7	4.8
Cook Islands	0.0	0.7	2.2	4.3	4.3	4.0	4.0
Federated States of Micronesia	−2.6	−2.9	2.0	4.6	8.8	2.0	4.1
Fiji	1.8	−2.6	0.2	4.5	4.8	4.0	4.2
Kiribati	−1.8	2.3	1.0	5.0	5.0	3.7	3.7
Marshall Islands	0.1	−0.8	1.0	4.1	11.0	4.0	5.5
Nauru	4.3	−6.6	1.2	2.3	2.3	2.2	2.5
Niue	2.4	2.3	...	...	...	...	...
Palau	0.6	0.7	0.5	4.3	10.2	4.2	5.0
Papua New Guinea	3.6	4.9	4.5	6.4	6.5	5.1	5.1
Samoa	2.2	1.5	−3.0	8.9	8.8	3.2	3.2
Solomon Islands	1.6	3.0	−0.2	5.0	4.0	4.0	4.0
Tonga	4.0	0.2	1.4	7.6	8.5	4.2	4.2
Tuvalu	3.5	1.6	6.7	3.8	7.6	3.3	3.3
Vanuatu	2.8	5.3	2.3	4.8	4.8	3.2	3.2

... = unavailable, ADO = Asian Development Outlook, PRC = People's Republic of China.

Notes: Data on Afghanistan was collected from international sources. Because of the uncertain situation, no forecasts are provided for 2022–2023 in Afghanistan.

Table A3 Current account balance, % of GDP

	2019	2020	2021	ADO 2022	2022 Update	ADO 2022	2023 Update
Developing Asia	**0.8**	**2.0**	**1.3**	**0.9**	**0.7**	**1.0**	**0.7**
Developing Asia excluding the PRC	**0.8**	**2.3**	**0.9**	**0.3**	**-0.3**	**0.8**	**0.5**
Caucasus and Central Asia	**-3.0**	**-3.6**	**-2.0**	**0.0**	**2.2**	**0.2**	**1.5**
Armenia	-7.3	-3.8	-4.0	-4.5	-5.0	-4.7	-5.0
Azerbaijan	9.1	-0.5	12.9	20.2	26.2	16.9	21.2
Georgia	-5.5	-12.4	-10.1	-10.0	-7.5	-7.5	-7.0
Kazakhstan	-4.0	-3.8	-3.0	-0.1	0.9	0.5	1.4
Kyrgyz Republic	-12.1	4.8	-8.7	-10.0	-10.0	-10.0	-10.0
Tajikistan	-2.3	4.3	2.6	-1.5	-1.5	-2.5	-2.5
Turkmenistan	...	...	0.6	1.2	4.2	2.4	5.0
Uzbekistan	-5.8	-5.0	-7.0	-7.0	-4.0	-6.5	-5.5
East Asia	**1.5**	**2.6**	**2.8**	**2.4**	**2.5**	**2.1**	**1.9**
Hong Kong, China	5.8	7.0	11.3	6.0	6.0	5.5	5.5
Mongolia	-15.2	-5.1	-13.0	-16.3	-19.5	-12.7	-16.8
People's Republic of China	0.7	1.7	1.8	1.5	1.7	1.2	1.0
Republic of Korea	3.6	4.6	4.9	3.8	3.5	3.5	3.2
Taipei,China	10.6	14.2	14.8	15.2	15.1	15.2	15.0
South Asia	**-1.2**	**0.5**	**-1.3**	**-3.0**	**-3.9**	**-2.1**	**-2.3**
Afghanistan	11.7	11.2	...	...	...	...	...
Bangladesh	-1.3	-1.3	-1.1	-2.7	-4.1	-1.8	-3.6
Bhutan	-13.9	-13.8	-22.0	-10.6	-15.0	-10.5	-7.5
India	-0.9	0.9	-1.2	-2.8	-3.8	-1.9	-2.1
Maldives	-26.6	-35.6	-9.2	-19.5	-20.0	-17.5	-19.0
Nepal	-6.9	-0.9	-7.8	-9.7	-12.9	-6.1	-8.1
Pakistan	-4.2	-1.5	-0.8	-3.5	-4.6	-3.0	-3.0
Sri Lanka	-2.2	-1.3	-3.8	-4.3	-0.8	-2.8	-0.9
Southeast Asia	**1.7**	**2.7**	**0.5**	**1.2**	**0.5**	**1.6**	**1.0**
Brunei Darussalam	6.6	4.5	12.5	16.0	16.0	12.0	12.0
Cambodia	-15.0	-8.5	-45.7	-21.5	-23.8	-16.1	-17.0
Indonesia	-2.7	-0.4	0.3	0.0	0.5	-0.5	0.0
Lao People's Democratic Republic	-12.2	-6.0	-5.0	-6.0	-4.5	-6.5	-5.5
Malaysia	3.5	4.2	3.8	3.3	3.5	3.0	3.2
Myanmar	0.4	-2.5	-1.3	-0.8	-1.8	-1.3	-1.3
Philippines	-0.8	3.2	-1.8	-3.2	-4.5	-3.1	-4.4
Singapore	14.5	16.8	18.1	17.0	18.0	17.0	17.0
Thailand	7.0	4.2	-2.2	0.5	-2.0	4.2	2.6
Timor-Leste	7.8	-12.7	-22.9	-58.4	-34.6	-72.8	-47.2
Viet Nam	4.6	4.4	-2.0	1.5	-1.5	2.0	-1.7
The Pacific	**13.7**	**11.0**	**9.2**	**13.8**	**14.0**	**12.3**	**12.8**
Cook Islands	33.2	-6.0	-12.5	-7.0	-7.0	5.1	5.1
Federated States of Micronesia	23.1	7.9	0.5	-10.2	-23.4	-8.8	-22.0
Fiji	-4.7	-12.1	-13.2	-13.6	-12.7	-8.3	-7.7
Kiribati	48.5	39.2	32.3	35.7	35.7	38.2	38.2
Marshall Islands	-24.4	20.5	23.5	3.5	1.7	2.0	-3.0
Nauru	4.9	2.8	4.1	...	...	...	...
Niue	...	...	...	...	...	...	...
Palau	-31.1	-48.2	-55.9	-51.3	-60.0	-30.3	-35.0
Papua New Guinea	22.1	20.2	18.9	26.5	26.7	22.1	22.9
Samoa	3.0	0.0	-15.9	-10.0	-10.8	-5.0	-5.5
Solomon Islands	-9.5	-1.6	-4.9	-12.0	-13.0	-12.5	-12.5
Tonga	-0.8	-4.3	6.5	-1.8	-5.2	-5.2	-17.7
Tuvalu	-16.9	3.8	-1.8	-5.1	-8.0	-1.2	-1.2
Vanuatu	23.0	6.4	-3.8	-10.0	-5.0	-7.0	-3.0

... = unavailable, ADO = *Asian Development Outlook*, GDP = gross domestic product, PRC = People's Republic of China.

Notes: Because of the uncertain situation, no data and forecasts are provided for 2021–2023 in Afghanistan. Some historical data for Turkmenistan are not presented for lack of uniformity.

www.ingramcontent.com/pod-product-compliance
Lightning Source LLC
Chambersburg PA
CBHW050242220326
41598CB00048B/7487